History of the World
From the Back of a Boat
Volume 1

Rob Peterswald

TABLE OF CONTENTS

~ DEDICATION ~

To Rosemary, Charlotte and Georgina for sharing this journey.

~ INTRODUCTION ~

'The ocean whispering on the shore, wind rustling the endless forest, a path winding upwards towards a light in the gathering gloom.'

From the back of a boat it is easy to feel close to the past, even the very distant past. The waves that surge around you and the wind that fills your sails are the same as those that carried the ancient Phoenicians to Carthage, Columbus to the new world and Cook to the Pacific. The horizons are little changed, memories of the past linger everywhere. The headlands you sail past, the mountains, the ports, the islands and the empty anchorages, all have their stories to tell.

When I was a young child, we lived in Taree, a small town in the mid-north coast of New South Wales. Once, after the Manning River had flooded, I found an old abandoned wooden dinghy half buried in the mud and mangroves of a nearby creek. It was leaky and unstable, but with a pole I could punt around the shallows, and with a paddle explore the mysteries of the far bank beyond the bend in the river. I had discovered a lifelong passion.

At thirteen, I tried to convince my parents to allow me to apply for the Naval College at Jervis Bay. At fifteen I decided to become a cadet patrol officer in Papua New Guinea. I think my parents would have been glad to see the last of me, but I was too young. At seventeen I started Law at the University of Sydney but threw that in when I was accepted as a cadet at the Royal Military College Duntroon. After graduation I was lucky enough to be posted as a lieutenant to Papua New Guinea, where I explored the great wild waters of the interior and the beautiful coral seas of the coast. I sailed in rough dugout canoes identical to those used by our forebears many millennia ago. With my new bride, Rosemary, (Ro) we bought our first boat— a small plywood half-cabin cruiser that we sailed in the reef-strewn ocean between Taurama Barracks and Port Moresby.

In 1969 I was a captain and second-in-command of a company of soldiers onboard the HMAS Sydney, a converted aircraft carrier heading from Sydney to Vietnam via the Great Australian Bight and the islands of South East Asia. In 1971 Ro and I were posted to Wewak and Vanimo on the north coast of Papua New Guinea. I spent time on the country's two great rivers, the Fly and the mighty Sepik and, sailed the south coast between Milne Bay and Port Moresby.

When my time with the army was up, we bought a farm in Tasmania and fitted out the *Charlotte-Rose,* a thirty-eight-foot Huon pine ketch which was great for exploring the east coast of the island. Before long we wanted to sail to the Whitsundays, so we changed to *Reveille,* a forty-four-foot fibreglass cutter rigged sloop. Later on, we fell in love with a lovely vintage Huon pine pilot-house ketch, the *Tasman Isle,* and continued to enjoy her until in 1999 we realised, that as our daughters had married and left home, we were free to follow our dreams. After a long search we purchased the very beautiful fifty-two-foot ketch, *Oceania,* which could take us anywhere.

We had long realised that we shared the sea, its ports and anchorages with the ghosts of all those sailors who had come before us, some by many thousands of years. We wanted to sail in their wakes. In doing so we discovered a world of endless enchantment and mystery, and we marvelled at how close we were able to feel to so many of the great men and women of bygone times.

~ TASMANIA 2001 ~

Oceania – The Hazards Tasmania

From the summit of Mount Misery we overlooked a wild and majestic panorama—the vast foam-flecked expanse of the Great Southern Ocean stretching away to the shores of the Antarctic. The horizon was buried in mist and dark swirling cloud. Behind us stood the ancient shrouded mountains of the Arthur Ranges and the

9

wilderness of south-west Tasmania. The icy south-westerly carried the rich tangy aromas of the storm-battered coast and the cries of seabirds wheeling in the sky around us.

For most of history the scene we overlooked had been empty. No human had ventured on this stormy sea or stood on this lonely mountaintop. Then, perhaps fifty thousand years ago, a nomadic tribe had struggled to where we now stood. Clad in animal skins and holding Stone Age tools, they had gazed over the empty expanse of desolate water, before turning away to seek shelter in the trees and ravines below.

For millennia after millennia nothing changed; the rain, the cold, the clouded sky forever driven eastward by the remorseless wind. Gradually the last Ice Age ended, the oceans warmed and the seas rose, and the beautiful island of Tasmania separated itself from the lands to the north.

Another ten thousand years passed; the ocean still remained devoid of any sign of man.

Then in 1642, some fifty thousand years after the first tribesmen and their families had stood where we now stood, two apparitions emerged in the distance—the small wooden ships of Abel Tasman's fleet. Two strange half-hidden objects battered by the heaving waves and obscured by the scudding cloud presaged the end of one age and the beginning of another.

Late in the summer of 2001, Ro and I sailed here in our ketch, *Oceania*, to begin a cruise from the bottom of Australia to the top. We would be following in the wakes of Abel Tasman, Mathew Flinders, George Bass, James Cook and other seamen—some of the greatest explorers the world has seen. This part of the coast, where European exploration of the east coast of Australia began, was the logical place for us to begin our voyage.

Below our wind-blown mountaintop was one of the world's finest cruising destinations. But apart from *Oceania* and two other yachts anchored in a small cove, the waterways of Port Davey and Bathurst Harbour were deserted. By the time we had stumbled down the faint path to the shoreline and rowed back to our yacht, dusk was beginning to fall, and the wind carried hints of approaching rain. The surrounding mountaintops were now invisible, hidden by dark clouds and it looked as if it would be another wild night. I went forward to check all was well on deck and lay my hand on our heavy anchor chain, which was fixed to a 120 lb CQR anchor embedded in the glutinous mud of the bottom.

'All's well,' I reported to Ro, before switching on our masthead anchor light and pouring us both a fine Tasmanian red.

Port Davey is a remote place and not easy to reach. You must come by yacht

10

or light aircraft, or hike along the rugged south coast walking track. In a yacht it's a long day's sail, seventy or so miles against the westerlies around the stormy south coast of Tasmania, from the last safe harbour at Recherche Bay; certainly not a passage to do while the westerly gales are blowing. The only sensible thing to do is to wait for a good weather window and do it as quickly as possible, keeping your fingers crossed that nothing goes wrong with the sails or the motor and nothing unexpected blows up.

Ro and I had come here with some old friends. Dave and Jill Henry, in *Sweet Chariot* a new Buizzen 48 in which they would later complete circumnavigations of Tasmania, Australia and the world. During their circumnavigation of the world they collided with a whale and lost their rudder near the Galapagos Islands, then sailed rudderless for over two thousand miles to the Marquesas. An extraordinary feat of seamanship during which Jill, who is a mere slip of a thing, lost ten percent of her body weight. I think this is a record for distance sailed without a rudder, although the bible says Noah was at sea and rudderless for a longer time.

Dave and I had dreamed of sailing here since we were cadets at Duntroon in the 1960s, so sailing in was a very satisfying moment for us both. Also with us were Don and Sue Clark who had been our neighbours and friends from the time we moved to Tasmania and bought a farm at Koonya on the Tasman Peninsula. Don had built their beautiful yacht in an apple shed on their farm. We had sailed many miles on *Cascades* as they introduced us to the wild and beautiful Tasmanian sailing waters, set in the path of the 'roaring forties', the howling winds that continually circle the globe around the latitude of forty degrees south.

Once you have passed into the protected waters behind the Breaksea Islands, you enter a harsh but beautiful wonderland. Sue Clark's description, 'a cathedral of nature', captures its essence. It has an overawing presence verging on the supernatural. A place where even the most brash must feel the insignificance of man.

Just inside are the first of many wonderful anchorages: Waterfall Bay, Bramble Cove, Schooner Cove and Wombat Cove, where the mountains wrap all around and there is some protection from most winds. But winds of over sixty knots are not uncommon, and then it becomes a soul-searching experience to be anchored here, cut off from the world by a raging ocean with towering waves that can approach twenty metres in height and are as fearsome as any in the world. After a few kilometres the channel opens into the grand expanse of Bathurst Harbour, surrounded by tough granite mountains with tumbling streams gushing into inlets around the shore. Melaleuca Creek leads off to an old mining area and a small light aircraft strip. There are tracks along the ridges leading upwards to rocky peaks where the climb is rewarded by grand panoramas of the sea and mountains.

We had a week or so before we were joined by our eldest daughter Charlotte, her husband Stephen, and eldest son, Hubert. Her second son, Rufus, was still in the womb, already with firmly held opinions. They had flown in by light plane from Hobart, which is a spectacular trip if you are visiting Tasmania—other good reasons to visit the state are: the great wilderness parks and walking trails, the best modern art gallery in the world (MONA—founded by the remarkable gambler and arts entrepreneur David Walsh), great seafood harvested from the pristine waters around the coast including abalone, Pacific oysters, mussels, scallops, rock lobster and a wide range of fish including the unsurpassed blue-eyed cod, beef and mutton—sometimes attributed not just to individual farmers but to particular paddocks—the equal to anything on hooves, brilliant cool climate wines that are the envy of the world, the historic Hobart waterfront, and of course, the world's cleanest air and water, and many other things…which I'm sure I will mention later.

Dave and Jill's two sons Rupert and Luke had flown in with Charlotte. Many years later, the same year Dave and Jill completed their circumnavigation, Rupert won his division of the Sydney Hobart race in his yacht *Chinese Whispers*, and his son Otto won an Australian dinghy title; a family of remarkable sailors. At this stage Rupert was still a carefree youth. However, Charlotte thought he would suit a girlfriend of hers, and in due course we attended their wedding on the shore of Sydney Harbour. Our party now had a much more youthful hue; there was more fishing, netting, lobstering, climbs to mountaintops and definitely more fun at night.

Often there was a party on one of the yachts. Later Dr Bob Wright and his wife Jenny sent us an extract from their log, which more or less captures the social scene.

'0600. Awoke at dawn to find the weather rotten and the crew fine.

1000. Meeting with crew to plan smooth departure the following day. Decision made to have a light BBQ lunch to guarantee an early night and perfect fitness for an early morning take off.

1200. Opened a bottle of light wine for lunch and were joined by the crew of Sweet Chariot. *Followed by more wine and the crew of* Jendire, *followed by more wine and the crew of a Melbourne boat whose name we had trouble reading.*

2400. Discovery made that the boats substantial wine cellar had disappeared. Considerable time spent assisting a bootless—and legless—skipper of a Buizzen steer his feet into his sea boots for the water ambulance trip home.

0930. Awoke a little after dawn to find the crew rotten and the weather fine.'

An entry from the log of Don and Sue's Cascades paints a more sombre scene.

0800. We awoke to the third day of gales. The morning report from Maatsuyker Island was winds of 70 knots and a seven metre swell. But the boat is barely moving tied to a log in Melaleuca Creek, Bathurst Harbour.

1000. Hail hit the deck, lying like frozen peas and floating in the tannin water (in late summer).

1800. A break in the sky. A platypus busily feeding a few metres from the boat.

2000. Replete with red wine and roast lamb. Who knows or cares what tomorrow brings?

With our time here running out and in search of some fish, we idled around to Spain Bay, a small cove on the shore of Port Davey. These waters are renowned for their abalone, a shellfish that grows well among the rocks and kelp of these surging waters. Mostly it is exported to China and Japan where the prices paid are astronomical, and prices it out of the local market. Generally, if you want to eat it, you or a good mate have to prise it off the underwater rocks yourselves, while keeping a couple of eyes out for one of the most fearsome predators of the sea, the Great White Pointer shark. The abalone flesh can seem tough to the Australian palate and needs to be very thinly sliced, or sliced and beaten, then lightly fried, sprinkled with lemon, and served as an entrée.

From our anchorage here, it was a short walk to the sand-dunes at Stephens Bay, where the winds have exposed huge middens hundreds of metres long. These have been made by the shellfish left behind from thousands of years of feasting by the Needwonee tribe, who roamed this coast and were perhaps only a few hundred strong. It is impossible to stand here, with the sound of the waves, the wind and the drifting sands, and not be taken back into the distant past to the old campfires, ancient ceremonies, dances and songs and not mourn the long-forgotten families.

It is estimated there were around two thousand aborigines in Tasmania at the time of European settlement, scattered in nomadic tribal groups throughout the island. Coastal shellfish was an important food source and most tribes found their way to the ocean at least during summer. But they were not a seafaring people and had only the most rudimentary canoes. Strangely, for at least for the last four thousand years, fishing which is one of the richest food sources on the island, seems to have been taboo.

After a few days at Spain Bay it was time to head back to Hobart and taking advantage of a day of moderate westerlies, we headed out in the half-light before dawn. There was still a large sea running as we followed *Sweet Chariot* down to South West Cape. It was cold and uncomfortable, the mountains again hidden in cloud as we were inspected by a wandering albatross or two, who after a cursory flyover peeled away riding the wind currents south.

The great Dutch navigator and explorer, Abel Tasman (1603-1659), bumped into Tasmania a few miles north of here on 24 November 1642 during one of history's epic voyages. He had sailed south from Batavia (Jakarta) to the island of Mauritius, and then followed the 'roaring forties' to Tasmania. Continuing east he discovered New Zealand, Tonga and Fiji before returning to Batavia along the north coast of Papua New Guinea.

He had two fine Dutch ships, built by some of the greatest shipwrights of his age: the *Heemskerk*, a one hundred and twenty tonne three masted 'war-yacht' with a crew of sixty, and the *Zeehaen* a two-hundred-ton three masted transport with a crew of fifty. In a second expedition in 1644 he sailed along the north-west coast of Australia to the tip of Cape York, then along the south coast of Papua New Guinea and back to Batavia.

In 2017 we sailed our new Dutch motor yacht *Linna of Jirnsum* (also built by some of the greatest shipwrights of the age) through the small village of Lutjegast near Groningen in north-eastern Holland, where Tasman was born and where he is still commemorated by a museum. We toyed with the idea of renaming our boat the *Eleanor of Tasmania i*n honour of him and our only granddaughter. But the next morning it didn't seem such a great idea, as it might have given us problems with our EU registration

It was not for another century and a half, on 13 December 1796 that the good friends Mathew Flinders and George Bass noticed '*the appearance of a considerable opening*' as they were blown past Port Davey in a westerly gale in the tiny *Norfolk*. They decided not to risk exploring it while the conditions were so wild but noted the small off-shore islands looking like '*white teeth erupting from the turbulent water*' and '*the mountains.... the most stupendous works of Nature that I ever beheld...are the most dismal and barren. The eye ranges over these peaks with astonishment and horror*'.

All very true on a stormy day, but it is not always hostile. Sometimes in summer in these changeable latitudes the air can be rich with the salty smells of the sea, the sun is warm on your cheek, the wind a gentle caress, the water a sparkling limpid blue. Then this bold dramatic canvas around you is something to set your heart soaring, to liberate your soul from the mundane cares of life.

Bass and Flinders were two of Australia's great maritime explorers. Both young men arrived in Sydney on HMS Reliance in 1795. Bass was a twenty-four-year-old ship's doctor and Flinders, a midshipman aged twenty-one. They were good friends and shortly after arriving explored the waters south of Sydney in the tiny *Tom*

Thumb, a rowing boat about eight feet long. Bass then sailed in a larger ship to Western Port in Victoria and was the first to surmise that Tasmania was a separate island. In 1799 Flinders was made captain of the *Norfolk,* a twenty-five-ton sloop. Accompanied by Bass they sailed along the north coast of Tasmania before circumnavigating the island and returning to Sydney.

Bass then resigned from the navy and disappeared on a voyage to Chile in 1803. His fate remains a mystery.

But for Flinders his great career was still ahead of him. He returned to England where he was given command of the *Investigator,* a three-hundred-and thirty-ton sloop, and on his voyage back to Sydney reached Cape Leeuwin on the south west tip of Australia on 6 December 1801. From there he explored the south coast of the continent arriving in Sydney on 9 May 1802. On 9 July he left Sydney, exploring the east and north coast as far as modern-day Darwin. By this stage the *Investigator* was leaking so badly he was forced to head for Sydney as quickly as he could, which he did via the west coast completing the first circumnavigation of Australia.

By the time we had rounded South West Cape on the western tip of Tasmania on *Oceania,* the sun was out and the wind gave us a comfortable angle as we rollicked along eastward, the large swells that had run halfway around the world surging under our keel.

The south coast is an important fishery, but the fishermen who work along the rocky coastline need to be lucky as well as being great seamen if they are to enjoy an old age. There are small inlets and gulches along the coast, but there are none that are really safe if there is any south in the wind. De Witt Island locally known as the 'Big Witch, and Maatsuyker Island are almost halfway across, a couple of miles off the mountainous coast. They have two or three small gulches that offer some protection for cray boats waiting between drops of their pots, but they are certainly not anchorages offering a peaceful night's sleep. Generally cray boats lay their pots in the mornings and will check and re-lay them again in the late afternoons. Sometimes it seems to be a job made in heaven. If you happen across a cray boat snugly anchored around mid-morning on a calm and sunny day you cannot help but be envious of the skipper idly admiring the beauty of the placid world around him. But watching the same man trying to retrieve his pots from close to the surging rocks if the wind and sea have come up late in the day, you can only wonder how any survive at all.

The son of a good friend of ours has been fishing this stretch of the coast for many years, and recently his mother, Margie sent us a description of an almost tragic episode which illustrates the dangers.

'It all started with oil Chris bought from a shonky oil company. It was wrongly labelled so wasn't even engine oil. The insurance company will sort them out. So the engine was giving trouble. Then it died at Maatsuyker. Luckily, he was at anchor. In a safe place but very vulnerable. Chris rang Kerry Tatnell. He is the angel of the story. He has three fishing boats—he skippers one, his twenty-two-year-old son Jack skippers one and Yanni, aged twenty-four, skippers the third. Tat rang Jack who had just got home after weeks out fishing. 'Get out of bed Jack, you have to go and rescue Chris'.

Seven metre swell and massive winds. Chris was the only boat still on the south coast. Jack and Yan unloaded their pots, fuelled up and headed down the channel from Margate. It took twelve hours to get to him, they were heading straight into the weather. Then they had to wait for day break. Tat rang Canberra to get permission to pull Chris's pots. No plotter to help, but they found them all but one. Pretty amazing. Then they had to wait for the swell to drop. It took them five hours to pull the anchor. Four young blokes, they could manage four hauls each at a time. But they got it in. It's still lying on the deck.

Then the tow started. Back to Recherche then straight across to Nubeena. It took twenty-one hours. All went without a hitch, Chris said the tow line never snatched. They got back to Parsons Bay, then they rafted up because Chris had no steering and Jack parked him beautifully. Paul was on the jetty, they passed the ropes and tied up. Paul said they would not have broken an egg.

Since them Chris has found another engine and Paul has put it in and it has been for a test run. Amazing engines GM Detroit. Paul says they're one reason the Yanks won the war, they ran them in everything, four in a tank!!'

The story tells a lot about the men involved. Their mate was at risk, they would save him. No crying to Canberra to do something. When we had first lived on the Tasman Peninsula, many years ago, Kerry Tatnell, the hero of the story, was a hardworking cheerful young truck driver who carted apples and fruit juice for us. We shared many cold dawns in our apple sheds as we loaded his truck, but until Margie had written we had not heard of him for many years. Good on you, Kerry!

Maatsuyker is surmounted by Australia's southernmost lighthouse; it became a beacon of comfort for sailors and fishermen after it was erected in 1881. Manned until 1996, in the early days the only emergency contact with Hobart was by carrier pigeon. Depending on the emergency up to three birds could be released at a time, it took them about three hours —if you were waiting to be rescued, a lot of patience was needed in those days. Indeed, the survivors of shipwrecks in more remote places could expect to wait for years—particularly if you were a lone European ship in the Pacific or Indian oceans.

Now I must confess that sometimes long watches on the helm can have a mesmerising effect and my thoughts can wander off on strange paths which probably explains why I started wondering about the pigeons. Their importance has waned in modern times. These days they are mostly associated with leaving white deposits on statues and window ledges and as a one-time ingredient in Christmas pies.

However, right up until modern times, they played a vital role in diplomatic and military affairs. Carrier pigeons were used at least as early as the 6th century BCE by Cyrus the Great of Persia to maintain communications over his far-flung empire. Most rulers of any note have followed suit. Certainly, Alexander the Great sent reports to his mother in Macedonia, Julius Caesar kept in touch with Rome while he was conquering Europe, as well as many Popes, the Venetian Doges, Napoleon and Bismarck to name just a few.

It turns out that some pigeons have become quite famous. During World War I a French pigeon named *Cher Ami* was awarded the '*Croix de Guerre* with Palm' for her part in the Battle of Verdun. She delivered a number of crucial messages (how do you say *'Mon Dieu, here come the bloody krauts again'* in French?) one after having been shot in the chest and leg and saving the lives of one hundred and ninety-four French soldiers.

From time to time after leaving Maatsuyker in our wake we were overtaken by clouds and the occasional rain squall, but in the late afternoon we rounded South East Cape and passed into the Tasman Sea. Before dark we had safely navigated the narrow entrance into Recherche Bay and our anchor was pulled into the sandy bottom. This is a great anchorage with very good all-round protection, which is very important if you want to sleep peacefully in this windy part of the world. It is named after the *Recherché*, one of the ships of the decorated French naval officer and explorer Jean Francois de Galauo, *Comte de Laperouse*, who disappeared in the Pacific after calling in at Port Jackson, Sydney in 1788.

In 1792 a French expedition sent in search of La Perouse (what was I saying about shipwrecked sailors needing to be patient?) called into the bay. The commander, Bruni d'Entrecasteaux recorded his impressions:

'It will be difficult to describe my feelings at the sight of this solitary harbour situated at the extremities of the globe, so perfectly enclosed that one feels separated from the rest of the universe. Everything is influenced by the wilderness of the rugged landscape. With each step, one encounters the beauties of unspoiled nature, with signs of decrepitude, trees reaching a very great height, and of corresponding diametre…. Some of the trees seem as ancient as the world and are so tightly interlaced that they

are impenetrable.'

Today Recherche Bay is still a remote and beautiful spot, fringed with thick native forest, stands of old pines and white sandy beaches. No roads go beyond here, only walking tracks that lead into the wilderness and eventually to the west coast. Anchored here you can still feel the call of the wilderness, and the power of nature when the wind whistles over the ridges and whips through the treetops.

Before turning in I went up to the bows to check the anchor and have a last look around. The wind had dropped out and the night was now perfectly still, and we were surrounded by a velvety blackness. There were no lights ashore, no sign of any other boat and we could have been the last people on earth.

Not far from where we lay is another bay which was one of the great crossroads of the exploration of the Pacific: Adventure Bay on Bruny Island. Many of the great explorers anchored there to take respite or to rendezvous with other ships: James Cook, Bruni d'Entrecasteaux, Tobias Furneaux, William Bligh—names that are immortalised in the charts of the Pacific. Tasman and Flinders both sought to anchor here but their ships were blown off shore before they could get in.

Fourneaux's log records his impression in 1773 after he became separated from Cook:

'To the south west of the first watering place there is a large lagoon which I believe has plenty of fish in it as one of our gentlemen caught upwards of two dozen trout and shot a possum which was the only animal we saw. There are a great many gum trees of a vast thickness and height, one of which measured in circumference twenty-six feet and the height under the branches was twenty feet.'

These days Adventure Bay has a small laidback village, popular as a weekend get-away and with fishermen. It is also the base for tours of the coast of Bruny Island in high speed inflatables and speaking as someone who has sailed many coastlines, they are world class and unforgettable. The coast is dramatically beautiful, prolific in bird and sea life. The close-up interaction with the seal colonies is breathtaking and you get the sense of the power of the great heaving Southern Ocean. There is nothing between you and Antarctica. This is another good reason to visit Tasmania, along with the cheeses made on the island—as well as the oysters and mussels grown around the coast.

After leaving Recherché Bay we had a short run past Southport. Australia's most southern town was settled in 1837 and now has a population of around three hundred and seventy. Then to Dover, with a population of over nine hundred, with the claim of being the most southern town of its size. It was established in 1856 and has a climate suited to those who enjoy temperate weather. The summer daily average is

18

6.8 to 16.4C, which is about par with summer in Holland, and 4 to 13C in winter. The statistics claim it rains every *other day,* but this is rubbish, summer sailing is great. The weather may help explain why it has a population of which ninety-one percent was born in Australia (probably nearby), five percent in the UK and 'less common nationalities' such as New Zealand, Germany and Greece about one percent each. Perhaps a multi-culture commissar should look into this dense concentration of Europeans—can it just be the cool weather?

Charlotte and family left us here, the Clarks and Henrys had already gone ahead, and we collected our other daughter Georgina, and her husband Simon, for the trip up the D'Entrecasteaux Channel to Hobart. It must have been the '*other day*' when we left, the sun was shining, the water sparkling, the wind behind us—a truly stunning day to be alive as we ran under sail across the broad expanse of the Huon River. The Huon and Derwent Rivers are undoubtedly the two finest rivers for sailors in Australia—they are expansive bodies of water with all-weather entrances, plenty of anchorages and striking surrounds. Not at all like the muddy creeks they call rivers in some places on the mainland, with their sandy bars that are death-traps if you try to cross at the wrong time of day or if there's a bit of swell.

Ro had had the idea of producing a 'coffee table book' on Tasmanian sailing waters, seafood and naturally wine, for some time. This summer trip had reinforced just how scenic Tasmania is, and as we were anchored that night near the mouth of the Huon, '*Tasmania – From the Sea*' went from being an idea, to a plan. And, as with much in our life, the credit for the idea and the determination to carry it through, goes to my lovely wife. It was a decision that has enriched our sailing and the rest of our lives, being the first of our five photographic coffee table books on sailing, seafood and wine and launched by the then, premier of Tasmania, Jim Bacon.

The Huon River was named after another French explorer, Jean-Michel Huon de Kermadec who was captain of the *Esperance* on d'Entrecasteaux's expedition. Unfortunately, he died from illness in New Caledonia not long afterwards, aged forty-four. In Tasmania his name lives on through the native timber Langarostrobos Franklinii (Huon Pine). It is certainly one of the world's premier boat building woods, being fine-looking, easy to work, and because of its natural oils, practically rot free. Unfortunately, in earlier times it was decimated in Tasmanian forests, but now thankfully is strictly protected. There is a limited supply for craft and boat building—there is still a wooden boat building school in the valley—of wood recovered from flooded dams and fallen timber.

There are a number of living trees that are over two-thousand-years old and one utterly remarkable stand near Mount Reed in western Tasmania is reputably in excess of ten thousand-five hundred-years old. A true wonder of the modern world, and…another reason to visit Tasmania. One of our household treasures was a dining table crafted from wood over two thousand years old. Resting my elbows on the lovely timber, with a glass of wine nearby, generally made me reflect on the wonders of the world.

Sailing, driving or walking through the fertile Huon Valley is always a joy. It was once a major apple growing area but these days there are more grapes, cherries, small fruits and craft farms of those seeking the good life in the country.

Our friend Don Clark's, great grandfather, John Clark, was one of the earliest settlers of this paradise. He was born in England in 1804 and travelled to China and the Americas before purchasing a hundred acres on the banks of the river in 1837 for twenty-five pounds. Fruit trees obtained from the Government Gardens were planted in the spring of 1838, and in 1840 he introduced a water-powered flour mill. In 1841 he began building a proper house of pit-sawn timber with a shingle roof. It was forty by thirty-three feet and had a large brick fireplace. He and his wife, Sarah, (nee Kellaway) became friendly with the Lieutenant-Governor of Tasmania, Rear Admiral Sir John Franklin, and his wife Jane, and called their first daughter Jane Franklin Clark. A bible presented to Jane by Lady Franklin at the christening is still in the family.

By the end of the 1840s their farm, Woodside was well established with an orchard of apples and pears, vegetable crops and wheat which was processed into flour and all transported to market in Hobart by their barge and a two-masted schooner, *The Brothers*. The farm continued to prosper, however John died in 1865 aged sixty-one. Sarah battled on for another twenty years before passing away, aged sixty. They had ten children, including twin boys, Aaron, and Moses who was Don's great grandfather, and who is believed to have been the first to bring a pair of horses (at a cost of one hundred pounds) to cart split timber to the waterfront.

Moses and his wife, Mary Ann, (nee Swinfield) moved to the Tasman Peninsula in 1882, where they planted the two mighty oaks that still stand at the entrance to Don and Sue's beautiful farm *Cascades*.

Sir John Franklin is widely remembered for his tragic disappearance and death while searching for the North West Passage linking the Pacific Ocean to the Atlantic across the top of Alaska. He was a remarkable man. In his earlier career he had fought at Trafalgar and in Greece's war of independence and had taken part in a number of Arctic expeditions. His wife, Jane, is fondly remembered in Tasmania for her involvement in family and women's issues, and she is universally admired for her courageous attempts to solve the mystery of her husband's fate.

We continued north on *Oceania* along the d'Entrecasteaux channel, the mainland to our left, Bruny Island to the right. On both shores the forested hills line the water's edge, broken here and there by small settlements and isolated houses. Tucked into sheltered places are Atlantic salmon, Pacific oyster and mussel farms producing world-acclaimed delicacies. For sailors there are plenty of havens in picturesque settings, and almost always a dinner of flathead waiting to be caught.

Mussels are still regarded as somewhat of a poor relation to the magnificent Pacific oysters of Tasmania. We have eaten them for years, simmered in a few herbs and white wine. But it was not until we relished them in a Belgium restaurant in the seaside town of Gruissan that we realised what could really be done. Cooked in a wide range of cheese sauces: blue vein, Edam and the other marvellous cheeses that come from that part of the world, curries, butter and garlic, white onion and parsley sauces, chillies, tomato, potato broth, you name it, and served hot by the half kilo with a bag of golden chips. Leftovers served cold with a salad or as nibbles. They are the most marvellously versatile seafood, and there are none better than those grown in the clear cold waters of Tasmania.

In the late afternoon we dropped anchor at Kettering Bay and later went ashore to the Kettering hotel set on a hill at the top of the bay. It seemed a good day for a long refreshing 'ale' so some of us started with a very fine stout from Hobart's Cascade Brewery, established in 1832 and Australia's oldest brewery. It brews with locally grown hops and uses the clear water running off nearby Mount Wellington. All that experience and the fine local ingredients can only result in one thing: a great drink and another place you should visit when in Tasmania. Afterwards we dined on oysters and salmon and enjoyed some excellent wine, all sourced within a mile or so.

We awoke to a morning of serene calm, the waters around us untroubled by any whisper of breeze or hint of wash. In the golden light of early morning the water was a mirror holding perfect reflections of the colourful yachts and launches, the jetties on the southern shore, the forested hills and the gulls floating motionless behind our stern. I have long thought that seagulls can read minds. It takes only the thought of food to have them appear from nowhere, watching the movements of those on board with eyes filled with malicious greed.

In due course the sea breeze came up and whisked us past the old pilot station on the bluff at Tinderbox, where the swells from Storm Bay that had worked their way into the Derwent River slid under us as we rollicked up the river to Hobart.

Ro and I have lived in Hobart for much of our married life and have found it a wonderful city. We have enjoyed it immensely. Large enough to have nearly everything the mainland cities can offer, it retains the charm of a picturesque seaport.

It is the second oldest Australian capital city, founded in 1803 as a defensive outpost and penal colony in reaction to the interest shown by the French explorers in the 1790s. There is no doubt that the deportation of British and Irish convicts to Sydney and Hobart was a brutal system. But it was one of the most successful systems of corrective punishment ever implemented. The vast majority of the convicts became free and prosperous citizens of a wonderful country

Prior to the British arrival Hobart had been occupied by the Mouheneener tribe for at least eight thousand years and possibly much longer. Australian aborigines are believed to have arrived in northern Australia some fifty-five thousand years ago.

Hobart has always been maligned—along with Tasmania in general—for its weather. However, the average temperatures are only slightly below Melbourne's and Hobart escapes the oppressive summer that is inflicted on that city, while at the same time having more hours of sunshine! Hobart winters are mild, winter minimums near the water average around five degrees Celsius, which is warmer than winter minimums on the mainland tablelands well into Queensland, and up to ten degrees warmer than say, Canberra (minus six is not uncommon) or Goulburn (recently minus ten). That said, it always pays to take a pullover if you contemplate a walk around the block.

The Derwent is one of the world's great harbours and can take just about anything afloat. The Hobart waterfront is undoubtedly the most charming in the country, with much of its early 1800s architecture preserved, framed against the majestic backdrop of Mount Wellington, which is often covered in snow in winter.

The city overlooks the harbour from the surrounding foothills of the mountain. Many of its Georgian and Victorian buildings have been preserved giving it a very old-world feel, particularly the suburbs close to the CBD. South Hobart, Salamanca and Battery Point are full of delightful heritage-listed houses, from the grand to restored fisherman's cottages. In recent years it has developed a reputation as a great *destination*. It is a vibrant centre of the arts, has fine dining based on the island's superb local produce and wines, and great open fires to dine beside in winter. Jump in a car and heritage-listed parks and renowned walking tracks are not far off. The Cradle Mountain walk through the highlands; the Bay of Fires walk along the mid-east coast; the Three Capes on the Tasman Peninsula and the South Coast track are all experiences which will live in your heart forever. Enjoy wine? There are dozens of wineries within easy drive.

The Museum of Old and New Art was established by the remarkable David Walsh in 2011. The museum is one of Australia's landmark buildings, carved out of a sandstone bluff on the banks of the river. The exhibitions of modern art are world-acclaimed, as are the festivals hosted on the waterfront, showcasing public art and live performances. The Hobart Museum and Art Gallery has an outstanding collection of colonial and aboriginal art, and the Maritime Museum gives a unique insight into the city's seafaring past, from the early whaling days to its links to Antarctica.

Hobart also hosts world-renowned events. The Sydney Hobart Yacht race finishes in Hobart around the New Year and stands at the pinnacle of world ocean racing. The Wooden Boats Festival held later in January is undoubtedly the finest maritime show in Australia and in the early New Year the Taste of Tasmania is an epicurean delight. Targa Tasmania is a vigorously competitive event, as is the bi-annual Three Peaks Sailing (and mountain running) Race.

We planned to continue sailing to the north of Queensland towards the end of the year, and before then we wanted to publish *'From the Sea'*. As the cold months slipped by, we slaved on the text, selected photographs for scanning—this was before the age of the digital camera—took more photographs, agonised over layouts and organised printing.

In the spring the book was launched in a pavilion at Constitution Dock by Jim Bacon. The Premier's wife, Honey, was an old shipmate who had sailed across a rough Bass Strait with us some years previously. And had enjoyed it so much she broke the world long-jump record when rushing to escape from our yacht *Reveille,* at Eden.

'From the Sea' was very well received in Tasmania, as it did capture a great deal of the beauty and romance of the state, and most Tasmanians dearly treasure and are proud of what they have. It was promoted and supported by the local bookstores, and probably with their connivance was reported as topping the best-selling lists across the state for a couple of weeks. We were a bit suspicious about this as it was competing against a new Harry Potter novel, but very appreciative of the helping hand. The first print run sold out quickly and we ordered a second.

All very satisfying, and we decided to give the east coast of Australia the same treatment, which in due course resulted in a second book *'Beyond the Shore'.*

In November we headed north. The plan was to spend the summer sailing to Sydney and leave *Oceania* on a mooring outside David and Jill Henry's home at Birchgrove over winter before heading north as spring approached. We had plenty of time and wanted to savour everything as much as possible. We had learned that good photography takes time and patience, and the special convergence of light and subject.

With Georgie at the helm we left the Hobart Docks in the early morning so the normal land breeze blowing down the Derwent would get us well into Storm Bay before the afternoon sea breeze set in. Storm Bay was named by Abel Tasman because of the storm that prevented him landing at Adventure Bay. It is an apt name and the bay can be uncomfortable with winds from any direction, which means it is often uncomfortable and frequently dangerous.

Charlie Watson, another old army friend, crossed Storm Bay in 1982 in the MV Cape Pillar a two-thousand-ton lighthouse tender, while part of the NATMAP bathymetric survey of the continental shelf. He recalls standing on the bridge wings outside the wheelhouse, about fifteen metres above the waterline, and looking up at the swells towering above him.

We were heading for the small fishing port of Nubeena on the southern shore of the Tasman Peninsula, where we planned to spend a few days catching up with old friends we had made when we farmed at Koonya

One of our first introductions to the Nubeena community was when we were invited to attend 'The Badger Creek Regatta' in 1982. Now, certainly Australia's best-known whimsical regatta is the Henley-on-Todd Regatta, otherwise known as the Todd River Race. This is held annually on the typically dry sandy riverbed of the Todd River at Alice Springs in central Australia. 'Boats' are made from anything that tickles the fancy, and 'rowers' run with them over the hot sand.

Lots of fun and boisterous well-lubricated laughter.

The Badger Creek Regatta is in this tradition, although Badger Creek is actually a delightful saltwater inlet, perhaps two hundred metres long by thirty metres wide on the wooded western shore of Nubeena Bay. The organisers were the Shoobridges, an old Nubeena farming family who were cousins of the English writer Evelyn Waugh and shared his literary genes. They all seemed to write, sing, paint or recite poetry while having a good time and wishing well to all humanity. Great people in other words and definitely with a whimsical sense of humour.

The regatta lasted from mid-morning to late night, and I have to admit that most competitors—and everyone competed at something, regardless of age or sex—indulged themselves in the eat, drink and be merry philosophy more than they probably should have. Barracking was loud and sometimes ribald, and the physical co-ordination of some competitors somewhat impaired.

The morning was given over to aquatic events: rowing, paddling, swimming; the highlight generally being the across the creek all breeds dog race. Followed by a long lunch. The afternoon was for farm and domestic competitions, bobbing for apples and that sort of thing, wood chopping—though I was a bit dubious about handling sharp axes and chain saws after lunch - generally only the men deemed themselves sober enough—arm wrestling, post tossing etc. Followed by a long dinner. Followed by a cultural night of storytelling, poetry recital, exaggerations, lying—that is telling lies—lying in the Biblical sense came after the singing.

The farm we bought when we moved to Tasmania in 1980 was north of Nubeena, across a few miles of rolling green hills. It overlooked beautiful Norfolk Bay, named after Flinder's fine ship, which was the first to anchor there. We made many friends in the area, and still at times regret ever having left. We have sailed many miles and watched many sunsets with Don and Sue Clark, Paul and Margie Hanson and the local doctor and his wife, Phillip and Carmel Thomson. Sue and Margie were city girls who were lucky enough to snare two local farmers—both farms veritable Edens. Sue has been on the board of Port Arthur for many years, and Margie is the custodian of one of Hobart's jewels, *Summerhome*. The house and garden was created as a summer retreat by the prominent Hobart businessman, Henry Hopkins in the 1840s. The large garden—one and half hectares—is still intact and Henry was so passionate about it he left it to his daughter, who he thought best able to care for it. Since then it has passed down from daughter to daughter, Margie being the great-great-great granddaughter. The garden still has a number of original plantings: a box hedge has been there for one hundred and sixty years, as has a Cabbage Tree and what is almost certainly Tasmania's—could be Australia's—oldest grapevine, growing out of the old hothouse.

We had a few nights anchored in the bay before we set off again. The stretch of coast beyond Nubeena is probably the most dramatic in Australia, with three majestic prominences facing the might of the Southern Ocean. The first is Cape Raoul which stands about three hundred metres above the heaving sea and ends in a spectacular fluted tip. A seal colony has long been established just inside the tip, where there is just enough shelter for them to leave and enter the sea from a slanting ledge of rock. From here they lounge, glancing suspiciously at passing yachts and wondering if there is a fisherman with a rifle aboard, planning retaliation for the fish they have stolen.

Once Cape Raoul is passed Cape Pillar and Tasman Island stand on the horizon, and the panorama is always unforgettable. At dawn on a clear day it is enchanting, coloured a misty blue and tinged with rose. Or at other times it can be wrapped in low storm clouds and lashed by wind, the most hostile place on earth.

Halfway across the cliffs open to reveal the narrow entrance to Port Arthur, a noble tree-lined port with a number of attractive anchorages. When we were living at Koonya in the 1980s we used to try to sail here each summer and leave the boat for a few weeks before completing a circumnavigation of the Tasman Peninsula. We always loved it, the water is clear and exquisite—perhaps a little on the fresh side—the colours enchanting in the morning and afternoon light. The fishing was always good, and we could count on dinners of flathead fillets cooked on the wood-fired barbecue. When fishing for flathead in Tasmania you attach three hooks—baited with anything until you caught a fish, which you then used—to a line, with a sinker to take the lot to the bottom. In the early days it was common to catch two flathead on a single cast, and on some memorable occasions, which had everyone cheering, there might be three fish hooked.

Port Arthur is one of the most significant heritage areas in Australia. The ruins of the old penal settlement are the best surviving reminder of the large-scale transportation and settlement of convicts in Australia in the 18th and 19th centuries. They are set in beautiful park-like grounds with very interesting interpretation centres. A day spent here is deeply engrossing and reveals a dark side of our heritage. But I do have a theory, that the harsh experiences of our convict ancestors helped form some of what we would like to think of as national characteristics. Our egalitarianism, the concept of a 'fair go', 'mateship'. Self-reliance and a sardonic disrespect for authority were incubated in those who survived the terrible ordeal of transportation to the other side of the world, inhumane incarceration and on their release, the struggle as free colonial settlers in a wild and hard country.

From 1833 to 1877 it was the prison for the hardest of the convicted British criminals, re-offenders and the rebellious as well as a number of Irish political prisoners. I have sometimes wondered if my old *alma mater* of Duntroon, was not modelled on Port Arthur.

There were a couple of interesting pieces of nineteenth century technology in Tasmania at that time. The first signal station in Hobart was set up at Mount Nelson in 1811, followed by one in Princes Park at Battery Point, only a few steps from where we once lived. These were used for ship-to-shore communications and the code books listed three thousand different signals. By 1836 a series of semaphore stations had been set up to enable speedy communications between Port Arthur and Hobart, a distance of 60 kms or so by line of sight. In clear conditions a short message could be sent, and a reply received within fifteen minutes. This probably put the pigeons out of a job at Port Arthur—but not the 'stool' pigeons, of course (sorry).

Also, in 1836 a 'carbon neutral' tramway was established between Norfolk Bay and Port Arthur, a distance of around twenty-five kms. This is probably something that should be re-looked at, as it provided useful employment for the prisoners who were pushing the trams backwards and forward. And there were no emissions—well, perhaps a few unmentionable ones.

Even on calm days the ocean between Port Arthur and the narrow passage between Cape Pillar and Tasman Island is lumpy, it surges with an uneven rhythm as the forces of the southern seas work against winds and currents coming down the coast. It is a tad eerie even on a calm day, and unnerving if it is a bit stormy. It is the only stretch of water we have sailed over where the ship's motion is such that Ro is lost for words, even unable to give advice, due to seasickness!

But the fishing here is legendary. Sue and Don's son Marcus is one of those people who have magical powers over fish. He is to the fish of Tasmania what Casanova was to the ladies of Venice. They cannot seem to resist him. It is rare indeed to ever dine at Cascades without sampling some of the freshest, tastiest Bluefin or Yellowfin sashimi that has ever been put on a plate. If sashimi is not on the menu you can be assured that the tantalising aroma from the wood-fired barbecue will be Albacore or Striped Marlin, Blue Warehou or Striped Trumpeter or Morwong or Barracouta or perhaps the tastiest of all, the giant flathead lured from the seabed seventy metres down.

It was always good to put Cape Pillar and the rugged spire of Cathedral Rock behind and to enter the anchorage behind the old wreck in Fortescue Bay an hour north. Thick forests completely envelop the bay and giant eucalypts line the rocky shore. The clear waters, at this time, were dense with giant seaweed fronds where a diver could be rewarded with a feast of crayfish—I think they actually come out and shake hands with Marcus—mussels or abalone. At night there is rarely the sight or sound of man; only the wind, the wash on the shore and the occasional cry of a hunting owl.

During the night a southerly front moved through and in the morning the sea was speckled with white caps as we ran northward, staying in close to the steep rocky coast, passing lobster boats setting their pots amongst the gulches and the reefs.

On the way we passed the site, in a small rocky bay near Dunalley, where a modest memorial marks the place where the Dutch flag was planted, and the newly discovered land claimed for Holland by Abel Tasman in December 1642. Tasman had followed the coast this far before heading east, discovering New Zealand not long after. The journals of the voyage reveal an amazingly democratic and consultative expedition. The crews were masters of their trades: seamen, sailors, carpenters, navigators, blacksmiths, and all exhibited a calm and rational approach to the daunting tasks they faced. It is inspiring that men such as these existed and could achieve what they did, while on the other side of the globe Europe was racked by the bloody religious and sectarian disputes that were the genesis for the great exodus of people to the New World. There was the establishment of an English colony in Jamestown, Virginia in 1607 and the Pilgrim Fathers in 1620.

Members of our distant families, who in due course would settle in Australia, were embroiled in the troubles of these times.

The cataclysmic Thirty-Year War raged and decimated the population of the German states. Over a quarter of their total population died, many were killed in the bloody battles, but most died through famine and disease as much of northern Europe became hell on earth. Georg and Bernard Peterswalde were being driven from the lands where their family had lived for centuries as Catholic and Protestant armies burned, pillaged and ravaged the countryside.

England was home to a bunch of ancestors; the Taylors, Watsons, Wightons, Bottrils, Hadleys, Grays and Cartwrights. Scotland home to more, the Keiths and the Mackenzies. The English Civil War—1642 to 1651—had begun. The Battle of Edgehill had been fought between Parliamentary forces and the Royalists supporting King Charles I, and the country would be racked by a bloody war for a decade.

In Ireland, the land of the Earngies, Fultons and Ro's family the Esmondes, the Rebellion of 1641 had developed into a brutal war between Irish Catholics and English and Scottish Protestants, that eventually led to the invasion of Ireland by Oliver Cromwell. The Esmondes still have a dining table at which the great man was very reluctantly entertained, and which still bears his initials carved in the wood—by whom no one knows.

Only in France, where the de Sainte Croix family resided was there some semblance of normality, although French armies were fighting on the Catholic side of the Thirty-Year War.

These thoughts of long-gone relatives were forgotten as we romped north with a south westerly wind behind us, but they should not have been. We all owe an immense debt to those early explorers and settlers who helped create the wonderful free nation that is ours.

By early afternoon we were close to Maria Island, gliding through the translucent waters of the Mercury Passage. This has long been one of our favourite Tasmanian islands. The north and south ends are separated by a narrow sandy isthmus, which is bordered by the sweeping crescents of two gleaming white sandy beaches. If the weather is from the north or west there is a beautiful anchorage in Riddle Bay, where perfect security and splendid isolation is almost guaranteed. At the very northern end of the bay is a very small anchorage, called Whalers Cove, just large enough for two yachts. We often used to overnight there, our then yacht *Charlotte Rose* rafted up with *Cascades*, when returning from further up the coast. If there is any east in the wind, Chinaman's Cove on the other side of the isthmus is equally enchanting, but sometimes you may have to share with another yacht. If you cannot catch enough flathead for dinner with a couple of casts of the line, something is very wrong.

The high peaks of Maria Island were now silhouetted against a perfect sky, their heavily wooded slopes tumbling down to the gleaming sands and thickly forested foreshore. We followed a rising tide through the shallow entrance into the small village of Triabunna and tied up among the fishing boats, not far from a friendly pub. This was Georgie's last night on board on this leg, and we had a tear in our eyes after we waved her off in the morning. On our first trip to Queensland on *Reveille* a decade earlier Georgie (and her then boyfriend Simon) had come all the way with us, and we knew we would miss her.

Not long after sunrise a few days later, when the tide was high enough to see us out through the channel, we continued northwards. With us were Don and Sue Clark, and Peter Knight, another friend of our youth.

I met Peter at Duntroon, but before that he was at school with Ro's brother Eugene, and for a time was lucky enough to date their sister Vivienne. His family lived in Canberra, and it was a home away from home for a group of us cadets—I have no idea how his parents put up with the rowdy mob who seemed to live there. Peter, and his lovely wife, Sue, had sailed with us from Sydney when we were sailing north in *Reveille* for a Christmas at the Gold Coast in 1990.

We cleared Cape Bougainville, named for the famous French naval officer and explorer who anchored here in 1772. Louis Antoine de Bougainville was born in Paris in 1729 and in 1763 was the first Frenchman to circumnavigate the globe. He could well be France's pre-eminent seafarer—Napoleon made him a count, he has had thirteen French naval ships named for him, numerous parts of the world, as well as of course, the beautiful South American climbing shrub, the Bougainvillea.

Onwards, into the dancing waters of Great Oyster Bay, accompanied most of the way by schools of boisterous dolphins that surfed our bow wave and cavorted under our hull. Early in the afternoon we anchored beneath the Hazards in Coles Bay and two days later passed through the Schouten Passage, which is another place where we spent a lot of time with *Cascades*. There are lovely anchorages off sandy beaches on both sides of the passage where over the years we often cooked crayfish over campfires, sometimes wrapped in seaweed and steamed in the coals, before rowing sleepy children out to the yachts.

We followed the rocky cliffs of the Freycinet Peninsula named for another French naval officer, who sailed with Nicholas Baudin and went on to make a great name for himself in his own right, to stunning Wineglass Bay. The name keeping up the French connection in these parts. The French navy, as you would expect travelled with wine, while the ruffians of the Royal Navy were given a 'tot' of rum (seventy-five mls) each midday. *Tot of Rum Bay* doesn't have quite the same ring to it, does it?

This is one of the world's most beautiful anchorages, and although it is open to the north-east it is a lovely place to be when the weather is from the south or west— which it is most of the time. The water is superbly blue and laps the shore of the virginal white sands of the glittering beach. It can only be reached by sea, or by foot over the surrounding mountains and rocky bluffs.

Many days you will be the only yacht, although often there will be a cray boat or two idling away the day between setting and retrieving their pots in the early mornings and late afternoons. In these days in the remote places it was still generally possible to trade for a cray or three, and fresh lobster eaten on the aft deck accompanied by a dry Tasmanian white under the gentle light of a swinging lantern, is close enough to paradise for us.

Sue and Don seemed to be on good terms with every fisherman we passed from Triabunna to Flinders Island, so we continued to eat like royalty on fish and lobster until we were on the other side of Bass Strait. After that we did not do so well with the fishing, and although we trolled a line some two thousand nautical miles, we only jagged one fish the whole way, which must be some sort of record.

The wind stayed in the west and the next day we reached up the coast carrying our large genoa, mainsail and mizzen, averaging seven knots, a good speed for our beautiful yacht. As the wind was blowing off the shore, we were able to stay close in and enjoy the panorama of the passing coast. The rugged headlands with the sun lighting up the spray, the rich reds of the lichen covered rocks, gleaming white beaches, the mountains of the Ben Lomond National Park, the wind chasing wispy white clouds overhead. On we sailed past Bicheno with its picturesque anchorage in 'the Gulch', the entrance over the infamous bar at St Helens, Binnalong Bay and the Bay of Fires

We dropped anchor in a small bay below Eddystone Point as dusk was falling. It is a safe enough spot while the wind stays in the west, but not the sort of place to evacuate at night. There are a lot of rocks and reefs about. There was a cray boat already anchored, which is a good indication that all will be well.

We had stopped here when we sailed our newly acquired *Oceania* south from Mooloolaba two years previously and had been thankful to have found peace from the abating westerly gale that had brought us across Bass Strait. We had been waiting in Snug Cove in Twofold Bay for the right weather to cross. In those days it was difficult to get a forecast for a two-day window in the Strait, and we were relying on our friend and neighbour in Hobart for advice. Hedley Calvert, sadly no longer with us, and his brother Don were sailing royalty in Tasmania. We were pretty sure Hedley had a direct link to God. So, when he told us that the next day would be good to go, we left before dawn. We were already into the Strait when the wind began to pick up, and it was blowing a moderate gale by nightfall. There followed a very uncomfortable passage, and it was not until we were behind Eddystone that we got Hedley's change of forecast, that we had missed by leaving too early.

We had been lucky enough to have my brother Richard and Mark Towers, *Oceania's* previous owner with us. Without them Ro and I would have been struggling to get across in one piece. Mark had given up sailing and had sold *Oceania*—with a life time guarantee that hasn't really been worth the paper it *wasn't* written on—to take up campervanning. But a couple of weeks later while on their first expedition, Mark became nervous about *Oceania* crossing Bass Strait without him and joined us in Sydney for the crossing. Not too long after that they sold the camping gear and bought another yacht *Knot Again,* and we were to spend a lot of time with them in Queensland and the Mediterranean.

We had no sooner dropped our anchor than two grinning fishermen arrived in their dinghy. This was nice in itself, but even better when they—more friends of Sue and Don— handed up two good sized lobsters. They joined us for a tot of rum and then left us to enjoy our dinner: Ro's famous Lobster Mornay.

Bass Strait is a dangerous stretch of water with an evil reputation. It is relatively shallow, and the east-west tidal flows and the strong westerlies of the 'roaring forties,' can create murderous sea conditions. There have been hundreds of shipwrecks and a number of ships, some quite large, have disappeared without trace. Not so long ago the yacht *Charleston*, carrying the husband of our friend Pam Corkhill, set off not far from where we were anchored, and disappeared. No sign of the yacht has ever been found.

We had previously crossed Bass Strait twice in our own yachts, and both times we had endured gales, which on a dark and stormy night in an angry ocean many miles from any help, is not a pleasant experience. One we were determined to avoid this time as we sailed north on *Oceania.*

If you leave Hobart and sail directly to Eden the first secure port on the mainland, you need to cover a bit over 700 kms. At a speed of 10 kph this means it will take three to four days to get across if all goes well. During this period, it is more than likely you will be hit by a south-westerly weather front, which more than likely will bring some gale force winds with it.

This time we had broken the journey up the east coast of Tasmania and planned to stopover at Flinders Island on the way across. Our plot was not to leave one port until a southerly front had passed over, and then sail north with the moderating southerlies that normally follow. These days, with weather maps, forecasts and radar pictures on the internet, this is a much easier thing to do. However, all this was still in the future and we had to rely on radio forecasts from scattered shore stations.

The early morning forecast from Mersey Radio predicted strong westerlies moderating later in the day, so after a conference over breakfast we decided to leave mid-morning, which would get us to Jamieson Bay, a small snug anchorage about 50 kms away on the eastern tip of Cape Barren Island well before dusk.

But it was a wet and uncomfortable passage. The wind stayed over twenty knots and working against the tide produced a steep swell with lots of spray and breaking water, until we were into the smoother water in the lee of Clarke Island. At Jamieson Bay we were comforted to see two cray boats already anchored, protected from the westerlies by high rocky bluffs. We had hardly anchored before we had another welcome visit from one of the fishermen, bringing the biggest cray I have ever seen. Much too large for any of our pots, but fine baked in the barbecue and garnished with pernod and olive oil, after we had shared a tot or two of rum on the aft deck.

Later the wind built to a south-westerly gale and we let out some more chain and prayed it would not back further to the south. Pity about the forecast.

In the morning it had eased enough to tempt us on our way, and we set off for another 50 km hop to an anchorage off the beach at the north eastern end of Flinders Island. Our fishermen friends from the previous night were already at work near the tip of Cape Barren and we waved goodbye as we rounded the cape and picked up a strong tidal flow going north. For a while we were flying—18 kph with the toe rail burying in the foaming wash.

We stayed well out from the shore of Flinders Island to avoid the dangerous shoals known as the 'Pot Boil' and by mid-morning the high peak of Babel Island had emerged from the light blue haze. The 'mare's tails' beginning to streak the western sky warned us that stronger winds were on the way.

We anchored a little south of Babel Island where we had reasonable protection unless the wind came in from the southeast, in which case we could move to the northern shore. Shortly afterwards we were joined by two large fishing trawlers and three cray boats. To our amazement the crew of one of the boats recognised Sue as they inspected us on the way in. She had taught one of the men when she was a young teacher at Tasman Primary School —funny how men remember beautiful blondes—and later they came across for a chat bringing another lobster dinner with them. God bless all fishermen!

By dusk the day had taken on a sullen expression and the wind was still picking up. We let out all our heavy chain (one hundred metres) and prepared for a stormy night.

Flinders Island is the largest of the fifty-two islands of the Furneaux Group at the eastern end of Bass Strait, where they are battered by the continual westerly winds and waves that drive through.

They were first recorded by Tobias Furneaux, the captain of Cook's support vessel the HMS Adventure in 1773, and later mapped by Mathew Flinders and George Bass in 1798. In the late 18th century it was a rough and lawless place, populated by sealers and mutton birders, many with kidnapped aboriginal women. Between 1830 and 1847 the surviving Tasmanian aborigines were relocated to the island at Wybalenna, before being moved again to Oyster Cove south of Hobart. It was not until late in the 19th century that freehold land was allocated for grazing and farming and a veneer of civilization took hold.

However, these days it is a great place to visit. The island is uniquely beautiful with great walks along the windswept stretches of white sandy beaches and rocky coves, or to the top of Mount Strzelecki where the views go on forever over the vast ever-changing seascape. You can fossick for semi-precious stones, dine on sensational seafood and renowned Flinders Island beef and mutton, curl up beside a wood fire as the wind rattles the windowpanes, and the world is a million miles away.

On board, the wind howled off the beach all the restless night and by dawn it was still gusting around forty-five knots. Although we were only three hundred metres from shore, we were surrounded by rushing whitecaps with our bow digging into each surge and the anchor chain drawn taut as a quivering bowstring. During the morning both the large trawlers dragged their anchors and came back in to re-anchor, with sheepish expressions as we looked on smugly.

We congratulated ourselves for being more or less safely anchored, thanks to our immense 120 lb CQR anchor and, settled down to catch up on some sleep and wait for calmer weather.

On 8 January 1797 Mathew Flinders would have been anchored in pretty much the same spot.

A six o'clock. Mr Bass went on shore to the small, south-eastern islet; whence he brought a boat-load of seals and gannets. Besides these, the islet is inhabited by geese, shags, penguins, gulls and sooty petrels; each occupying its own separate district and using its own language. In the confusion of noise amongst these various animals which induced me to give the name of Babel Isles to this small cluster...'

Late that night the wind finally blew itself out and after getting a forecast from Mersey Radio—which so far had not exactly been a great deal of help—we left early the next morning, laying a course for Eden, which was now two hundred miles north on the New South Wales coast. There was still a large cross sea running but with all our sails set there was enough wind to keep us steady and we were soon making a good rollicking 12 kph.

After the gales the air was crisp, freshly washed, as sweet as air can be. There was virtually nothing up wind of us before the coast of Africa. The sea sparkled, an albatross looked us over, some dolphins played for a while, in the distance seagulls attacked a school of fish. Freshly brewed coffee, a light lunch, a warm sun before a red sunset heralded a star-filled evening. In the late night we caught the gloom of Little Rame Head lighthouse on the Victorian coast and in the sunrise the spire of Gabo Island lighthouse climbed out of the shining water, lit by the golden orb of the rising sun. A breakfast feast—plates heaped with bacon, eggs and toast.

In the late night we had crossed the 1770s track of Captain James Cook's Endeavour. The first European recorded sighting of the east coast of mainland Australia was made at dawn on Thursday 20 April 1770, nineteen days out of New Zealand, by Lieutenant Zachary Hicks, in whose honour Point Hicks on the Gippsland coast was named. Hicks was the second-in-command and an able and intrepid man. Unfortunately, he died on the way home and was buried at sea. He was only thirty-one years old and denied the rewards he should have enjoyed.

Cook was on the first of his three great voyages. He had left England in 1768 and came via Rio de Janeiro, Cape Horn, Tahiti and New Zealand and would return home around the top of Australia, Sumatra and the Cape of Good Hope.

Cook's Journal records this momentous moment in his usual understated manner.

'At 5 set the Topsails Close reef'd and 6 saw land extending from NE to west at a distance of 5 or 6 leagues having 80 fathoms of water and a fine sandy bottom ... the Southernmost Point of land we had in sight ... I have named Point Hicks, because Leuit. Hicks was the first to have discover' this land...'

To the Southward of this point we could see no land...makes me doubtful whether they are land or no: however, everyone who compares this journal with that of Tasman will be as good a judge as I am...'

Meanwhile, back on Oceania the crew was more loquacious. More coffee as the coast drew near and after some discussion, we reached the conclusion that probably no yacht had ever sailed from Hobart to Gabo and dined as well as we had: crayfish every night since Triabunna. Not even Queen Elizabeth II, who once crossed the strait in the royal yacht Britannica and lunched at Wine Glass Bay on the way, could beat that.

We know delightful Twofold Bay and the town of Eden quite well, having spent a fair bit of time anchored here either waiting for good weather to head south across Bass Strait or celebrating a safe arrival. As I mentioned, on one occasion when we were approaching the jetty after having arrived safely, Honey Hogan, wife of Premier Jim Bacon, who had made her first and only sea voyage with us, left her seasick berth and easily broke the world long jump record in her eagerness to be done with the boat.

Mathew Flinders recorded his impressions of Snug Cove on 9 April 1798 on the *Norfolk*.

'Soon after a man made his appearance. He was of middle age, unarmed, except with a 'waddie', or wooden scimitar, and came up to us with careless confidence. We made much of him and gave him some biscuit; and he presented us with a piece of gristly fat, probably a whale. This I tasted; but watching for an opportunity to spit it out when he should not be looking, I perceived him doing precisely the same thing.'

And later.

'I was preparing the artificial horizon for observing the latitude, when a party of seven or eight natives broke out in exclamation on the bank above us, holding up their arms to show they were unarmed ...and we sat in the midst of the party. It consisted entirely of young men, who were better made, and cleaner in their persons than the natives of Port Jackson usually are; and their countenances spoke both goodwill and curiosity, though mixed with some degree of apprehension...our visitors returned into the woods, seemingly well satisfied with what they had seen.'

We had also spent some time here after crewing on a folk-boat owned by an old friend, Paul Mench, when we were living in Canberra in the 1970s. Not long afterwards Paul, who had been destined for greatness, fell to his death in the Border Ranges. Coming back here always reminds us of great times we shared and the tragedy of his death. That aside it has always been a great place to visit. The clubs and pubs are hospitable, with showers for smelly sailors and fine pub fare for hungry ones. The bay has a number of sandy beaches where children can be amused and there is protection from most winds.

We tied up amongst the fishing boats at the pier and were absolutely delighted to find the marvellous HM Bark *Endeavour* Replica moored close by. As Cook and the *Endeavour* had been much on our minds over the last couple of days, we couldn't believe our good luck to be able to clamber all over this remarkable reconstruction. It is now mostly moored at the Australian National Maritime Museum in Sydney and makes a grand outing that will be immensely enjoyed by both grandparents and grandchildren.

We needed to replace the navigation light at the top of the mast and to run an eye over the rigging in general. If there is only Ro and myself on board this often poses problems. It is a much harder thing to do than change an average light bulb, so it is not something you can confidently expect a girl like Ro to handle. On the other hand, I am a heavy weight for her to haul up, and on the way up I always start to wonder if she's up to it, and the deck starts to look a long way down. But with a crew of five, one of whom was quite a light weight and an engineer, the choice was easy. By a vote of four to zero with one abstention Peter Knight was hauled aloft. Soon all was shipshape.

Prior to the arrival of Europeans, the Thawa aboriginal tribe were the only inhabitants of the area. By 1791 whaling ships were operating out of the bay and the first whaling station was built in 1828. A strange arrangement is said to have developed between the whalers, the Thawas and the killer whales—orcas—of the area, in the pursuit of the great and oil rich humpback whales.

The orcas liked feasting on the harpooned whales, a godsent opportunity for a free feed as far as they were concerned, but the Thawas refused to kill them. Instead they encouraged orcas to trap the humpbacks in the large bay where they were easily harpooned, and the orcas then rewarded with parts of the whale carcasses. The orcas were led by 'Old Tom' a ferocious specimen about seven metres long and weighing six tons and said to be thirty-five years old when he died. Whaling remained an important part of the town's economy until 1930, as was tuna canning until 1999. Sawmilling and the collection of wattle bark to be used in tanning leather was also an important industry.

There are only a couple of all-weather ports before Sydney, so it was a popular stopover for many sailors from the earliest days of settlement. By the 1840s the commercial advantages of developing the port were well recognised and in 1843 permanent settlement began, although it was not proclaimed as a town until 1885.

We also have a family connection with Eden. James Watson Keith who had been born in Dundee, Scotland in 1831 landed at Eden around 1856 with his wife Margaret (nee Taylor 1833–1872). In due course they had eight children. The second youngest child was Jemima who married William Peterswald. They were my grandparents.

James went on to become a pioneer of the Monaro district, possibly attracted to the area by the Kiandra gold rush (1859-1860) and appears to have led a long and productive life, eventually dying in the southern highlands in 1923. There is some mystery about his younger days as described in the publication '*The Monaro Pioneers*'. Arriving in Melbourne in 1854 at the age of twenty-three, he is said to have been a sailor who reached the rank of captain in his earlier life and having invested twelve thousand pounds sterling—now worth about seven million sterling—in a Victorian goldmine.

At first, I thought that if both these facts were correct, and he was a millionaire at such a young age, he must have been a very successful pirate. But on discovering that the other side of the family were slave owners in Jamaica prior to the Abolition Act of 1833, it occurred to me there could be another explanation. Many fortunes were made in the slave trade to the USA up until the American Civil War.

This is certainly not enough evidence to convict anyone, let alone my great-grandparent, so perhaps we should just remember him as a 'mysterious sea captain'. A photograph probably taken around the time of his arrival in Melbourne shows a handsome young man with neatly trimmed, glossy dark hair and moustache, large soulful eyes, neatly tailored coat and waistcoat and a tie with a jewelled pin. It was probably taken before his fortune was lost and he definitely doesn't look like a slave trader. A card sharp? Perhaps.

Whatever the amount of his fortune, it was lost, and he came on to Boydtown in Eden, and thence to what must have been a hard life in the high country.

On my mother's side of the family, her father Stanley Earngey (married to Etta Hadley) had been the local chemist here in the 1930's, and we have a number of photos of her family relaxing around a large fishing launch with an inboard motor. In some of these my father is present, his fine physique displayed in speedo swimmers with shoulder straps. He was courting mum's elder sister, Kath – I'm not sure what happened there.

Our next stop over was Bermagui, a small snug harbour about forty miles further north. This stretch of the coast is only a dozen miles from the edge of the continental shelf and is famous for its game fishing. We paid particular attention to the setting of our lines and lures, quietly confident, with our bottomless pool of optimism, of a good catch. But alas, the fish remained safe – again.

We arrived at the bar earlier than we had planned and the tide was still a bit low and we bumped the sandy bottom a couple of times as we crossed. No damage done and we were lucky enough to get a spot on the jetty a short stroll to the town centre. Here we bought—as we always really knew we would have to—freshly caught baby snapper, which were delicious grilled on the barbecue under the watchful eyes of a number of baleful-looking pelicans.

A light southerly stayed with us the next day and after the early morning haze cleared, we had a lovely view of the picturesque rocky coastline broken by numerous beaches, all framed by green rolling hills and the great hump of Mount Dromedary. Before long we were off Broulee Island where we have sometimes anchored. The names of the small villages we were passing; Mossy Point, Malua Bay, Potato Point, Sunpatch all brought back many memories of escaping from the drudgery of the Defence Department in Canberra and holidaying on this part of the coast when Charlotte and Georgie were toddlers.

Cook's Journal 21 April 1770:

'Winds Southerly a gentle breeze and clear weather with which we coasted along shore to the northward ... we saw smoke of fire in several places a certain sign that the Country is inhabited ... at 6 o'clock we were abreast of a pretty high mountain laying near ... which I named Mount Dromedary ...an open Bay wherein lay three or four small islands bore NWBN distant 5 Leagues this Bay seem'd to be very little sheltered from the sea winds and yet is the only anchoring place I have seen on this coast.'

Late afternoon we dropped anchor behind one of the islands he mentioned, Snapper Island, off the entrance to the Clyde River. There was already a fishing boat there and he assured us that all would be well. As twilight gave way to night the lights of Batemans Bay reflected coloured patterns across the calm water while we enjoyed the ambience, the aroma of prawns cooking on the barbecue and the echoes of old memories, of laughter and our children when we all were young.

Cook's Journal 22 April 1770:

'... (we) were so near the shore as to distinguish several people on the Sea beach they appear'd to be a very dark or black colour but whether this was the real colour of their skins or their Clothes they might have on I know not...the land near the sea continues of a moderate height forming alternately rocky points and Sandy beaches...

Onward on *Oceania*. To the manmade harbor at Ulladulla which was also, for a period, home to Stanley Earngey and family. Then to the lovely calm waters of Jervis Bay where we anchored at the 'Hole in the Wall', another favourite spot off the beach inside the southern headland. We had sometimes towed our little trailer-sailor named '*Prauwin*'—Pidgin English for 'Following Wind' although it was often mistakenly called '*Prawn*' by those unfamiliar with Papua and New Guinea and the language—here from Canberra.

Two days later the towers of the Sydney central business district loomed on the horizon taking our minds back to Captain Cook who was to make his first anchorage in Australia at Botany Bay, and his first contact with Australia's aborigines.

Cook's Journal 29 April 1770:

'...we stood into the bay and anchored under the southern shore (of Botany Bay)... saw as we came in on both points of the bay Several natives and a few huts, men, women and children on the south shore ... to which place I sent boats in the hope of speaking to them ... as we approached the shore they all made off except two men who seem'd resolved to oppose I landing – as soon as I saw this I ordered the boats to lay on their oars in order to speak to them but this was to little purpose for ... (we) could not understand one word they said. We then threw them some nails (and) beads a shore and they seem'd not ill pleased in so much as they beckon'd us to come on shore but in this we were mistaken for as soon as we put the boat in they came again to oppose us upon which I fired a musket between the two which had no other effect than to make them retire back where bundles of their darts lay and one of them took up a stone and threw at us which caused my firing a second musket load with small shot and altho' some of the shot struck the man yet it had no effect on them ... immediately after this we landed which we had no sooner done so than they throw'd two darts at us this obliged me to fire a third shot soon after which they made off... we found a few small huts made of the bark of trees in one of which there were four or five small children with whom we left some strings of beads... three canoes lay upon the beach the worst I ever saw they were about 12 or 14 feet long made of one piece of bark of a tree drawn or tied up at each end and in the middle kept open by pieces of sticks...'

Cook's Journal 1 May 1770:

'In the PM ten of the natives again visited the watering place. I being on board at this time went immediately ashore, but before I got there they were going away, I follow'd them alone and unarm'd some distance along the shore but they would not stop... we left several articles such as Cloth, Looking glasses, Combs, Beeds, Nails etc... after thus we made excursions into the country... a great part of it might be cultivated.'

Cook did try, at great personal risk, to establish friendly relations with the Australian aborigines. In 1779, on his third voyage of discovery, he was killed by Hawaiians while trying to do the same there. On 6 May Cook continued north, having failed to make friendly contact, but importantly had established the presence of a fine harbour, which he named Port Jackson.

Entering Sydney Harbour on a yacht is an unforgettable experience. The passage through the towering cliff faces of North and South Heads is dramatic, and suddenly you are in one of the world's great harbours and surrounded by one of the world's great cities. From being alone on the heaving ocean, remote from your fellow man you are suddenly surrounded by the buzz, the energy, the excitement that is Sydney. The harbour is alive with colour and movement and your eyes are drawn to two of the world's iconic structures: the Sydney Harbour Bridge and the Sydney Opera House.

It is amazing that not so very long ago, in 1788 a fleet of eleven small wooden ships brought a little over one thousand men, women and children, including seven hundred convicts to Sydney Cove. They did not bring much with them: seven horses, twenty-nine sheep, seventy-four pigs, seven cattle, six rabbits—which had proliferated to ten billion by 1920—some fruit trees and seedlings and sixty-five thousand litres of rum. They knew their priorities.

This entire invasion army would have been easily carried by one Manly Ferry, although Health and Safety Regulations would have required the rum and the animals left behind, and the heavy steel leg shackles removed from most of the invasion force.

Very few, if any, were here because they wanted to be. The convicts were being sent into exile and the remainder were under orders of the British Government. The first governor, Captain Arthur Phillip, was invested with the power of the British Government and on arrival issued orders that the native aborigines, who had been the sole occupants of the land for some fifty thousand years, were not to be offended or molested and were to be treated with every mark of friendship. This was strictly enforced by Philip, who soon hanged a convict for the murder of an aborigine. Sadly, these ideals were not always met, and over the years there were many conflicts, some bloody, between the indigenes and those who kept arriving from all over the world. European and Asian diseases and alcohol decimated those who had never before encountered them.

When considering the interaction of the new arrivals and the indigenes the following opinion of Arthur Findlay in 'The Curse of Ignorance' is worth noting.

'Europe at the close of the 18th century, could certainly not be called civilised, as we now understand the word. The roads between the towns were infested with highwaymen, and the dark filthy streets by gangs of thugs ready to strike down any unprotected person. In Britain, Dick Turpin and men like him, made travelling dangerous, and a journey from St. Pauls to Westminister at night was a hazardous undertaking. Street brawls were common, blows were readily given and returned, drunkenness was accepted as something quite natural, tempers were hasty, and there was little self-control.

Baths were unknown, and the poor were filthy and verminous. Children, in rags, swarmed the filthy smelly city streets, receiving neither education, care nor attention from their elders, whose moral standards were of the lowest order. Socially, Britain was backward, and the condition of the poor was deplorable ... Under such conditions both corruption and apathy flourished in Church and State, so much so that Sir Robert Walpole and William Pitt condemned their fellow politicians for their entire lack of ethics and social conscience.'

It was a very different world from the one we are now so lucky to enjoy.

After two years the colony was in danger of starvation but they were saved by the arrival of the second fleet in 1789 and the third fleet in Sydney in 1791. Among the arrivals was a convict Charles Hadley, one of whose descendants was Etta Maria Hadley who was my mother's mother, seen many years later sitting near my father in a fishing launch owned by the chemist Stanley Earngey.

A few years later on 11 January 1800 when the Reverend Henry Fulton—my ancestor through the Earngeys and Hadleys—arrived in Sydney, the population of the settlement had only grown to around three thousand. It still had a makeshift and transient air. Buildings were mainly constructed of roughly dressed wood, the streets muddy tracks; it was not until 1803 that a stone bridge was built over the Tank Stream. Sydney's oldest surviving building, Cadman's Cottage was not completed until 1816, Hyde Park Barracks in 1819 and St James Church in 1824.

Henry Fulton had been born in 1761 in Lisburn, a town in the Lagan Valley a few miles south of Belfast in County Antrim, Ireland. Fulton was originally a Scottish name but by the seventeenth century had become common in England. It is most probable that Henry Fulton's family came to Northern Ireland as part of the relocation of English settlers—known as planters—by the British Crown, which had begun under Henry VIII and continued through to Oliver Cromwell's time.

I do not know when the family actually arrived in Ireland and whether they regarded themselves as English or Irish. However, they had become wealthy damask manufacturers, and when Henry Fulton was a young man he must have identified as an Irishman. In the rebellion of 1798, he put his life at great risk in the support of an independent Ireland, and during his life in Australia he considered himself, and was also regarded by those in the colony, as an Irishman.

In 1788 he entered Trinity College, Dublin as a full paying student—known as a pensioner—and graduated in 1792 with a BA with no specific theological qualifications. At this time, students could either be 'sizars', who were generally from poorer families—often the clergy—and received financial assistance in return for doing some menial work to keep the university functioning, or a 'fellow commoner' who paid double fees and enjoyed some privileges including a three rather than four year degree course, and were often from the nobility.

Sometime after graduation he was ordained into the Church of Ireland by Bishop William Knox and by the late 1790s was a clergyman in the Diocese of Killaloe, a picturesque town at the bottom of Loch Derg on the Shannon River in

County Tipperary. Only a few kilometres from what would become Ro's family home Drominagh, a century and a half later. By this time, he was certainly a sympathiser, and had probably become a member of the Society of United Irishmen. In 1795 he married Ann Walker the daughter of a prominent clergyman and by 1798 there were two children, James and Jane.

In Ireland during the 1780s Sir Henry Grattan—an ancestor of the Esmondes—a liberal member of the Irish parliament organised the Irish Patriot Party and campaigned for the reform of parliament so as to lessen the influence of the English and to extend the voting franchise for Catholics and Presbyterians.

By 1784 the attempts at parliamentary reform had collapsed and those seeking reform were forced to follow a more radical path, which was influenced by the situation in France and the beginning of the French revolution in 1789. A number of radical organisations were established with the aim of achieving self-rule. One of these was The Society of United Irishmen. Most of the initial membership was Protestant, but it was soon linked with Catholic political movements, and an important ideal was that of religious equality and Catholic emancipation

The movement's strategy was to proclaim its ideals by pamphlets, leaflets, newspapers and ballads as well as by personal proselytisation. By 1793 its popularity had grown to such an extent, although it was divided in many of its aims, that the authorities banned it and it was forced underground to become a determined force of revolt against British rule.

A rebellion in Leitrim was bloodily suppressed.

Tensions became more extreme when the French declared war on Britain and links were established between the Society and the French. In 1796 a French fleet carrying fifteen thousand troops was wrecked when attempting to land at Bantry Bay. The British responded by imposing martial law and beginning the brutal suppression of the Society and all dissent to their rule.

By 1798 the Society membership had grown to two hundred and eighty thousand sworn members, and in 1798 Henry Fulton was arrested for administering the 'Defenders Oath' to recruits of the United Irishmen, which was an illegal act after the banning of the society. In August 1979 he was found by the Tipperary court to be guilty of sedition and sentenced to transportation for life.

After his trial the English judge, Sir William Osborne, made some comments that clearly indicated he thought Henry Fulton had used his position as a clergyman to further the cause of the United Irishmen: *'I cannot conceive of a more Compleat Wolf in Sheep's clothing,'* and *'one of the last Men I would turn loose amongst the people'*. However, he did concede that he was a careful and thoughtful pastor of his flock, humbly visiting them on foot. It would be hard for an Irish patriot to receive a greater compliment and escape with his life.

Two of Ro's ancestors, Sir John Esmonde and his cousin Esmonde Kyan, were not so lucky, and were found guilty of sedition and hung as rebels from Carlisle—now O'Connell—Bridge in Dublin.

Sir John had been a leading member of the Society of United Irishmen and had commanded rebel forces in County Kildare, including in the Battle of Prosperous. At 2 a.m. on the night of 24th May 1798 he led a rebel force of about sixty men in an attack on the British garrison at Prosperous, which consisted of members of the Cork Militia and a detachment of a Welsh regiment, the 'Ancient Britons'.

The rebel attack was preceded by the infiltration of a small detachment who, probably aided by Irish girls visiting the soldiers, scaled the walls, killed the sentries and opened the gate. The barracks were then surrounded and torched and, the trapped garrison given the choice of dying in the flames or leaping onto the waiting pikes. About forty of the garrison were killed. The next day British forces retaliated by massacring thirty-four suspected United Irishmen at Dunlavin Green, County Wicklow.

The merchant ship *Minerva* sailed from Cork on 29 August 1799 with Henry Fulton on board. Also, on board were one hundred and sixty male convicts—of whom seventy, including him, were classed as political prisoners and twenty-six female convicts, and a detachment of twenty New South Wales Marine Corps as guards.

Ann Fulton and the two children joined the ship as free travellers and the Fulton family shared a cabin with the family of Joseph Holt who had been a general for the United Irish rebels in County Wicklow. He had avoided John Esmonde's fate by agreeing to self-exile in lieu of punishment. Both he and Henry must have considered themselves lucky, particularly Henry who had actually been convicted of sedition, to be recognised and treated as political prisoners and to be alive and travelling in comparative comfort. The *Minerva* reached Rio de Janeiro on 10 October and arrived safely in Port Jackson on 11 January 1800.

It was now twelve years since the arrival of the first fleet and the colony was now in a more sustainable situation. Farming practices had been adapted to local conditions, harvests were better, and the near famines of the early nineties were now only bad memories.

The role of the NSW Corps was to ensure that the Governor had the power to govern, but this had been subverted by the increasing economic and commercial power of members of the army. Through both official and unofficial means, they controlled the import and distribution of ship's cargoes—including rum which was commonly used as currency and resulted in the NSW Corps being known as the Rum Corps—and the sale and distribution of what was produced in the colony, including the illegal distillation of rum. Through land grants and purchase many had become large land holders benefitting from convict labour and what it produced.

The number of Irish convicts and their families, many of whom had been deported for association with the Irish Rebellion, now made up nearly a fifth of the population. This added another level of concern for government, on top of the normal security considerations of the penal colony.

Henry Fulton and his family had made good friends amongst the officers they had travelled with, particularly Captain William Cox and the ship's surgeon JW Price, both of whom made representations to Governor Hunter on their behalf. Within the year he was appointed to carry out ministerial duties in the Hawkesbury region, which after the departure of the Principal Chaplain, the Reverend Richard Johnson, in October, left him placed behind the Assistant Chaplain the Reverend Samuel Marsden in the ministerial hierarchy in the colony.

However, he did have his problems. In 1801 the Church of England and the Church of Ireland were united by an act of Parliament to become the United Church of England and Ireland. This left Henry as a convict and a minister in a church which no longer existed. Serious social and theological handicaps. It was not until 1811 that he was given a Crown Commission as Assistant Chaplain in New South Wales, but I can find no record of him becoming an ordained minister of the Church of England, despite his original benefactor Bishop Knox later making personal representations to the Archbishop of Canterbury. All of which would explain the very poor recognition he has received in the annals of that church.

He and Marsden did not get on. Partly, but certainly not entirely, for the reasons outlined above. Since his arrival in 1794 Marsden had followed the lead of the Rum Corps officers and had made himself into a large and wealthy landholder and was very much part of that 'club'. It was common for ministers to act as magistrates, but in Marsden's case he had made himself infamous for the use of the lash, not just as punishment but for interrogation. Although Marsden, whose father had been a labourer, had attended university before ordination, his education did not match that of Fulton's. More-over Fulton was primarily interested in the welfare of his parishioners and a love of scholarship, rather than the pursuit of wealth and power. He was to accumulate an extensive library dominated by works on science and mathematics.

In March 1801 Henry Fulton was conditionally pardoned by Governor King and sent as chaplain to the new penal settlement at Norfolk Island, which was in part established to isolate the most dangerous of the convicts. King's opinion of Fulton was that since arriving in the colony he had conducted himself with great propriety and in a most exemplary manner. Although pleased with his pardon he found it difficult to uproot himself and his family from the community in the Hawkesbury region, where he had been ministering and where he felt at home, to go to a remote outpost which was a 'very disagreeable place for a person who has a growing family.' It was a harsh environment and very tragically his four-year old daughter Jane died there.

By May 1803 he was authorised to be paid an assistant chaplains' stipend. Governor King continued to be impressed by his 'exemplary' conduct and in 1807 Governor Bligh described him as 'a good, moral man, becoming his situation'. Despite this he too would have preferred a Church of England minister—who was not an ex-convict—which is easy enough to understand.

In 1806 he was unconditionally pardoned and recalled to Sydney as Acting Chaplain. He was to take over from Marsden who was returning on leave to England. Amongst other things he was supposed to speak in support of Governor Bligh's reforms, which were aimed at weakening the hold over the colony by the Rum Corps and improving the situation of the emancipated settlers.

Fulton and Marsden did not get on well during the handover. Marsden's resentment had not abated, and he later reneged on an agreement to share his stipend while he was in England. Marsden was glad to get away. His finely tuned political antennae could see trouble coming. He wrote: *'I considered this circumstance a highly favourable dispensation of Providence towards myself ... being aware that a great political storm was fast gathering in which, if I remained, I could not well avoid being involved.'*

On the 26 January 1810 the officers and men of the Rum Corps led by Major George Johnston, marched on Government House and arrested Governor Bligh. Fulton was with the Governor when the soldiers arrived and bravely attempted to bar their access. As he had in Ireland, he saw his duty as standing up for his parishioners and the reforms that Bligh was instigating. For his actions he was also placed under house arrest, although he was later released, and suspended by the military from all the chaplain's duties.

He remained loyal to Bligh, writing to London in his support and acting as his personal chaplain. Rowland Wilson of the London Missionary Society described his suspension as the *'silencing of a most sound divine'*. In a letter to Viscount Castlereagh on 20 July 1808 Fulton had revealed his motivation in supporting Bligh, arguing that Bligh's reforms were bringing genuine benefits to the struggling and indebted settlers in the Hawkesbury region, his parishioners.

He later returned to England to testify in support of Bligh and subsequently returned to NSW where he continued to play a prominent role in public affairs as a minister, magistrate, emancipist and as an educator. He established the Castlereagh Classical Academy where young men were taught Latin, Greek, French, English, Writing and Mathematics to equip students for careers in education, commerce, the military or navy.

His wife, Ann, died in 1836 and he followed her a few years later in 1840, aged 79. Their son John married Elizabeth Cartwright. Their daughter, Henrietta Fulton, married William Hadley and their daughter Etta married Stanley George Earngey, whose youngest daughter was my mother Hazel.

In 1840, the same year that Henry Fulton died a twenty-year-old Irishman, James Earngey, and his wife, Catherine, had arrived in Sydney aboard the *Lady Clarke*. His immigration certificate is a little hard to decipher, but it appears to say that he was 'reading divinity' and there were no complaints about him. In due course their son George married Kate Bottrill, and their son was the chemist from Eden and the south coast, Stanley George Earngey.

I only met grandfather Earngey once when I was six or seven and he was well into his seventies. There was a gathering of the Earngey clan at 'Gull Cottage' in George Street Avalon, near Careel Bay. This was the home of his only son, Edison, who had spent most of his life in the merchant marine as a radio operator and had never married, and a daughter Kathleen who had divorced her husband many years before.

In those days the area was quite bushy, certainly not the exclusive area that it is today. There were always koalas in the trees or wandering clumsily around the garden if they happened to be awake, which was not often. The mud flats at Careel Bay were alive with soldier crabs and their burrows. A marvellous place for a young boy to enjoy himself poking around in the mud, chasing crabs, and getting wet and dirty.

Both Eddy and Kath were keen artists and about this time Eddy, much to everyone's delight, was 'hung' in the Archibald. I still treasure an impressionist portrait of myself done some years later at the end of my first year at Duntroon.

Grandfather Earngey was camping in a sleep-out in the backyard of the fibro cottage and I have vague memories of he and I prospecting for either gold or jewels in the scrub near the rear fence. He had been an entrepreneurial man. At one stage he was quite prosperous, with a number of commercial properties along the south coast, some of which he operated his chemist shops in. He became worried about the amount of estate duty his wife would have to pay on his death and transferred all the property into Etta's name, paying the required stamp duty. Unfortunately, Etta died first, and the estate duty was paid, and then paid again on his death. This put a big dent in his wealth, and I can imagine how annoyed he would have been.

So, the Peterswalds have multiple connections with Sydney since the very early days—1791—, although it was not until the 1920s that my paternal grandfather, Police Superintendent John Peterswald who was born in 1863 in Adelaide, settled permanently in Sydney after a career as a country policeman. In the course of which he had courted and married Jemima Keith, daughter of the mysterious sea captain, miner and pastoralist in the Monaro high country, James Keith.

My father John Peterswald was one of their seven children and married Hazel in 1933. They spent much of their lives in country New South Wales, mostly in Taree on the mid-north coast. We moved back to Sydney in 1954, when I was eleven. How the Peterswalds came to arrive in Adelaide in 1853 is quite a saga, which was not fully fleshed out until after the fall of the USSR and the arrival of the internet. It is a story best told a little later on.

Meanwhile, back in the present aboard *Oceania*, we had picked up a mooring in front of Dave and Jill Henry's home at Birchgrove, celebrated our arrival and started to think about the next leg. Along with Don and Sue Clark we returned to Tasmania for a brief winter, and Peter Knight returned to Canberra.

~ THE CORAL SEA 2002 ~

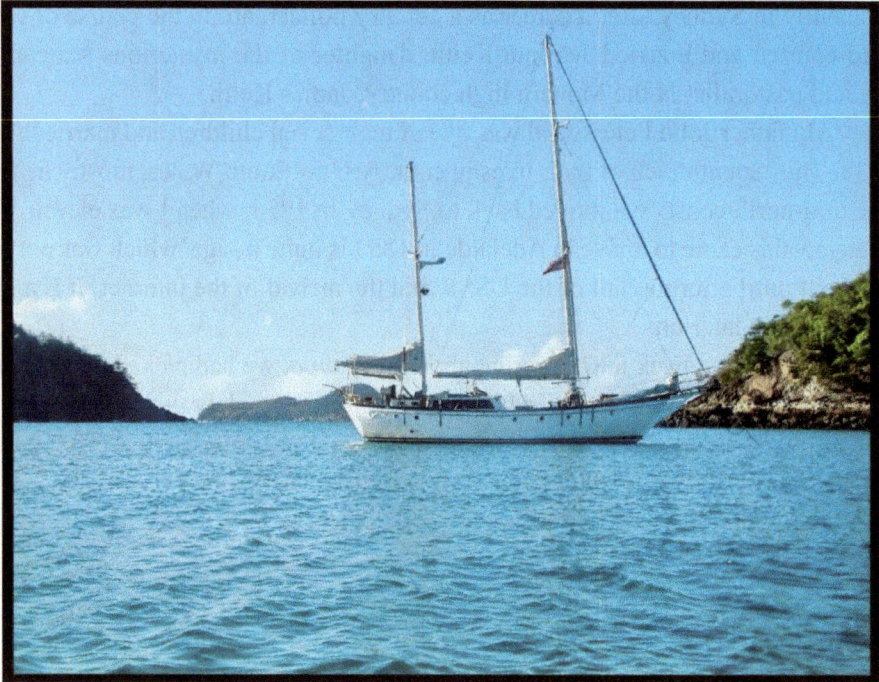

Oceania – Whitsunday Islands Queensland

At the beginning of spring we were back onboard *Oceania* and ready to head north. Our last night in Sydney Harbour was spent anchored in Spring Cove, a lovely spot near the old Quarantine Station just inside North Head. Most of the foreshore is a lush green reserve framing the whiteness of Store Beach, which is still washed by the spring on the hillside above that gave the cove its name in 1788. It is a remarkably peaceful anchorage for one located in the heart of one of the world's great cities.

A weather front passed over in the night, and the next day we had a lovely brisk run up the coast to Broken Bay. We stayed close in to enjoy the views of the coastline that held so many memories for us both. My family had lived at Freshwater after we moved from Taree to Sydney in 1954, and I had spent my teenage years on the northern beaches. As a boy I had surfed at every beach and clambered around every headland. Ro had good friends who lived at Whale Beach and had had many happy holidays there.

Ro's remarkable family did not arrive in Australia until 1954. Not so long ago that made them very recent arrivals, but now it's getting to be more years than I like to count, and she is definitely a very proud Australian.

The family was originally among the Viking warriors who conquered the Normandy region of modern-day France. In due course they became Norman warriors in the service of William the Conqueror and were in his army at the Battle of Hastings in 1066. They were rewarded with land and titles in England.

In 1169 Sir Geoffrey de Estmonde was among thirty or so Norman knights who crossed to Ireland to aid the King of Leinster, but later joined the army of the Earl of Pembroke—Strongbow—who invaded Ireland to assert the rule of Henry II. The family established themselves in Wexford and over time, built castles at Johnstown in 1240, Ballynastragh in 1300, Lymbrick in 1602 and at Huntington in County Carlow in 1625. The castles at Ballynastragh and Huntington remain in the family to this day, and Ballynastragh is still the seat of the seventeenth Baronet.

They became Norman-Irish warriors, more proud of their Irish heritage than the Irish themselves. It seems that in almost every generation an Esmonde gave their life or their freedom in the cause of Irish independence and the castle at Ballynastragh was burnt to the ground twice—once by Oliver Cromwell. But at the same time, and who can explain the contradiction, they were fierce warriors in the armies of England and Great Britain. They fought in the Crusades and have the appropriate coat-of-arms to prove it, in Europe and India, at Trafalgar, the Crimean War and both World Wars and along the way won awards for valour, including two Victoria Crosses and a Distinguished Service Order, perhaps the equal of any other family in the British Empire. But they were not just warriors. The family history is littered with writers and poets, doctors and politicians, judges and bishops and is deeply woven into the history of Ireland.

Many of Ro's forebears deserve special mention, but perhaps the most deserving are the Victoria Cross recipients, the first being Captain Thomas Esmonde of 18th Regiment during the Crimean War. This war was fought from 1853 to 1856 between Russia and a coalition including France, England and Turkey. The main object of the war was to prevent Russia taking control of the Bosphorus and the sea route from the Black Sea to the Mediterranean from the Ottoman Empire. The climax of the war was reached in 1855 during the Siege of Sevastopol and the Battle of the Great Redan, and it was here that Captain Esmonde distinguished himself.

His citation reads:

For having, after being engaged in the attack on the Redan, repeatedly assisted, at great personal risk under heavy fire of shell and grape, in rescuing wounded men from exposed situations; and also while in command of a covering party two days after, for having rushed with the most prompt and daring gallantry, to the spot where a fireball from the enemy had just been lodged, which he effectually extinguished, before it had betrayed the position of the working party under his protection – thus saving it from murderous fire of shell and grape, which was immediately opened upon the spot where the fireball had landed.

Dates of Acts of Bravery 18th – 20th June 1855.

Captain Esmonde received his cross from the hands of Her Majesty the Queen at Portsmouth on Monday, 2nd August 1858. He left the army ten years later but died from injuries sustained in a riding accident in 1872. He is buried in Bruges.

During World War II Squadron Leader Eugene Esmonde took part in two of the war's epic naval battles and was awarded the Distinguished Flying Cross for his part in the 'Hunt for the Bismarck' and the Victoria Cross for the role he played in the 'Channel Dash'.

In May 1941 the German battleship, Bismark was ordered to break into the Atlantic and attack allied shipping. The allies were aware of the danger and tried to prevent the *Bismarck* leaving the Baltic Sea. At the Battle of the Denmark Strait the British battleship *HMS Hood* was sunk and the *HMS Prince of Wales* damaged. Although there was damage to the *Bismarck*, she was able to escape into the Atlantic and in company with the cruiser, *Prinz Eugen* headed for the French port of Saint-Nazaire for repairs.

The Royal navy ordered all ships in the area to join in the pursuit. In all there were six battleships and battle cruisers, two aircraft carriers, thirteen cruisers and twenty-one destroyers committed to the chase.

By 10 p.m. on the night of the 25 May the aircraft carrier HMS Victorious had closed to within 120 miles of the *Bismarck*. It was approaching dusk on a wild and stormy night and the seas were rough. Although this was close to the extreme range for the nine Fairie Swordfish torpedo bombers of 825 Naval Air Squadron their commander, Lieutenant-Commander Eugene Esmonde advised the captain of the *Victorious* that they would be able to launch a successful attack. The majority of his pilots were inexperienced, and some had not yet even undertaken an operation off an aircraft carrier. Notwithstanding the awful conditions, he managed to locate the *Bismarck* in the rough seas and gathering gloom and led his pilots through a wall of anti-aircraft fire into the attack, despite his own plane having already been damaged by the fire. All planes dropped their torpedoes, most were near misses, but one struck the *Bismarck* amidships, causing enough damage to slow the ship's speed to 12 knots. This damage enabled a later attack by aircraft off the *HMS Ark Royal* which damaged the steering of the *Bismarck* and led to its eventual destruction. For this operation he was awarded the Distinguished Service Order, an award for gallantry second only in prestige to the Victoria Cross. He had previously been aboard the *HMS Courageous* when she was sunk and would be on the *HMS Ark Royal* when that ship met the same fate a little later. He was Mentioned in Dispatches for his conduct in this catastrophe.

By anyone's reckoning he had already survived a harrowing war and must have considered himself lucky to still be alive and in one piece. However, he was about to play a tragic role in a battle that was to become known as the Channel Dash.

On the night of 11 February 1942, a German naval battle group including two battleships *Gneisenau* and *Scharnhorst*, a heavy cruiser *Prinz Eugen* which had survived the Bismarck episode, six destroyers, fourteen torpedo boats and twenty-six E-boats slipped out of the harbour of Brest in Brittany heading north. Air cover was provided by thirty-two bombers and 252 fighters. The German battle group represented a potentially calamitous threat to the allied war effort and their destruction was of paramount importance. It had been assessed that if they broke out of Brest their most likely route would be up the Channel, and as part of the response to such a move 825 NAA Squadron, still commanded by Eugene, was moved to Manston in Kent, close to Dover.

It was not until mid-morning on the 12th that the German flotilla was located, and they were already off the French coast near Boulogne. Around midday they came into range of British shore batteries at Dover, who opened fire but caused no damage. Cloud cover was making attacks by conventional bombers ineffectual and Motor Torpedo Boats could not get through the German destroyer and fighter screen.

Three squadrons of RAF fighters had been allotted to give protection to Eugene's squadron as they launched their attack, but by 12.20 pm they had not yet arrived overhead at Manston. Eugene realised that he would have to go alone if he was to reach the target and took off. Remember that he had recently survived the anti-aircraft fire of one battleship and was now about to face a flotilla of forty ships and a swarm of enemy fighter planes, so he knew the danger of what he was undertaking. At 12.28 pm he did meet up with one squadron, but it was soon forced off by the German fighter cover. The other two squadrons did not arrive until after the event. Eugene, who led in the first section of three planes, was forced to run the gauntlet of the massed enemy fighters unaided before he faced the firepower of the mighty German flotilla. Every gun in the fleet was firing at them, the air was filled with exploding shells and arcs of tracer fire. It had probably always been a suicide mission, but now there was no doubt of their fate. Disregarding his safety, he pressed on. He got close, but not close enough to launch before his plane exploded. Perhaps it was his brave determination that allowed his companions to get within range, and they did manage to launch their torpedoes before they too were shot down. The second section of three planes crossed the destroyer screen before disappearing from view, never to be seen again.

Subsequent attacks by both the British navy and the air force were marked by disorganisation and poor coordination and failed to prevent the German flotilla from passing through the channel. The event was a devastating blow to the prestige and morale of both the armed services and the country as a whole.

Perhaps the only thing to be proud of was the gallant sacrifice of the men of 825 Squadron.

Admiral Sir Bertram Ramsay, commander of the Dover area said: '... *in my opinion the gallant sortie of these six Swordfish aircraft constitutes one of the finest exhibitions of self-sacrifice and devotion to duty the war had ever witnessed.*'

The German Vice Admiral Ciliax who was aboard the flotilla: '...*the mothball attack of a handful of ancient planes, piloted by men whose bravery surpasses any other action by either side that day.*'

The citation for Eugene's posthumous Victoria Cross:

3rd March 1942.

Madam,

I am commanded by My Lords Commissioners of the Admiralty to inform you that the King has been graciously pleased to award the Victoria Cross to your son, Lieutenant-Commander (A) Eugene Esmonde, D.S.O., Royal Navy, for valour, in the action in which he lost his life.

On the morning of Thursday, the 12th of February, 1942, Lieutenant-Commander Esmonde, in command of a Squadron of the Fleet Air Arm, was told that the German Battle Cruisers Scharnhorst and Gneisenau, and the Cruiser Prince Eugen, strongly supported by some thirty surface craft, were entering the Straits of Dover, and that his squadron must attack before they reached the sand-banks North East of Calais.

Lieutenant-Commander Esmonde knew well that his enterprise was desperate. Soon after noon he and his Squadron of six Swordfish set course for the enemy, and after ten minutes flight were attacked by a strong force of fighters. Touch was lost with his fighter escort; and in the action which followed all his aircraft were damaged. He flew on, cool and resolute, serenely challenging hopeless odds, to encounter the deadly fire of the Battle Cruisers and their Escort, which shattered the port wing of his aircraft. Undismayed, he led his Squadron on, straight into this inferno of fire. Almost at once he was shot down; but his Squadron launched a determined attack, of which at least one torpedo is believed to have struck the Battle Cruisers, and from which not one of the six aircraft returned.

His high courage and splendid resolution will live in the traditions of the Royal Navy, and remain for many generations a fine and stirring memory.

I am to express their Lordships' pleasure at this, the highest mark of his Majesty's appreciation, and their deep regret that your son did not live to receive it.

At the end of the war he was remembered in Churchill's famous victory speech on 13 May 1945.

'When I think of these days I also think of other episodes and personalities. I do not forget Lieutenant-Commander Eugene Esmonde VC DSO, Lance-Corporal Kenneally VC, Captain Fegen VC and other Irish heroes that I could easily recite...'

How was I lucky enough to meet Rosemary, a scion of such a family? Circumstances had left me without a partner for the Queen's Birthday Ball at Duntroon in 1965. But I had already noticed the charms of the youngest sister of my friend, Eugene Esmonde (who was born in the year of his uncle's death). Eugene wasn't all that excited about allowing a date, but against his better judgment he relented. It was just my lucky day.

We can leave the memories of those famous old warships, and the brave men who gave their lives, and return to our beautiful *Oceania*, sliding through the sunshine along the northern beaches.

After rounding Barrenjoey Lighthouse we anchored in Refuge Bay for a late lunch, enjoying the afternoon sun and the embrace of the surrounding sandstone cliffs.

We spent some time in the winding waters of Broken Bay and Pittwater before Don and Sue Clark joined us again, and early one morning well before dawn, we headed out. There were flashes of lightning out to sea behind the Palm Beach peninsula as we hoisted the sails, persuading us to put a precautionary reef in the mainsail. Daylight found us well out to sea beneath a leaden sky with patches of storm clouds away to the south.

During the morning the breeze freshened, sweeping away the dullness, chasing the wispy white clouds overhead and flicking the crests off the following waves. We rollicked along and in the early afternoon the prominences of Yacaaba and Tomaree Heads, which mark the entrance to Port Stephens began to peep over the horizon. By dusk we had edged into Shoal Bay and dropped our anchor in four metres on a clear sandy bottom. The entrance into this beautiful harbour had been quite spectacular. High rocky headlands battered by the southerly sea, spray-flecked offshore islands, but once inside a calm bay encircled by a gleaming white beach.

Captain Cook didn't stop here but recorded it in his journal.

Cook's Journal 11 May 1770:

'Winds southerly in the day and in the night Westerly a gentle breeze and clear weather. At 4pm past at a distance of 1 Mile a low rocky point which I named Port Stephens that appeared to me from the mast head to be sheltered from all winds ... We saw several smooks a little way in the country...'

Port Stephens is another place with lots of memories. In 1976 we had hauled *Prauwin*, our 22ft Boomeroo sailor/trailer, up here from Canberra and set off to explore the Myall Lakes. We had a crew of six, ranging in age from Georgina, aged five to Poppy age seventy-three, with Charlotte, Ro, myself and sister Wendy in between, plus our dog, Gatsby. It was a bit crowded at times, but fine at night once we had a tent set up on the shore and a campfire going.

The freshwater lakes cover an area of around nine thousand hectares and are connected to Port Stephens by the Myall River which is shallow (as are the lakes themselves) and only navigable in small craft. Most of the shoreline is now national park, lined with sandy beaches and coastal scrub. It is a wonderful and safe place for a family beach holiday.

After a night at Shoal Bay on *Oceania* we moved around to Fame Cove. A place we had fond memories of from our 1976 trip. We had spent a few days with the girls and had a couple of raucous nights with Harry Smith MC, who was the Australian company commander at the Battle of Long Tan, the most famous of the Australian battles of the Vietnam War.

On board *Oceania* our planned two-night stay drew into three as we waited for strong northerlies to abate and watched a pair of sea eagles refurbish their nest high up in the tall eucalypts surrounding the cove. The eagles seemed to be on good terms with the flocks of white galahs that were also nesting there, unconcerned by the great birds as they came and went.

The wind finally returned to the south, and although there was still a strong wind warning, we decided to make the short hop to the enchanting anchorage of Sugarloaf Bay near the small village of Seal Rocks twenty-five miles north. We reefed the sails and set off, past Broughton Island which is a few miles offshore and provides a few remote and often solitary anchorages, untrodden beaches and a breeze always rich with the tangy aroma of seaweed. A few of the local seagulls sensed breakfast was in the offing and left their rocky crags to wheel overhead, screeching complaints at the cook to hurry up.

Ro, who is a great cook in normal circumstances, is unsurpassed in rough weather. With the galley heeling, surging up and down as the chasing swells caught us and pushed the stern high, then surged beneath us, tossing the bow as they rolled on, she worked her miracles. Toasted fingers of cheese, tomato and salmon topped with delicious relishes, freshly brewed coffee—what a woman!

There was very little left for those rude complaining gulls, who flew back to their crags to sulk—these days they would have reported us on Trip Advisor but fortunately this was well before all that.

By the time we edged into Seal Rocks the wind had built up to a wet and freezing thirty knots, and we were very glad to get out of it. There was a bit of a roll in the bay and although the wind howled all night, we felt reasonably secure—you can never really not worry completely – well, perhaps I could when I was young. I have become rather famous in later life for the over large anchors I use—in this case a 120 lb plough. Let them laugh!

In the morning the wind had eased a little and from time to time the sun broke through the chasing clouds, turning the waters of the bay into translucent blues and greens. It was calm enough for a fisherman to troll along the inside of the headland, but outside there was still a large sea running, the white caps at times gleaming, but grey and bleak when dark clouds covered the sun. Mid-morning we recovered the anchor and set off for Crowdy Head planning to arrive there on a rising tide with enough water to clear the bar. It was almost dark when we finally tied up alongside the jetty. The wind was howling again, and we were glad to be secure and to enjoy a snug meal in the cabin.

When I was a boy my family lived in nearby Taree where I had been born in

1943. After the war it was a quiet country town of weatherboard houses and corrugated iron roofs, spreading along the northern bank of the expansive Manning River. It was a few miles upstream from where it flowed through sandy beaches into the ocean, close to where we were now moored.

On the other side of the river the rich alluvial river flats were dotted with dairy farms, the farmhouses resting on high wooden piles with a somewhat dilapidated air. To the west the horizon was the thickly forested slopes of the Great Dividing Range.

The Sydney to Brisbane railroad ran along the fringe of town, not far from where our house sat on a suburban block, opposite a park and a rugby league oval. The town's public schools were a short walk across the park near the town's commercial centre, astride the Pacific Highway that ran through the town a hundred metres or so from the river.

Our home was a small Federation style cottage with partially enclosed verandas on three sides. It sat behind a picket fence and a small garden of roses and annuals. There was a detached wooden garage at the end of our driveway, but no car. I think there had been one pre-war, but a car was then a luxury we did without.

My mother cooked dinner of meat and three vegetables on a wood stove, breakfast was cereal and toast, lunch was sandwiches. She did the household washing in a wood-heated copper and had an ice box to keep a few things chilled, there was no telephone and one radio. Television was still years away. Some nights my parents might have shared a bottle of beer with dinner, but I cannot remember there being wine in the house until the 1960s.

My father, John Peterswald, was the assistant manager of the local Bank of New South Wales, a position he held for many years, foregoing transfer and promotion to allow us to finish our schooling in one place. Although his job gave him some status in the town his salary did not run to many luxuries, and it was not until 1950 when he was forty-seven years old that my parents purchased their first home. The purchase in Chatham, a new suburb on the fringe of town, was enabled by a small inheritance from my mother's father—the Eden chemist, Stanley Earngey. Thereafter my mother became an enthusiastic player in the property market, badgering Dad into many moves he was not too keen on.

Taree Primary School was a mixture of solid red brick buildings built before the war and some semi-detached wooden classrooms built to accommodate the children of a growing town, soon to be augmented by the first of the baby boomers. The classrooms were grouped around a bitumen quadrangle. At lunchtime bare-footed boys competed ferociously at games of marbles and cricket, with a bit of scuffling and wrestling thrown in. The girls, more sedately, skipped.

56

The teachers carried canes and most days some child copped a caning, either on the hand or on the backside and I certainly had my share, and more. I was good at sport, captain of the schools under four and a half and five and a half stone rugby league teams and, one year was chosen in the 'possibles and probables' of the NSW country schoolboys' team. I was also captain of one of the school 'house' cricket teams, until I was sacked by teachers for supposedly using go slow tactics to avoid defeat in one game. Causing me to take up tennis instead.

I had a canoe on the river and used to 'borrow' my brother's sailing skiff; for a while I mucked about in an old wooden dinghy that we rescued from the mangroves. We swam and surfed, explored the countryside on foot and bike, terrified birdlife and rabbits with catapults and air rifles with a kelpie cross in tow and generally had a fantastically carefree childhood. I grew up independent and used to going my own way and with a love of the water that was to last all my life.

My parents were nominally Church of England, but rarely went to church, although I can remember them very bravely attending a Catholic Christmas service with some Irish friends. This was in the days when it was generally believed that that this was on a par with fighting for the Japanese in the war. Periodically I attended Sunday Schools which were run by the various Christian denominations in the town. Over time I was a guest of the Church of Christ, the Church of England, the Methodists, the Baptists and I think others.

In 1954 Dad was offered a promotion and a transfer to Sydney which he decided to accept—on orders from my mother. Both Wendy and Richard had left school and as it is with most country children their prospects were much better in Sydney than the bush. Richard, who had been captain and dux of Taree High School wanted to study law and Wendy had a chance of a job with the ABC in Sydney. I finished primary school at the Freshwater School in Sydney and the following year started at Manly Boys High School.

But back to our fine ketch—*Oceania*.

The next day, when we were confident there was enough water over the bar to leave Crowdy Head Harbour, we eased ourselves out into the boisterous sea. The southerly was still blowing, catching eagerly at our sails and intoxicating us with the salty, heady smell of the untamed ocean. Past the familiar face of Point Perpendicular, guarding the entrance to enticing Camden Haven. Past Port Macquarie with the strong wind still over our stern.

In the twilight we nosed into a sandy anchorage behind Korogoro Point near the small village of Hat Head where we enjoyed the beauty of the high rocky headland and the sweep of the long white beach. A glorious sunset, and in the morning another delicious dawn—the water clear, over a shiny sandy bottom, the wind still fresh, pushing a gentle swell into our corner.

Stronger winds were forecast for later in the day and we thought it best to go around to Trial Bay where Smoky Cape—another of the many landmarks named by Cook, gave a little more protection from the south. Outside, the beautiful dawn had been already swallowed by grey sullen clouds and a lumpy uncomfortable sea. Smoky Cape was shrouded in cloud and rain, exactly why Cook named it 'smoky', although it was one of many areas where he reported seeing 'smooks' or aboriginal fires. It was an awe-inspiring sight as it came and went behind dark rolling clouds and veils of passing showers. By the time we had given the off-lying rocks a wide berth we were all soaked, cold and muttering about the bloody weather.

Rounding Laggers Point, dominated by the imposing stone ruins of the old Trial Bay Jail, we were greeted by the very welcome sight of the wide smooth expanse of Trial Bay.

Soon the skies cleared, and although the wind was still blowing a gale we were once again happy with our lot and absorbed in a late breakfast of pancakes and fruit. Later we went ashore to investigate and had a fish dinner at the township of South West Rocks, enjoying the fine view over the bay to the lighthouse on Smoky Cape. The views from the lighthouse are one of the most beautiful and dramatic along the coast. Rugged hills running to a rocky foreshore broken by small sand-fringed bays. To the south, mile after mile of beach edged by tossing ocean.

Up early and away for Coffs Harbour. A cloudy dawn soon gave way to a sparkling morning with a good wind from the south-west. After some hours of beautiful sailing, patches of storm cloud began to form behind us and an hour out of Coffs we were overtaken by squalls and rain. Once again, we were soaked and the sea ominous, with lots of breaking water and we were very glad to surf into the relatively calm water behind the breakwater. By nightfall we had registered gale force gusts from the east and were grateful that we were in one of the few protected places along this part of the coast. There are no all-weather ports between Broken Bay and the northern tip of Fraser Island in southern Queensland. The entrance to Coffs can be closed in dirty weather and all the rest have bars or shallow water which can be impassable because of storm or tide.

Strong northerlies kept us in Coffs for the best part of a very enjoyable week. The marina is in a most attractive situation, joining the green hump of Mutton Bird Island to the mainland. While we were there the first of these remarkable migratory birds were arriving back from the northern hemisphere to nest and breed along the east coast as far south of Tasmania—which also has at least one Mutton Bird Island.

There are good walks, good beaches and a number of convivial restaurants within an easy stroll. If you are inclined to go further afield the hinterland varies from lush farming land to the heavily timbered ranges—all of which goes to explain why it has been officially registered as one of God's waiting rooms —but this certainly doesn't mean you cannot have fun here.

Eventually the northerlies began to abate, and we set off in mid-morning, planning to do an overnight hop to the Surfers Paradise Seaway, timing our arrival to give us a rising tide to cross the notorious bar.

The sun was out, the water sparkling, our hearts sang. Dolphins played around our bow, shearwaters skimmed the wave tops and the occasional gull investigated us, circling over our wake before gliding off. Further out a whale was 'blowing'.

By mid-afternoon we were clear of the Solitary Islands and by dusk the wind had swung into the west. As night settled the lights of the fishing fleets from Evans Head and Ballina began to glow in the darkness, strung across our front like a chain of fireflies. Overhead the sky was ablaze and as we neared Cape Byron we thought we caught the first gentle fragrances of the tropics.

For a yacht going north it can be hard work getting past Cape Byron. The northerly current is often strong here, running at three or four knots. On our first cruise north, with Georgie and Simon as crew on *Reveille*, it took the whole night to edge past the cape, struggling along at about two knots across the ground—and being abused by the fishing boats for getting in their bloody way. Then, as we finally put the cape astern, *Reveille's* unreliable motor had broken down, again! Shortly after that, while I was down below cursing and fiddling with the motor, a strong northerly blew in and it looked as if the Gold Coast Seaway would be closed. Thankfully, Simon's helming got us there and Georgie's prayers to any god that was listening, kept the seaway open. They closed it shortly after we reached safety and she had stopped the incantations.

This night on *Oceania* it was a different story, there was almost no current and the steady westerly pushed us along at six to seven knots. We were past the lighthouse, the most easterly point on the Australian coast, before the sun's first rays began to light-up its tall white tower, the Border Ranges and Mount Warning along the western horizon. We had a comfortable entry through the Gold Coast Seaway and by nightfall were happily tied up at the Marina Mirage.

It was wonderful to be met at the marina by Michael and Dianna Battle, friends for many years. We had a few too many drinks on the balmy aft deck before dinner at their apartment close by.

Mike and I had been friends at Duntroon, and at the end of our first year we were among a group who rented a house for a couple of weeks on the Gold Coast, at Mermaid Beach. In 1962 it was just a laidback beachside suburb with understated holiday homes, and rentals had to be cheap to fit the very meagre budget of RMC cadets. On our first morning I had been for a swim at the nearby beach and was drying myself, admiring the view and the two very shapely girls lying in the shade of a nearby beach umbrella. A gust of wind uprooted the umbrella and sent it cartwheeling off. I captured it, and naturally we got to talking. With a little persuasion they agreed to drop into the party we were having that night. There Dianna met Michael, and four years later they were our best man and bridesmaid at our wedding in a thatched church in Taurama Barracks, Papua New Guinea.

At that time accommodation was always very difficult to find in Port Moresby, and while Michael and myself were required to live in the barracks, we struggled to find roofs to keep over the girl's heads. Before the wedding, Ro and Diana had shared various rooms and flats. Port Moresby was a pretty rough frontier town and some of the accommodation was in retrospect, quite horrifying. One flat was actually within a car junkyard, surrounded by barbed wire and a rusted detritus of cars and trucks. On the other side of the fence was a village of half-naked natives who had drifted into the town from the wilds. Mike and I were away a lot of the time and the girls had to fend for themselves. We must have all been mad.

Mike and I served together in the Pacific Islands Regiment, then again with the 5th Battalion in Vietnam. After that Mike had decided he had had enough and left the army. He completed a law degree at Queensland University and a masters at Oxford and came back to practice law in Queensland. On the side he speculated in property and established a college to allow students to bridge between school and university.

Then one day he received a call from one of his old soldiers from Vietnam. He had bought a commercial fishing boat and had some problems with both his health and finances. He was in a bad way. Could Mike help?

Of course, he could. Michael's not-so-secret passion has always been fishing, so he gave law away, and for the next five years became a commercial fisherman working the reefs in Far North Queensland, and like all fishermen he was away from home most of the time. Professional reef fishing has its own particular modus operandi. There is a mother ship which provides accommodation and sustenance and tows a fleet of five or six launches. These launches fish independently among the reefs with hand lines during the day and return with the catch at night. Once the mother ship gets past Cooktown it is very hard for it to tow all the launches south against the strong southerlies that blow through to November. It is also difficult to just hand over the operation and duck home for a visit if you are a thousand miles up the coast.

Finally, Di who is the most understanding and tolerant of women—and of course also being deliciously beautiful and a prodigiously talented artist — threatened severe repercussions if he did not return home and help with the four children.

The next day at Southport we were joined by Ro's brother, Eugene and his wife Jenny, later both our daughters and families, and my brother Richard and his wife Franny.

Don and Sue headed back to Tasmania for Christmas, planning to re-join us further north after the cyclone season had passed. We followed them south a few weeks later, leaving *Oceania* securely berthed at Marina Mirage.

In April the next year we were back, ready to press on northwards.

We enjoy the shallow sandy waters, with their winding channels lined by mangroves and sandbanks that link the Gold Coast waterways with Moreton Bay and Brisbane. But we needed to be careful with tides and had calculated that on the next high tide we would have ten centimetres under our keel at Jacobs Well. In fact, we found that we had to slide *Oceania's* full keel across the sand for about thirty metres with the engine flat out. Pale faces and fixed smiles at the thought of being grounded for two weeks until the next tide high enough would float us off.

In the narrow channels we motored past small craft of every shape and size snuggled into secluded bays and backwaters, and others such as ourselves migrating, north or south. By late afternoon we had taken a berth at the Royal Queensland Yacht Squadron and were making plans for dinner.

In late July 1799 Mathew Flinders was the first to find his way into Moreton Bay and on 28th July recorded his impression of a group of tribesmen:

'I am happy to say (the aboriginals) were all friendly, which is attributable to their opinion of us having undergone a salutary change from the effect of our fire arms at Point Skirmish. These people are evidently of the same race as those at Port Jackson, though speaking in a language which Bongaree could not understand. They fish almost wholly with cast and setting nets, live more in society than the natives to the southward, and are much better lodged. Their spears are of solid wood and used without the throwing stick. Two or three bark canoes were seen; but from the number of black swans in the river, of which eighteen were caught in our little boat, it should seem that these people are not dexterous in the management of either canoe or spear.'

After a few days we continued north, overnighting between the beautiful strip of beach and the wrecks at Tangalooma. It was perfect weather for barbecuing on the aft deck, listening to the gentle lap of the water on the sand and admiring the loom of the mainland lights running for miles and miles along the western sky. In the morning a steady south-easterly followed us through the Spitfire and North West Channels across the top of Moreton Bay and back to the ocean.

Here we re-joined the track of the *Endeavour*, where on the evening of the 17 May 1770, Cook was entering the following observations.

Cook's Journal 17 May 1770:

'At sunset the northernmost point of land bore NBW, and the breakers NWBW distant 4 Miles and the northernmost land set at noon which form'd a point which I nam'd Point Lookout ... on the northside of this point the shore forms a wide open Bay which I named Moreton Bay ... at this time we had a great sea from the south ward which broke prodigious high ...there is a small space where we could see no land (and) some on board was of the opinion that there is a river there because the Sea looked paler than usual ...'

He had not found an anchorage since leaving Botany Bay, and even for this most equable of men you can sense a little frustration in his entries.

Our next stop was just up the coast a little at Mooloolaba, a place we know well and have enjoyed for many years. There is a bar over the river entrance which, as with all bars, deserves respect. Actually, we give all bars so much respect that we avoid them completely whenever possible.

All the river entrances along the New South Wales coast have bars and there are a number of immutable rules for crossing them in a yacht—for me anyway—if you do not want to end up wrecked and/or drowned. In any case I have a bit of pedantry for you, which will be of *no* interest to anyone not planning to sail over a coastal bar.

The most basic thing about crossing a bar in a yacht is to make certain beforehand, that the water will be deep enough at the time you want to cross. This means you must consult an up-to-date chart of the entrance that covers depths and channel markers, and a current tide chart. Bars and channels are constantly changing so up to date information is vital. If possible, speak to the appropriate shore station at the bar entrance before you finalise your plans and departure from the last port. Consider driving up to have a look and a talk.

You need to time your crossing for the last couple of hours of a making tide. This means the tidal flow will help you in, and more importantly you mostly avoid the dangerous waves created at the entrance by the outwards tidal flow. Often, particularly with large rivers, this flow will continue for some hours after the tide starts to rise. You need to time your departure from the last port to arrive at the appropriate time, there is no sense in hanging around outside for hours. Mornings, before a sea breeze builds up the waves is better than later. Daylight is better than night.

Check the wind and wave conditions are safe.

Make sure you speak to the appropriate shore station well before you come in. When you are ready to go in have your engine running, if possible, a bit of sail up to steady things and get you through if the motor stops. Carefully study the wave pattern to pick the best route in and wait for a favourable set of waves. Make sure all the hatches are shuts, small kids below, everyone with life jackets and tied on.

All that seems to be a lot of trouble, but yachts have deep drafts, move more slowly and pose more problems than a fast boat with a shallow draft. Even if you survive one bad experience you will find your partner will probably not want to sail with you again. Ask any lone sailor, or even ask our good friend Mark, about the Clarence River Bar.

So after all that we arrived at Mooloolaba and found the channel markers had been moved, so we waited round for a while and followed a fishing boat in—another very sensible tactic I forgot to mention. No problems at all. We anchored in the river and spent a few days catching up some more with Mike and Di.

Mike had volunteered to provide local expertise for our next hop, which would involve crossing the Wide Bay Bar one of the more notorious bars along the coast. We had done it once before and scared ourselves enough to welcome any assistance.

It is about fifty-five miles from Mooloolaba to Wide Bay. As well as needing to choose a high tide and daylight—preferably in the morning as the leads are almost impossible to see with the afternoon sun in your eyes—for that crossing we needed a high tide to get out of Mooloolaba. There were a number of possibilities involving leaving at absurd hours and sailing overnight. But we all agreed that leaving on the morning high tide, a daylight hop to Double Island Point, anchor there overnight and an early morning crossing the next day was the way to go.

After getting a report from the Tin Can Bay Coast Guard on the bar we headed off beneath a cloudless sky. Off to our portside the long sandy beaches of the Sunshine Coast ran parallel to our course, to seaward the perfect ocean stretched to the distant blue horizon. By midday Noosa was well astern and the twin humps of Double Island Point were clearly visible, and a light sea breeze was flecking the water.

Late afternoon saw us anchored behind Double Island Point and as the sun slid behind the long-deserted sweep of Rainbow Beach, it coloured the western sky a gentle mauve, and highlighted the wispy clouds a pale amber. The still night embraced us; the glow of our lamp's flickering flame cast a golden cocoon about us. The small swell coming around the point rocked us gently. In the darkness we could hear the wash of the surge on the shore and the splash of hunted fish around us. Lots more reminiscing and laughter.

We were up early the next day, the morning light playing on the high cliffs of coloured sand behind the beach and the water still alive with splashing schools of tuna. We still had a few miles to go to the entrance and the leads across the bar were hard to pick up, but we finally got them aligned and headed into the mile and a half run through the first leg of the channel with broken water on each side of us.

Although the conditions were calm, and it was near the top of the making tide we still found large swells standing up behind us before they surged through. Four or five times the yacht surfed as they broke around us, carrying us forward on the breaking face of the wave. It is imperative not to lose control and let the yacht broach, or swing across the front of the wave, which could lead to capsize and swamping.

After what seemed to be a long time, we finally reached the marker for what is known as 'the mad mile' and turned hard left into the leg running behind a sandbank. Here the last rush of the outward tidal race and the wash of the waves coming in over the sandbank churned the water to a maelstrom and we needed to gun the engine to keep steerage and avoid running aground.

Finally, a right turn near Inskip Point and into the protected waters of Wide Bay Harbour behind Fraser Island. Relief and elation. In due course we deposited the other half of our bridal party at Tin Can Bay, a small town, marina and fishing hub on the western shore, before turning our bow northward up the narrow tidal channel that winds its way for some seventy miles between the mainland and Fraser Island the world's largest sand island.

The island is another one of those places whose beauty is impossible to do justice to. The blues of the sky and the warm translucent waters, the green fringes of the mangroves, the glistening sandbanks, the teeming birdlife, the surf and beeches on the outside all go to make many kinds of paradise. And although I do not catch many fish, when we came through here a decade before in *Reveille*, I did catch a few dinners of Blue Swimmer crabs. In fact, with all due modesty, I am not a bad crabber at all— sometimes I think Ro might be getting a bit tired of being reminded of this.

We anchored in a small sandy inlet and with nonchalant expertise I threw some lines in, baited with bacon, and reminded God what a good boy I had been.

We had just enough time to cook and chill the delicious, succulent, mouth-watering crab while having a cool wine before dinner. Thank you, God. I didn't say much about my crabbing ability, well just a little bit, but I couldn't help noticing the admiring glint in Ro's eyes.

We spent two days in this delightful spot. Watching yachts making their way up and down the channel, the rise and fall of the tides, the flow of the currents, the flocks of bird life, pelicans surveying life from comfortable perches and drying sandbars, schools of fish passing, and at dawn and dusk dingoes patrolling the water's edge. And when night settled, another dinner of chilled crab.

About halfway up the channel there is a shallow hump, at a place known as Boonlye Point, from which the falling tide flows northwards on one side and southward on the other. There is only enough depth for us to cross at high tide. So, the procedure is to follow the rising tide up to arrive at Boonlye Point at the appointed hour, cross the hump with a prayer on our lips, then follow the falling tide north.

Running aground in these sandy channels is always a risk and all eyes must be on the depth sounder, the channel markers and the water colours which hint at depths. If you run aground with a rising tide you may well be able to back off, but with a falling tide you could be stuck until the next rising tide floats you off.

A grounded yacht is a very uncomfortable place to be, as the keel means the boat will lean over at an acute angle. It will be bloody hard to get off and on, there is nowhere to sit or lie, all sorts of things leak and fall over, you cannot use the gas, water may not pump. Indeed, there are lots of things to swear about if you are so inclined. The heavy unsealed batteries, for instance, which need to be unhooked, manhandled to a flat spot and kept upright, man-handled back in place etc etc.

All these factors will inevitably lead to a discussion about whose fault it was.

Yes, I am speaking from personal experience! Though not on this trip.

Thankfully all went well and by late afternoon we were anchored behind Woody Island, near the entrance to Hervey Bay. We had only one other yacht for company, and as night fell there was no other sign of man other than some distant riding lights on the Fraser Island shore.

The next morning, we left as the sun rose over the island and by the time we were clear of land we were enjoying light southerlies and clear blue skies. The shallow waters of the bay were translucent, glistening, the sandy bottom shining and so clear we seemed to be floating on air. We shook out the sails and set the self-steering for the mouth of the Burnett River, brewed a coffee and shortly after clearing the fairway buoy we were delighted by the passing company of a small pod of whales.

We coasted on, just enough wind to keep the sails full. From time to time indolent dolphins loitered alongside—too lazy to play, just saying hello. Some brightly coloured butterflies flew by, a few pausing on the rigging for a moment before fluttering off, unconcerned the next landfall was New Zealand.

As the day passed the wind slowly picked up, out to sea some fluffy white clouds drifted past and on our left the coast gradually came closer, and eventually we picked out the channel markers into the Burnett.

We spent the night at the Bundaberg Port Marina, filled our tanks and had a fine meal at the marina restaurant. Bundaberg is famous for Bundaberg Rum—a cold 'bundy and coke' is as Queensland as XXXX Beer, the smell of the sea, suntan lotion, cane toads and beautiful girls in bikinis. It was also a very popular drink in Papua New Guinea—and we rarely have one without it bringing back memories of good times, 'Hey Mr. Tambourine Man' thatched roofs, fans rotating slowly overhead, geckos and liar dice.

The Bundaberg Brewing Company has been producing the best rum in the world since 1889; brewed from local sugar this smooth dark drink has an aroma and a taste that is never forgotten—just mix with good memories or make new ones. Sugar is one of Queensland's major rural industries and the extensive cane fields an intrinsic part of the tropical countryside.

We cleared the channel markers before the sun rose over the pink horizon, bringing with it another perfect day. Our course to Agnes Waters and the Town of 1770 took us well off the coast and it had slipped below the horizon before the hills near our destination were visible. The wind came up to a good breeze, our sails filled, and *Oceania* cavorted along, a little anyway as she is a staid lass and needs the right music and a bundy to really get going.

We were once again on Captain Cook's track, and he was about to make his first anchorage since Botany Bay.

Cook's Journal 23 May 1770:

...we were abreast of the South point of a large open bay ...we anchored at 8 oClock in 5 fathoms of water (on) a sandy bottom...

... I went ashore with a party of men in order to examine the Country ... we landed at little lagoon within the South point of the Bay where there is a channel leading into a large Lagoon ...here there is room for a few ships to lay very Secure and a small Stream of fresh water. After this I made a small excursion into the woods while some hands made three or four hauls with the Sain and caught not above a dozen very small fish ... as yet we had met no people but saw a great deal of smook coming up from the west side of the Lagoon ... (we) found 10 small fires in a very small compass and some cockle shells laying by them, but the people were gone... The country is visibly worse than at the last place we were at, the Soil is dry and sandy ... Here there are plenty of small oysters sticking to the Rocks, stones and mangrove trees and some few other shell fish such as large Mussels, Pearl oysters, Cockels...

In the late afternoon we anchored pretty much on top of where the *Endeavour* would have lain, under the lee of Round Hill headland. We have previously anchored in the lagoon Cook mentions but the entrance had silted up a bit and the tide was not that good. It was actually very nice to be able to drop 'the pick' with plenty of room to swing and not have to worry about tides and running aground.

A bundy or two, thought about Cook, discussed plans for the next day, lit the lantern and the barbecue, thought how great life was.

We took the dinghy ashore for a cup of coffee in the morning and later motored the dozen miles to Pancake Creek sheltered from the south by Clews Point. Secure and beautiful, easy to enter, lined by golden beaches and lush forests, this is always a lovely stopover. There are warm bath-sized rock pools ashore that are great for basking in, and the crabbing was again successful. Very tasty baked in the shell.

Two days later we tied up in the marina at Gladstone and congratulated each other on having achieved it without a contretemps—our previous attempt in *Reveille* some years ago had been mishandled and some unfortunate words were bandied about. I think the word 'divorce' may have escaped someone's lips. If possible, it is much safer to come in at slack tide; a strong tidal flow and a wind can give a yacht a mind of her own.

Gladstone has changed quite a bit since we last went through. Then it was a laidback Queensland country town, a few pubs, life moving at a gentle pace, sitting on the edge of a pretty bay. The marina was relaxed with a good restaurant serving great local steaks and reef fish. Certainly, a place to linger and enjoy. In fact, a few years later Mike Battle's restless soul led him to acquire a very nice residence on the waterfront south of town, where he could fish to his heart's desire from a very beautiful classic launch that he had fallen in love with.

The port was first noticed by Mathew Flinders, but it was not closely examined until 1823, when John Oxley had a good look around. He thought that the harbour was too difficult, the country too dry and the timber useless. In 1827 there was a failed attempt by ninety odd soldiers and convicts to establish the 'colony of North Australia', and it was not until the 1850s that settlers began taking up land in the area. These days it is Queensland's largest multi-commodity shipping port.

There are three options for a yacht leaving Gladstone harbour and going north. The sensible and unexciting thing is to go back through the main southern entrance that you came in by, out through the long row of leads and turn north. This is what all the commercial shipping does. The second option is to leave by a long winding shallow passage inside Curtis Island. It is so shallow that one spot along the route is called the 'cattle crossing' and at low tide it is a couple of feet above water level. This obviously means waiting for the right tides and the chance of going aground. We didn't like this option either. The third option is a shallow, but not as shallow, passage between Curtis Island and Facing Island. We still needed to wait for a rising tide, but there was more latitude with tides and timings, and it is quite a picturesque route.

So we left a few hours before high tide and by early afternoon we were anchored below the lighthouse on Cape Capricorn a picturesque spot with great views up the coast and protection from the southerlies.

On 17 August 1803 Mathew Flinders, who had been unable to find another vessel to continue his exploration, was returning to England as a passenger on the *HMS Porpoise*. When they were approximately four hundred and fifty kilometres east of where we were anchored, the *Porpoise* and another vessel accompanying them ran aground on an uncharted reef. Both vessels were lost, and the crews marooned. However, the ship's small cutter survived, and Flinders sailed it back to Sydney to arrange the subsequently successful rescue of the stranded crews. He was then given command of a leaky schooner, the *Cumberland*—at twenty-nine tons about the same size as *Oceania*—to return to England. When he reached the French island of Mauritius in the Indian Ocean he was forced to put in for repairs. War with France had broken out again, and despite his scientific credentials he was held captive for over six years. His health suffered and he died a few years after his return home, still a young man of forty, and before his widely acclaimed book and atlas, *A Voyage to Terra Australis* was published.

Prawn trawlers were working close in around the rocky foreshore and when towards sunset they hauled their nets we went across to say hello, and to see what we could barter for a bottle of Bundy and a couple of cans of Tasmanian Cascade beer. We had a few laughs about cane toads and in-breeding in the Apple Isle and came away with more large banana prawns than we could eat and a good-sized red emperor. In the morning we moved a few miles west and anchored in a spot near the channel between the mainland and Curtis Island, where the fisherman assured us even Tasmanians could catch a few fish and crabs.

We only had two days there before the Met Office at Rockhampton began forecasting a patch of bad weather, and as it was almost time to rendezvous with our friends and previous owners of *Oceania*, Mark and Rem Towers at Rosslyn Bay Marina, we headed in. A good reach across Keppel Bay under foresails and mizzen saw us through the channel into the marina at high tide, where Mark and Rem were ready to take our lines.

Mark had quite a remarkable business career. As a young man he came to Australia on a working holiday. It was in the early 1990s and computers were beginning to transform the way every industry operated, and he saw the opportunity to revolutionise the storage and distribution of goods. Within a few years he had a dozen acres of warehousing and was handling a number of international labels Australia wide. He was still only in his early thirties when he was made a generous offer for his business. He accepted, bought *Oceania*, went sailing and devoted his spare time to assembling the world's largest private collection of music! Periodically, he updates a collection of fifty thousand of his favourites on an iPod for me—which now goes everywhere with us. Of course, he was inspired in his endeavour by the beautiful girl he met after arriving in Australia, his wife, Remy.

As I mentioned before, after selling us *Oceania* they had bought another yacht *Knot Again*, and we were about to sail together to Port Douglas. Over a few drinks and some fiery Moreton Bay Bugs and chillies on the terrace of their home overlooking the marina, we made some plans.

But the next morning the winds were gusting around thirty knots and we were happy to leave *Oceania* snugly tied up in the marina while we investigated the township of Yeppoon.

When the wind abated, we followed *Knot Again* out of the marina with the excited faces of Holly and Sasha, Mark and Rem's two Labradors, leaning over the deck rail. Dawn was breaking and outside an uncomfortable sea was still running; the sky was sullen with patches of low cloud trailing misty tendrils of rain. The Keppel Islands were only grey shadows on the horizon, sometimes lost to sight behind the curtain of passing showers. The tide was running strongly northward, and we bowled along at a great pace, and by the time we cleared Cape Manifold the sky was starting to clear and the sun was beginning to sparkle on the tumbling waves.

However, despite the beauty the waters here can be treacherous with strong currents creating dangerous eddies, standing waves and overfalls. Particularly in the warmer months localised thunderstorms can develop with surprising speed, and a peaceful afternoon transformed into a dark maelstrom within minutes.

On our previous passage on *Reveille,* calm seas had lulled us into towing our sturdy aluminium dinghy, rather than stowing it on deck. Before we had appreciated what was happening a dark thunderhead had formed and began marching towards us, hurling ferocious gusts as it came. The sea, which only minutes before had been placid, was a jumble of breaking waves as the wind fought the tide. Before we could do a thing, the dinghy was capsized, the doubled towing lines snapped, and it was last seen, half afloat, being driven towards the beach as the gale drove us northwards under bare poles.

We were then faced with the prospect of not being able to get ashore until we reached Mackay (neither of us were too keen on swimming in and out to shore in an area notorious for its saltwater crocodiles) which was still a long way off. Luckily when we anchored that night we were visited by the crew of an American yacht who were having troubles with their engine, and we decided we would do well to stick together as we headed to Mackay.

However, that was in the past. Today all was good.

We sailed past the entrance to Port Clinton and by the time we were nearing our destination of Pearl Bay it had turned into a beautiful afternoon. The rocky coastline, broken by small coves and islands clothed in Norfolk Pines, was bathed in a golden light.

The water was a patchwork of blues and greens, the wave breaks along the reefs and the cliff faces the purest white. Pearl Bay is protected by the heavily timbered hills that rise steeply behind the crescent of its white beach, and a cluster of small islands a few hundred metres offshore. We anchored on a sandy bottom in five metres of crystal-clear water and let the beauty of the bay wash over us. So enchanting, that for this moment at least, no more could be asked of life. The afternoon drifted into night and the golden crescent of the waning moon hung suspended over the dark hills. Overhead the night sky blazed and the only sound that reached us was the gentle wash of the waves on the shore.

In the morning we followed the sweep of the bay northward, staying close inshore to appreciate the string of small golden beaches, each lying within its own pine clad headlands. Each one was perfect, but each seemingly more beautiful than the last.

By midday we had anchored in Island Head Creek a large and safe sandy estuary, and spent the afternoon walking along the ocean beach to Pine Tree Point. The coastline here is still a pleasant mixture of beaches, headlands and rocky islets. Thick stands of tropical forest, paper-barks and casuarinas line the beaches, framed between dramatic green headlands decorated with clumps of Norfolk Pine.

Some other yachts came in during the afternoon, and in the dusk we could pick out their riding lights, tucked well up the bay and protected by banks of drying sand.

Our path took us around Townshend Island and across the mouth of Shoalwater Bay (where years earlier I had spent a gruelling month on the last training exercise before leaving for Vietnam) to the Duke Islands forty miles to the north. The weather was still idyllic with a calm sea and just enough wind to keep the sails pulling. The tidal range along this coast is often over four metres, which meant we were either flying along with strong currents behind us, or barely making headway once the tide changed. We anchored in a pretty spot off Hunter Island.

Flinders at Broad Sound late September 1802:

*'There are kangaroos in the woods, but not in numbers. The shoals all over the sound are frequented by flocks of ducks and curlews, and we saw in the upper part some pelicans ... Many turtles were seen in the water about Long Island, and from the bones scattered around the deserted fireplaces, this animal seemed to form the principal subsistence of the natives; **BUT WE HAD NOT THE ADDRESS TO OBTAIN ANY.** Hump-backed whales frequent the entrance to the sound and would present an object of interest to the colony. **IN FISHING, WE HAD LITTLE SUCCESS WITH HOOK AND LINE;** and the nature of the shores did not permit the hauling of the seine.'*

Good to see other sailors had their bad days at fishing!

Oceania rested quietly during the night, the only movement her gentle swing to the change of tide and, in the morning, we awoke to find the distant mainland a grey stripe against the clear pale sky. The sun rose and the colours ripened, and by the time we weighed anchor the sea stretched a rich blue to the curved horizon. So still it seemed a painted canvas that, if we chose, we could have easily strolled upon it. We motored off and set a course for the Percy Islands, twenty miles further on.

The water was still unruffled when we dropped the anchor off the palm-lined beach in West Bay on Middle Percy Island. We spent the last of the golden afternoon ashore, idling in the warm water and inspecting the famous mariners' hut, rich in memorabilia of passing yachts. We could not remember what sign we had left of *Reveille's* passing, but if we had we could not find it. Later, under the soft light of our hurricane lamp, we entertained Mark, Rem and the dogs on our aft deck and barbecued a mackerel that Mark had hooked on the way across.

Mathew Flinders was having even more trouble than us with his fishing when he was anchored at the Percy Islands. 3 October 1802.

'...there were deserted fireplaces upon all. The Indians probably come over from the mainland at certain times, to take turtle, in which they must be much more dexterous then we were; for although many turtle were seen in the water, and we watched the beaches at night, not one was caught.'

The Met Bureau was again forecasting strong winds on the way and, as we were shortly due to meet my brother and his wife Franny, at Laguna Quays, we thought it best to get in while we could do so. Richard had not sailed on *Oceania* since he had come with us across Bass Strait on the delivery voyage, when he maintained that it was his prayers that saved her us going down. It would be great to see them.

We were away at dawn and by early morning we had some wind behind us. The crater of Digby Island slid by, and when Prudhoe Island was abeam we could make out the hump of our destination for the night St Bees Island which would be a run of around sixty miles for the day. An hour before sunset we were snugly anchored in Egremont Passage between St. Bees and Keswick Island. We anchored as close as was prudent to St. Bees, but the fringing reef still kept us a good four or five hundred metres out from the densely forested shores. When we settled down, we were amazed at the cacophony of bird calls that floated out to us, loud even at that distance. They reached a crescendo at dusk, gradually settling as darkness fell. The wind came up for a while during the night, and with the slop from the tide gave us a restless sleep.

The southerly stayed with us as we sailed up the Hillsborough Channel to Repulse Bay.

The first thing we did when we reached Laguna Quays was find a carpenter to have a look at the main mast. When we were pulling up the mainsail at Pearl Bay one of the cleats had come away from the wooden mast, and to our alarm we discovered a small patch of rot. We needed an expert to check it out. These days wooden masts are a rarity and marine carpenters scarce, and we were lucky to find a convivial craftsman from Proserpine. He chiselled out the rot, which was quite significant, and glued in some teak. He assured us that it was now as good as new, but I wondered if there was any more rot lurking behind fittings higher up. I resolved to take it a bit easy until we could un-step the mast and inspect everything carefully at Port Douglas.

Strong winds arrived with Richard and Franny the next afternoon. Laguna Quays was a difficult marina for us to leave when strong winds were blowing from the south. It is at the top of a long shallow bay that would be very hard for us to beat out off with an iffy mast, if we had a problem with our engine. And we were now having engine problems. Marine algae were growing in the diesel tanks and clogging our filters. I needed to check them every hour when the motor was running, and I had to change them frequently. Changing the filter meant bleeding the air out of the system and was not something you wanted to do in a rush in rough weather on a lee shore, if it could be avoided. Our stainless-steel tanks had no inspection ports and cutting into them in so the tanks themselves could be thoroughly cleaned was a major end of season job, along with the mast.

That night over drinks I reminded Mark about his 'lifetime guarantee', but he muttered his usual spiel about verbal guarantees and reading the fine print and poured me another wine. Unfortunately, my lawyer brother agreed with him. Who can you trust these days? Over time we were to find that the fine print had more and more exclusions! But she was a beautiful creature, well worth putting up with trifles like dodgy masts and engines.

At the time of our visit the Laguna Quays golf course, which was adjacent to

72

the marina, was reputed to be one of the best courses in Queensland, a luxuriant tropical paradise —emerald fairways lined with thick rainforest. It was so attractive that I was talked into making up a foursome. As usual it was not long before I had to search in the rainforest for my ball and I remembered why I had had enough of wandering around the steamy dripping jungles of New Guinea and Vietnam. After I had lost half a dozen balls in the first few holes, and had got myself scratched and muddy, I decided to just enjoy the walk.

Laguna Quays is an excellent example of the best sort of foreign investment. The beautiful golf course, with its resort facilities and international standard airfield, was built during the period when the Japanese economy looked set to conquer the world. The value of real estate in Tokyo was greater than that of all the USA. Reputedly something approaching $200 million was spent on Laguna Quays before the wheels fell off. It was sold for less than half that, then an astute Tasmanian acquaintance picked it up—and thus it became Australian owned regardless of what you think of Tasmanians—for about $15 million or less.

The wind was still blowing when Richard and Franny had to head back south without us getting out of harbour, and a few days later Max and Viv Doerner, old friends from Tasmania, arrived.

I have known Max and Viv since Max and I sat next to each other in the first year of high school at Manly Boys High in 1956. The school had only been established in its current site in Abbott Road, North Curl Curl two years earlier and, the large brick buildings sat rather forlornly on about ten acres of un-landscaped paddock, with an untamed hill of scrub and rocks at the back.

Max has a theory that the school was staffed by teachers volunteering from established schools, and that precedence was given to seniority. Because the school was in a virtual beachside location in Sydney, it was popular with senior teachers approaching retirement. The fact that our science teacher often regaled us with his stories from Sir Douglas Mawson's 1911 Antarctic Expedition, and he was certainly not the oldest on staff, lends credence to this theory.

The result was a certain lack of energy, so that in these early years it cannot be said that the school assiduously strived for academic excellence. Classes went through their motions, but on a sunny day when the surf was up in the afternoon, quite a number of faces would be absent.

The only problem in escaping from the school after the roll was marked in the morning was crossing the large paddock without being spotted. Max and I solved this by forming the school Flora and Fauna Society to protect the rocky scrubby hill at the back of the school, from where it was easy to slip through the back fence undetected.

Sadly, our early role as environmentalists, many years before Bob Brown got on the bandwagon, has never really been acknowledged.

Often in my last year I did not even make it to school and if I did, would slip over the scrubby hill to the beach, or to a tennis or squash court or occasionally the nearby Dee Why Hotel for a beer in the company of some legally aged layabouts. It was not uncommon for some of the 'old' school staff to be propping up one end of the long bar, while a few students would be amongst the mob of no-hopers at the other end. As neither group could admit being there, each turned a blind eye.

I started off with a demanding curriculum: Mathematics 1 and 2, Chemistry, Physics, French, Latin and English, but at the end of five years I had worked my way down to a much easier one; General Mathematics, Modern and Ancient History, English and Economics. The bare minimum in those days to get into university. My only vaguely academic success was as the lead speaker for the school debating team which won the Sydney inter-school competition.

But I was not a complete wastrel if you count sport as a productive occupation. I surfed a lot if the weather was good and the waves were up, played rugby league for the Collaroy Lifesavers (premiers 1959 and 60) plenty of squash and tennis (my only regular attendance at school was inter-school tennis, which often meant travelling all around Sydney most Wednesdays). On Saturday mornings from the time I was fourteen I was an assistant coach at Keith Walker's Tennis School where I was paid ten shillings for the morning's work.

Keith (Whacker) Walker was a sporting legend. He must have been in his early thirties at this time and was famous for the challenge he left on the table, internationally as well as in Australia, to all comers to contest five round ball sports. As a tennis player he was in the same cohort as the Australian greats of the time, he was the Australian Professional Squash Champion, a scratch golfer, Manly snooker and billiard champion and a top-grade table tennis player. If there were any other games requiring hand eye co-ordination, if he was given five minutes, he would have been a champion in those too. A lot of famous sportsmen took him on and to the best of my knowledge he was never beaten, but being a competitive bastard, he could have kept going too long. He was an outstanding person and very generous to me in many ways. He spent a lot of time working on my squash and tennis, and because of him I was playing in the top senior grades of both when I was fifteen and, had won the state schoolboys squash championship. At the NSW lawn tennis championship at White City I had cleaned up Bill Bowery, a future Australian Open champion. Wacker was not too keen on me wasting my life in the army but, never-the-less gave me a great sporting reference which certainly did not hurt my chances of getting into Duntroon, where I was lucky enough to win the squash and tennis trophies each of the four years I was there.

After finishing school Max went to university and I went to Sydney Law School and then Duntroon, and our paths did not cross until we both ended up in Canberra a decade or so later, and then by coincidence we both went to Tasmania in the early 1980s. Ro and I had gone there to buy an apple orchard, but Max while working for the Trade Practices Commission had identified a much smarter opportunity, if you did not mind swimming with Great White Pointer sharks. He bought an Abalone License for fifty thousand dollars. Within a couple of years, the market in Asia had boomed and its value had trebled, then trebled again. Against my strong advice not to trust a government license and to sell and take the windfall, he held on. The value trebled again, then again, and within a decade was worth around seven or eight million dollars and returning a million a year.

Max leased out his license for a fortune, retired from squash, we were calling ourselves the '*lapuns*' (pidgin English for old and decrepit) by this stage and took up golf. Within a couple of years, he had a handicap of two. Yes, his family has good genes, his father had been captain of an Australian Olympic water polo team and his brother was a junior Davis Cup player.

I probably should say a little more on the risk and rewards of abalone diving in the 1980s.

First the rewards: in a good day's fishing a diver could harvest one thousand kilograms of wild abalone, for which an average sort of price landed at the jetty was around forty-five dollars per kilogram. Will I work that out for you? Yes, that's right, forty-five thousand dollars for a day's scuba diving in the 1980s. Not bad at all, in anyone's book. Why bother being a brain surgeon or a leading silk?

Now the risks: you must spend the day swimming underwater in often murky and freezing conditions with poor visibility, dressed in a black wetsuit and flippers so that you look as much like a seal as possible! Seals are the favourite lunch of Great White Pointer sharks, the most dangerous of the shark species and common in Tasmanian waters.

Adult sharks can grow to in excess of seven metres and weigh over two and a half thousand kilograms and can surge at speeds of sixty kilometres an hour. Can you imagine what that would look like, if you saw one coming!

Sometimes I used to think wistfully that I could have bought three abalone licenses for the price of our lovely orchard. But the reality is I would have been far too terrified and busy looking over my shoulder for white pointers to have had time to harvest any abs at all. Max has a few shark stories. My favourite is where he puts a gloved hand on a big greyish rock to steady himself while prizing off an ab—and the huge rock blinks. He claims he was saved by a disgusting brown stain in the water, which put the shark off lunch.

We were not surprised when he arrived to board *Oceania* at Laguna looking relaxed and prosperous with a large and awkward set of golf clubs, and lots of scuba gear. Whenever we were walking on a beach Max was always kicking over shells looking for abalone. Surprisingly, everyone thought it would be much too warm, he did find a few tiny ones. But not enough to invest in.

Peter Langford, who has been a friend since Duntroon arrived the next day. He had not so long ago become a bachelor again and we were pleasantly surprised when he arrived with a very attractive friend—well Max and I were probably more pleasantly surprised than our wives. She made a habit of sunbathing topless in a G-string on the deck near the companionway—where she had to be stepped over by anyone coming on deck or going below. We only had one electronic chart and that was down below, and I was always stepping over her to check where we were in relation to reefs and sandbars. It seemed to worry Ro and Viv more than me. I didn't really mind that much.

However, I was not all that surprised to find that before long the G-string had been mysteriously blown overboard.

Eventually the wind dropped and we set off to explore the Whitsunday Islands and their magnificent coral reefs which are one of Australia's great sailing destinations. They were named by Captain Cook who sailed through the islands on Whitsunday in 1770.

Our first stop was Thomas Island and by mid-afternoon we were anchored inside the lagoon on the north side, where we had good protection from the southerlies and the choice of three beautiful beaches for an evening barbecue. Around dusk the wind had dropped out and we had an aromatic driftwood fire going on the beach. Above our deserted island, with only the glowing embers of our fire in the darkness, the immense orb of the night sky blazed with the light of uncounted millions of stars. It was one of those nights when the vastness, the limitlessness of what surrounds us is manifest.

In daytime a sailor can forget there is anything beyond the horizon or above the sky. The world is just you, the blue dome overhead and the tossing sea. But on nights such as this you are reminded of the beauty and immensity of the universes.

During the next couple of weeks, we picked our way through the islands. Over the years we have spent a lot of time among them and it was not possible to do justice to them in such a short time. There are seventy-four islands, most have a charming place to anchor and many are away from other boats and are surprisingly remote. There is generally a beach of gleaming sand cleanly washed by the tides, and a handy coral reef alive with the colours of the coral and the fish. Our favourite places, all with entrancing beauty, include; behind Burning Point on Shaw Island, the north bay on Lindeman, Whitehaven and Sawmill Bay on Whitsunday Island, Happy Bay on Long Island, the north bay on Border Island, most of the bays on Hook Island, the northern bay on Double Cone Island and Double Bay on the mainland north of Airlie Beach—which itself is always good fun after dark. But having made that list I can think of a lot which should be there, as should the islands to the south which we bypassed this trip, including Goldsmith Island and convivial Brampton Island.

Mathew Flinders 9 October 1802 discovered the wonders of the reef:

'In the afternoon I went upon the reef with a party of gentlemen, and the water being clear around the edges, a new creation, as it was to us, but imitative of the old, was there presented to our view. We had wheat sheaves, mushrooms, stag horns, cabbage leaves, and a variety of other forms, glowing under water with vivid tints of every shade betwixt green, purple, brown and white, equally in grandeur the most favourable grandeur the most favourable parterre of the curious florist. These were different species of coral and fungus, growing, as it were, out of solid rock, and each had its particular form and shade of colouring; but whilst contemplating the richness of the scene, we could not long forget with what destruction it was pregnant.

And coral bleaching?

'Different corals in a dead state, concreted into a solid mass of dull-white colour, composed the stone of the reef.'

We have lots of good memories of Airlie Beach as it was a pick-up and drop-off point during the winter, we had here on *Reveille* in 1991 and we spent quite a few nights exploring the nightlife with people coming and going. Charlotte and Georgina, Don and Sue Clark, Carmel and Phil Thomson, Margie Hansen and others all spent a couple of weeks.

Reveille was a fine yacht that had been built by an engineer for his own use. It was elegant, solidly built, handy to sail with a good cutter rig. But he had overcomplicated the engineering of the fuel lines and filters and the cooling system of the diesel motor. Consequently, we often had stoppages from air in the system and overheating. These were within my range of capabilities to remedy—just—but one day while Margie was on board, we developed an engine noise that was new to us and defied our diagnoses. Worried, we sought an anchorage and had a serious look at the motor, but with darkness falling we had gotten nowhere. In desperation we 'phoned a friend'. Margie's husband Paul is a magician with diesel motors, so we gave him a ring and let him listen to the noise over the phone.

Now, another bit of over engineering was that instead of a gear box it had a variable pitch propeller, so that you went forward or backwards by changing the angle of the propeller blades. These have never really caught on—although someone once said they were used by the USA Navy—probably because they are always giving problems. In our case it could jump out of its setting so that you went nowhere, and if you were trying to manoeuvre at a jetty you could never be sure whether you were going to go forward or backwards until the boat actually started to move.

Now, you have probably guessed Paul's diagnosis, and really, we should have worked it out ourselves—it was a bloody noise from the propeller shaft.

I was sick of it all by this stage and left it to have a look at in the morning, although I was worried about the bottom which was very coarse sand with lumps of dead coral. During the night the wind came up and by first light we had dragged onto a coral reef. Luckily, a small miracle actually, the wind stopped and, the tide started to rise just as we touched the coral and we were able to drag ourselves off without damage. Very relieved, we were able to sail back to Airlie Beach and have the shaft looked at by an expert.

Not long after this we thought we should return to Hobart and do something about earning our keep. We left *Reveille* swinging forlornly on her mooring and wondering why she was being deserted.

Once in Hobart we became trapped by work and, with deep regrets, decided to sell her.

There is an old saying that 'the only days you enjoy a yacht are the day you buy it and the day you sell'. I do not agree with this—although it is true that yachts are holes in the water that you throw money into—as yachts do become part of the family no matter how much trouble they have been. But I have to admit that in our case the losses on sales have always been enough to make you weep anyway.

About a month after we put it on the market, we received an offer of the full asking price if we traded on an apartment at Noosa. It seemed too good to be true, but we took it anyway. Two years later, in one of the price surges that the Queensland market has every so often it doubled in price, and for once we had made money on a yacht. For this reason alone, *Reveille* has always had a special place in my heart—as has Airlie Beach, as this was the place where the miracle occurred.

Back on *Oceania* we continued up the coast. Beyond Airlie Beach there are a number of rocky islands south of majestic Gloucester Island which is separated from the mainland by a shallow sandy passage. Inland the coastal ranges still run close to the shore, covered with patches of dense forest among the rocky crags. *Oceania*, who

78

may have been wondering about her fate while we had anchored off Airlie, ran north under the genoa hoping we had forgotten about the mast and the contaminated diesel tanks.

We tarried for a while at the northern end of the passage, anchored beside Mark and Rem in *Knot Again* off a delightful beach. It was just a short stroll to 'Montys' a convivial beach restaurant with a lovely view across the shimmering water to the heavily forested slopes of Mount Bertha on Gloucester Island.

Onwards, across the large expanse of Edgecumbe Bay to Bowen where, after a bit of juggling in the crowded fishing boat harbour we deposited Max and Viv, the golf clubs and the diving gear and they set off to explore the local golf courses. The rest of us topped up with water, fuel and seafood from the fishermen's co-operative and motored around the point to Greys Bay, where we baked the freshly purchased mud crabs in the barbecue for dinner.

I must report that Peter, who spends much of his time trout fishing in the Southern Highlands and likes to pass himself off as an expert, was still fishless. To no avail he had spent hours trolling around the edge of reefs with an intent look on his face. This made me feel a bit better about myself.

Sometimes after a few wines we could not help ourselves and would reminisce a bit about the long-ago days at Duntroon. It was to Australia what West Point was to the USA, it trained officers for the army who would be ready to fight and risk their lives in the service of their countries. If you Google 'West Point Honour Code' you will find quite a lot about honour, including a committee and a charter, 'A cadet will not lie, cheat, steal or tolerate those that do'. The ethos of Duntroon was much more about mateship. Duntroon (commonly known by the inmates as 'Clink') had a lot of irksome rules which because we all had a bit of larrikin in us, we were happy to bend a bit if we could get away with it. Mostly they were rules that inhibited our social life. Hotels and licensed restaurants were out of bounds, alcohol was verboten, you could not entertain visitors, there was no leave at all during the week and on Saturday and Sundays there was a curfew, cars were not allowed, the list goes on and on. Rules more appropriate for a monastery, most of us thought. So, as we were not training to take divine vows, we thought that if you needed to break a few rules to enjoy a night with your girlfriend or, to tell a fib so a mate could do the same, that was definitely okay. If you were caught it was all part of the game, but 'mateship' within our class was much more important than a few anti-social rules. It has meant that nearly six decades since we all marched into Duntroon there is still a mob of us, ranging from some who saw the light and left in the first year to generals with a lifetime's service, having a cheerful lunch at the 'Kingo' pub in Canberra every first

Thursday of the month. Even more amazing, every second Wednesday the 'First Wives Club' (which actually includes some 'exes' as well as a few second and third wives) meet at a somewhat posher restaurant.

This is how it worked for us. One evening during the week a friend was 'over the hill' visiting his girlfriend. His company commander came looking for him and asked class-mate Hughie Conant if he knew Harry's where-abouts.

'I think he's training for the cross-country, sir.' (An OK lie).

'Really, tell him to come and see me when he gets in'.

An hour or so later, after being told his presence was required. 'How's the training going Harry?' the company commander asked.

Option One. 'OK thank you, sir.' An OK half-truth, as there was no direct question as to where he was.

Option Two. 'I was actually AWOL, sir.' Slow thinking, and unnecessary information.

'Really' said Captain Ted Chitham, who was a good sport and could remember his own time at Clink—and later at the age of eighty rode a push bike from Brisbane to Canberra—'I thought you were training for the cross country, but now you have told me that you were AWOL you had best put yourself on a charge.' Ted was also at one time our lecturer in Peace Administration—abbreviated PA on the timetable. This was an incredibly boring subject dealing with the minutiae of administration and the endless number of forms it spawned in the peace-time army. It was often programmed after lunch in a heated lecture room, and it was very hard to stay awake. Only the 'boggers'—those that loved 'spit and polish' and there were a few in every class—made much attempt.

'Sleeping' was generally referred to as having a 'Z'—that is the Z from dozing or snoring. So if you were asked, 'What are you going to study in the upcoming free period?' Your answer would probably be, 'Oh, I think I'll just have a Z.' With so many having a Z during PA, Ted's lectures soon became known as PZ. Which he found as funny as the rest of us.

Years later Ted endeared himself to me forever when I overheard him speaking to my boss at the time. 'How were you lucky enough to get him?' he had asked in an amazed tone. I think he was talking about me, but perhaps not. Nevertheless, I have felt sorry for Z'ing in his lectures ever since.

Harry also tells a funny story of when he was the Cadet Duty Officer in our senior year.

One evening a classmate told him he was going AWOL to celebrate his birthday, and to keep an eye out for him if there was a bed check. Later in the night

Harry was woken from his sleep by thumping on the heating pipes, which was the warning that an officer was beginning a bed check to discover anyone AWOL—it really was a bit like Port Arthur during convict times.

Realising that he would have to act quickly if he was to save his mate, he made a dash in the darkness to his friend's room. He was naked, as everyone slept that way to save washing, and jumped into bed so that it would be seen to be occupied. However, in the dark he had picked the wrong room and a startled fourth class was woken by a naked intruder jumping on top of him. The scheme had failed, and the fourth class maintained for the next fifty years that he had been psychologically damaged by the shock and horror of the naked, panting Harry jumping on top of him!

Back to the present on *Oceania*.

The next day was a forty-mile run to Cape Upstart, yet another Cook named feature, dominating the low-lying shore along this part of the coast. With Mark's guidance we found some delightful spots along the northern side of the cape, small white beaches dominated by towering granite buttresses. There is a scattering of isolated houses along this remote shore. Some are quite entrancing, half-hidden amongst the rocks and trees beside deserted beaches. There are no roads; everything must come in by water.

These were new waters for us, but Mark had sailed *Oceania* to Port Douglas a few years before and his firsthand knowledge was invaluable. The charts rarely tell the whole story and it is nice not to have to worry whether you have chosen the right bay or whether the next is better, or not.

Continuing on, we stopped at the low-lying deserted sand bar that passes itself off as Cape Bowling Green and had a restless night with the swell working its way into the anchorage. The anchor was up as the sun peeped over the horizon, tinting the flimsy clouds a pale lavender, and in the late afternoon we had a high tide to take us over the shallow channel into Townsville Marina.

Townsville has had a long association with the army and in the old days used to be a bit of an ugly duckling, but it is now a very pleasant place to visit. A lovely foreshore, fine eateries, elegantly restored period buildings and located in a dry tropical zone, which has excellent weather for sailing. Cook sailed past, named the prominences and kept going. The area was first settled by Europeans in the 1860s but prior to that a number of indigenous groups, including the Wulgurukaba, Bindai, Girrugubba, Warakamai and Nawagai lived in the area. The population is getting up towards two hundred thousand and the city has a large technical base which is also good for sailors.

Over the years it has provided many beautiful girls to the army as brides.

Suzie Knight, Peter's wife and Leslie Eley another friend of ours being two that spring to mind, but with a bit of thought I could easily name a dozen. A short stroll around the town assured us that they were in no danger of running out of pretty girls.

We managed to get a berth for a week and settled in for an enjoyable stay, our only worries being which choice of a picturesque route for a morning walk and which restaurant to visit for dinner—though Remy usually decides these things anyway. After a couple of days Peter Langford and his beautifully browned, but thong-less friend headed south and shortly afterwards the super experienced team from Koonya, Don and Sue Clark arrived. I tried to get Sue to take over the role of lolling around the companionway topless, but she told me to grow up.

One of the local treasures is the bold and beautiful Magnetic Island lying a couple of miles off the city—named by Captain Cook because of the magnetic interference he experienced while passing. We tucked ourselves as far up into Horseshoe Bay on the outside of the island as we could get, where we had fine protection from the southerlies. Much of the island is national park but there is still a vibrant island community of Townsville commuters, sea-changers and holiday makers, and we spent an enjoyable few hours inspecting it from the local bus.

Onwards. Almost every day the southerly comes up about mid-morning, so there is not much sense in leaving too early unless there is a long leg to complete. Generally, we would motor for the first hour or so to charge the batteries and run the eutectic refrigeration and then use the wind when it came up. It's best to anchor while the sun is still reasonably high while you can still see what is under the water in the way of sandbanks, rocks and reefs. By seven the wind has dropped out and it's generally ideal to light the barbecue and discuss the meaning of life.

As we sailed across the shimmering water of Cleveland Bay, Townsville was sprawled below the great rocky crag of Castle Hill, the colours changing as the sun played across its face. Before long the wind was tossing white caps and we cavorted along under the genoa, a reefed main—still nursing the main mast—and the mizzen. We entered Steamer Passage running between Great Palm Island covered in rainforest and dominated by the cloud-covered peak of Mount Bentley, and a group of smaller in-shore islands.

After a beautiful day gliding past the emerald green tropical islands, alone apart from the odd fishing boat in the distance, we anchored in Little Pioneer Bay at the northern end of Orpheus Island. To our north were the great mountains of Hinchinbrook Island, while at the head of our small bay, a beach was edged by the luminous green of the mangroves. After a walk on the beach, keeping eyes out for crocodiles which might have liked Mark and Remmy's dogs for dinner, or us for that matter, we retired to the aft deck to enjoy a rich golden sunset as the sun sank below the mainland mountains. Then dusk, under the soft light of the hurricane lamp as the aroma of Barramundi (bought in Townsville) in crusted cheese drifted deliciously from the barbecue. But be prepared, we are shortly to catch our first fish of the trip whilst trolling!

In the morning we took a rising tide through the shallow approaches to the Hinchinbrook Channel keeping a watchful eye on the depth sounder as we edged cautiously through the treacherous sand banks. Once inside there is plenty of water provided you pay attention to the channel markers. In the early morning-light the still water was rich in the reflections of the surrounding mountains and the dense foliage along the shore. As the tide fell the tangled trunks and roots of the mangroves formed tangled webs, inverted by their reflections in the mirror of the water.

We anchored inside Haycock Island and as the sun dipped it became a place of overwhelming beauty. The ripening colours of the placid winding waterways lined with the latticework of mangroves roots. The mountain peaks clothed in mist, their slopes decorated by dramatic lichen covered rock faces, the valleys and ridges with impenetrable rainforest. All clothed in a mantle of absolute serenity. The beauty was supernatural.

In the still night while we were enveloped in our cocoon of darkness, Mars shone with an unnatural radiance and the whole sky was a shining brilliance. In the quiet of the next morning, while the sun still hung below the mountains, the whole scene was cooler and paler, all again captured perfectly in the still mirror of the placid water.

In this mood the Hinchinbrook Channel is one of the truly great beauties of the natural world—bewitching and seductive. But in the twisting mangrove channels one of the world's great predators proliferate—the fearsome saltwater crocodile. Swimming would be madness and even walking the dogs on any of the banks exposed at low tide would be extremely foolhardy. As would going on the water in anything less than a substantial 'tinnie' and certainly not an inflatable.

This area is more or less in the centre of the tropical cyclone belt and it is not really a sensible place to be cruising for pleasure between December and April. In 2011 one of the most destructive cyclones ever recorded crossed the coast at the north end of the channel.

Cyclone Yasi had a huge diameter of fourteen hundred kilometres and brought wind gusts of two hundred and ninety kilometres per hour. It caused extensive damage over a large area of the coast, and to appreciate the danger of being caught in a cyclone it is worth looking at the damage to the Hinchinbrook Marina and the yachts moored there. There is really no way of protecting yourself from something as fierce as Yasi, but fortunately they are relatively infrequent. The traditional way of riding out lesser cyclones is to take your yacht to a 'gunk hole' in the mangroves and tie onto the roots. This is safer than many marinas, where the pylons are not high enough to keep you in place during a high tide storm surge, apart from the destructiveness of the wind itself.

Anyway, we had no intention of being around for a cyclone or swimming with crocs for that matter.

We had a few enjoyable days at the marina, which was relatively new, and we fell in love with a block of land on the promontory above the entrance, with breathtaking views across the channel to Hinchinbrook. Good sense prevailed and we sailed off across Rockingham Bay towards Dunk Island with our money metaphorically still in our pockets.

As usual Don rigged up his rod and started towing a lure. No one gave it much thought, just part of an unrewarding ritual.

But . . .

But this time, after twenty minutes or so there was a strike, and minutes later we had a beautiful mackerel flapping on the deck. The first since Koonya, which was really quite remarkable, because Don who had sailed with us for most of the distance, often fishes at home and would very rarely return to Cascades without a good feed. He is a good recreational fisherman. But as we know, his son Marcus, is a freak and could catch a feast out of a puddle in the road. I can only put it down to my poor technique putting Don off. I know I have that effect on golfers, who at the end of a round, can be hacking, slicing, hacking, hooking and cursing almost as badly as me.

In the afternoon a northerly blew in, the first for ages, and we anchored on the south side of Dunk Island towards the westward tip. The water was shallow, and shelving and we had to anchor a long way out where it was quite choppy, and the wind made cooking a bit difficult. But it didn't diminish the joy we felt as we hosted the crew of *Knot Again*, and served superbly cooked, fresh mackerel steaks. The next day the wind was still against us, so in the morning we dropped the crab pot near a likely-looking bank of mangroves and then set off to inspect the island. We wandered around the tropical gardens of the resort, followed a track to the top of the rain-forested hills, found we were thirsty and had a light lunch at a bistro overlooking the beach. Towards dusk I retrieved the empty crab pot.

The wind returned to normal and by mid-morning the southerly was back with us for an interesting run past two groups of coral islets to Mourilyan Harbour. We motored in to the fully enclosed bay through a channel lined by high thickly-forested hills, and dropped anchor into a lovely muddy bottom, which warmly embraced our big plough anchor. We felt very secure and could see that the shores of the harbour were enclosed with thick mangroves that were obviously crawling with large crabs.

In the late afternoon, after we had set the crab pot, I enjoyed forty winks secure in the knowledge that nothing untoward could happen here. But the tide had changed while I had been dozing and it was slowly carrying a trawler on a collision course with us. He was now quite close, and the only ones aroused by my shouts were our own idle crew. There was still no sign of life on the trawler, and damage from its heavy steel trawling gear was imminent. There were a few moments of panic before a dozy fisherman, rubbing sleep from his eyes, appeared on deck. Calamity was averted.

In the morning Don and I were up early to collect our crabs, but as our fellow fisherman Mathew Flinders had remarked at the Percy Islands, we still 'had not the address to obtain any' and had to motor out the channel with our plans for dinner still up in the air. As it turned out we made Fitzroy Island before dusk, anchored off one of Australia's great beaches, and had a very nice meal ashore.

Strong winds were forecast and had started to chop up the water off the new Marlin Marina at Cairns, and we were glad to be in before they became a real problem. Even so, with the help of the strong tidal current pushing us away from our berth, I still managed to make a hash of docking and we were glad when we were finally tied up. We had not been in Cairns for a few years and were impressed with improvements and the new 'swimming lagoon'. Cairns has always been blessed with plenty of good eateries. The climate, great local seafood and beef, tropical fruits, the proximity to the Atherton Tableland, and tourism, have all helped to create a plethora of interesting and romantic places to eat—many within a short stroll of the wharf. Behind the city the dim outline of coastal mountains has always invoked a mysterious air as the sun sets, and the twinkling lights on the water remind you that the oceans beckon. Asia is not far off.

Before we knew it, the time had come for Don and Sue to leave us again. They had been with us nearly all the way and it would not be possible to find better shipmates. We then had a short hop by ourselves to Port Douglas, another of our favourite places, where *Oceania* was going to have her mast and diesel tanks taken out and fixed.

'The Port' still retains much of the charm of earlier times, when it was a working port. Originally servicing the goldfields and the sugar industry it has also always been home to a fishing fleet. More lately it is become a major tourist hub, carrying tourists from all over the world to the Great Barrier Reef. It has a few great pubs where you can rub shoulders with drinkers from the ends of the earth, still including plenty of genuine North Queenslanders. You can eat great food in expensive milieus, great food at the old open-air yacht club, or great food in a tin shed on piles over the water. It was a good place to catch up with some old friends: Eric and Eileen Tang from Papua New Guinea, Sally Cerny from Tasmania, and Roddy and Annie Reid who we first met years ago in Canberra and were now living in Cairns. Charlotte and Georgie both came up to help celebrate my landmark birthday, and we discovered the delightful *Silky Oaks* north of Mossman. Mark and Rem were sailing home on *Knot Again* and we made a plan to rendezvous in the Whitsundays the following winter.

The repairs to *Oceania* meant she would be out of commission for the rest of the sailing year, so we decided to sail to Thursday Island in the Torres Strait on the *Trinity Bay*, a cargo vessel that ran a weekly service supplying settlements north of Cooktown.

We sailed from Cairns late one afternoon, and we were enjoying the cool breeze on the aft deck as we sailed past Trinity Beach, which is about twenty kilometres north of Cairns, and has now become home base for Georgie, Simon, Joseph and Eleanor.

I want to digress here and talk about my uncle Keith Peterswald, because it was at the Atherton Tablelands and at Trinity Beach that he and thousands of other men did their final training before fighting in Papua New Guinea in World War II, and where a number came back for rest and recuperation at various stages of the war.

Keith's father—my grandfather—spent much of his career as a town cop in country New South Wales. Keith was born at Dubbo in 1913 and lived in a number of towns before his father ended up in Sydney as a retired superintendent. After leaving school he was employed by the Commonwealth Bank.

He joined up soon after Australia entered the war and was in Egypt with 2/9 Battalion of 18 Brigade in April 1941, just before it was sent to Tobruk with the 9th Division. He was a private soldier, one of the famous Rats of Tobruk who defended the port until they were relieved on the 23 August 1941. He then served in Palestine and Syria at Aleppo near the Turkish border.

In 1942 18 Brigade was recalled to defend Australia from the Japanese, and arrived in Adelaide in March 1942, after traveling in an unescorted convoy. Keith, now promoted to corporal went with the 18 Brigade to Milne Bay in Papua, where he took part in the Battle of Milne Bay. This battle was the first defeat of the Japanese in the war.

Along with some other experienced men he was then seconded to 25 Brigade as a sergeant and fought with them in both the retreat and the advance back over the Kokoda Trail ending up at Buna on the north coast of New Guinea. Here he was minding his own business when he was spotted by the commander of his old brigade Brigadier Wooten, who allegedly said:

'What the bloody hell are you doing with this mob Peterswald, you're coming back with me.' He re-joined 18 Brigade just in time for the heavy fighting that saw his battalion decimated from a strength of around one thousand to one hundred and twenty men.

American forces had been attacking the fortress at Buna since 19 November, but by the middle of December when the 2/9 Battalion entered the battle little progress had been made.

The Japanese were in strongly prepared positions in terrain that favoured the defenders. Patches of open kunai grass and coconut plantation gave them good fields of fire and swampy creeks made other approaches almost impossible. Although the Australians were supported by limited artillery and some tanks, the battle continued until 1 January and came down to brave men assaulting prepared positions. The casualties were horrific.

It is impossible to justify the Brigades losses of fifty-six officers and eight hundred and forty men killed and wounded, which was forty-five percent of the strength that arrived at Buna. The Brigade was then reinforced by some one thousand men, most with only limited training, and on 12 January joined in the Battle of Sanananda which so far had defied the attacks of other 7 Division units.

The 2/9 Battalion pushed up to the main Japanese positions, losing the two lieutenants leading the attack. The Brigade continued to struggle forward through deep swamps, mangroves and creeks flooded by torrential rain. The retreating Japanese continued to fight hard, still taking many Australians with them. On 19 January the battalion lost four dead and twelve wounded, and the next day, thirteen dead and eighteen wounded.

On the 22 January the last of the Japanese defences were destroyed. The cost to 18 Brigade of the Sanananda battle was a further one hundred and fifty-five dead and two hundred and sixty-five wounded.

The total for the beachhead battles was horrific. In a month they had lost ninety-six percent of their original strength through battle casualties and illness. This included four hundred and twenty-five dead and over eight hundred wounded, a greater toll than in the whole of the rest of the war and similar to the total of the Australian army losses in the whole of the Vietnam War. A great, great tragedy, particularly at this stage of the war for men who had already given so much.

18 Brigade left New Guinea on 10 March 1943. In General Vasey's words they had taken part in 'one of the greatest epics of the AIF'. But they had paid a hideous toll and the question will always remain as to why so many lives had been wasted because of the irrational urgency and disregard of the high command for their men's lives, and who had sent poorly supported infantry against heavily fortified positions that could have been reduced by siege and attrition.

In 1944 as part of 7 Division they returned to the Lae area in New Guinea where they fought in the battles in the Markham and Ramu river valleys and the Battle of Shaggy Ridge.

In 1945 Keith returned for a third time to the Atherton Tablelands before serving in Borneo. He was demobilised as a warrant officer at Enoggera in December 1945.

After the war he bought a sheep property near Bourke, married Winsome, a glamorous model who made him move to Sydney in 1960. He was a fine man, a second father to me.

Many years ago when I was a major commanding an outstation of the Pacific Island Regiment in Vanimo, Papua New Guinea, I was hosting a visit of the then Chief of the Defence Force, Lieutenant-General Mervyn Brogan. I had just shown him to his bedroom—which was mine, but generals of course take precedence—when he scratched his head searching through his memories. 'Any relation to Keith?' he asked. 'A very fine man, I knew him well during the war. Don't make'em like him anymore.'

Back onboard *Trinity Bay*. During the night, while we slept soundly in our comfortable cabin, we passed by Endeavour Reef, where Cook and all his crew so nearly lost their lives.

Cook's Journal 11 June 1770:

... a few minutes before a 11 when we had 17 (fathoms) and before the man at the lead could heave another cast the Ship Struck and stuck fast – Immediately upon this we took in all our sails and hoisted out the boats and sounded round the ship... the Ship being quite fast upon (the reef) we went to work to lighten her as fast as possible which seemed to be the only means we had left to get her off... At a 11 oClock in the AM being high water we thought we try'd to heave her off without success ... not twith standing by this time we had thrown over board 40 or 50 tun...

Cook's Journal 12 June 1770:

Fortunately we had little wind and fine weather and a smooth Sea all these 24 hours, which in the PM gave us an opportunity to carry off two bower Anchors ... it was 5 oClock in the PM, the tide we observed had begun to rise and the leak increased upon us which obliged us to set the 3rd pump to work ...

At 9 oClock the Ship righted and the leak gained on the Pumps considerably however I had resolved to risk all and heave her off ... and about 20' past 10 oClock the Ship floated and we hove into deep water having at this time 3 feet and 9 inches water in the hold...(we) got up the fore topmast and fore yard warped the Ship to the SE and at 11 got under Sail and Stood into land with a light breeze at ESE some hands employ'd sewing Ockham wool etc into a lower Studding sail to fother the Ship, others employ'd at the Pumps which still gain'd upon the leak...

Cooks Journal 13 June 1770:

...we kept edging in for the land. Got up the Main topmast and Main yard and having got the sail ready for fothering the Ship we put it over under the Starboard fore chains where we suspected the Ship had suffered the most and soon after the leak decreased so as to be kept clear with one Pump with ease, this fortunate circumstance gave new life to every one on board...

In justice to the Ships Company I must say that no men ever behaved better than they have done on this occasion animated by the behaviour of every gentleman on board every man seem'd to have just sense of the danger we were in and exerted to the very utmost...it was happy for us that a place of refuge was at hand; for we soon found that the ship would not work, and it is remarkable that in the whole course of our voyage we had seen no place that our present circumstances could have afforded us the same relief.

Cook and his crew were to spend seven weeks at what was to become the site of modern day Cooktown while they repaired the Endeavour and replenished their supplies. While they were there the scientist Joseph Banks, and naturalist Daniel Solander collected and documented over two hundred species of new plants.

Cook's Journal 18 June 1770:

... Fresh gales and clowdy with showers of rain. At 1 PM the Ship floated and we warped her into the harbour and moor'd her alongside a Steep beach on the south side. Got the anchors and Cable and All the Hawsers a shore- In the AM made a stage from the Ship to the shore – erected two tents one for the Sick and the other for the Stores and Provisions...

Cook's Journal 19 June 1770:

This afternoon I went on one of the highest hill over the harbour from which I had a perfect View of the inlet or river and adjacent country which afforded but a very indifferent prospect – the low lands near the River is all over run with mangroves among which the salt water flows every tide and the high land appear'd barren and stoney – In the AM got the remaining guns out of the hold and Mounted them on the quarter deck ... set up the smiths forge and set the Armourer and his mate to work ...

89

to repair the ship –

Cook's Journal 24 June 1770:

In the Pm the Carpenters finished the Starboard side and at 9 oClock heeled the ship the other way and hauled her off about 2 Feet for fear of neeping ...I saw myself... one of the animals ... of a light mouse colour and the full size of a grey hound and shaped in every sense like one with a long tail which it carried like a grey hound ... but for its walking or running in which it jumped like a Hare ...

Cook's Journal 3 July 1770:

... In the evening the fishing party returned having got as much fish as came to 2lb a man ...At noon the Master returned and reported he had found a passage out to sea between the shoals which lies out ENE from the Rivers mouth ...

Cook's Journal 4 July 1770:

...At high water hove the ship a float ... trimming her upon an even Keel intending to lay her ashore once more to come at her bottom under the larboard Main chains...

Cook's Journal 9 July 1770:

...he saw a great number of turtle three of which he caught weighing 791 pounds ... all hands feasted.

Cook's Journal 10 July 1770:

In the AM 4 of the Natives came down to the sandy point on the north side of the harbour, having along with them a small wooden canoe with outriggers in which they seemed to be employed striking fish... at length 2 came in the canoe so near to the ship as to take some things we throw'd them, after this they went away and brought over the other two and came along side ... and took such trifles as we gave them. After this they landed close to the Ship and all 4 went ashore carrying their arms with them ... most of us went to them and made them again some presents and stay'd with them until dinner time when we made them understand that we were going to eat and ask'd them by signs to go with us but they declined and as soon as we left them they went away in their canoe, One of these men was something above Middle age, the other three were young, none of them were above 5 1/2 feet high and all their limbs proportionally small, they were wholly naked their skins the colour of wood soot or a dark chocolate ... their hair was black lank and crope'd short ... Some part of their bodies had been painted with red and one of them had his upper lip and breast paint with streakes of white... their features were far from disagreeable, the Voices were soft and tunable and they could easily repeat many words after us...

Cook's Journal 1 August 1770:

Strong gales ... with clowdy weather ... we could see nothing but breakers all the way from the South round by East as far as NW ... after having well view'd our situation from the mast head I saw that we were surrounded on every side with shoals and no such thing as a passage to Sea but through the between them dangerous in the highest degree ...

Finally, after nearly two months 'on the dry' they managed to get underway again. It was an amazing achievement. To drag the badly damaged boat off the reef. In imminent danger of sinking they manage to get her ashore. Repair the boat themselves, feed themselves by hunting and fishing, survive the climate and arduous labour, continue their scientific exploration, sail the boat some thirty thousand or so kilometres home across the dangerous seas, many still uncharted.

Cook's Journal 4 August 1770:

The wind continued to Moderate all night and at 5 oClock in the morning when it fell calm this gave us an opportunity to warp out. About 7 we got under sail... we stood out to sea...having the Pinnace ahead sounding...

The next recorded European expedition to the area was by Captain Phillip Parker King in 1819 but it was not until after the discovery of gold that a township was established at Cooktown in 1873. Today it remains a small picturesque village nestled beside the river and surrounded by rainforest. In the sailing season there are generally a few yachts and fishing boats in the river and the old Cooktown Hotel is a vintage Queenslander.

Once Cook got his ship afloat again he kept edging along the coast. He still had a few scares before he was out of these dangerous waters, and it all makes you realise just how vulnerable these sailors were. If they lost their ship there was little prospect of rescue, even if they made it ashore. In his future voyages he insisted on, and was given two ships, which did improve the odds a bit.

But before long it looked again as if they were doomed.

Cook's Journal 16 August 1770:

... we had hardly trimmed our sails before the wind came EBN which was right upon the Reef and made our clearing of it doubtfull ...we ... stood not above 2 miles to the SSE (of the reef) before it fell quite Calm ... there was no (bottom at) 140 fathoms ... a little after 4 oClock the roaring of the surf was plainly heard and at daybreak the vast foaming breakers were too plainly to be seen not a Mile from us towards which the Ship was carried by the waves surprisingly fast ... (there) was not an air of wind ... there was no possibility of anchoring ... at 6 oClock we were not above 80 or 100 yards from the breakers ... all the dangers we had escaped were little in comparison with being thrown on this reef where the Ship must be dashed to pieces in a moment ... at this critical juncture when all our endeavours seem'd too little a small air of wind sprung up, but so small that at any other time in a Calm we would

not have noticed it, with this and the assistance of our boats ...

Then at Cape Flattery it appeared he was completely surrounded by reefs. He went in the pinnace to Lizard Island then sailed through a passage he had spotted. But again, the ship was soon in grave danger and safety had to be found inside the reef.

Meanwhile on the *Trinity Bay,* things were very much more comfortable for Ro and myself than they had been for Cook. Not having to worry about running on reefs is a great advantage—as is a bit of ice in your rum. Off Cape Melville we were in awe of the colours of the great piles of boulders in the dawn light. And as the sun climbed higher, the blueness of the sea flecked with dancing whitecaps. Around us lay the pale outlines of sunken reefs, fringed by the whitewash of breaking waves, and golden cays and islets laced with tossing palms. It was a mesmerising and beautiful scene. But in 1889 the area was struck by the most violent recorded hurricane to strike Australia. Fifty-nine ships anchored in Princess Charlotte Bay were destroyed and three hundred and seven lives lost. The tidal surge was twelve metres.

Cook's Journal 17 August 1770:

... a few days ago that I rejoiced at having got without the Reef; but the joy was nothing Compared to what I now felt at being at Anchor within it.

Cook continued edging north inside the reef and on 21 August 1770 Cook had finally cleared the point of Cape York, the northern extremity of Australia.

Cook's Journal 22 August 1770:

...Gentle breezes at East by South and clear weather. We had not steer'd 3 or 4 miles along shore to the westward before we discover'd the land ahead to be Islands detached by several Channels from the mainland ... I made the Signal for the boats to lead thro' the next Channel to the Northward ...

They had almost reached Endeavour Strait and had completed their exploration of the east coast. Cook then completed the circumnavigation of the globe by sailing home to England via Java and the Cape of Good Hope. Meanwhile on the *Trinity Bay* we were still surrounded by extraordinary beauty, we passed Restoration Island which was Captain Bligh's first landfall after the mutiny on the Bounty. The next morning saw us nosing in Cook's wake up the Albany Passage close to the tip of Cape York. Again, the beauty concealed a tragedy. Here the *Quetta* was lost with one hundred and thirty-three lives, and in a pretty palm fringed bay the rainforest has smothered the tragic settlement of Somerset, which was planned to be the hub of the north.

Cook still had two incredible voyages ahead of him. In 1772-75 he was commissioned to lead another scientific voyage on behalf of the Royal Society. His explorations covered huge areas in the wild seas of the southern oceans, and he completed another circumnavigation. His final voyage lasted from 1776-79 and was primarily concerned with finding a passage across the top of the American continent but it included crossing the Pacific Ocean from around fifty degrees south to seventy degrees north. He was killed in a dispute with native Hawaiians in 1779.

He was an exceptional seaman and commander of men. In these voyages and earlier commissions in Canada he demonstrated that he was a supremely skilled cartographer and left behind maps which were signposts of the world. He might not have always known what lay ahead of him, but he knew where he was every mile of the way. And left it recorded for history. I think this is the quality which gives him my vote for the greatest explorer, on land or sea, that the world has seen. He came from humble beginnings—the second of eight children of a Scottish farm labourer, who was apprenticed as a shop boy to a grocer, before giving that away to become a merchant navy apprentice. He studied algebra, geometry, trigonometry, navigation and astronomy and by 1755 he had been given command of a small trading vessel. In June of that year he volunteered for the Royal Navy and was enlisted as an able seaman. He was promoted to master's mate, then boatswain and by 1757 he was qualified to command and navigate a ship of the Royal Navy. He subsequently earned his promotions and appointments by his own diligence and ability, and by the time of his return from his second circumnavigation he was a national celebrity. It says a lot about England and her navy that such ability could be recognised and rewarded.

The following is a description of Cook written 1779 by Heinrich Zimmermann, a thirty-seven-year-old able seaman on Cook's third voyage:

'I do not believe that England ever had a braver sea-officer than Cook. In times of the greatest danger he was the bravest, the cheeriest, and the most resolute; and at such times his chief concern was to keep calmness and order on the ship. In this he was so successful that for most part all eyes were fixed upon him' and *'On Saturdays he was usually more affable than at other times, and on that day he frequently drank an extra glass of punch, pledging a toast to all beautiful women.'*

That evening from *Trinity Bay* we had drinks ashore on Thursday Island to celebrate the end of our odyssey, and as darkness settled, Papua New Guinea and the memories of our lives there in the 1960's and early 70's seemed very close. Most of that story belongs in later chapters, except for one part.

In July 1606 two Spanish ships heading west across the Pacific to Manila, the *San Pedrico* and *Los Tres Magos* commanded by Luis Torres discovered Basilak Island and Milne Bay on the eastern tip of Papua New Guinea. They then sailed along the south coast of PNG, naming Orangerie Bay a little further on, before continuing past present day Port Moresby, the Gulf of Papua and the island of Daru, before passing through what is now named Torres Strait. There is still a question mark over whether or not he actually saw Australia without realising what he had seen. He definitely sighted 'islands' to his south, which could have been where we were sitting on Thursday Island or, perhaps the tip of Cape York.

In 1972 as a young and newly promoted major, on our second tour of duty with the Pacific Islands Regiment in Papua New Guinea, I had once unwittingly followed in the wake of these Spanish Ships. At the time Ro, Charlotte and myself were stationed in Wewak on the north coast—where, if we had been there in 1643 we may well have noticed Abel Tasman sail past on his way home after discovering Tasmania and New Zealand—and were anxiously waiting on Georgina's arrival. However even births as important as this one didn't rate in terms of the army's comings and goings, and I had been sent off with my soldiers to patrol in the mountains around Milne Bay and to then walk across to the south coast.

The plan was that we would rendezvous with a 'Landing Craft Large' then sail and walk along the coast to Port Moresby. When we eventually staggered out of the jungle for our rendezvous it was at Orangerie Bay, where our ship was waiting with the welcome news that both Ro and the new baby Georgie, were doing well. We then sailed westward, stopping at every place we could get ashore, which meant we were probably travelling at much the same speed as Torres and his ships, and probably anchoring in many of the same bays. It was a very enjoyable cruise, although at the time I had no idea whose wake we were following, and I was very anxious to get home to meet our new baby.

In the next chapter we go back in time quite a few years, to 1966 when Ro and I first lived in Papua New Guinea, that mysterious land not far to the north of where we celebrated the end of our voyage on *Trinity Bay*.

~ PAPUA NEW GUINEA 1966 ~

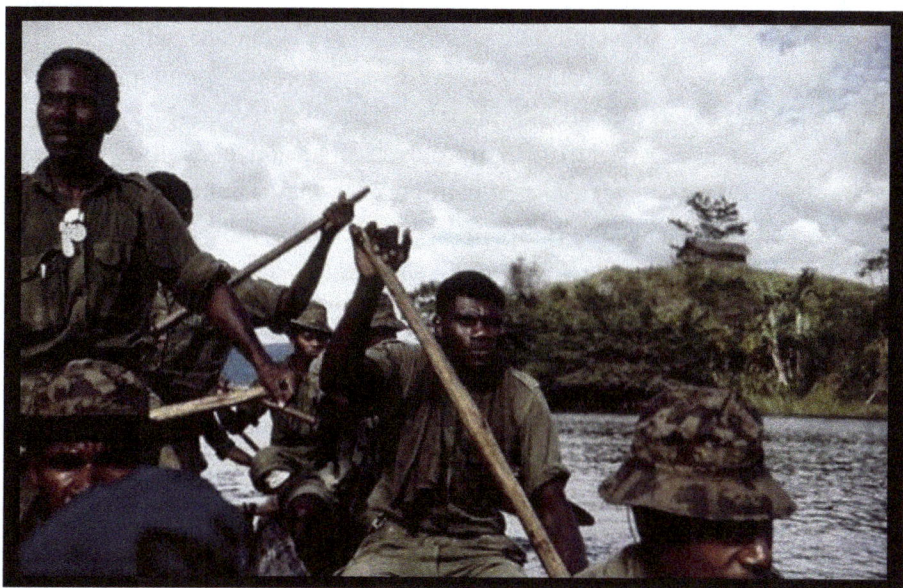

A Dugout Canoe on Lake Kutubu PNG

The canoes were large hollowed-out logs, very similar to those first used by our ancestors at least ten thousand years ago. By the time my heavily laden soldiers were on board, we were floating rather low in the muddy water of the small creek that led into Lake Kutubu. Even the owners, painted tribesmen dressed in penis gourds with boar tusks through their noses, looked a bit dubious of our chances of reaching the other end of the lake.

It was 1966 and I was a new lieutenant serving with the 1st Battalion Pacific Islands Regiment. A few weeks earlier my platoon had been flown in to the grass airstrip of the remote government outpost of Mendi, in the Highlands of PNG.

In those days it was mainly a collection of thatched huts, with a few small prefab buildings that served as the headquarters of the District Commissioner. It was overlooked by the cloud-covered ridges of the Owen Stanley Ranges and nearby, the jagged peak of Mount Giluwe at 4367 metres, the second highest in the country. There were no vehicular roads in or out, just walking tracks linking nearby villages. The Highlands Highway was still only a distant dream.

Extending law and order over this wild country was done by gradually establishing a network of small outposts in the more remote areas. The patrol officers—*kiaps*—who ran the patrol posts were extraordinary young men who did a remarkable job and deserve the thanks and admiration of everyone who has an interest in Papua New Guinea. Accompanied by only a small detachment of police, and sometimes by an even younger assistant patrol officer, they would literally carve their small settlements out of the jungle. An airfield that could handle small aircraft would have to be hacked out of the rainforest and walking tracks extended. The authority of the law had to be established, with the patrol officer acting as both magistrate and police commander. Remember his citizens had settled their disputes, including domestic ones, by violence, murder and cannibalism for thousands of years. They could still be cannibals, their belief systems being embedded in the Stone Age. Schools, hospitals and trade posts would be established. Money would be introduced into the society by payment to the tribesmen and women for work on government projects and for the supply of foodstuffs.

This was all difficult and quite dangerous work, all carried out in remote isolation. When I was around fifteen, I had read about patrol officers along the Fly River, in the Western District, and it had so captured my imagination that I took myself off to North Sydney for a job interview. I was politely told to come back when I had grown up a bit.

What were we doing in Mendi? We had been sent to walk and map a route through an area that had largely not yet been explored. From Mendi via a circuitous route to the patrol post on the northern end of Lake Kutubu, and then in a long loop north to the small native village of Tari.

Our route began as a narrow dirt track leading south-west, winding its way through the green hills of the Mendi Valley towards the lattice work of mountain ridges and dense jungle that enclosed Lake Kutubu. For the first few days the track

96

led through small native villages. Some of the villagers would follow us, yodelling and chanting until they reached the edge of their land, where the people of the next village would greet us and take up the chant. All the while the beat of tribal drums preceded us, alerting the tribesmen further along the valley that we were coming.

Many of the them were decked out in their traditional finery. Elaborate headdresses made from the brilliantly coloured plumes of the Bird of Paradise, their faces tattooed and painted in reds, yellows, ochres and black. They carried evil-looking barbed spears, had pig tusks in their noses, wore large mother of pearl shell discs around their necks, penis gourds two feet in length, and a clump of bush-grass between their buttocks. Their arms and legs were decorated with armlets of bone, carved wood and platted vines. They were magnificent, and still answered to the gods from another age. Only a couple of the men were marred by approaching civilisation and wore dirty cotton shorts and perhaps a tattered shirt or singlet. As well as spears, most carried razor-sharp machetes.

The women wore grass skirts and were bare-breasted. Their faces were painted, and they too had bones through their noses. Many wore 'fez' like caps sewn from small shells, armlets of platted grass and neck plates of large gold-lipped mother-of-pearl shells. The shells, brought all the way via the age-old trade routes from the Papuan Gulf, were a traditional form of wealth, and greatly prized in the mountains. The number of shells worn attested to the father's wealth and the 'bride price' that must be paid to possess her.

Sadly, a few of the women wore loose fitting 'merri' dresses, usually introduced at the behest of missionaries who did not approve the lascivious nature of traditional dress. Some of the girls carried and played flute-like instruments made from split bamboo, and some men had slim double-ended drums with python-skin heads.

It was a light-hearted festival as we passed through, good-natured and boisterous. Neither the villagers nor my soldiers, the harbingers of the new world, were aware of the impending death of this civilisation that had prospered in these mountains for thousands of years. In the early mornings it was cool, but by the time the sun had climbed above the surrounding mountains it burned with a remorseless intensity. By midday all, including ourselves with our jungle greens soaked black with sweat, had retreated to the coolness of some shaded place, a thatched hut or a stand of timber. During the afternoon clouds would start to gather on the ranges, and the valley would be blanketed in torpid humid air. With the onset of night, we would be drenched by a deluge, cool and refreshing for a while before the darkness found us cold and shivering.

The land was rich and much of it was cleared, interspersed with native gardens of yam and sweet potato, fenced with sharpened stakes. There were copses of trees that had been harvested for firewood for more generations than any could remember. Their farming practices had preserved these trees for at least five thousand years.

The villages were only a few thatched huts built around a patch of bare earth, sometimes enclosed within a palisade of sharpened stakes, which was dusty when it was dry, and muddy as soon as the rain fell. They were dominated by a large '*haus man*' or men's house, ripe with the smell of unwashed bodies and the smoke of cooking fires and twist tobacco.

All the while the great central range lined the northern horizon, sometimes proudly but mostly dark under a curtain of cloud. In the afternoon of the third day we had left the last village behind and the path gradually dwindled into a faint footpad, winding up a long spur to the tree line above.

As night approached, we camped on the edge of the high rainforest where we could enjoy a majestic view over the long valley we had come through, to the shrouded bulk of Mount Giluwe. Ahead, hidden under the dark canopy of the forest lay a barely trodden hunting path that led higher towards the mountains, and eventually to the mysterious waters of Lake Kutubu, the halfway point in a six-week patrol. Then on to the village of Tari, tucked away under the escarpment of the Owen Stanleys.

There had been a Government patrol from Mendi to Lake Kutubu in 1953 following a more direct route than we were planning, but most of what we would see from here on would be unexplored territory. We were near an area where cannibals had killed and eaten a patrol officer only three years before.

As always there was a quiet bustle when it was decided to make camp. There was much to do before nightfall brought the evening rain. Peacetime patrolling in Papua New Guinea, although it was through some of the most daunting country on earth—towering jungle-clad mountains, vast waterways and dark malarial swamps— did have some advantages not available to soldiers in a wartime situation.

One blessing was that most of the time you could sleep 'off' the ground, above the mud, spiders and reptiles of the jungle floor. The Pacific Island soldiers were adept at building their versions of the common soldier's shelter, 'the hutchie.' This required a considerable amount of timber to be cut, and the noise involved was much more than could be tolerated in a situation where you might be shot at—in which case it is much smarter to be with the leeches in a wet hole, than aloft in an improvised hammock.

These 'hutchies' were such wonderful and dry comforts that they deserve a full description. As much as any other reason they allowed us to live in the jungle for months at a time, under very extreme conditions, with remarkably few health problems. That they could be built says much for the abundance of straight timber in the rainforest—three hundred and sixty straight, strong poles about seven feet in length would be required to house a platoon of thirty men, and these could normally be cut close to camp.

Firstly, two pairs of stout poles were driven into the ground about two metres apart. Each pair crossed and tied with vines to form two X-shaped supports, like bed ends, upon which a stretcher made from two more poles and an inflatable ground sheet was fixed. This was the bed and was low enough so that you could sit on it with your feet comfortably on the ground if you wanted to cook, write or clean a weapon.

Above it a waterproof sheet was drawn tightly between six more poles to form a gabled roof with the ridgeline about three feet above the centre of the bed, and the 'eaves' extending a couple of feet. Once erected by my hardworking batman, Wafiaga—he received certain perquisites to balance the extra work involved—I would hang my pack facing inwards at the foot end and my webbing and weapon at the head end—and there was perfect protection from the worst of storms. With a mosquito net hung and wrapped inside a blanket with a waterproof covering—if you were in the high mountains—there was protection from leeches, snakes, malarial-carrying mosquitoes, spiders, ants and the myriad of other nasties of the jungle.

Wafiaga was a young soldier from the Sepik district, and one of the newer cohort of recruits who were better educated than most of the older soldiers. At this stage he had been in the regiment for a couple of years and I was keen to keep an eye on him with a view to getting him promoted to lance corporal, the second-in-charge of a section of ten soldiers, if he was as good as he seemed. This was the first step on the way up in the army, and for many soldiers the most important. Although called a 'batman,' (a hangover from the British Army, not the movies) and although there were some menial tasks associated with his job, a batman was an important cog in the system. Working closely with the platoon sergeant and the platoon commander was a part of their education.

He was an enthusiastic and cheerful young man, with a beaming white smile— although chewing betel nut, which turned teeth a startling red was outlawed in the army, it did not automatically translate to Hollywood smiles. His good English was also an advantage, for although I made it a rule to speak *pisin* whenever possible, there were often times where it was very helpful to be able to be understood in English, and for soldiers to be sure that certain things could be explained clearly to me.

While the bustle of making camp was underway, I would draft a report to be sent in morse code by HF radio to Port Moresby and, mark up the route map covering the day's march. These were to supplement the army ordnance maps which were missing a lot of detail, in some cases whole mountain ranges were blank areas notated as 'obscured by cloud'. Orders for the next day needed to be prepared and a wander through the camp to check all was ok with the men.

Meanwhile the signallers would be stringing aerials high overhead, anxious to establish communication before the atmospheric interference of the tropical night made signals impossible. The medic would be holding sick parade, latrines were dug and a water point designated where drinking water could be taken. Soon food was cooking on small solid fuel stoves and the aroma of curry, sweet potatoes and rice wafted in the air.

There are over eight hundred and fifty tribal groups in PNG, all speaking their own language. Language note, not dialect. This diversity developed because the country was at the end of the migratory trail from Eurasia, and any ethnic group heading east could go no further without seagoing craft. And further, the impenetrable terrain separating the tribes restricted interaction and assimilation. My thirty-something soldiers were drawn from many tribes. The aim was to create a national army that owed allegiance not to one tribe, but to the nation. Hoping to avoid the common situation in Africa where tribal armies trumped national loyalty, and has resulted in, and continues to, bloody coups and uprisings.

My platoon sergeant was also from the Sepik district where the mighty Sepik River flows from the great central massifs of the highlands to the north coast near Wewak. He spoke three languages: reasonable English, his tribal language, and the *lingua franca* of the nation, *Pisin*. My corporals came from Manus Island in the east of the Papua New Guinea archipelago, Milne Bay on the east of the main island of the country, and from Mount Hagen in the Central Highlands. Some of the soldiers spoke 'police *motu*' an inter-tribal dialect common in parts of Papua.

Most of the soldiers were quite young with varying degrees of sophistication; some had been educated in mission schools, a couple had come from the northern highlands, where only two years before the patrol officer had been killed and eaten. Some were from villages that had had only little contact with modern life and still harboured a belief in the Cargo Cult, which explained that the wealth of the white man was delivered by planes sent by our dead ancestors. There was no concept of the creation of wealth through manufacturing and service industries. In some forested valleys nets were still strung high among the trees to try and capture the planes which brought our wealth. Lyndon Johnson, the US president at the time was regarded as a god in some places.

They all had one thing in common, that you could forget at your peril. They were tribal warriors to a man. In their villages and in the surrounding jungle they would be carrying bows, spears and murderous clubs, and their role in life was to protect what was theirs and kill those whose path crossed theirs in anger. Murder and payback were a central part of life. When they were happy, they were laughing and boisterous, but a simple slight could make them sullen and dangerous. They wore their hearts on their sleeves and they had no deceit. Their smiles and their scowls were always the real thing.

The common language of the army was Pidgin English (now *Pisin*) a language that had evolved through the interaction of English and German administrators and the islanders since the European nations had first colonised the country in the late 19th century.

After a gruelling day's walk carrying a pack weighing over thirty kilograms, where at times it seemed almost impossible to drag one foot past another, to luxuriate in a camp and feel the aches of the day drain away, was a feeling as good as life itself. To take off the sweat and rain-sodden clothes, wash if there was a creek handy or otherwise a 'bird bath', and dress in my second set of jungle greens that were kept dry no matter what, was a luxury beyond imagination.

Some days I would find the time to wander into the bush in the last hour before nightfall and find a spot away from the bustle of the camp where I could sit quietly and hope to see some of the wonders of the jungle. If I was lucky, I might catch a glimpse of the great ballerina skirts of a Bird of Paradise as a male bird postured, danced and sang for his female admirers, or the silver headdress of the beautiful Crowned Pigeon. Once I saw, coiled on a high limb among coloured lichen and orchids, waiting silently for its dinner, a beautifully coloured Golden Python. Perhaps the Giant Frogmouth owl with its baleful eyes and horrendous jaws as it flittered through the darkening forest in search of the beautiful Birdwing butterflies, or a flock of Cuckoo Tailed Parrot feeding in the deep foliage above.

Possums were quite common and once I was confronted by a giant Cassowary that stood almost as tall as myself, and for a moment I thought he might have attacked me. They are magnificent birds, with bright plumage around the neck and face, but dangerous and are known to have disembowelled men with their frightful talons. These birds were highly coveted by the natives—a grown bird was worth a wife, if she was young and pretty, or two years of labour. In the high moss forests, there were somnolent sloths, tree kangaroos and Flaming Crested Bower Birds who built metre-high nests on top of gardens of moss.

On the jungle floor there were many species of dangerous snakes. The deadly and aggressive Black Taipan, Death Adders, Whip Snakes and the highly poisonous blacks and browns were more than enough to make sure I watched where I put my feet. The plentiful number of scorpions and spiders made it essential to carefully shake and inspect your boots before entrusting your pale and blistered foot to their safekeeping.

As darkness closed in a mug of sweet white coffee and a check of the camp – then to bed, surrounded by the impenetrable darkness of the jungle and the loud cacophony of calls of the darkness. In the jungle danger can often be heralded by the sudden silence of the night.

'Patrolling' was a regular feature of service with the Pacific Islands Regiment. I have been often asked what the purpose was of sending us off to the remote reaches of PNG two or three times a year to wander around the jungle for weeks on end.

The most valuable aspect from a soldiering point of view was to maintain the ability of the soldiers to live and fight in the jungle, and to not lose the skills first developed during the Kokoda fighting in World War II. The patrols also served to show the embryo nation their new national army and to help pull together the hundreds of tribes locked away in the remote ranges and islands of PNG. There was also an element of exploration; many of the patrols would be in areas not seen by Europeans and rarely trodden by even the indigenes.

To me they were far and away the highlight of my service in PNG. I loved the wildness and the challenge, the unexplored paths through the wilderness, the remote campsites, awe inspiring views, the exotic flora and fauna and the companionship of the soldiers 'on the trail'.

Normally only the platoon commanders were sent off, while the captains and the majors luxuriated in a fixed camp somewhere comfortable, probably close to a 'club', and ran things over the radio. But as I rose to these exalted ranks, I always continued to take every opportunity to enjoy the wildness and the adventure of the mountains and jungles. After two tours and five years of this, not too many would have humped a pack over more of the country or spent more nights inspecting important parts of their anatomy for leeches.

The next morning, we began following the barely discernible path leading westwards into the mountains. It was rarely used, probably only by the occasional hunting party from the last village, and by mid-morning it had petered out. From now on we relied only on our compass to maintain our general direction, while trying to find the most practical way forward.

This part of our route would take us over a series of parallel mountain ridges, some nearly 3000 metres high. These were spurs of the central range, the Owen Stanley Range, that run the full length of the country from the border with West Irian to the Bismarck Sea. We would take an air resupply at the Erave River, then press on over more of the same topography to Lake Kutubu.

With some use of machetes, we made reasonable time, although it is hard to maintain a sense of progress in the jungle. Your immediate surroundings do not seem to change. You can usually only see a few paces, sometimes it would open out a little and at others close in even more. There is a sameness that makes the patch of jungle you were in five minutes ago, or an hour, or two hours ago, indistinguishable from where you are now. The watercourse, or gully, or ridge that you cross is no different from all the others, and probably not marked on the large-scale ordnance map that you have been equipped with.

In these days before GPS technology, distance was largely measured by counting paces or hours. On a difficult route that climbs and falls and is continually changing direction, both are extremely inaccurate. After time you do develop a sense of how many metres you have covered in varying conditions. But often this will be way out when you are able to confirm where you are from an identifiable feature.

Another source of reference was a local guide, in our case a local policeman from Mendi. Guides can have their drawbacks, however. The average tribesman, carrying a few spears while his wives toil behind him with heavily laden *billums*, will cover distances much more quickly than overladen soldiers. This will often lead to widely optimistic estimates of times to reach places, often exaggerated because of my obvious eagerness for the destination to be close. The locals, like most Greek taxi drivers, do not like being the bearers of bad news. Hence a place that is actually two day's hard march away, may well be, *'em close to lik lik, masta'* (it's pretty close) or *'em e no long way too mus'* (it's not too far).

Guides may well not have travelled a route for years. On one occasion we employed an elderly man, a *'lapun'*, who had not walked a track since childhood, and since then it had changed beyond recognition because of landslips and flooding. He had as little idea of where we were as we did!

We climbed steadily upwards for most of the morning and reached the top of a ridgeline just after noon and in the afternoon slid down the other side to a rocky stream, where we camped while there was still enough light. We were carrying a week's supply of patrol rations, including two days' emergency rations—two blocks of chocolate. Patrol rations came in self-contained packages for each day, but weight and space meant they were invariably broken down so that each individual carried only what he wanted and threw away or swapped the rest. I normally carried one 200gm can of meat, half a cup of rice and some dried peas or beans for each day. My batman would carry the same and we would share for breakfast and dinner, generally flavoured with curry and sweet potato if any could be bought along the way. Lunch was a small packet of dry biscuits and a cup of sweet tea.

I was a fit eighty-five kilograms when I started and an emaciated seventy-six when I got back to Port Moresby.

The weight of our equipment was always a problem. At the start of each patrol, despite culling and culling all that was not essential, the load would be around thirty kilograms. It was a struggle even getting my pack on my shoulders. The first few days march were always hell, but eventually your body adjusted, and the burden became just bloody torture. It was always bliss to drop your pack at the end of a day and feel for a moment that the laws of gravity had been suspended—something Sir Isaac Newton missed, by the way—and you were actually floating.

As far as we knew there were no tribes in the area we were crossing for the next two weeks and we did not expect to meet anyone, except perhaps a hunting party. So, it was unlikely we would be able to buy any local 'kai kai', although everyone was already carrying a few delicious red or purple yams and a succulent sweet potato or two.

For three days there was no change in the rhythm of the march. We rose before sunrise, packed our gear while breakfast was being cooked, and were on our way before the sun penetrated the thick canopy. The day was still cool. Normally we would march for two hours or so, have a twenty-minute break for a cup of tea, and march for another two hours so that we had broken the back of the day before the heat of midday. If possible, we would have a long break for lunch, but if we were in a swamp, crossing a river, it was pouring rain or we were climbing a precipitous cliff face, we would generally press on.

On a good day, we would then do another couple of hours, and hope to camp early, in a congenial spot. Water close by, which for a place where rain mostly falls in bucketful's, was sometimes difficult, reasonably flat—bloody difficult—with timber for 'hutchie' poles, and if we were in a populated area, near a village so that we could do some trading and public relations work with the locals. I loved to camp somewhere with an outlook, perhaps a distant view of craggy mountains, a tumbling mountain stream or just an open glade, where I could contemplate the approach of evening, and if we had done more than an hour after lunch and came across somewhere enticing, that was good enough for me.

Many locals may have never seen a white man, or anyone from the government or army and may not have realised either existed or have even seen someone from another tribe. With the number of languages spoken in Papua New Guinea, conversations were often slow and laborious – my *pisin* to a soldier, his police *motu* to the constable, the constable's tribal language to a villager who had picked up a second language, the villager to the headman, and back the same way. Half an hour to say, 'good afternoon, you have a lovely place here', and another hour for 'how much is your sweet potato?'

They all understood how markets work and loved to drive a hard bargain. They knew that if you wanted to negotiate a deal you must be prepared to walk away from it. More than once I would see locals throw produce into a river rather than sell for less than the price they wanted—which in these cases was actually outrageous. But in any case, we had no concerns about negotiating with villagers for a while

After a few hours on the morning of the fourth day, to our great relief, we found that our path continued downwards. We had crossed the watershed to the Erave river.

We camped early and sent out some men to explore the crest east and west, to see if we could see any signs of life. They returned by dusk having seen nothing.

The short day, the packs a fraction easier to carry, the prospect of a downhill run for a while, all cheered everyone up. The soldiers were mostly a genial bunch anyway, and happy to be away from the tedium of the barracks and doing something they really enjoyed. Even if it was hard work. The rhythms of the days, exploring little known areas, meeting villages and tribes with different customs.

Spirits were still high when we set off downhill the next morning, although in reality it is really just as hard going down with a heavy load as it is going up. Slipping and falling, on muddy or moss-covered rocks or tree roots concealed by mud or rotting vegetation, was always a problem. With a heavy pack, once you start to fall there is no recovery. It is only a nanosecond before you are on your bum—as I indicated before, a heavy pack greatly magnifies the laws of gravity. This happened more often to me than to the soldiers. In my case they didn't make a great deal of it and smirks were suppressed—rude to laugh at the physically challenged—but if it was a fellow soldier, his misfortune was greeted with howls of laughter.

As we descended the country began to gradually change, and by the time we reached the valley of the Erave we had entered a distinct microclimate. Locked between two sets of mountains it seemed almost like a coastal valley—hot and steamy with lusher vegetation and patches of high kunai grass. That evening we made a pleasant camp in a stand of reasonably open timber adjacent to a patch of kunai that would be suitable for our food drop the next day.

We were only a stone's throw from the river, and I strolled down to get a feel of it. It was quite a sight. It seemed bottomless and was about eighty metres wide and coloured like chocolate from the sediment it was carrying. Although it was moving sluggishly, a knot or so, there were a few dangerous eddies along the banks and as I watched, a large tree trunk partially covered in branches was carried past. It was not flooding, but the water was right up to the banks, and it would be a difficult monster for heavily laden soldiers to cross.

I wondered what was happening upstream. Were the waters on the rise? I hoped not, it would be difficult enough to cross as it was. When I returned to camp, I sent men to see if there were any better crossing places nearby, or if there were any villages with canoes we could hire. They returned just on dusk with mixed news.

Upstream the river was no easier and there were no signs of any villages, although there were stands of bamboo, which would make raft building much easier. Downstream the news was bad. Within a few miles the river narrowed, and the current picked up. Ominously, in the distance there was the roar of cataracts or waterfalls.

With the approach of darkness, mist and cloud drifted over us and the heavens opened up, the rain beating like drumsticks on the taut roof of my hutchie. Puddles began to form around it so that it was almost an island. Was it my imagination that the noise of the river seemed louder—you should have camped on higher ground, idiot! Apart from how the rain would affect the river crossing, rain or low cloud tomorrow would almost certainly mean no ration drop. Although not a calamity, I knew that the terrain ahead would be very bad for a drop, and if we wanted rations we would need to hang around here.

There was nothing sophisticated about our aerial delivery. The ration packs were left in the light aluminium containers they came in. These were placed in sandbags and padded with grass. They would then flown in by a chartered single engine Cessna, which flew over the drop zone as low and slow as the bravado of the pilot allowed. Flying among these rugged mountains is dangerous enough at the best of times. But trying to come in at tree height after a difficult descent to a drop zone, followed by a difficult climb out, tested every pilot's nerve.

Waiting on the ground we would curse if the drop was too high, which guaranteed damaged goods, or off target which could well mean the rations were lost completely. Army ration accounting was one ration per man per day and did not recognise loss or damage —we just went without. If you were taking an air drop in the mountains, particularly if you were on a 'knife-edge ridge' it was not uncommon for rations to disappear into an abyss never to be seen again.

The next morning, although the rain had stopped during the night, we were

106

shrouded in mist and the hopes of an air drop nose-dived. HF radio contact was good however and all was ready to go if the weather cleared.

'What's the cloud like at your end?' Headquarters wanted to know.

'Oh, a little mist that looks to be lifting.'

'OK, will call you at 10.00 hours to see what the situation is.'

While we were waiting, I took a walk down the river. We had only two options for river crossings like this. One was for individual flotation. Everyone bundles their gear into their waterproof shelter, together with the partly inflated inserts from his bed, along with lots of long grass, to create a bundle that will float with enough buoyancy to support him for the crossing. The river was just too formidable and the chances of a drowning too real for this.

The second was to build rafts which sounds easy, but in practice is quite difficult from what is generally available. But with bamboo close by things would be much easier. Highland trees were mostly as buoyant as rocks and it was always a struggle to build anything that would take a load.

Anyway, I mulled these thoughts over as I followed the tracks of last afternoon's patrol, at least it was cool under the cloud cover. We were not so far from camp when I became aware of the low roar ahead of us. Gradually it built in volume and thinking we must be close to the source of the noise we cut our way through the tall pit pit grass at the river's edge to see what was there. Nothing. The river narrowed and ran faster, but no signs of rapids.

We pushed on again; the roar growing gradually louder and after a while I again cut through the thick undergrowth to the riverbank. There was a gigantic fallen tree lodged by floodwaters that provided a view up and down the river. It looked a bit insecure and was covered with moss. I thought of sending Corporal Kanai, who was an agile youngster, out to have a look downstream. But I caught his glance and knew that it was something he thought I should do.

I left my rifle and 'bum' pack on shore, and scrambled out along the gargantuan tree, sure that at any moment I'd slide into the eddying brown water below. Further out the tree was not as firmly fixed to the bank as it had seemed and flexed with the flow of the current. When I was perhaps fifteen yards from the bank I could go no further, but I had a clear view downstream. But there was still nothing to see— only the brown flow of the river that was now an irresistible force of nature, rather than the sluggish flow it had been upstream. The roar from downstream was loud and ominous and I now knew without doubt it would be a death trap if it caught any of us.

The mist still hung low over the river as we scrambled back to camp, but by 10.00 hours it had indeed cleared a bit and an hour or so later we picked up the drone of the Cessna's engine in the distance. But alas the drifting mist had shrouded us again and although we could hear it circling overhead trying to find the drop zone, it was invisible. After a few minutes it flew away to the east.

There was little chance of the weather improving during the afternoon, but we had no alternative but to wait here for the drop. I had some biscuits and a cup of tea for lunch, produced by my batman Wafiaga who was grateful he had not been dragged down the river and back, and I told Pokoi to send a party up the river to start cutting bamboo for rafts. Then followed an afternoon like so many in the army—waiting.

The afternoon brought only rain, and apart from the bamboo cutters the rest of us sat around under our hutchies, drinking what tea or coffee we dared, depending on our optimism of a rapid resupply. I lay in my dry clothes in my hutchie, and continued my 'Letter to Ro,' that I hoped to post from the patrol post at Lake Kutubu. Later I strolled upriver to encourage the bamboo cutters, wrote up my notes and worked on my map corrections, wondering if they would ever find their way onto a map. Probably not.

The next morning the mountains lived up to their unpredictability, and when the sun finally climbed above the ridges it was greeted by a clear blue sky, and before long, dappled sunlight was streaming through the green canopy above us. It was an opportunity to get everything dry for a change. If rain or rivers did not soak things, they were always just as wet from sweat.

We were on the radio first thing and by mid-morning we could hear the distant drone of the Cessna. Being able to hear a plane does not automatically mean the pilot will find you; not by a long shot. But no problems today. The Cessna made one trial pass and then began dumping our rations. Only one drop went astray into the tall trees two hundred yards beyond us, but most of that was recovered. The rations were quickly distributed under the watchful eye of Sergeant Pokoi and we set off up the river, planning to lunch when we had joined the bamboo cutters. The first few meals after a drop were often feasts as soldiers tried to gulp down what they preferred not to carry. There was also plenty of trading; a can of bully beef for tinned fish or tea for coffee.

While the frameworks of our rafts were being lashed together with vines, we started to swim a line across the river, using some of the strong swimmers from the coastal tribes—the Highlanders, generally short and nuggety were as buoyant as their trees. By this time the rafts were ready and with much laughter the first raft set off, the strong swimmers pulling it along the safety line and the Highlanders hanging on grimly. Halfway across things were looking grim as the lashings started to come apart from the strain, but to ironic cheers they struggled into the reeds on the far side and pulled themselves up the steep bank. Next was platoon headquarters, perhaps we should have gone first and shown the way, I thought. Too late now!

Despite having strengthened our lashings we did no better than the first raft but made it across— just. On the far shore I could see Pokoi shaking his head and sending soldiers into the trees to cut more lashings. Looking around I began to take in our surroundings. The steep bank we had climbed from the water led to a narrow strip of relatively flat ground, perhaps twenty metres wide, beyond that the slope rose steeply. Beneath the dense canopy of the rainforest the ground was rocky, huge trees sprouted from fissures between great cracked boulders. I wondered how such a forest as the one we stood under could be sustained.

I returned my attention to the crossing, as the soldiers on my side began to lay out a campsite. By now it was getting late, darkening clouds were shrouding the mountains and the last of the sun had gone. Finally, the last two rafts crossed safely and Pokoi was pulled across on the safety line.

The ground made it difficult to plant the poles for our hutchies, which was a taste of what was to come. But Wafiaga had commandeered a flat patch of land with a fine view over the river for platoon headquarters, he was definitely showing leadership potential. It was unusual for us to light wood fires, generally the rainforest timber was too wet to make it worth the trouble, and of course fires were totally forbidden if we were 'tactical' or training for active operations. For cooking we carried tablets of solid fuel, called hexamine.

Tonight however, some fires were lit as we were all cold in our sodden gear. It was a peaceful scene, the flicker of the smoky fires with soldiers sitting around them, the barely discernible river running away into the unknown. Around us the dark forest—quieter it seemed, because of the fires and the smoke. Wafiaga and I shared a tin of bully beef, curried with rice and peas, and I listened to the banter about the crossing; these boys could have taught the Australian cricket team a lot about sledging.

A full stomach, a hot brew, warm in my second set of jungle greens carefully kept dry in the crossing. Ah, soldiering was great.

The next morning the going was very difficult right from the start. It was not possible to walk, we had to scramble and climb across steep rock faces, still covered with tall forest and a thick undergrowth of leafy vines. Gradually we left the river below, but for much of the day we could still hear its roar, and occasionally we had a glimpse out over the valley it followed.

By midday of the second day since leaving the river, we had not come across

109

any running water. This was starting to get serious. We all carried two plastic water bottles attached to our webbing and could normally fill up from creeks and small water courses fairly regularly. Each man had a small canvas filter bag and chlorine tablets to make the water safe. But on this rocky mountainside there was nothing; the rain disappeared down the crevasses without trace.

In the late afternoon we were still on the rock face and we had found neither water, nor a place to make camp. Although we had all collected a bit from the run-off from the hutchies and cut vines, we were now desperate for water. There was little left to drink, let alone cook the brown rice which was the bulk of our diet.

We pushed on until darkness was almost with us, then accepted there would be another night perched like shags amongst the rocks and hoping that it would rain hard enough for us to catch some water in our waterproof 'hutchie' sheets.

After it was dark, and I had crawled around the platoon and checked everyone was okay, I rolled into a crack between two boulders, cold, wet and thirsty, hoping I would have captured enough water from the vines draining into my mug and water bottles to get me through the next day, and wondering what the hell I was doing on this godforsaken mountainside.

The mist hung around us like a shroud, but the rain regular as clockwork most nights, there was none. In the morning, cold and stiff from a night on the ground, the impenetrable white blanket still covered the mountainside. Pokoi moved among the men, encouraging them with the thought that today we would reach the pass and after that it would be all downhill to Lake Kutubu.

We continued to scramble upwards, and after a few hours were rewarded when we broke through the mist and could look to the south over a gleaming sea of whiteness. Below a pale blue sky, the mist stretched away for miles and miles, a glimmering carpet lit by sunlight and broken in places by mighty crags covered in dense green foliage. We sat for a while, awed by the view and warmed by the sun; such a friend after the cold damp night. But soon to be a torment again, as it climbed higher and the forest gradually became a steaming sauna.

Climbing mountains in PNG was always a matter of overcoming the heartbreak of false crests. In the dense forests, where you could rarely see very far ahead, it was impossible to know whether the crest you were climbing or had actually arrived on, was the magical top of the mountain or just a false crest somewhere below it. In a day's march upwards there could be twenty or thirty crests. By number nine or ten everyone would be praying, 'Dear God, let this one really be the top'. Then would come number eleven, twelve, then thirteen and ever upwards. The only course was dull acceptance of the pain of dragging one foot above the next. To enter a catatonic state, where your mind wandered free from the pain of the body. The common expression being 'mind in neutral, head down, bum up' – there are coarser versions which you don't need to know.

So, it was on the third day. A dozen times it seemed a crest was the pass we sought. A dozen times we were disappointed to find that after a short distance the path rose upwards again. We were still tortured by thirst. Beneath the damp foliage of the high canopy there was no water for those on the march.

Finally, in the early afternoon, we reached a place where we had walked for fifteen minutes on ground that was reasonably level, and gradually we realised that we had reached the crest. There was nothing here to mark the event. No distant panorama, or canyon walls pressing in from both sides – still only the thick canopy of the high trees and the same dense under story.

Pokoi and I looked at each other, and he nodded. 'This is it, boss.'

We decided to make camp here. It was level and there were plenty of vines to see us through the night as far as water was concerned, if we couldn't find anything better.

For a number of minutes, we all collapsed. Too exhausted to even take the packs off our backs we sat with them resting against tree trunks and rocks. Before long energy returned and we set about making a camp, and most urgently sending out parties to scout for water. Surely, now that we were on some sort of plateau and the run-off was not so precipitous, we would be able to find something. After an hour one party returned with the news that they had found a small spring. With great relief we sent off a water party, taking every water bottle in the platoon to be filled.

Sometimes I don't think people really appreciate how hard is the lot of the poor infantryman, as opposed to those lucky souls who drive around in tanks, or fly planes or lounge around in the artillery. So, while lugging my pack around, with my mind in neutral of course, I have developed some rather pedantic mathematical formulas to help explain things, in the hope of eliciting some sympathy for the benighted souls who make up the army's backbone. Here is the formula for walking around the jungle-clad mountains anywhere in Papua New Guinea.

Firstly, forget the word walk. If you are going up a trackless mountain and down the other side what you will be doing is climbing. You always will need at least one handhold and a foothold before you move your other leg.

Forget the words level and straight. It is either up or down, crabwise left or right, scrambling over or under fallen trees, pushing or cutting through vines or foliage. You must visually select each spot you place your foot amongst the mossy, muddy latticework of roots and rocks and decaying foliage you are climbing through.

Many of the vines, including the infamous 'wait-a-while' are covered with spikes that will rip your hands and clothes. In some places the ground cover is not so dense that you must cut your way through, but often it is, particularly if a fallen tree has let the sunlight in.

Remember you are carrying a pack and equipment which mostly weighs over thirty kilograms. How heavy is that? About the same as having four cartons of beer cans on your back. I know that Sir Isaac Newton says something along the lines of things falling at the same speed—but we already know this is a load of b***s***! If you slip with four cartons of beer on your back, your bum hits the ground much faster than if you're carrying nothing.

How high is a three thousand metre mountain? About as high as a building with one thousand floors, say two thousand flights of stairs, say eighteen thousand individual steps. So, if you were climbing stairs it would be eighteen thousand steps up, but you are not climbing stairs you are winding your way up a mountain. It will take at least forty thousand steps to get to the top. Then another forty thousand down the other side, which means a total of eighty thousand steps.

Now, if you were on flat ground eighty thousand steps would take you about seventy kilometres. But unfortunately, by the time you have gone up and down the mountain you will only have advanced about six kilometres forward. And, while climbing the mountain it is impossible that you could have walked in a straight direction towards your goal, so you've probably made only four kilometres. Now, let's say—taking a conservative estimate—it takes three times the effort to climb rather than walk, so our four kilometres has expended the same energy, as walking two hundred and ten kilometres on level ground. Then, if I was being completely pedantic—I know that is hard to believe—we would have to talk about slippery mud, tenacious vines etc etc etc and we are looking at five hundred kilometres along a highway —and if you are not carrying four cartons of booze you would need to walk from Sydney to Brisbane, at least, for you to be as buggered as a stupid grunt hauling himself over one three thousand metre mountain in PNG—and I forgot to factor in the energy-sapping heat and humidity etc etc. Now I have to admit that three thousand metre climbs were not common, but they make the maths easier; and there were plenty of two thousand metre climbs.

Did I ever say I enjoyed this? I did, but as I said before there were also a lot of times, I wondered what the bloody hell I was doing.

By dusk the campsite had worked its recuperative magic. Sitting under my hutchie, dry, fed, my chores and reports done, surrounded by the muted sounds of the camp, I was happy with my lot. More importantly so were the soldiers—it had been a hard few days—but there were plenty of smiles, no sullen faces and no injuries or sickness to speak of.

One of the necessities for staying healthy in the jungle, more so for a European but still important for the soldiers, who had some inherited advantages for living in these conditions, was a constant obsession, bordering on hypochondria, with your physical well-being. The most likely causes of sickness were polluted water, malaria, or an infected wound or tropical ulcer.

We always imposed strict water discipline and were very careful where we took water —never down-stream from a village, and always at least treated it with chlorine tablets. Sometimes, of course, you just had to take what was available.

Malaria is perhaps the deadliest of the tropical diseases and it is estimated that some one million—yes, one million—die from the disease each year. At this time there was no medication to prevent contraction of the disease, but we took a paludrin pill which effectively suppressed the symptoms. So most of us would be carrying the infection, caused by the bite of an anopheles mosquito, relying on our own immune system to cure us. I wonder what long term effect this had? Paludrin was taken by every soldier every morning under my direct supervision, seven days a week. We slept under mosquito nets whenever feasible, wore our sleeves rolled down and covered ourselves with repellent. So effective were these precautions that it was a chargeable offence to come down with the symptoms, as paludrin was supposedly one hundred percent effective as a suppressant.

The major source of infection and tropical ulcers was leech bites. In some areas they were so bad I would inspect my legs, crotch and armpits at every stop and burn them off with a cigarette. If I took my boots off there would be a number of bloated and, crushed leeches, which had sucked their fill and been squashed within my boot when they stopped feeding.

Once my hutchie was erected and it seemed probable that I could stay dry for the night, I would remove the sodden mud-soaked jungle greens, socks and underpants I had worn during the day and inspect myself for any more leeches, particularly around the scrotum. There was a scary rumour that they were attracted to the urinary passage, which was a worry for a young man.

I then removed them by either burning them with a cigarette or pouring salt or squirting with mosquito repellent—pulling them off would leave a poisonous residue which invariably became infected. At this time, although I did not know it, I still had another decade where much of my time was to be spent in the jungle. Despite my care, forty years after I last pulled on a pair of muddy boots, my legs are still scarred by hundreds of small white spots that the leeches left behind.

That done I would wash myself, often in a creek but at least by sponging with a damp camouflage scarf that we all wore and then drying myself as well as possible with the same scarf. Starting with my feet, treat all the leech bites, blisters, chafing between my toes, bites, stings, cuts and scratches, chafing in the crutch and from my pack on my shoulders and back, with either antiseptic powder, cream or liquid; I carried a small container of each and a few band aids. Once anything became infected you had problems, but I found with this quick routine, a few minutes a day, I could stop any serious infection. Most of the soldiers would go through the same routine automatically, but it was also the job of the NCOs and myself to make sure they did.

Then the exquisite pleasure of a dry set of jungle greens and thongs and hanging my wet canvas boots upside down on two of the hutchie poles in the hope the next morning they would be only damp, rather than sodden. The dry clothes were carried in the inner most sanctum of my pack, wrapped in everything waterproof I carried, and would stay dry even when the pack was completely immersed in a river or through a day's torrential rain. A dry night's sleep was luxurious, and as necessary as food and hygiene to staying fit and healthy.

This done I would think about the next day, when I would be changing back into my 'walking set' of greens. If possible, I would have washed them when I was washing myself, but at least I would hang them outside the hutchie to be either washed by rain or aired and dried somewhat—whatever nature decreed. But there was very rarely any escape from climbing back into clammy wet clothes each morning, even if some of the mud had been washed off.

Every day we came across assorted poisonous creatures: snakes—but most often non-poisonous pythons and tree snakes—spiders, centipedes and scorpions, but bites from these were not common. The real problem was always fighting the infections from the wear and tear of the march and being wet so much of the time.

When we set off the next day, we found after a while that we were following the ghost of a trail. Whether it was just an animal pad, or had been trodden by humans, it was hard to say. But it was going our way, across the spine of the range we had climbed. The going was much easier, relatively flat—by PNG standards—and we had left behind the rocks and great boulders of the ascent. Once again, the ground was soft underfoot, damp earth covered with a thick layer of decaying leaves.

Our packs felt lighter; they were, nearly half our rations had been eaten and we made good progress. In the early afternoon we came across a small rivulet, bubbling over a rocky bottom between clean low banks. The water was cool and clear. It was the first sight of abundant water we had seen since the river crossing, and to all of us it was like stumbling across a rich seam of gold. We stood and admired.

Pokoi, who normally brought up the rear to ensure there were no stragglers, was mysteriously at hand to ensure the right decision was made.

'*Sir, em e good pella place to mus,*' was his sage advice.

In Pokoi speak this meant, 'This is a great spot, don't be a bloody idiot and go past it. We are overdue a rest day anyway—which everyone is keenly aware of— so let's stop and spend tomorrow as a 'make and mend' day'.

To preserve some dignity, I pretended to consider the options for a few moments, before giving orders to make camp. To be honest I was there barracking for a rest day as much as anyone – but there was no need for everyone to know that. It was a bit like the end of the working week. An almost festive air enveloped us— remembering we are thirty odd Pacific Islanders and one white man, in the middle of the jungle and a long march from any grog.

Talking about the passage of time.

It certainly leaves some scars. But sometimes in compensation it leaves many great memories. Fifty years after this patrol I have clear recollections of most of the places we camped, and the feeling of the remoteness and pleasure of being there. Give me a map and I can trace the many jungle miles of the other PNG patrols, and point out where we stopped and something of it. The same with sailing. With a chart I can trace the thousands of miles we have sailed and the hundreds of places we have anchored and conjure back memories of them nearly all.

But back to the Highlands of PNG.

The soldiers, and for that matter most Pacific Islanders, have an obsession with eating pig. Pigs, apart from being good eating, are a measure of wealth in their society. Piglets are raised on the wife's teat next to the baby and if there is a choice as to who gets mother's milk, it is probably the pig. And, if eating pig is a luxury, hunting wild pig with army rifles and ammunition is every soldier's dream. Their only real chance to do this is 'on patrol.'

But just a minute. The army carefully counts ammunition expenditure, and what is taken on patrol is expressly forbidden to be used for 'hunting.' Is there an answer?

Of course there is. The sergeants 'club' is in charge of accounting for ammunition, and this mob always have a way around inconvenient rules (that officers should not stick their noses into) and Pokoi, with a nod and a half smile to me, is seen moving into the bush. With him are two of his 'one-talks'—from the same tribe—and two Highlanders who may not be great swimmers but know where to find pig in the mountains.

The platoon commander continues to luxuriate in the cool clear water of the rivulet, contemplating clean walking clothes for the first time in a fortnight; in fact, by tomorrow night, everything will be clean, for a while.

While the hunting party is away the usual chores go on. I write up my reports, draw map corrections, check the signallers are stringing their HF radio aerial, walk around the platoon and have a chat to whoever crosses my path. But while I am doing this the real work of the afternoon goes on. On the explicit orders of Sergeant Pokoi, a *'muu muu'* pit is being dug, flat rocks and firewood are being collected, and another team of Highlanders have been sent to gather the leaves and native roots necessary to cook a pig in the traditional 'highland' style.

The *'muu muu'* pit is the same as a shallow grave. Once it is dug it is partially filled with rocks; preferably ones which are not so waterlogged that they will explode when heated, and then the best fire it is possible to conjure up under the conditions is lit. The aim is to have a bed of red-hot stones in the pit.

The party sent to gather leaves and roots is the first to return. Among their spoils, and the only thing I can identify, are a quantity of broad banana leaves. It is possible that Papua New Guinea has more varieties of banana than it has spoken languages. They range from the large and sweet to the small and tasteless, but every variety has its place in traditional culinary. The leaves are essential for a *muu muu*, for they are used to wrap the meat and keep it moist and tender for the many hours it will be buried steaming in the pit.

Just on dark the hunting party returned laden with two pigs. Pokoi is wearing the small smile he often has when he is pleased with the way things have turned out, and the Highlanders are positively puffed with pride that their mountains have provided such bounty—not to mention it was them that led Pokoi to the pigs.

Now things get serious, and nearly everyone has a job; of course, there is nothing I can be trusted with. The pigs are dismembered with machetes and wrapped in parcels of banana leaves, together with the wild herbs. About half the hot rocks are pulled out of the pit with sticks, amidst much laughter and hooting, as it is not an easy thing to do without burning yourself.

Then the bottom rocks are lightly covered with earth and then a layer of banana leaves and other greenery. Now the parcels of meat are placed on the leaves and covered with more dirt. After that the remainder of the hot rocks are returned to the pit so that they are covering the feast. Finally, more dirt is mounded over, and a fire kindled on top.

Sometime later steam begins to rise from the pit, and later still the delicious aroma of the cooking pig meat. The meat will be allowed to cook slowly overnight, and everyone can look forward to a great feast tomorrow. By now the night was well

116

advanced, and the scene was partially lit by four campfires, and the soldiers were sitting around cooking their dinner of army rations while talking of tomorrow's pig and other feasts in other places.

After the rest day and, the great feast, we continued on the faint trail that was following the grain of the country northwest. We did not know where it led, but it was heading more or less in our direction and that was enough. We continued to make good progress over the next two days, and in mid-afternoon it seemed we were beginning to drop down into the Kutubu valley.

We began clambering down a steep stretch covered in thick jungle, and we found that our trail had disappeared, swallowed by the lush greenery. It was hot sticky work, with the forward scouts trying to cut a path for us to follow, and the moisture-laden air as hot as a steam bath. There was a brief shower that cooled us for a few minutes, but soon the wet forest floor was steaming again, and the sweat ran off us in rivers.

We continued to push through the thick vegetation, much thicker and hotter than it had been on the higher ridges, but before long it levelled out and we came to a creek running along the edge of the escarpment. The forward scouts waded across, and almost immediately the cry came back.

'Road e stap.'

I moved forward to investigate, and sure enough, we had come to a maintained track that showed signs of human use—perhaps a 'road' in local parlance, but it was only about a metre wide but not one that was capable of taking any form of vehicular traffic. One of the first jobs of the *Kiaps* when they moved into an area was to improve the existing network of tracks between villages. The villagers were coerced into widening them to perhaps two metres, and footbridges were built. These were known by the locals as 'roads', and each village was responsible for maintaining its own stretch. In due course many were improved enough to carry vehicular traffic—and some, with government assistance, were eventually sealed with bitumen.

There was room for a camp between the creek and the 'road' and while it was being set up, I sent some men upstream to see if there was a village. They came back within the hour, preceded by some heavily laden *meris*, to report that the track ended at a native garden.

Most native villages have a number of vegetable gardens, which are worked mostly by the women. The gardens are operated on the slash and burn principle. A patch of bush is cleared, and the fallen timber and undergrowth burnt. The ash is worked into the ground as fertiliser and crops of sweet potato and bananas—and taro in the lower regions—are planted and tended daily by the village women. The men may accompany them to the gardens to 'protect them' and then proceed on the 'men's business' of hunting, or then again, they might lounge round the *haus man*, smoking and telling lies. Like men in bars and coffee shops the world over.

After a few years when the soil is worked out, the garden is abandoned, and a new one cut out of the jungle by the *meri*s. No doubt the menfolk decide where it will be. There are old disused gardens, many with some self-seeded crops to scavenge, all over PNG. Many remain long after the village they served has been forgotten.

The *meris*, carrying *billums* full of sweet potato were not keen to chat, and scooted past platoon headquarters sited near the track, with eyes averted. Nevertheless, Pokoi must have caught a gleam in someone's eye, because shortly afterwards he suggested he should follow them to their village and have a chat to the headman about buying some potatoes and bananas. Taking some Highlanders as interpreters and porters he set off, a small smile on his lips.

He returned at the conclusion of not very fruitful negotiations at the village, but accompanied by a number of curious villagers, mostly men and children. It turned out that after the government patrol post had been established at the other end of Lake Kutubu a bible society 'mission' had been established nearby. Bible society missions were located in a number of remote villages in Papua New Guinea for the purpose of translating the bible into tribal languages, as well as converting the locals to Christianity. That some languages might well have only a few hundred speakers did nothing to dull the ardour of the missionaries for their task, and no doubt in due course their efforts will be the only record of a number of the tribal languages.

Some, often young families, would spend years living in very trying conditions in some of the remotest areas of the country. I could not help but being impressed by the dedication, and the belief in their task that enabled them to live in such wild and remote places. Invariably they were kind and generous people, happy doing the Lord's work.

Unfortunately, it seemed to me that there were a number of adverse spinoffs from these missions. The first was the encouragement they gave to Cargo Cult mentality amongst the locals. In seeking a reason why Europeans were so relatively wealthy—why they had so much 'cargo'—many thought the explanation was a religious one. Europeans are followers of Jesus. They have lots of cargo. If we become Christians, we will be rewarded too. This idea was not always discouraged by the missionaries.

More importantly, the imposition of the Christian religion seemed to take something important out of the tribal society. Not just the good humour that I found to be an almost universal trait of the 'natural' villages, but something deeper. The fact that all their age-old beliefs were rendered obsolete by the stories of the bible, which they didn't really understand, destroyed the underlying cultural bonds that had held tribes together for thousands of years.

Of course, it wasn't just religion, there were many other factors pulling apart the tribal bonds—the lure of the growing towns and cities and the growth of a younger educated generation that tended to sideline the older leaders, and perhaps worst of all the introduction of alcohol into a society with no tradition of its use.

Over my time there I found that the army was never really welcome at most mission villages. I did lecture my men periodically on the need for good behaviour and to stay away from the women, but they were all lusty young fellows and I'm sure some succumbed to temptation whenever possible. Sometimes it was difficult to trade with villages that had been 'shaped' by the missions. Often they wanted very high prices for their produce—not that they can be blamed for wanting to do the best they could, but at times they were bloody minded.

Pokoi had returned with only a few sweet potatoes, shaking his head at his lack of success, and we had to rely on trading with the curious visitors who trickled in during the afternoon. Before dusk we ushered the last of them outside the camp perimeter and checked again that all our men were accounted for. But everyone finally got a good meal of sweet potato, and the mood in the camp was upbeat; only one more day along a good track to the shores of Lake Kutubu and another day in hired canoes to the patrol post at the far end.

The next day was a stroll, a firm flat track that you could actually walk on without carefully placing each foot in a safe spot, the vegetation cleared, and best of all—light packs, we were just about out of rations. We camped not far from a village built on the banks of the mouth of a creek that discharged into the lake, and Pokoi, the native constable and myself went to discuss hiring canoes. Our aerial reconnaissance of the patrol route had established that there were canoes here, and I hoped they would still be available for hire. We could now see Lake Kutubu and its mountainous surrounds, and it was obvious that if there were none available there would be some hard slog to reach the far end of the lake.

I need not have worried. The canoes were there, and it was a delightful and friendly village. Strange how one village, a day's march earlier, had been so different.

The canoes were large hollowed-out logs, with about an inch of freeboard after we were loaded. Those who had experience paddling canoes were given paddles; the Highlanders sat grimly holding the sides of the canoes with white knuckles. Apart from the natives living around Lake Kutubu there would be no natives in the whole of the PNG highlands who could be trusted to do more than just hang on.

It was a luxurious feeling, being paddled across the still waters of the lake under a high blue sky, after two weeks of slogging through the undergrowth under a thick green canopy. About halfway along the lake we were taken close to the western shore so that we could be shown the tribal burial ground.

Here an almost sheer cliff rose perhaps a hundred metres from the water level. Along the face of the cliff, suspended in loosely woven wicker burial baskets, were the remains of the more recently deceased, picked clean by carrion and ants. Eventually, as the baskets rotted and broke, the remaining bones would drop into the reputed bottomless water below the cliff.

I suppose there are worse ways of returning the earthly remains to nature.

From some distance we were able to make out the government patrol post, sitting on a commanding promontory at the north end of the lake, and in the early afternoon we disembarked at a small landing below it. There to greet us was the young district patrol officer, who made us feel very welcome and led us to a campsite on the edge of the small outpost.

It only consisted of a few buildings mainly built of local materials: woven bamboo walls, thatched roofs and roughly dressed timber floors, arranged around a grass parade ground. At one side stood a three-room residence with a wide sheltered veranda overlooking the lake. Opposite, with the Australian flag flying from a white flagpole was the district administration office and nearby, a lock-up and a medical post. Away to one side were a few houses for police and local government employees, such as a medic and schoolteacher. A short light aircraft landing field had been constructed along part of the promontory.

Port Moresby has always had a number of drawbacks as an administrative and commercial centre. The most serious is that it has never been connected by road, apart from a few nearby villages, to the rest of the country. A few rough tracks, the Kokoda Track being by far the most famous, wind their way into the interior, but they have been of no importance to commerce or governance. In the 1960s, only a beginning had been made on the Highlands Highway running inland from Lae along the spine of the country.

The isolation of the capital meant that the administrative districts that were created to develop and govern the country were critically important. Moresby may have been where the Administrator lived, but it was the District Officers in the districts—which were to eventually evolve into provinces—who really applied the law and gave the impetus to move the tribes from the Stone Age towards the twentieth century.

At this time the district's capitals were already reasonably developed towns with most of the comforts of modern life, and the coastal towns of Wewak, Madang and Lae had been trading centres with some infrastructure for most of the century. Mostly the streets were still full of tribal men and women in their traditional rigs, and a short distance out of town would take you back to tribal societies.

The recently established Lake Kutubu station, was one of the remotest of the patrol stations at the time, pushing out the fringe of government control into areas where no government had previously existed, and where inter-tribal and village relationships were often marked by bitter feuds, and in some cases open warfare. It was part the role of patrols such as our own to provide a demonstration of the power of the central government and bolster the prestige of the patrol officers and help make their jobs a bit easier.

We spent a few days at the post recovering from the wear and tear of the previous weeks. We took a resupply and by way of 'civic action' helped rebuild a few nearby footbridges. In the evenings I enjoyed the patrol officer's hospitality, revelling in the chance to watch the sun go down with a beer in my hand and to eat freshly cooked food at a table.

But we were soon on our way again, taking canoes across the lake and up a long arm to the head of the track that we hoped would lead us in the direction of the small outpost of Tari —our final destination.

It was quite late in the day by the time we were all across and ready to face the trials of the track again, and rather than push straight on we spent the evening at a pleasant spot on the shore of the lake. Campfires were lit and the soldiers began the serious business of eating all the fresh fish and vegetables that they would not be able to carry the next day. It was a still clear night, washed clean by late afternoon showers, and it was cool away from the fires. The lake stretched away in the blackness, its calm surface twinkling with reflected starlight.

Before the sun had risen, we had begun to climb the high ridges that cradled the western side of the lake. Once again, our packs were full and heavy, and my body protested vehemently as we dragged our way upward once more. My pack straps dug into my shoulders and my pack jarred against my lower spine, each pace was agony on my knee and my wet trousers chafed.

A couple of months after arriving in PNG I had fallen and broken my right leg. The tendon attached to the knee ripped a piece of bone from the top of my shin bone, and it had required a lengthy period in a plaster, from crutch to ankle. Even for the army I thought my subsequent treatment was a bit hard-nosed. The plaster had barely set before I was discharged from hospitable and re-assigned as the Assistant Quartermaster—almost certainly the least sought-after job in the battalion. No time for rest and recuperation, no physio, just get on your crutches and report to the Q store where all the army stores are held and accounted for.

I was made responsible for conducting the annual rolling stock take, which involved sighting and counting every item in the large Q store, every item in every room of every house, every barracks, every kitchen, every dining hall, the officers mess, the sergeants mess, the medical centre, the transport yards etc etc. Every item from teaspoons to trucks were counted and recorded in large ledgers where items were categorised in an incomprehensible order; 'spoons tea special mark 55' would be pages away from 'spoons tea general service,' and pages away from 'forks three pronged large for eating', which could well be between 'blankets GS' and 'sheets tropical service green'. Much time was spent hunting through the ledgers and distinguishing between 'pots large special' and 'pots large GS'. When everything was counted and recorded the totals were compared against what should be on hand. This required numerous recounts and re-identifying 'brushes toilets for the cleaning of' to 'brushes kitchen scrubbing'.

A thankless task at the best of times in the hothouse atmosphere of Port Moresby, but much worse on crutches with pencil and stock sheet clamped between my teeth, swinging on my crutches from place to place. There was still no time allowed for rehabilitation and physio, I was required to spend a full day on the job. Eventually I could get by without the crutches which made life easier, and I became quite mobile, swinging along with a great white plaster-casted leg.

In fact, I became quite agile. So much so that one day I had the inestimable satisfaction—after a bet being laid without my knowledge by one of my fellow lieutenants—of beating a smug visiting officer at squash with my leg in plaster. Oh, the joy. But it did not enhance my popularity with the hierarchy much. Later on, long after I was plaster-less my fellow lieutenant used to make good money betting on me in 'flippers'—still not the smartest thing to do, but it seemed funny at the time.

After my plaster had been changed a couple of times, I had lost so much condition in the broken leg that the slim-cut trousers that were the fashion to wear after dark, fitted equally snugly over both my good leg and the plaster-cast. And unfortunately, the leg gave me trouble for years; I probably should have stayed off the squash court.

The one blessing of my broken leg was that Ro, still just only nineteen, had been allowed to come to PNG. So that at least I had a bit of mothering and a driver for my TR4, a sports car with plenty of grunt but known as the 'flying brick', because it didn't turn corners all that well.

Meanwhile, climbing the ridges out of Lake Kutubu, by midday things had settled down. I had gotten into the routine of 'head down, bum up, mind in neutral'.

The track petered away to nothing, and for much of the day we followed the course of a small swiftly running creek that splashed its way below the thick overhanging rainforest. At times we slithered along its stony bottom, walking up to our knees against the force of the water and stumbling among the smooth slippery rocks. At other times we climbed its slippery banks and followed the ridgelines above it.

By late afternoon we had reached the top of a ridgeline and I called a stop at what appeared to be the source of the creek we had followed, where cool clear water bubbled from a rocky spring.

We made a welcome and pleasant camp, and once things had settled down a call of nature took me to the pit latrine that had been dug thirty metres or so from the camp boundary. It was sited in a nice private spot, surrounded by a thick clump of trees with a mass of low hanging branches, and offered a view down the creek line we had followed. While I was squatting and reflecting on the events of the day, I suddenly had the strongest sensation that someone was watching me. I peered around and could see nothing. There was no one in sight and the only sounds of life were the muted noises from the camp.

Still the feeling persisted, a shiver in my spine.

What was it?

I let my gaze climb into the foliage above me, and suddenly my eyes focused on the unwinking gaze of a huge python that was strung out in the branches above, its colours making it almost invisible to the casual glance.

In the nanosecond it took to launch myself to safety, bellowing with shock, I registered that part of its main trunk seemed almost as big as the body of a man, and it seemed to go on forever.

My shout attracted most of the platoon, who arrived on the scene armed with machetes, rifles and whatever else had come to hand. The python which most probably had absolutely no ill intent towards me, decided it was time to decamp and took off towards the creek—not in apparent alarm, but with a casual insouciance appropriate for a lord of the jungle.

This now posed a problem for the soldiers.

Here was enough fresh meat for a great feast, but the average Pacific Island soldier had a well-developed fear of snakes—as I certainly did and still do. The lack of medical facilities in the jungle, or their villages for that matter, makes snakebite a life-threatening matter. Even nonvenomous snakes are treated with some trepidation.

I have seen a soldier on sentry duty behind a machine gun frozen with fear and unable to move as a harmless tree snake wrapped itself around the gun's barrel. And despite the very politically correct atmosphere of the times, the European subalterns of the battalion sometimes used a rubber snake to rupture the self-importance of one of the Pacific Island officers— who at times acted as if he was already in charge of the PNG Defence Force. A rubber snake dropped on his plate during dinner in the mess would give him such a fright that he would become airborne, change colour from black to pasty white, and some swore that he would levitate for twenty metres or so before he came down to earth. We sometimes joked that rubber snakes would be more effective than hand grenades in PNG.

In any case, the desire for fresh meat and the thrill of the chase won the hearts of a dozen or so soldiers, who set off in pursuit of the python, catching up with it as it entered the stream. Two of them grabbed the beast's tail and were soon joined by two more. For a second it seemed they might hold the monster—it seemed at least six metres long—but it swivelled backwards, and the soldiers released their grip, shouting in alarm. The python continued on its way, the soldiers tried again, and were again frightened off. By now the chase had developed into a game. The snake was evidently only interested in escape and did not seriously intend to attack its pursuers, and the soldiers, yahooing and laughing to overcome their nervousness, were only interested in exhibiting their macho lack of fear; a bit like running with the bulls.

Eventually the snake had the good sense to swerve out of the creek and into the thick undergrowth and was able to make good its escape.

We all returned to the camp, where amidst much laughing and boasting, there were numerous replays of the event— including my inglorious exit from the latrine. In the future I paid much more attention to my surrounds when nature called.

The late afternoon deluge continued during the night, the rain beating down through the thick overhead canopy and turning the campsite into a quagmire. Thunder rolled overhead and the jungle was lit by great flashes of lightning. Thank God for my hutchie and a relatively dry bed.

By morning the rain had cleared and the sun filtering through the green canopy lifted everyone's spirits. We continued on our way, and in the afternoon two days later we started to become aware of the distant roar of the mighty Hegigio River, the next major obstacle in our path. Hoping to reach the river in time to camp beside it we pressed on. But after two hours when the sun began to slide behind the mountains and the river still sounded no closer, I decided to take advantage of a delightful glade bounded between two clear streams, and we made camp.

I had long since learned that it was a risky business passing up a good camping spot. Few things annoyed the soldiers as much as subsequently being forced to sleep rough or wet, or worse still stumbling around in the dark, because the platoon commander didn't have the sense to know a good place when he saw it.

Night fell over a contented camp, small cooking fires flickered in the gloom outlining the tight groups of soldiers hunched over their meals. Pokoi made a show of pointing out where the latrine was—much muffled laughter from the circles around the fires.

Crossing of the Hegigio River was the greatest unknown of the patrol. Prior to my aerial reconnaissance it had the reputation of being 'uncrossable' for much of its length, and from the air I had confirmed that it in places it was truly awe-inspiring. One stretch, which I thought was still further north of us, was well over a hundred metres wide and rushing with such force there were 'rises', where the water flowed over submerged rocks, that were higher than a man. Crossing in such a place was inconceivable, and I was still wondering how such a violent body of water could be tamed enough to cross.

The *Kiap* at Lake Kutubu had said that he had heard rumours of a bridge in the general area we were heading towards, but I could not believe that any native bridge could have crossed the river I had seen. He had been unaware of any inter-tribal contact across the river since he had been at Lake Kutubu. There was no sign of any track or crossing on our map, but then again, there was no sign of most things on it.

The next morning, we had been walking for a couple of hours when we reached the edge of a broad canyon, with precipitous sides plunging hundreds of metres to the mighty Hegigio River. It was the same monster I had seen from the air— a wide impassable torrent. Even this far above the river, its roar made speech difficult as its churning water flung itself onto the great boulders in its path. In places the races of water were deep, flowing with a smooth irresistible force. In others it broke into spray and mist or rose in high waves over submerged rocks.

It was a force of nature that took my breath away. Even growing up on the coast of the Pacific Ocean where often the beaches and headlands were beaten by huge waves and powerful storms had not prepared me for a show of such brutal natural power. No one could cross this death trap.

I withdrew from the edge and ordered a 'smoko' while I squatted on my pack and considered our options. There were no good ones. If we went upstream it would certainly be a long way before the beast had shrunk enough to cross, and we could then be immersed in the steep ravines of the main range. Going across the grain of the country there could well be impossible.

Heading downstream looked forlorn. Possibly we could find a calmer stretch of water when the river disgorged from the mountains or failing that at least some villages and eventually an airstrip. But that would seem to be a long way off and would probably mean we would fail to reach our goal. The worst option would be to admit failure and return to Kutubu.

Pokoi sauntered across, an evil smelling smoke of trade store tobacco hanging from his mouth. I invited him to sit.

'What do you think, Sergeant Pokoi?'

'Em e no gut fella tu mus, boss. Yu me best behind im road e go on top.'

Just what I had thought: follow the river upstream. It was always a boost to know the sergeant and myself were on the same wavelength.

'No long way tu mus bridge e come up.'

I looked at Pokoi, then back towards the river. A bridge across this monster. Was he mad? Did the locals know something the *Kiap* didn't?

Seeing my expression, he smiled.

'Tru boss, em e close tu lik lik.'

Oh well, there was nothing to be gained by voicing my opinion of his sanity. I returned his smile and gave the order to go on. Walking twenty or thirty metres from the edge of the cliff, we headed off in single file, winding through large old trees with a heavy canopy and thick undergrowth on the forest floor. The river growled away on our left, contemptuous of us.

After an hour or so I fell into the rhythm of the march, mind pretty well in neutral, trying to forget the pain in my shoulders from the pack and the ache in my knee. By mid-afternoon we were still threading our way through the thick forest and it had closed in more around us, the twisting vines and dense undergrowth pulling at us as we pushed through. The sound of the river was more muted. Then we seemed to have struck a faint footpad, barely distinguishable on the leaf-covered forest floor.

The noise of the river had now almost vanished, and I signalled the leading section to stop, and went forward to see why we were drifting away from it. When I reached the forward scout, he gestured to a latticework of timber and vines a few paces ahead of him.

'Bridge e stap, sir.'

Looking closer I could see that it was a native structure of some kind. Timber had certainly been cut and tied with vines. But a bridge? Where was the river? I couldn't hear anything. But the faint path did lead towards it.

I edged further forward. Yes, it was a native bridge. It was not more than ten metres across and held together by twisted ropes of vine. It looked fragile and unsafe. Possibly disused for some time it must have been built to cross a tributary of the river.

126

Pokoi must have mistaken this for a bridge over the Hegigio itself.

I walked up to the edge and gingerly looked over the bank.

At first, I could see nothing. Then in the darkness far below I could just make out a mass of churning water, and suddenly the river was roaring in my ears again. For a moment I stood mesmerised by the impossibility of what I was seeing; the mighty river we had stood beside a few hours ago was being forced into the narrow chasm below me. It didn't seem possible that so much water could be squeezed into such a narrow space. The forces, and pressures down there would be unimaginable.

Stepping back from the flimsy support on legs which were suddenly shaking I signalled a halt and shrugged off my pack. Pokoi came up from his position at the rear of the line. With a nod he graciously forgave my thoughts about his sanity and moved on to study the bridge.

At some stage it must have been capable of carrying lightly laden natives, but now it was certainly not up to getting thirty heavily burdened soldiers across. If it was to be crossed repairs were needed, and that would take some time. It was obviously rarely used. The small path we had followed for only a few hundred metres from the south certainly didn't go anywhere and was probably only an animal footpad in any case. There was no track going north.

We made camp and soldiers were dispatched with machetes to cut suitable timber and vines and Pokoi—who was in charge of things—began to lay out the rope he always carried. Before anything was done this would have to be taken to the other side, so that things could be pulled across to strengthen the timber work. The first one over would test the bridge and take the rope.

While this was happening, I inspected what I could of the bridge from our side and gave a few exploratory tugs at the main vines. Nothing gave, but I was certainly not confident that it would take even one soldier.

I was standing in front of the old bridge, still a bit doubtful if it was worth the risk of crossing. If anyone fell there was absolutely no chance they would survive, and having the platoon split on both sides of an uncrossable river would not be a good look. While casting my eyes around for the lightest and nimblest soldier in the platoon, and guiltily wondering if I should be leading by example, Pokoi edged up to me, trailing his rope.

I think I could see him thinking, 'No, not you, sir. You are the heaviest and clumsiest bastard in the platoon' as he beckoned to a nimble young Highlander. By nightfall there was a masterpiece spanning the chasm and Pokoi was wearing that small self-satisfied smile of his.

The next morning, hoping that I was exhibiting a nonchalance that I did not feel, with the safety rope securely tied around my waist, I edged onto the bridge. There was an interested group of grinning soldiers on both sides.

'Hold the bloody rope tight.' I shouted, thinking it too important to risk any misunderstanding of my pidgin.

The bridge sagged under my weight as I started to shuffle across, holding tightly to the two higher rope vines, and gingerly sliding one foot forward at a time. The wooden footpath was still very narrow—more so once I was on it—and the cut trees round and slippery. Trying not to look down I crept forward, only moving one hand or foot at a time, the roar of the water loud in my ears.

It seemed an age before I reached the far bank and stepped onto firm ground with a sigh of relief. It took a while for my legs to stop shaking. Once there I stood looking down at what I had crossed. It was fearsome, and the sheer power and malevolence of that river has never left me.

Applause and laughter on all sides.

It took some hours to get everyone across, soldier by soldier, and we camped that night not far away.

Recently I have pored over modern aerial photographic maps to try and pinpoint the location of the bridge, and I have not been able to find a fit. But I do have an old photograph to prove its existence, and I can only assume that over the years the mighty flow of water has knocked off half a great hillside. However a modern Hegigio River bridge has been put across since we passed through the area, over fifty years ago.

Our route lay north again, towards the looming bulk of the Owen Stanley Ranges, which were visible in the distance from time to time through gaps in the foliage. There was still no track, but on the second day after the bridge our way led us back to the river. It was still a raging torrent a hundred metres or so wide, but on each bank, there was a rocky bed of boulders, rounded like giant marbles. To think that at some stage perhaps two or three times the volume of water must come down the river was something almost impossible to comprehend.

Although it was difficult walking across the rocks, it was a change and probably quicker than through the dense jungle further back. We took another airdrop in a small clearing beside the river and shortly afterwards crossed the much more manageable Tigari River at its junction with the Hegigio and began climbing a narrow valley leading north. If our map reading was right, this would lead us to a village and eventually a track to Tari.

After a few miles the sides of the valley began to close in around us, and not long afterwards we were confronted with a precipitous cliff, and we were forced to backtrack to a place where we were able to climb a high slope to the ridgeline above. It was now late afternoon and we were only halfway up when the heavens opened. The rain bucketed down, turning the slope into a treacherous, slippery quagmire.

As I dragged myself upwards, exhausted, morale again on the rocks, close to collapse, I found myself asking, yet again. 'How, the bloody hell, did I end up here?'

It had all begun five years or so earlier.

When I was about to matriculate from high school, Dad and my brother, Richard, had arranged for me to be 'articled' to his old firm of Sydney solicitors. Being the brother of my brother, I was welcomed with open arms. Then in January 1961, recently turned seventeen and dressed in my one and only suit, I caught the bus from Collaroy on the northern beaches to the city, for my first day at work. Shortly afterwards I started lectures at the Law School of Sydney University; each morning from 8.00 to 9.00 and in the afternoon from 5.00 to 6.00.

This meant I was on the bus at 6.30 each morning, and home around 8.00 pm, often standing both ways in a haze of cigarette smoke, as it rattled and lurched its way through the creeping traffic. Then I studied until late. My days at work were spent as a cross between an office drudge and messenger boy for the office manager. From my immature perspective she seemed an ancient battle-axe but was really just a long-suffering legal secretary who treated me much better than I deserved. The lectures were in a drab hall to a large bunch of uninterested students, and I did not seem to be actually absorbing anything that was likely to be useful in an exam.

It did not take long for the routine to pall. I was used to living a very free and easy lifestyle, playing lots of sport, surfing whenever the mood took, with only the odd bit of study during the day. My nights had been free to court the fair maidens whose paths I crossed.

Autumn turned to winter, the morning and evening travel began and ended in the chilly and smoggy Sydney darkness. My evenings of footy training and squash had long since given way to nodding off over 'Constitutional Law' or 'Torts'. I began to have serious misgivings over my choice of career. The five-year course seemed to stretch forever into the future, and with exams twice a year; failures could stretch it out much longer. It was rumoured that there were article clerks who were still grinding away after a decade.

Was there a way out of this predicament? Yes, there was.

In the mornings my rattling green double-decker bus dropped me off at Wynyard Park, from where I had a ten-minute walk through the grey city streets to the Law School. By this time, they were reluctantly coming to life and in an hour, they would be crowded and the crush difficult to fight your way through. In the evenings after lectures I followed the same route back to the bus along with many others who looked equally crushed by the day and the prospect of a long trip home.

Morning and night, I passed a recruiting centre for the Australian Army, alive with epic photographs of exciting places and action heroes. Among the displays that had caught my eye was one for the Royal Military College Duntroon, with photographs of boys not much older than myself in glamorous uniforms, escorting beautiful girls who gazed adoringly into their eyes, and other photographs of them playing rugby and tennis and visiting exotic locations in Asia.

At first, when a famous career at the Bar had beckoned, I had strode past with barely a glance. But as winter settled over us and the realities of life as an articled clerk lay drably on my shoulders, my eyes were drawn more and more to the seductive windows of the recruiting office.

One lunch hour I could resist no longer and presented myself there to find out more. The officer who talked to me made it sound irresistible. A free university education, free accommodation and a living allowance which would make me completely independent of my family. Plenty of sport, good mates, an honourable and well-paid career as an army officer that could lead anywhere; overseas postings, perhaps even in later years an appointment as a state governor or as governor general.

'What about entrance qualifications?' I had asked.

And so here I was in the treacherous mountains of PNG, the lies and exaggerations of the recruiting posters revealed, climbing up a dark and slippery slope, wet and exhausted. A metaphor of my life?

It was common for us to have to climb like mountaineers, using both hands and feet, sometimes with a safety rope. This is always hard with a heavy pack and a weapon. But on this slope, it was impossible to get a grip without digging in a bayonet or entrenching tool and using it to drag yourself up a metre or so; the going was appalling and slow. The further back in the line you were the harder it was, as those in front ripped out more and more foliage from the bank and made it even more slippery.

Landslips are common in the mountains, and as darkness started to envelop us and the rain beat down, it became a real concern. Eventually a shout from above told us that the top had been reached. Thank God, I thought, and continued to drag myself upwards. An hour later, with the aid of weak torchlight I was able to check that everyone had made it, and we huddled on a small false crest.

It was a cold wet night, spent lying in the mud wrapped in our groundsheets. By daybreak the rain had been replaced by a cold mist, but a least we were able to cook breakfast and have a cup of tea before moving on. The ridge we were on became

130

quite narrow and covered in kunai grass, but we could not see much of the lie of the land because of the shroud of mist. But we knew our path was upwards—doesn't it always seem to be—so we trudged on hoping to find some sun and some water to clean our mud sodden clothes and gear.

But the rain returned, falling steadily without let up, and we had to camp, wet and muddy again. The next day the kunai eventually gave way to rainforest, the trees ghost-like in another still morning mist. With the approach of midday, it began to lift and shortly afterwards our prayers were answered; the sun peeked through and our path crossed a fast-running creek.

Pokoi came up to survey the spot.

'Gut fella place tu mus,' he opined.

Yes, it was a great spot and it would be a good spot to camp. Within an hour we were at peace with the world again. Our mud-caked clothes were washed and hanging on trees to dry, sodden muddy boots washed and drained, hutchies erected, food cooking—spirits restored.

While Wafiaga was preparing to cook our rice, I took a stroll up the track and within fifteen minutes came to the edge of the forest. Ahead was another broad bank of kunai surrounding a roughly fenced native garden being tended by half a dozen stooped *meris,* digging energetically for *kau kau.* We were approaching civilisation again. The next night we camped near another small village and two more days marching along well-maintained tracks brought us to Tari, surrounded by the majestic Owen Stanley Mountains.

The patrol left me with lasting memories and was my first taste of what it was like to be in the remote jungle on a completely independent assignment. The only link to the outside world, an HF radio that didn't work at night, and the nearest help in an emergency would be via some small airstrip perhaps a week's walk away.

After a few days working on small 'civic action' projects we flew out to Port Moresby, and most importantly reunion with the love of my life and bride-to-be.

I had first arrived in Port Moresby earlier in the year, and when Ro came up a few months later we discovered a world that was totally new and unimaginably different to anything we had experienced. The Pacific Islands Regiment had grown out of World War II, when men from the Papuan Infantry Battalion and Royal Papuan Constabulary fought alongside the Australian Army. In 1966 it was still a part of the Australian Army but was destined to become the national army of PNG on independence. At this time Papua New Guinea was still governed by Australia as a United Nations Protectorate.

Taurama Barracks, the home of the 1st Battalion, was more of a small town

131

than a barracks. It was pleasantly laid out in landscaped gardens, although the army still could not resist painting rocks white to edge the roads, and lawns that were still relatively green despite the long dry season. There was a sentry at the main gate with a fixed bayonet who challenged all arrivals. The officers' mess was a pleasant older building, with a cool sitting room open on three sides, a bar where all drinks were put on a tab and a dining room with long polished wooden tables. After not too long, the girls found, after good sense had departed late on dining-in nights, that such tables made great stages for cabaret performances.

A month after arriving back from the Highlands, Ro and I were married under a canopy of flowers in the old thatched roof chapel at the barracks. Ours was the first European marriage at this venue for some time. The next couple to be married was Michael and Marlene Jeffries. Michael went on to have a brilliant army career followed by appointments as Governor of Western Australia and Governor General of Australia. Perhaps there was some truth in the recruiting posters after all!

Married accommodation was very scarce at this time, Ro had already shared three flats with Di Battle before our marriage. But we were lucky enough to organise a ramshackle flat in town at Boroko for two months, then a 'leave house' for another couple of months, followed by a barely-furnished flat on top of Paga Hill overlooking Port Moresby, then to our own married quarter in the barracks—that's seven moves for Ro, if you haven't been counting. Next, we were sent to Lae at the eastern end of the mainland, and another married quarter—eighth move. During this time, Ro had to fend for herself two days out of three while I was either out in the bush or at the Jungle Training Centre at Canungra in south-east Queensland.

By now Charlotte was nearly with us. So, it was back to Canberra and Sydney—two more moves for Ro before she was too pregnant to fly, and into the officers' mess for me. How were our removals arranged? Mostly we did it ourselves in the back of an army truck. They really spoiled us in those days. Late in 1968 I was finally posted back to Australia, saw our new baby Charlotte, and Ro a couple of times during the final hectic months of the preparations and training with the 5th Battalion Royal Australian Regiments before it deployed to South Vietnam. Fortunately, when I returned twelve months later, Ro was still waiting for me, but Charlotte wasn't too happy with this strange man in the—eleventh— house.

Michael and Dianna Battle, Rosemary and Rob.
Officers Mess, Taurama Barracks 1966

~THE WESTERN MEDITERRANEAN 2008 ~

Sea Dreams – Sardinia

After we had completed our voyage north on *Oceania* we continued to cruise in the tropical waters of north Queensland, until in 2006 we found ourselves back in the Whitsundays. By this time, we had started thinking about sailing to the Pacific islands, possibly via Papua New Guinea or following our friends Dave and Jill Henry, who

134

were planning to sail *Sweet Chariot* to the Mediterranean.

Unfortunately, a heart condition that I had been controlling with medication worsened to such an extent that I could no longer consider cruising on a yacht as a practical lifestyle. We were devastated contemplating a life without *Oceania*, but there seemed no alternative. Back in Hobart things continued to go downhill until I could hardly walk as far as the front door. Eventually we decided to undergo the two procedures that offered a possible fix. They proved to be an incredible success and I am forever in the debt of the surgeon, Professor Paul Sparkes, who literally gave me back my life. Within a week I could walk down to the docks and back and I soon wanted to go back to sea. As we had no boat of our own, we decided to take a cruise from Hong Kong to Istanbul. It was fantastic. On the way we passed Jill and Dave Henry on *Sweet Chariot* somewhere in the southern Aegean, fell hopelessly in love with the Med and decided we had to have a yacht of our own again.

We bought a new Beneteau 50 which we christened *Sea Dreams*. The name was inspired both by our constant dreaming and by the painting of a wistful boy standing beside a blue ocean and an old walled town, by Marie Lucas-Robiquet, circa 1930. It had been in Ro's home while she was growing up and has had a place in our hearts for many years. The first time we saw *Sea Dreams*, she was in Gruissan a small town in the south of France. She was still wrapped in the factory's plastic and sitting in the shipyard of Alaine and Martine; a tenacious French couple who were to transform her into a most graceful swan. They were working with a ferocity and determination that you do not see so often these days. Alaine had no English and Martine just a few words, which made her the linguist of the group. '*Oui Oui,*' she would say with a laugh and smile when we asked, in our tortured French, when *Sea Dreams* would be ready. Alaine remained scowling and mute, as if no Frenchman should waste time with the language of the bloody English.

We had flown in from a beautiful Tasmanian autumn and were now wondering what was in store for us in the infamous Gulf of Lyon—a stretch of water renowned for its gales. We had brought lots of wet weather gear, but the wind had an icy edge, sharper than the winter wind at home and a shock after the hot, humid climate of far north Queensland. At this time of year, the mistral can roar down from the Toulouse Gap with such ferocity that the old men and women of the village can hardly walk against it as they struggle through the winding streets and along the wind blasted quay; their crooked backs a reminder of a lifetime's toil. It is a freezing wind blowing straight off the snow-covered Pyrenees, sometimes gusting over sixty knots. The vineyards of the Languedoc had yet to flower. The hills were hard and rocky, the surrounding fens, grey and forlorn.

In the mornings while we waited, we would amble across the windy Place de Minihirs, which was sometimes brightened by brief glimpses of the sun between the scudding clouds, to collect baguettes from *Le Briochon Patisserie* and the Herald Tribune from Le Tabac. Carrying them back to our small kitchen table we could watch the morning rituals of the town square while making our own plans for the day.

We spent a lot of time scouring Narbonne for all we required to make *Sea Dreams* our home and buying the extra nautical things we needed: a tender, more chain and ropes, a heavier anchor, safety gear, flags, flares. But we found time for a few touristy things. We inspected the Canal du Midi, drove through a bit of Catalonia and visited the old walled city of Carcassonne. It was still protected by the great ramparts erected in medieval times to safeguard religious beliefs, as much as the citizens. This region has spawned some esoteric Christian sects which were seen by the Roman Catholics as heretical and resulted in bloody conflicts. Many believed, and some still do, that Mary Magdalene escaped to here from the Holy Land, accompanied or perhaps not, by a child. The Knights Templar were powerful here, and rich, until they were brought down by their King. Some believed the Holy Grail was secreted close by.

At night we enjoyed the food and wine around the quay: rich and steaming *cassoulets maison au confit de canard*, and mussels in a steaming soup of blue vein cheese— (*specialte et frite)*—prepared by a gregarious Belgian couple, Janette and Claude in their small harbourside café, *Le Champhitte*. We had not realised that Belgians are supreme in all things mussels and were assured that this remained the truth in Paris and even Amsterdam.

But it seemed only a blink of an eye before *Sea Dreams* was ready for sea, indeed a beautiful swan, moored alongside the town quay. She had been christened, all systems were working, and she was stocked with food and lots of local wine from the town's *cave*. Late in the afternoon we cleared customs and sailed into the grey, white capped Mediterranean. The Romans called it *Mare Nostrum*, meaning 'Our Sea' and before too long that's how we came to think of it. Looking back through the gloom of the gathering clouds we could still just make out the old tower overlooking Gruissan. It is all that remains from a tenth century castle that had been built to watch over the approaches to the city of Narbonne, and as a refuge from bloodthirsty Muslim pirates.

By nightfall on our first day back at sea the wind had built to forty knots and with reefed sails we surged towards the island of Mallorca 300 kms ahead. Within the first few hours we knew *Sea Dreams* could handle a gale in the Gulf of Lyon and, she had started as she was to go on. Over the next nine years there was not one structural failing in the boat as it had come out of Alaine and Martine's' shipyard. All the essentials were totally reliable: the engine always started on the first turn of the key, the anchor always came up and down on command, the sails always furled and unfurled, not one drop of water leaked into the hull, not one piece of rigging failed. We loved her from the start to the finish—you could trust her with your life.

During the night, wearing all the woollies we owned beneath our wet-weather gear, we ran past the lights along the Spanish coast and were eventually greeted by a cold grey sunrise. The sky was shredded with scudding clouds, the ocean flecked with grey breaking seas, and away in the distance on our northern horizon a sight that could never be forgotten. The great snow-covered massifs of the Pyrenees. And later in the day another unforgettable memory. Still behind us the white snowline of the mountains framed against a pale blue sky, while ahead the tips of the hard, rocky peaks of Mallorca peered over the horizon.

We arrived at Palma, the capital of Mallorca, a bit after midnight on the second night out and were directed to a berth on one of the long jetties running out from the quay in front of the centre of the city. It seemed to me that there were more yachts here than in the whole of Australia, and I would not be surprised if there were more British yachts, of all shapes and sizes, some huge, than in all of Great Britain. To own a berth for a large yacht costs millions.

Part of the deal in buying *Sea Dreams* was a month's berthing to fit a genset and a water maker. We were really looking forward to exploring the island and it was love at first sight. Mallorca is rich and beautiful and has attracted man since beyond antiquity. Its history reflects most of the ebbs and flows of the Mediterranean.

There are Neolithic burial chambers that were here thousands of years before the Phoenicians; a seafaring people from the Levant arrived in their galleys in the 8th century BCE and established numerous colonies. Later it came under the control of Carthage, which was the principal Phoenician city in the western Mediterranean. In 123 BCE, after the defeat of Carthage, it was occupied by the Romans. It prospered under their rule and many of the existing towns and cities were established during this era. Horticulture, and of course viticulture flourished.

The Vandals, a Germanic tribe who probably originated in the region of modern day Silesia captured the Balearics in 429 CE—as well as Corsica, Sardinia and Sicily. But Rome managed to re-establish its rule in 465 and in 534 the Eastern Roman—Byzantine Empire took over. With the returning Romans came the Christian Church which had become the official church of the Empire in 380.

From 707 it was increasingly raided by Muslims as they drove their empire westwards along the north coast of Africa and across the Straits of Gibraltar into

Spain. They were finally halted on the Loire River in France by Charles—the Hammer Martel—grandfather of the first Holy Roman Emperor, Charlemagne at the Battle of Tours in 732. But this did not prevent Mallorca and most of Spain being incorporated into the Caliphate of Cordoba.

The Spanish Reconquista began in the north of Spain in 722 and over the succeeding centuries fought its way south. The islands were eventually liberated by King James of Aragon in 1229, and Valencia in 1238. If you are interested in more detail, please examine the Time Lapse Maps. But in the beautiful spring of 2008 none of this old 'bloody' history was on show. The waterfront at Palma was lined with restaurants, night clubs and bars. Most of the day, and well into the night, it was crammed with people from all over the world having an exuberant time. *Sea Dreams* was moored only a short walk from the old town which has kept much of its ancient character, and restaurants offering traditional dishes as well as magnificent modern Spanish tapas plates.

During the days we took trips through the rugged mountains along the north coast, where the roads hung suspended from the sheer sides of the cliffs and pine forests and olive groves open to reveal breathtaking views of the sea, the coastal headlands and mountain peaks sometimes shrouded in mist. We explored the charming stone villages perched on ridges and tucked into small valleys; we ate wild boar at remote mountain restaurants and drove through the home village of the great Rafael Nadal. And fortunately, we arrived back alive after many near-death experiences on the roads, certain that Spanish drivers must all have death wishes and be the most reckless in the world. The first is possibly true, but we were to find that there is fierce competition around the Mediterranean for the title of 'Most Reckless Driver'.

It was closer to six weeks before *Sea Dreams* had her new genset and water maker—50 litres an hour—and was right to go, but we had had a great time while waiting. Our daughter, Charlotte, who was now living at Lake Annecy in France, came to check out the new boat. Michael and Di Battle stopped by while on a cruise.

We spent many nights exploring Palma after dark with Lenny and Helen Griffin from Newcastle in Australia, also new owners of a Beneteau.

It seemed Lenny had a grandmother who came from the island, although on some occasions it seemed she might have come from the Spanish coast. Together with a local grandmother and many *'holas' 'muchos' 'sis'* and *'tantos'* and his usual big smile, Lenny soon had friends everywhere. Later in the year we found that Lenny had grandmothers from Sardinia, Corsica and Elba—and then we got to Italy and Croatia.

Wine is generally thought to have been first made in Armenia, Georgia, Iran or perhaps China around 6-7000 BCE and was certainly being produced around the shores of the Mediterranean and on the islands around 4500 BCE. It was while Lenny and I were exploring some of the old vineyards in the mountains and afterwards having a well-earned glass of wine on the waterfront, we wondered if these dates told the full story. There were certainly ancient winemaking traditions and examples of early technical ability all over the Med. Could it be possible, we asked ourselves, that 'the man who invented red wine' actually came from *Mare Nostrum*? We decided to keep our eyes open and do more research.

It took a bit of adjusting to the normal Mallorcan working hours. Nothing happened before 11 am, full stop. But a bit later on some locals might arrive at a cafe nearby, have a gossip, volubly solve the world's problems, perhaps stroll to work and shuffle some papers. Then lunch and siesta through to around 5 pm. Then back to work for an hour or two where there could just be something which could not possibly be put off any longer. Then thinking about dressing for dinner for a date around 10 or 11 pm. Followed by a party afterwards until late. That was the routine until the summer holidays, which were all July and August, and then it was almost impossible to get anything done. And they wonder why their unemployment rate is over twenty percent and fifty percent for the young.

However, this regime allowed everyone to have a great time, not just the tourists. I was particularly impressed by the exuberant savoir faire of one restaurant near the yacht –which relied mostly on English speaking tourists—to proudly display a sign reading 'No English Spoken Here'. Lucky we generally had Lenny, who was more or less family as far as the restaurant was concerned, to speak for us. But it does help to explain Brexit, and a reluctance by the norther Europeans to bail out the Mediterranean economies.

From the deck of *Sea Dreams*, we had a nice view of the great Catalan-Gothic cathedral that was begun by King James to give thanks to God for the liberation of the island. It is a magnificent and imposing structure that took nearly four hundred years to complete. Perhaps the siesta was already an institution in medieval times. The cost in money and labour must have been truly enormous.

This was the first time I had stood on ground that been overwhelmed in the first great rush of the Muslim invasion. Mohammed had died in 632 and the seemingly irresistible surge westward began only a few years later. Christianity had then been established as the official religion in the old Roman provinces for only a few hundred years.

What made Islam such an explosive force?

While sitting in the back of *Sea Dreams* as she has wound her way across miles and miles of Mediterranean waters and lay at anchor in peaceful coves and bustling old ports, I have given this much thought. At times I must admit, with the help of a glass or two of fine local red. Here's the short version.

Firstly, it was a new and a simple religion to understand. Allah had given his laws directly to his single prophet, Mohammed. These were clearly codified in the Koran. On the other hand, Judaism the basis of Christian dogma had been around since Abraham was an old man, around 1,400 years. Jesus left no written words and his earliest teachings had promised his imminent return and a better world. There had been no sign of either for over six centuries. His teachings had been passed down in a confusing and contradictory collection of scriptures.

Secondly, the Koran demanded conquest by the sword and offered substantial rewards to Muslim warriors. This was a natural and very appealing doctrine in the patriarchal world of Arabia and along the North African coast—Allah and Mohammed knew their target market. When Jerusalem fell in 638 CE Caliph Omar, an Arab, rode through the gates on a white camel. When Carthage fell the person riding through the gates was a Maghreb tribesman with a bloody scimitar in his hand. Along the North African coast most warriors were savage and rapacious tribesmen, spreading the word among like-minded savages. They were entitled to the booty and slaves of conquest—not to mention heaven and seventy virgins if something went wrong. They were entitled to four wives and these could be divorced at will. Men were masters and women were men's chattels. All a very natural and an appealing license as far as the tribesmen were concerned. On the other side, the Christian Church allowed only one wife for life and was for peace and turning the other cheek. What self-respecting tribal warrior was going to buy that!

Thirdly, they were lucky with their timing. At the outset the Byzantine and Persian Empires were exhausted from war and plague. Later, internecine warfare within the Christian world was so endemic that they rarely presented a united front.

In the long and bloody struggle over the next thirteen centuries the Muslims came very close to subjugating Europe. If Malta or Vienna had fallen, or the Battle of Lepanto lost, our world could easily have been a Muslim one. But by the late nineteenth century it seemed that the war had been finally won by the west.

The separation of Church and State and the emergence of liberal democracies in the west eventually created an industrial and technical power that was irresistible. The western monogamous family unit and the relative liberation of women created a healthier and more dynamic society. If they were less inclined to fight for God, they were still willing to fight for their nations and the great freedoms of democracy—and many for love.

But after a decade sailing in the Med, I think perhaps that victory may have been illusionary.

However, no time to brood. Being an old soldier who was brought up on Robert Grave's poetry, a visit to his house and grave at Deia was mandatory. It brought back to me these eternal lines, and the need for another wine with sunset.

'I've watched the Seasons passing slow, so slow,
In the fields between La Bassee and Bethune;
Primroses and the first warm day of Spring,
Red poppy floods of June,
August, and yellowing Autumn, so
To Winter nights knee-deep in mud or snow,
And you've been everything.'

Graves served on the Western Front from the age of nineteen, alongside Siegfried Sassoon and was wounded on the Somme. He became one of the leading literary figures of the age, Professor of Poetry at Oxford, and a long-time lover and resident of Mallorca.

Eventually our new genset and water-maker were installed; the chap installing our gear was actually a Pommie vehicle mechanic, but he had adopted local customs and despite having booked him months earlier he didn't turn up until almost the end of the month. We headed out to explore a few local anchorages and check all was good. After a couple of days, and happy all was well, we headed off to Ibiza the most western of the Balearics. The party island of the Med. We anchored in the clear warm water of cala d'es porcs on the north coast after an uneventful passage.

There were two other yachts anchored here, but the only sign of life was a group of naked kayakers who had pulled their craft ashore and were desultorily beating bongos in the shade of some old stone boathouses. The bay was overlooked by a sprawling hacienda with a white crenelated tower, which looked as if one day it may have been a real place of refuge if Moorish pirates stopped by, but now was for enjoying the sunsets with an aperitif in hand. It was surrounded by lush wooded gardens; olives and palms mingling with flowering shrubs and vines.

Ibiza was first occupied around 3000 BCE and was settled by the Phoenicians in the 6th century BCE. Showing great prescience, they dedicated the island to the gods of music and dance—which is pretty much what the it is known for these days. But along with most Mediterranean islands its history was not always thus. Each of the great empires took their turn at looting her and the Muslims ruled from the 9th to the 13th centuries, when there would not have been much singing and dancing at all.

In the late afternoon we swam ashore to explore some caves on the southern shore. These could well have been home to some of the first inhabitants of the island, with ancient soot blackened caverns and high galleries only accessible by ladders. The north coast of the island is rugged and beautiful. High rocky headlands dappled with the greens of pine and olive groves, small indented bays provide beautiful anchorages in calm weather but are mostly open to the north. We loitered west along the coast, stopping here and there while the weather remained good.

In due course a northerly forced us to find shelter in Puerto de San Antonio where we anchored in shallow water close to the waterfront. This proved to be a noisy choice as it is very much a party town, but we were rewarded with great seafood and a lovely view over the harbour. The locals claim that the ancient general Hannibal was born on a small island we passed close by as we came in, but I have not been able to find any corroboration. Carthage on the African coast is generally regarded as the place. Nevertheless, for the purposes of the history from the back of a boat, I think we should give the locals the benefit of the doubt.

Charlotte lived for a number of years in the French Alps and one autumn we drove up to the pass over the Alps Hannibal most probably used to cross into Italy. Reading about his army crossing the Alps with their war elephants in mid-winter is inspiring stuff. But to actually see what it involved, realising how freezing it must have been when you see last winter's unmelted snow still on the ground at the end of summer, eyeing the sheer precipitousness of the valleys and mountains, takes admiration to a whole new level.

Then to think when he finally dragged his army into Italy, having lost many of his starving and exhausted men and elephants, he engineered some of the greatest military triumphs ever recorded, against the best Rome could throw at him.

At the Battle of Trebia, fought in the middle of the winter of 218 BCE when Hannibal had first emerged from the mountains, he decimated a Roman army of equal size—around forty thousand men—inflicting around thirty thousand casualties. The next year, in perhaps the largest ambush in military history, he destroyed another army at the Battle of Lake Trasimene, killing fifteen thousand and capturing another fifteen thousand. In 216 BCE, in what is regarded as one of the greatest tactical feats in warfare and one of the worst defeats in Roman history, he destroyed another army twice his size at the Battle of Cannae. Roman casualties were variously estimated as between eighty and fifty thousand with up to another twenty thousand captured.

After the battle, the Romans were in complete disarray. The Roman historian Livy had this to say: *'Never when the city was in safety was there so great a panic and confusion within the walls of Rome... The consul and his army had been lost at the Trasimene the year before, it was not one wound upon another which was announced, but a multiple disaster, the loss of two consular armies, together with the two consuls: and now that there was neither any Roman camp, nor general nor soldiery than at Apulia and Samnium, and now almost the whole of Italy, were in the possession of Hannibal. No other nation surely would have not been overwhelmed by such an accumulation of disaster.'*

The historian William Durant sums it up: *'It was the supreme example of general-ship, never bettered in history... and it set the lines of military tactics for 2,000 years.'*

Hannibal's armies remained in Italy for a further sixteen years, during which time the Romans declined battle relying on the fortifications of their cities and towns to keep them safe. He was virtual master of the countryside until he returned to defend Carthage from the Roman general Scipio Africanus. But he was defeated, and Carthage subjugated at the Battle of Zama in 202 BCE. The Romans were surprisingly lenient to one who had caused them so much misery and heartache, and he was allowed to stay on in a position of power for some years.

But Hannibal was eventually exiled and spent the rest of his life in the East—at Ephesus, Armenia, Crete, Bithynia and remained Rome's bitter enemy to the very end. He died around 181 BCE possibly from fever, but some think poison. He left behind a mocking letter: *'Let us relieve the Romans from their anxiety that they have so long experienced, since it tries their patience too much to wait for an old man's death.'*

Was there a woman in the life of this great general?

The Roman historian Livy (64-59 to 12-17 BCE) records that Hannibal married a woman—who may have been a princess—named Imilce from the wealthy Spanish city of Castula. The bride and infant son were sent back to Carthage before he marched for Italy, *'fixing her eyes on the shores of Spain until the ship's progress hides them from her sight.'* The only other reference to her relates to the decision by the government of Carthage, some time before the Battle of Lake Trasimene and on the urging of Hannibal's enemies to try to bring him down, to sacrifice Hannibal's son as part of a ritual sacrifice to the god Baal. Imilce fought the decision and the sacrifice was delayed until Hannibal buried it, promising to sacrifice a 'thousand enemies' instead.

So, unfortunately there is not much on which to build a love story. But she is not entirely forgotten. The female figure of the Los Leones fountain at Baeza in Spain is said to be of Imilce.

In the morning we sailed around the small lump of rock that may or may not have been his home and headed to a bay on the extreme western tip of the island, overlooked by the towering peaks of Isla Vedras. We then turned east and followed the rocky shoreline towards Puerto Roig. The imposing cliffs were dotted with beautiful villas, enjoying views across the turquoise waters to the island of Formentera, ringed by glistening beaches. Steep paths cut into the cliffs led to small secluded coves or to rock ledges with steps or ladders to the water. Puerto Roig was quite a snug anchorage lined with old stone and timber boat sheds built below steep sandstone cliffs, coloured in layers of rich ochre and pale gold. By nightfall only a few yachts remained to share the beauty and tranquillity of the night.

In the late afternoon a couple of days later we ghosted into an anchorage off the long beach of Los Trocados on Formentera. The last nature lovers were strolling, in varying degrees of undress along the sand towards Puerto Sabina the main town on the island. As the sun dropped towards the distant silhouette of Isla Vedras we were treated to a truly spectacular sunset. The sun, a molten ball of gold glowing amber, the sky a great dome of red, the distant island dark and mysterious, the ocean simmering with greys and golds.

We lingered off the beach for some days. The water was delicious, there was a light sea breeze in the afternoon that took the edge off the midsummer heat—each sunset seemed more beautiful than the last. The nearby port was a pleasant laidback place for an aperitif and congenial dinner with Ibizan house wines served in litre jugs.

We had been entrusted with Charlotte's two eldest sons and by now old shipmates, Hubie, aged ten, and Rufus, six, for a couple of weeks. Their arrival changed our evening routine a bit. We had to cut down on the philosophising and concentrate on things that would interest both six and sixty-year-olds. We settled on poker. This has been a family game forever, and we started the first of our World Series games off the beach at Formentera. They have continued at every family gathering since. Some of our friends have been critical of teaching poker to six-year-olds. But I ask you, when is it too early to learn that the world is full of lying and duplicitous people—even at times your grandparents? We also started them off on chess and continued playing, even over the internet, with all the grandkids, for years. I have to admit that after a while prize money had to be offered to maintain enthusiasm.

Our days were pretty much the same: a bit more fishing, swimming and walking. In due course we had to give them back to their parents in Annecy. Along with their poker winnings.

Our track back to Puerto de Ibiza took us through the group of small islands off the northern tip of Formentera and before long we could make out the high walls

144

of the grand citadel built to protect the harbour in the sixteenth century. We were lucky, miraculously so, to find a berth for the night. The harbour was awash with boats and ferries all with a license to kill, and we were very relieved to be safely—we hoped—tied up.

The streets were thronged with mostly young and beautiful holidaymakers wearing nothing much at all. The sidewalk restaurants were packed, there was laughter and noise, music and conversation, delicious aromas floated on the salt-tanged breeze.

But before long we were spotted by the gendarmerie who checked our passports, discovered we were over eighteen-years-old and didn't smoke dope and ordered us back to the boat. On the way we had a wander through the old town, the citadel, the cathedral built around the thirteenth century and the subterranean burial chamber dating from Phoenician times. Actually, I felt more at home with the laughter and noise.

The next day I paid the price of a Rolex for the overnight mooring fee and we continued along the coast to the deep-sided inlet of Cala Llonga, an hour or so away. We found a vacant table overlooking *Sea Dreams* and dined on grilled sardines washed down with a fresh local white. It was relaxed and peaceful after the frenetic port.

We had arranged to pick up a friend from Tassie, at nearby Cala Talamanca. When we got there, we discovered there was more shallow water than appeared on the chart, and a not so easy to spot reef with less than a couple of metres over it in the middle of the bay. We avoided the reef, anchored and settled down to while away the time until Sandy's late-night arrival.

The sun was quite low with lots of glare off the water when a modern charter yacht came in. There were four guys of Spanish/Italian appearance onboard, all gesticulating and shouting at their mobiles; one of them may have been steering. I could not attract their attention.

You've got it!

No one saw the reef and they went aground doing about six knots. They went hard aground, but more or less still upright. Plenty of help arrived and it looked as if all would be okay. However, it is not hard to damage the keel bolts that fasten the keel to the hull. Six knots are more than enough to do plenty of damage. After a while the yacht started to list a bit, and by the time I went in to pick up Sandy it was lying at about forty-five degrees and had long since been deserted by the crew. It was well past midnight on the way back and it had slipped partly off the reef and only a little bit of the rigging was above water.

145

This gave us plenty to think about regarding the advantages and disadvantages of long keels versus deep keels and caused us to keep even a better eye open for whales and semi-floating shipping containers. We actually had no idea there were any whales in the Med, but a few weeks later on the way to Sardinia we passed within patting distance of a mother whale and her baby. It turns out they are quite common.

Anyway, we had better things to talk about than running aground. We were keen for news from Tassie and the couple of weeks Sandy had spent in France. This called for drinks on the aft deck and it was very late by the time we got to bed.

In the morning someone had marked the wreck with a buoy.

We spent the next few days exploring the many small bays along the eastern end of Ibiza, most enclosed by steep hills and heavy forests. Old stone watchtowers still cling to the precipitous rocks ready to warn of Barbary Pirates. Some modern villas and ancient monasteries enjoy majestic sites overlooking the romantically rugged mountains and the limitless sea.

The distance from Ibiza to Mallorca is around 80 kms. After an early start we had a delightful passage across on the back of a mild southerly and arrived at Cala de Santa Ponsa, near the western tip of the island by mid-afternoon. We had dinner at the palatial Club Nautico de Santa Ponso, beside a long narrow inlet off the bay and discussed our plans for exploring Mallorca.

The next morning, we moved around to Carla Portals a beautiful three-fingered bay on the way to Palma. We arrived early and anchored off the beach in the centre of the largest finger. As the sun climbed higher more and more yachts and motor boats squeezed in (it was a Sunday) until by afternoon it was almost possible to step from boat to boat. The bay hummed with laughter, beautiful people posed on their decks and splashed in the water. As the sun fell towards the horizon motors were started, anchors raised (much more posing on the bows by pretty semi-naked girls) sails set and by sunset we had the bay almost to ourselves.

The old Phoenician tombs cut into the sandstone cliffs were swallowed by the darkness and we lay quietly, where boats had lain since the very dawn of history. If you counted the years since the first Phoenicians anchored here and had cut a wharf into the cliffs, it would mean that some million nights would have elapsed. It was humbling to think how many boats would have dropped their anchors here, their crews gossiping or haggling on the shore and like us, watched darkness settle?

We had known Sandy and her partner John since we had first moved to Hobart in 1986. Very sadly John died prematurely and after some years of mourning she found herself being courted again.

Mac was an engaging and charismatic American who had fallen in love with Tasmania and had decided to make it his home. Already wealthy when he arrived, he became more so by the successful start-up and sale of a telecom company. He bought a beautiful waterfront farm overlooking an enchanting anchorage. It had a heritage-listed house set in beautiful gardens with a deep veranda that looked out over the anchorage to majestic Mount Wellington.

On the fertile rolling hills of the farm he established a large cherry orchard, choosing varieties which suited the conditions and were emerging in popularity. He practiced the latest in horticultural techniques and employed men with local knowledge and experience.

Then, at an equestrian event in southern Tasmania, his eyes were drawn to one of the riders. She was astride a fast-stepping grey, blonde locks spilling below a black helmet, sparkling azure eyes above a laughing smile. She rose and fell in the saddle in harmony with her mount and the zest of the fresh summer's day. Her long legs clasped firmly, her figure enhanced by a close-fitting riding jacket. A goddess on horseback. All eyes followed Sandy as she cleared a jump.

Mac had become widely known as the 'Big American'—he was six feet three or four and strongly built—and everyone knew Sandy, or at least wished they did.

So, an introduction was arranged, and the pursuit commenced.

Sandy had no intention of beginning another relationship. But Mac was charming and handsome. He had been in the running for Governor of a large state in the USA before he had thrown it over to come to Australia after a break-up with his wife. He had a lot in common with Bill Clinton, though bigger and better looking, and it was rumoured he could have also gone all the way. So, he knew how to get things done, and his pursuit was unwavering.

It might not have been the dizzying overpowering passion of first love, but overtime Sandy developed a deep fondness for her pursuer. He built stables, a dressage arena, and post and rail fenced paddocks for her horses on his farm. In due course they became a couple, united by a comfortable affection. There were frequent trips overseas and Mac agreed to her investing her savings in the farm so that she would have a complete sense of partnership in the blossoming undertaking.

Under her hand the old farmhouse became a sparkling jewel, the gardens something to marvel at. They had a wide circle of friends. An invitation for the weekend, to watch the sunset behind the mountains, to dine on the wide veranda or in front of the ancient hearth and listen to an in-siders views on Washington across flickering candles, was something to savour.

However, there were a few flaws in the glittering facade.

147

Being a very litigious-minded person who knew what he wanted, Mac was happy to fight in court for what he couldn't obtain by negotiation and persuasion. His divorce settlement was still in the courts and was actually quite ugly, there were some questions relating to the sale of his businesses, he was suing the local council over subdivision approvals. In fact, at one stage there were several matters before the courts and even if she personally was not actually being shot at, Sandy was certainly in the trenches. Mac had to make a number of overseas trips by himself, and the mortgage had to be increased to fund the court cases and the expansion of the orchards.

Clouds continued to gather over what had been a wonderful relationship. The court cases dragged on, finances were becoming strained, there were long separations while Mac jetted off overseas. It turned out that his political career had been pretty well what he had said, and he had been on track to political power and perhaps a presidential nomination. However, he had neglected to mention that his career had been derailed by a much-publicised episode involving a pool party and naked teenage girls.

Despite everything, Sandy continued to stand by him. But then he confessed that on his frequent overseas trips he had started a relationship with another woman, and she realised it was time to put it all behind her. She is a strong woman, and it was not long before she was able to laugh about it all.

I must admit that I had already gone off him a bit by this stage. You had to wonder about someone who was so proud of avoiding service in Vietnam by sitting out his national service in Anchorage, Alaska.

Slipping out of our anchorage after farewelling Sandy we headed across the Bahia de Palma towards the east coast of Mallorca. Summer was still at its best, the breezes gentle, the water enticing as we swam off the back of the boat at every stop. We overnighted at Puerto el Arenal on the edge of the bay, and enjoyed a few days in cosy Porto Pedro where we could take the dinghy into the old stone wharfs and enjoy a leisurely sunset before returning to *Sea Dreams* in the calm twilight.

As we sailed eastward along the coast it seemed that behind every headland was another enticing anchorage. Each night we anchored in sheltered bays with the water so clear that we could see the anchor dug into the sandy bottom fifteen metres below. Anchored below the high crags behind Cape Farrutx on the eastern tip of the island we were overwhelmed by their majesty and awed by the ancient stone watchtowers that stood as immutable testimony to the bloody past.

During the night we were hit by the blasts of howling wind gusts roaring down the steep slopes like screaming banshees heralding our destruction and laying *Sea Dreams* on her beams. The anchor was on a rocky bottom and we had an anxious night before dawn brought calm and we were able to enjoy the glint of the new sun playing on the freshly washed sea and the coloured sandstone cliffs of the bay.

It was a short sail across the bay to the ancient city of Alcudia, founded by the Phoenicians three thousand years ago. The Phoenicians, like the later Venetians, were mostly interested in defendable harbours for their trading fleets rather than vast expanses of land. Here they had a narrow peninsula with harbours on both sides. The Romans liked it also and it was an important place until it was sacked by the Vandals in the dying days of the Western Empire.

We moved around to the Bahia de Pollensa and anchored in a very pretty spot overlooked by a beautifully restored castle. There was a 'for sale' sign above a small beach. We liked the look of it and enquired about the price—even though we knew that real estate prices on the island were outrageous. But one hundred million euros took our breath away and we thought we would have to think about it! We were still thinking about it some years later when we recognised it as the magical getaway of the 'worst man in the world' in the TV series based on John le Carre's 'The Night Manager'.

It was now late July, the height of summer, and the beachside bars and cafés in the small coves around the large bay were all packed with people having a terrific time. Most had moorings, but you had to be very early or very late to get one. The cruising habit of most of the local and charter yachts was to spend the night at a marina and motor out to a mooring the next morning once they had recovered enough from their hangovers. Very few would anchor overnight.

We took a strong south westerly across the strait to Menorca the most eastern of the Balearics. Our intended destination was the long narrow Porto de Ciudadela on the western tip, but when we got close there seemed to be too much swell blowing in for comfort. There was no alternative but to haul off and hunt for somewhere along the north coast. Eventually we found good protection from the wind in Cala Binimalia where there was a nice spot off a beach at the head of the bay. The wind eased in the late afternoon and we enjoyed another golden sunset in the company of a dozen or so yachts. I would be hard pressed to look back on our anchorages in the Balearics and think of a single one that was not so beautiful that at moments it could hold you spellbound—content in its beauty, wanting nothing more.

There are still megalithic stone monuments on the island which are evidence of prehistoric settlement, and there are memories of just about all the major historic players, from the Minoans onwards.

The Muslims were expelled in 1287 but as late as the sixteenth century, the notorious Muslim admiral/pirate/murderer/slaver/homicidal maniac known as

Barbarossa terrified the island as well as the whole Mediterranean. There were actually two brothers of this name. The elder was famous first, but he was captured and decapitated. His younger and smarter brother then assumed the title and raped and pillaged until he was an old man. He was reportedly over eighty when he sacked the Port Mahon on the eastern end of Menorca. Aficionados of Captain Jack Aubrey will recognise this as the British Naval Station where Jack is introduced to the reader by Patrick O'Brien in his novels. No one knows how many were murdered or sold into slavery by the brothers, but it is estimated in the tens of thousands.

Our peaceful night ended an hour or so before dawn when we were awoken by a swell beginning to work its way into our once calm and serene bay. The dawn was grey and sullen with an unpredicted north-easterly blowing and there were now some white caps breaking on the other shore. The more exposed boats pulled anchor and ran for the angry-looking sea. We were faced with the choice of staying, there was still a chance we would be okay if the wind remained where it was or going to sea before things got worse.

The boats nearby started to go, and that decided it for us. There was plenty of broken sea outside as we retraced our course of the previous day—we needed to get on the south side of the island to find any protection. The wind continued to build and by the time we had passed Ciudela it was blowing a gale and we were pleased to get in the lea of the land.

Port Mahon was crowded with yachts flying the flags of every European nation and many super yachts flying the flag of wherever registration was cheapest. We wanted to refuel here before we made the overnight hop to Sardinia – but it was not easy. The fuel berth was surrounded by yachts jostling to get in.

We had already discovered that the French, Spanish and Italians have no sense of queueing; it was an Anglo-Saxon invention introduced after they had conquered England. After a few months of pottering around the Med I had come to realise that not all sailors share the courtesy, good manners and modesty that comes naturally to us Australians. Apart from just not understanding the concept of 'waiting your turn' they could at times be quite aggressive. We learned quickly that the only way to get into a fuel berth was to put Ro up the front with a shotgun!

Now, I certainly do not want to appear racist or intolerant. Or pedantic for that matter. But even a not so astute observer will soon identify some national characteristics.

No-one could argue that it is not very dangerous to get between a French yacht and one of the last vacant moorings in a harbour or an empty berth on a quay. Or no matter how close to the shore (or another yacht, for that matter) you anchor, there will always be a Greek yacht which will squeeze in between, so that even the gentlest change of wind will threaten a collision.

The German standing on the bow of his yacht waving you away will be very obstreperous to anyone who anchors within his three hundred metres radius of swing. This is partly because he has finally managed to dig-in his anchor after fifteen attempts to get it to hold while applying 500 hp of reverse pull. Spanish yachts need a semi-naked goddess in the bows while anchoring, while Russian yachts have the right to anchor anywhere, and if that interferes with anyone—stiff. Ditto for super yachts with lots of noisy jet skis.

We eventually filled up with diesel and found a spot to anchor some distance from the town and came in later for a wander around. The old fortifications on the headland at La Mola were interesting and we strolled past Golden Farm where Lord Nelson and his lover, Lady Hamilton — with Napoleon and Josephine the most famous couples of their age—were once guests. Later we retired to the aft deck and watched the lights of the town and wondered what it would have been like a couple of centuries ago when it was full of the British Navy and their mighty 'ships of the line'.

If you were to make a short list of British heroes, Admiral Lord Viscount Horatio Nelson would be on it, and if you were to make a list of Great British Romances — yes, I know, those words don't really go well together; perhaps Great British Scandals has a more genuine ring to it—he would be on that also. Emma Hart was a great beauty, a model and dancer. By the age of fifteen she was already attracting plenty of attention, on one occasion dancing nude on the dining room table at a party given by Sir Harry Featherstonehaugh. She became Sir Harry's mistress and a famous artists' model and before long the mistress and then wife of Sir William Hamilton, a wealthy patron of the arts and British envoy to Naples. His Palazzo Sessa in Naples was famous for its refinement and hospitality, and Emma soon became its beautiful centrepiece. She set fashions, famous artists were infatuated, she was invited to star at the Royal Opera in Madrid. She was the close friend of Queen Maria Carolina, sister of Marie Antoinette the wife of Ferdinand I of Naples and was fluent in French and Italian.

Nelson and Emma met briefly in 1793, and in 1798 he returned to Naples after his victory at the Battle of the Nile. Approaching forty, in poor health and having lost an arm in battle, he was already a national hero when they met again. In admiration and alarm at the toll his exploits had taken on him, she gasped, 'Oh God, is it possible?' before fainting in his clasp.

They soon fell in love. Their affair was tolerated and perhaps encouraged by

151

the elderly Sir William who, as well as his love for Emma had a deep admiration for Nelson, which was warmly reciprocated. The three were widely feted as they travelled together on a 'grand tour' back to England, and Emma and Nelson were the most famous couple in the British Empire.

The three lived openly together and the affair became common knowledge and a great scandal—Nelson's wife Lady Fanny, was after all alive and well. Emma gave birth to Nelson's daughter, Horatia in January 1801 and Sir William died in 1803.

The ardour of the romance waned. Nelson returned to sea and on 21 October 1805 won the great naval victory at the Battle of Trafalgar. After his death and despite the great posthumous honours heaped on him, Emma received no help from the Government, and she ran through her inheritances from both her husband and Nelson. She died ill and destitute in 1815. A tragic end for such a beautiful, talented woman who came from nowhere to be, for a while, the belle of Europe.

Back to the great harbour of Mahon, where we were once again waiting for the weather.

After a few days the forecast was for a moderate northerly, which would be ideal for the two-hundred-mile crossing to Sardinia. We set off as the sun began to flush the clear eastern sky. A few other yachts were leaving also, and we had company for much of the morning, but different speeds and courses eventually left us alone on the sparkling blue ocean. The wind stayed true, the sky cloudless, the sea kind and we averaged a good seven to eight knots for most of the day. Towards sunset we surprised the two whales I mentioned earlier and not long afterwards the wind died out and we needed the engine.

In the middle of the night we picked up the lume of the Capo Caccia light marking the entrance to Porto Conte and in the dawn we slipped into the calm waters of the bay and anchored off the beach in the eastern corner. It was a beautiful scene with the warm morning sun lighting up the golden sandstone of the immense cliff at the entrance, surmounted by the lighthouse. The bay has some of Europe's best dives, with dozens of submerged grottos including the famous Nereo Caves.

Not far from our landfall the old port city of Alghero was settled in prehistoric times and there are still traces of the Phoenicians. The actual city fortifications date back to 1102 CE when the area was colonised by the Doria family of Genoa, and there is much to see and enjoy in the old town still nestled behind the walls.

From Porto Conte we motored north over a calm turquoise sea, passing fishermen around the many rocks and shoals along the coast. Thirty miles brought us to the Passaggio di Fornelli, a rock-strewn shortcut through some outlying islands into the Bonifacio Channel. After safely negotiating this we thought we would top up out tanks and check into Italian customs at the sleepy village of Porto Torres. But we arrived at the beginning of the siesta and the only sign of life around the port was a disinterested dog. We pressed on and before long we were rewarded with a fine view of Castelsardo, a fortified town and castle on a high bluff above a small marina.

There was life here, but no anchorage, so we were obliged to take our first marina berth since Ibiza. There was also an empty fuel berth, so we topped up before docking, completed the formalities and set off to explore the town. It was quite a slog through the old town up to the eleventh century castle, but once there we were rewarded with sweeping views across the water towards Corsica and over miles of emerald coast and hinterland. There was plenty of bustle, it was a working town, and lots of places for our first taste of Sardinian cuisine. We selected a restaurant where we could feel like the masters of all we surveyed and sampled a traditional dish of malloreddus pasta with grated goats' cheese, shared a honey brushed pastry and a carafe of local white. Going down was much easier, but we had to watch our step.

The Bonifacio Strait is a notoriously windy place. The 'mistral' blows through the south of France, across the Gulf of Lion and out into the Mediterranean, where it batters the west coasts of Corsica and Sardinia, and blasts through the Bonifacio Strait which separates them. At times it can reach speeds of more than one hundred and sixty kilometres per hour and builds up very dangerous seas in the relatively shallow waters.

While the weather was still good we skipped along the coast and rounded the cape at the eastern end, where we could find shelter among the rugged windswept islands of the Maddalena Archipelago. The archipelago is named, of course, in the honour of Mary Magdalene. There is a local legend that the ship carrying her anchored in one of the bays as it passed through the archipelago while fleeing to France after the crucifixion. Certainly, the islands were on one of the sea routes to France in Roman times.

This legend is also widely believed in the south of France, where many still think she took refuge in a mountaintop cave in the Sainte-Baume mountains not far from Aix-en-Provence. The cave is now hidden by a monastery called the Sanctuary of Mary Magdalene and pilgrims have been making the journey there since the fifth century—including kings, popes and saints. King Louis visited in 1447 and 1456, praying to Mary Magdalene for a son. She made him wait, but in 1470 Charles VIII was born. Within the cave is a reliquary housing her bones, resting beneath her statue.

There are seven main islands and a number of smaller ones, covered with hardy stands of native marquis and outcrops of red and grey granite, in the archipelago. It is a beautiful place, but hard and dangerous, the sparkling clear waters laced with half-hidden rocks and reefs. There were exhilarating walks on the islands, with the salty tang of the wind in our faces, the aroma of wild herbs and the ever-present cry of the sea birds. When the wind came up, we found a lovely spot on the south side of Santa Maria island and it was here where Helen and Lenny on *Fourth Dimension* caught up with us.

It turned out that somewhere along the way Lenny had got chatting to the father of the proprietor of a rustic restaurant on the island and was keen that we try it out. That sounded good. He booked for lunch and the next day we followed an overgrown track through the rocks and scrub until we came to an old rough stone cottage covered with cascading bougainvillea. It was on a rugged hill with a lovely view over the glistening water on the other side of the island, known as 'Dead Man's Passage'. Very nice indeed, we thought.

We were a little bemused when we were ushered inside and up onto the terrace by the maître d'hôtel dressed in 'black tie'. Not very common in the low dives we usually patronise. The wine waiter attended us, also in formal rig and handed Lenny the wine list. He looked a bit abashed and, it takes a lot to abash Lenny, and he passed it to me. In the heat of the Mediterranean summer Ro and I had taken to diluting our wine with ice and water, and even before that I was renowned for my preference for cheap 'house wines'. So, I was certainly abashed by the wine list. The cheapest wine was one hundred and eighty euros. I reluctantly agreed on that, but it was out of stock, so we had to settle on the next cheapest, two hundred and twenty euros.

The restaurant had a set menu with no prices so even the slowest amongst us —I am speaking of myself here, just so there's no confusion —had deduced that it was not going to be a cheap meal. It was fresh, simple and delicious; seafoods gathered from around the island. Lenny assured me that I would remember the great food long after I had forgotten it was five hundred and fifty euros a head. But I can only remember that one course was sea urchins and we had two bottles of okay wine, and as you can see, I have no trouble remembering the price. We justified it all by taking some great food photos for the coffee table book, *Sea Dreams in the Western Mediterranean* we were compiling at the time.

We were not far away from the fashionable Porto Servo on the Costa Smeralda which is a port frequented by the very rich and famous and a number of Russian oligarchs, and which I knew was going to be very expensive. Here we did a bit of window shopping and then had a coffee at the yacht club. That was twenty-five euros a cup, and I was relieved when Ro agreed to have lunch on the boat. We had a night at a mooring in the bay only a couple of hundred yards away from the superyacht jetty and watched the comings and goings, the helicopters on the aft decks and the patrols of small armies of security guards. I have to admit, that sitting on our aft deck next to the most beautiful girl in the world, I would not have swapped places with any oligarch.

A little bit further down the coast we found a couple of very nice anchorages tucked into rocky bays on the island of Caprera. There was good protection from the still boisterous wind that swept down from the Bonifacio Channel. One of the anchorages was named after the great Italian patriot Giuseppe Garibaldi, who once had a home above the bay and is buried there. He was a lion of his era, and certainly deserves a mention by any passing sailor.

But first, to put things in context, we need a brief sketch of Italian history.

The Italian peninsula was unified under Roman rule in the third century BCE. When the Western Roman Empire collapsed in 476 CE it remained united as part of the Ostrogothic Kingdom. Later it became part of the Frankish Empire whose titular head was the Holy Roman Emperor, and the Emperor was also King of Italy. During this period Italy became a collection of city-states, with little sense of national identity and a lot of inter-city rivalry and warfare.

With the rise of the modern nation states of Europe the Italian city-states became prey to their ambitions and the political map of the peninsula was in a continual state of flux.

Just to take a snapshot in time. In 1810 Italy was divided into the following main components: the Kingdom of Sicily, the Kingdom of Naples taking in most of the bottom of the peninsula, the Kingdom of Sardinia, the French Empire controlled all the north west and the coast down past Rome including the Papal state, the Kingdom of Italy controlled only a slab of the north east. I have probably missed a kingdom or a duchy or two, and ten years before it would have been different—ten years later, different again. Time Lapse Maps if you would like more detail.

After Napoleon fell in 1815, Italy was largely returned to the control of the Austrian — Habsburg—Empire. Although there had been earlier stirrings of nationalism, this marked the beginning of the struggle for independence. There were many insurrections and confrontations that coalesced into three Wars of Italian Independence, before it was achieved in 1871.

Now, back to Garibaldi, and just to get an idea of his legendary stature. At the outbreak of the American Civil War in 1861, he volunteered to fight for the Union. But there were two conditions. Firstly, he was to be given command of the US army, now even someone with the ego the size of say Bono, or even Sting, would hesitate to make such an offer. Secondly, when he thought it appropriate, he would issue a

155

declaration abolishing slavery.

This was politely declined by the US government. But showing that he realised their hands were tied by local politics and that he took no umbrage, he penned the following polite note to Lincoln:

'Posterity will call you the great emancipator, a more enviable title than any crown could be, and greater than any merely mundane treasure.'

He might have had an ego, but he was a legend in his own lifetime – lauded by such celebrities as Victor Hugo, George Sands and Alexander Dumas. And he had certainly 'walked the walk'. Regarded as one of the fathers of Italy, he was born in 1807 and by 1833 had joined the 'Young Italy Movement' and taken an oath to liberate Italy from Austrian rule. Participating in a failed insurrection in 1834 he was sentenced to death and fled to South America.

Here he commanded revolutionaries, and fell in love with and married Ana Ribeiro da Silva, a beautiful revolutionary firebrand, who was expert with sword and gun and who fought in his battles beside him. Being an Italian his first words to her had been, *'You must be mine,'* and although they were passionately in love his Italian eyes could not help straying, from time to time. In 1842 he raised 'The Italian Legion' and commanded the Uruguayan fleet. In 1848 he won victories at the Battle of Cerro and the Battle of San Antonia de Santo.

Already famous he returned to join the revolution in Italy in 1848 and defeated a French army in 1849, but later while being hunted by his enemies in the mountains, his beloved Ana, ill from malaria and pregnant with their fifth child, died in his arms. He carried her memory with him, and years later in 1860 when he hailed Victor Emanuel II as king of a united Italy, he wore her scarf draped around his shoulders.

She is still remembered in Brazil as a heroine of republicanism and her statue and name adorns a number of public places in both Italy and her homeland.

In 1859 during the Second War of Italian Independence, Garibaldi was a general commanding the 'Hunters of the Alps' and won some famous battles in the mountains. In 1860 he conquered Sicily and declared himself dictator of the island in the name of Victor Emmanuel II. His army crossed the Messina Straits and took Naples, then uniting with the army of Piedmont greeted Victor Emmanuelle II as King of Italy.

Returning home to Caprera he had the time to make his offer to the Americans but was soon at war again in Italy and was wounded and imprisoned. In 1866 he raised an army of forty thousand men—The Hunters of the Alps again—during the Third War of Independence and defeated an Austrian army at Bezzecca. Still opposed to an independent Papal state he marched on Rome again, and was wounded at the Battle of Mentana. In 1870 the Franco-Prussian War resulted in the collapse of the Second French Empire.

Finally, in 1871 the reality of a united and independent Italy was realised.

A universally admired hero, Garibaldi died in 1882 aged 74 and was buried at his unpretentious house above our anchorage on *Sea Dreams*.

Our younger daughter Georgie, husband Simon, and children, Joseph and Eleanor, had arrived by this time and we strolled up the rocky hill a couple of times. From the house there is the sort of wild windswept panorama that seems appropriate for this force of nature.

In the evenings the Sardinia Texas Hold 'em Poker Championships were in play, with the grandchildren showing the same promise as their mother. We have a favourite photograph of Georgie aged about six, displaying a royal routine flush which won her a pot at a family game at Koonya in Tasmania. An immensely smug and delighted grin on her face.

Down the coast a bit was Porto Rotondo, where we were planning to leave *Sea Dreams* for winter, but we still had several days on the water before hiring a car and all of us setting off to explore the centre of the island. It is a rugged and beautiful place, but what really captures the eye are the hundreds and hundreds of stone towers, called Nuraghes which dot the landscape. They were built by the Nuragic people as part of tribal defensive works, from 1500 BCE onwards. The Phoenicians began visiting the island from around the ninth century BCE and there-after things went much the same as the Balearics, except the Muslims were repulsed around 1100 CE. For a while it was split into four semi-democratic states, but then became subject to various overlord ships: the Aragonese, Spanish and Savoyard, until it became part of the newly unified Italy in 1871.

For some reason Sardinia has never really received the recognition its beauty deserves. The coastline is superb, with countless glimmering white beaches set between rocky cliffs. Picturesque villages coloured in Mediterranean pastels enjoying sweeping views or sitting beside palm fringed quays. The countryside is green and hilly, with distant views to rocky crags and roads leading you from one secretive glen to another.

Sadly, as autumn began to wane, we put *Sea Dreams* to bed and made our various ways home, Georgie and family to Cairns and us to Tasmania. I arrived home fit, tan and feeling a million dollars only to be diagnosed with prostate cancer. I cursed the gods, opted for brachytherapy—implanting radioactive pellets in the prostate—rather than going under the knife.

All went well and at the end of April the following year we were back on board, with a slightly augmented medical chest, and heading north. We had Ro's nephew Godfrey Esmonde with us and sailing beside us was the sleek white hull of *Fourth Dimension*. The wind had heaped up an uncomfortable swell off the Costa Smeralda and we were happy to get into the shelter of the Maddalena Archipelago. We passed all the familiar anchorages of autumn and anchored again in Dead Man's Reef Passage where we tried out the beautiful but still chilly — 15C—water.

At least Lenny and Godfrey did, but their screams put me off.

The next day we picked up a buoy at the head of Cala Lunga, a long narrow bay on Isolo Razzoli lined with fantastically sculptured rocks and with a narrow entrance which kept it sheltered from just about anything.

The Bonifacio Channel lived up to its windy reputation and the forecast fifteen knots was twenty-five by the time we were across and approaching the township of Bonifacio lining the high cliffs on the southern coast of Corsica. The entrance into the harbour is a narrow chasm that is hidden until you are quite close, and even with the aids of modern navigation it is a bit daunting. I think this is the most western location claiming a link to Homer's Odyssey. According to local folk-law it was here that the fearsome Laestrygonians attacked Odysseus' ships and ate many of his sailors.

It certainly sounds like it.

'A curious bay with mountain walls of stone to left and right, and reaching far inland, a narrow entrance opening from the sea where cliffs converged as though to touch and close.'

The port and the impressive medieval citadel overlooking the harbour sit rather precariously on the very edge of the sheer cliffs that plunge the best part of a hundred metres to the turbulent waters of the strait. The quay is lined with excellent restaurants, and the old city is well worth exploring, with many reminders of the bloody and difficult times it has endured. We got to talking with the crew of a Dutch boat and ended up sharing a meal with them and for the first time heard what was soon to become widespread, a venomous dislike of Brussels and the hierarchy of the EU. Afterwards the younger members on board went nightclubbing and found it a bit hard to keep their footing on the way home through the steep and narrow streets.

Inland, the winding roads of Corsica led from one beautiful mountaintop village to the next, all built well back from the sea to try and escape the marauders who have terrorised the island throughout its history. It was never conquered by the Muslims, but the barbary pirates were a brutal threat for the best part of a thousand years.

158

It is hard rocky country but, in many places there are plantations of cork, interspersed with vineyards and olive groves, while every turn opened up stunning vistas of the snow-covered mountains and the distant sea.

Not wanting to get caught by a strong mistral while on the west coast of the island, we took off when presented with a three-day weather window. Our first day took us to an anchorage off a pretty beach near Anse d'Arana. The second was a sixty-mile passage to Girolata. Sailing past Napoleon's birthplace at Ajaccio, it was framed by the dramatic and hostile snow-covered central massifs which in places tumbled ridge after rocky ridge down to the sea. From one rocky bluff to the next old Genoese watchtowers gazed impassively as we edged past.

A brisk breeze continued to blow off the coast and as twilight began to fall we slipped into the tiny anchorage at Girolata surrounded by towering blood red cliffs. Further inland we could still glimpse the gleaming white peaks of the central range. There was a seventeenth century Genoese castle with a square tower rising above its crenelated walls overlooking the anchorage, built to guard from invaders, pirates and slavers.

In the morning we climbed through an enchanting stone village set between the beach and the castle, and up a spur line until we were rewarded with one of the Mediterranean's great views – the stone girt expanse of the Golfe de Porto and the great bold mountains framing the old castle sitting on its headland. We were surrounded by flowering shrubs and small fields clothed with wild herbs and grasses. The fresh breeze carried the fragrances of the sea and the wild bush and the calls of gulls circling the rocky foreshore.

During the last century this place was sometimes a Bohemian colony, sometimes a criminal refuge. I could see it would have been good for both. A day's sail north we found Calvi dominated by the jagged peaks behind the town, nearly three thousand metres high and still covered in snow in the middle of May. The approach from the west coast is unforgettable. The city ensconced behind its high stone walls and framed by the mighty mountains is both defiant and beautiful. It was controlled by Genoa from the thirteenth century until it was captured by the British in 1794. In the battle Horatio Nelson lost his right eye, which in later years was to become an important part of his legend. At the Battle of Copenhagen in 1801, Nelson, a vice admiral at the time, famously put his telescope to his blind eye to ignore commands from his superior to withdraw, popularising the saying 'turning a blind eye.'

Corsica is still a very reluctant part of France, with discontent simmering below the surface and a continuing hostility to foreign ownership, which can make property ownership a risky proposition. However, if you are just a tourist and not bent on buying up the island all is well, and Calvi will make you very welcome. The local cuisine and wines are a mixture of French and island traditions and there are plenty of fine restaurants tucked away in the winding cobblestoned streets.

A rendezvous with Charlotte in northern Italy at Genoa called us on. For centuries the great maritime rival of Venice their mutual avarice sometimes spiralled into war. They were one of the staunchest bulwarks in the fight against the Muslim fleets in the Western Mediterranean and sent ships to most of the big battles elsewhere. Today it is still a bustling city with one of the busiest ports in Europe, a thriving economy and still a great centre of the arts.

To me however, ever since I could read it had always been famous as the birthplace of Christopher Columbus, the European explorer credited with establishing and documenting routes to the Americas, which led to the irreversible linking of the new world to the old. These days it is generally recognised that his discovery was preceded by the short lived colonisation of North America—probably in the Gulf of St. Lawrence—by Leif Erikson in the 11th century. Erikson led an expedition from Iceland, a country which had been colonised by his Norwegian father Erik the Red. But it was Columbus's voyages that enabled the link between Europe and the Americas.

He was born into a middle-class family in 1451. His father was a tavern owner and perhaps his adventurous spirit was ignited by the talk of sailors gathered there, telling tall tales while quaffing fine Ligurian wine. He first crewed on a ship in 1475 sailing to the Aegean island of Chios. In 1476 he crewed to England, Ireland, possibly Iceland, and in 1447 from Ireland to Lisbon. There he settled for some time and married Filipa Moniz Perestreio, the daughter of a Portuguese nobleman. From 1482 to 1485, financed by his father-in-law he traded along the African west coast. His wife died in 1485 and he moved to Castile.

Columbus was an ambitious and charismatic man, self-educated in languages, astronomy, geography, history and with a knowledge of the bible. He had made himself a master mariner and understood the seas and winds of the east Atlantic.

Meanwhile the Portuguese were developing a trade route to Asia around the south of Africa. In 1488 Dias reached the cape.

In the 1480s Columbus and his brother Bartholomew began exploring the possibility, earlier suggested by the Florentine astronomer Paolo del Pozzo Toscanelli, that Asia could be reached by sailing west. This was by no means a new idea—except perhaps for the Catholic Church. In the 3rd century BCE Eratosthenes, a Greek mathematician, geographer, poet, astronomer from Cyrene on the North African coast had correctly calculated the circumference of the Earth and its tilt.

Since that time many geographers, including the great Ptolemy, had suggested various solutions as to the distances that needed to be travelled by sea. A difficulty was that it was not possible to calculate the distanced covered by the great land mass of Europe and Asia as it was not yet possible to measure longitude.

Columbus overestimated the distance to Japan travelling east overland, which meant he badly underestimated the distance travelling west by sea. He thought that Japan from the Canary Islands was around 3,000km where-as the real distance was 20,000km. He was wrong on distances, but he was right on winds. He could run with the easterlies going west, and by going further north for the return journey, northerlies would bring him back

He had a plan. But he still had to sell it.

In 1485 he presented his plan to John II of Portugal. He asked for three ships, and to be made the Great Lord of the Ocean if he pulled it off. He was rejected. In 1488 he was granted another audience. Another no. Diaz's successful voyage made his plan superfluous to Portugal. Not to be denied he tried Genoa and then Venice. Bartholomew sailed to England and had an audience with Henry VII.

In 1486 Columbus approached Queen Isabella and Ferdinand II of Spain. They desperately wanted to get into the trade with Asia but did not believe in his plan enough to buy it. But they took out an option by putting him on their pay roll. Finally, after continually pressing he got the go ahead in 1492. Isabell and Ferdinand also promised that if he succeeded, he would be made Admiral of the Oceans and Seas and governor of all lands he could claim for Spain, 10% revenue of new lands in perpetuity and more.

From 1492 to1503 he completed four round trip voyages between Spain and America. Maps of Columbus's Voyages. Not bad for the son of an innkeeper, and his tumultuous life was only beginning.

We managed to get a berth close to the city centre for a couple of nights, before spending some time with Charlotte along the northern Italian coast. It is still a maze of narrow streets surrounded by some beautiful castles, cathedrals, piazzas, museums, classical and baroque buildings. Lots to see and not enough time. But we gave it our best and had some of the grand northern Italian dining (Charlotte had by this stage developed much more refined tastes than her father, enjoying expensive wine) before slipping down the coast a little.

Portofino has been a favourite of the rich and famous since there were enough citizens of Rome wealthy enough to get away from the mosquitos in summer. These days it is very crowded and to get a mooring for a yacht is somewhere between very difficult and impossible. However, in calm weather it is possible to anchor off and to mingle with the beautiful sophisticates along the waterfront, admire the exquisite villas set amongst luxuriant stands of cypress and oak and sample some of the exquisite Ligurian wines (even their cheap stuff is great). The region produces a number of varieties of whites and reds that are perfect for the abundant seafood and salads harvested on the overlooking mountains.

We think Vernazza is the most beautiful of the Cinque Terre villages, but they are all stunning, as is the whole coast. There is a small fishing harbour with pretty good protection for the local fishing fleet, but there are some photos around the harbour showing what it could be like in a winter storm, and you would not want to be there. It was calm enough to anchor off, where you are centre stage of a great amphitheatre, with the rising terraces filled with the colour and bustle of the village. It is a bit crowded during the day in summer, but by the late afternoon the 'day trippers' have left, and as the sun sets the rich reds, ochres and yellows of the houses colour the light around the quay.

It is a magnificent spot for an aperitif. You can watch the colourfully painted fishing boats putting out to sea for the night, before dining on their catch with wines from the vines on the terraced vineyards on the mountains behind. As night settles the ancient village reclaims its soul. Children play, the old gossip, play cards and chess and sip wine. In the dawn the village shakes itself awake and teams of local men scrub up the old girl, including sweeping the beach, ready to face the onslaught of the tourists.

Our next stop, the very beautiful island of Elba is greener and softer than Sardinia and Corsica. The capital, Portoferraio has one of the great harbours of the Mediterranean. The fertile interior is densely covered with palms, cedars, olives and grapes – and as you would expect amidst such abundance, plenty of churches and some grand monasteries. It is of course famous as Napoleon's place of exile and a stroll up through the old town to the ridge overlooking the sea and the harbour will take you to his residence. It is certainly not what he had become used to as Emperor of France residing in the grand luxury of the Tuileries Palace, but it does have a lovely view.

Napoleon was born at Ajaccio on the west coast of Corsica in 1769; we had a glimpse of it as we passed by a month or so earlier. Although his family was of Italian descent, the island was part of France when he was born.

In 1779 he was admitted to a military academy at Brienne-le-Chateau—where an examiner reported he would make an excellent sailor—and in 1784 to the elite *Ecole Militaire* in Paris. In 1889, not long after he graduated, the French Revolution erupted. This provided exciting opportunities for young officers pursuing glory. In

1792 he was promoted to captain and he distinguished himself at the siege of Toulon. This caught the attention of the Committee of Public Safety, and he was promoted to brigadier-general at the age of twenty-four.

In October 1795 while defending the Tuileries Palace from a royalist insurrection he killed 1,400 royalists with cannon fire. This action earned him fame and wealth and the patronage of the new government. He was given command of the French army in Italy and fought sixty-seven actions and won eighteen pitched battles in the course of destroying the Austrian army. In part his victories were due to tactical brilliance, but also to his personal bravery. He was now a national hero.

In 1798 he invaded Egypt with an army of 25,000 with the object of establishing relations with the Indian princes and attacking the English possessions in India. He had victories in Egypt and invaded the Ottoman provinces with his remaining 13,000 men of his army. Retreating to Egypt he poisoned his own wounded (perhaps 500 men) with opium. He was now left with an army of less than 10,000 men suffering from the plague and disease.

Eluding the British Navy he left his men to their fate and returned to France in August 1799, to a hero's welcome again (I suppose the poor buggers he left behind did not matter in the grand French scheme of things). On 9 November he staged a coup d'état and drafted a constitution appointing himself First Consul for 10 years. It was approved in a plebiscite by 99.94 % of the voters.

In 1800 he returned to Italy and this time took possession of the country. In 1803 he was elected Emperor of the French, with 99 % approval, and annexed Piedmont. He was crowned King of Italy.

Madame de Remusat, a commentator on the times, explains his widespread support in France: *'men worn out by the turmoil of the Revolution ... looked for the domination of an able ruler'* and *'people believed quite sincerely that Bonaparte, whether as consul or emperor, would exert his authority to save (them) from the perils of anarchy'.*

After a brief peace, war broke out again in 1803—against a coalition of Britain, Prussia and Russia. The French *'grande armee'* now numbered around 350,000 soldiers of all arms and were well led. Hopes of luring the British Navy to West Indies to allow the invasion of Britain failed. The French Fleet was destroyed at the Battle of Trafalgar in July 1805.

Napoleon turned his attention back to the continent. The Austrians, Prussians and Russians were all defeated. The Battle of Austerlitz on 2 December 1805 when he defeated the combined Russian and Austrian armies, is regarded as a feat equal of the Battle of Cannae. Later at the battle of Friedland he wiped out most of the Russian army. Peace Treaties were signed at Tilsit leaving Napoleon master of Europe. When the Russian Emperor Alexander arrived at Tilsit his first words to Napoleon were 'I hate the English as much as you do.'

In October 1807, the Peninsula War began when Napoleon sent an army to Spain.

In 1809, the Austrians invaded Bavaria, but he crushed them again. In June, Napoleon invaded Russia with an army of more than 450,000. The Russians withdrew, generally avoiding battle and employing a 'scorched earth policy' until they finally faced him on 7 September at Borodino near Moscow. This may have been the bloodiest day of battle in history to that time. There were 44,000 Russian casualties and 35,000 French.

Napoleon said of it: '...the most terrible of all my battles was the one before Moscow. The French showed themselves worthy of victory, but the Russians showed themselves worthy of being invincible.'

The Russians burned Moscow and retreated. Napoleon had the option of starving or retreating. He began marching home five weeks later. Only around 45,000 of his army made it home. There was a lull before fighting began again. After early victories he lost the Battle of Leipzig, where in total there were 90,000 casualties. There was more fighting, but after pressure from his generals Napoleon was forced to abdicate on 6 April 1814.

He was exiled to Elba, but on 26 February 1815 escaped on the brigantine *Inconstant* with 700 men, and subsequently landed in France. The French 5th Regiment, led by his old mate, the famous Marshall Ney, was sent to arrest him and they met near Grenoble on 7 March. Napoleon approached the regiment alone, dismounted his horse and when he was within gunshot range shouted to the soldiers.

'Here I am. Kill your Emperor, if you wish'.

The soldiers responded with. 'Vive L'Empereur'.

Ney embraced Napoleon and together they marched on to Paris. Then onto Waterloo on 18 June 1815.

The above is a very sketchy description of his military career and does not even allude to the quite vast array of his marvellous civil achievements.

Napoleon was much more than a brilliant and brutal general. As the eminent British historian Andrew Roberts, writes:

'The ideas that underpin our modern world – meritocracy, equality before the law, property rights, religious toleration, modern secular education, sound finances, and so on – were championed, consolidated, codified and geographically extended by Napoleon. To them he added rational and efficient local administration, an end to

164

rural banditry, the encouragement of science and the arts, the abolition of feudalism and the greatest codification of laws since the fall of the Roman Empire'.

And although these days his fame is largely based on his military brilliance, it is these achievements for which he should really be remembered. But in any case, few Frenchmen no matter how great, would regard their life a success unless it was enriched by an epic love affair or twenty. And so it was with Napoleon and his relationship with Josephine, an older and sophisticated woman, who he fell passionately in love with when he was a young man.

'I awake full of you. Your image and the memory of last night's intoxicating pleasure has left no rest for my senses'.

They were married in 1796 but an early dalliance by Josephine while he was away during his Egyptian campaign took the gloss off things. Yet although he indulged himself with other women, he remained infatuated and she was crowned his empress and retained the honorific title when he later divorced her in search of someone to give him a noble heir. They still remained on good terms until her death in 1814, and while in exile on St Helena he is reported at saying. *'I truly loved Josephine, but I did not respect her.'*

A few hundred metres below Napoleons old abode, the quay at Portoferraio has a very pleasant ambience, and a day or so later it is here that we caught up again with Dave and Jill Henry who were here on *Sweet Chariot*, having sailed via Asia. Helen and Lenny on Fourth *Dimension*, who had taken a quick detour to France, also arrived. There were some interesting restaurants in the back streets serving traditional dishes of seafood soups and stews, accompanied by some fine local dry whites and sumptuous reds, which were ideal for some rather raucous catching up. Of course, Lenny didn't get to choose where we ate this time!

The harbour is large enough to get away from the town if you want a bit of peace and quiet, and there are also a few good anchorages on the south and east coasts with small attractive villages. Although it is a very Italian island it has been influenced by the tides of history that have washed over it; Iberian and Moorish influences are still evident. They have left a unique and beautiful place to visit, and a feeling that it would be a lovely place to live in. Although I must admit this is a feeling that many islands invoke.

One of Rome's earliest historians, Pliny the Elder, describes Elba as an area that produces a lot of wine which is a pretty good recommendation for any place. Wine production predated Pliny by many centuries and was probably first bought here by the Etruscans when Rome was still only a small village in a swamp. Nevertheless, Lenny and I agreed that this was probably not the home of 'the man who invented red wine' but we did agree to keep searching.

In good spirits we left for our next stop, the reputably beautiful island of Giglio, a short hop south.

We arrived at the small crowded harbour without incident and started hunting around for a spot. Most of the quay was taken with boats tied up alongside, two-deep. But there seemed to be a stern-in spot amongst a few fishing trawlers. We dropped the anchor and started to reverse in. It was a bit after midday, siesta time, and there was not a soul in sight. When we reached the quay, we found it too high for me to get ashore with a line – I'm the first to admit I'm not as agile as I was as a young man. A bit of swearing, still no sign of anyone. A bit more swearing, and a drowsy fisherman appeared on the deck of the trawler next to us. Ah, our saviour.

Shaking his head and waving his arms, he gave us a burst of Italian. I didn't understand a word, but I got his meaning.

After this rudeness I was all for giving Giglio a miss, but Ro is made of sterner stuff and was determined to explore the picturesque hilltop town. We eventually ended up anchored in a bay on the other side of the island. On the way out of the harbour I had cursed it and its fishermen. I was sorry I had done this, when within a few months my incantations were answered and, a large ocean liner went aground near the entrance. The Italian captain had been distracted by a pretty girl.

Onwards again. The wind a light north-westerly, the sea a sparkling blue and soon we were romping along at seven knots, heading for Anzio about a hundred miles to the south. In the afternoon, as we were abeam of Rome, a lone patrolling thunderstorm zeroed in on us and we were buffeted for an hour or so. It passed, summer resumed, the air was fresh and clear.

Later in the afternoon we were off an undistinguished part off the coast where, mythologically speaking, one of the most important events of Roman history took place. According to both Greek and Roman legend Aeneas the son of a Trojan prince and the goddess Aphrodite, made landfall in Italy after escaping from the fall of Troy. In Homer's Iliad, as the second cousin and lieutenant to Hector, the principal Trojan warrior who is slain in battle by Achilles, he plays a small but honourable role. Nevertheless, it is apparent that on a number of occasions, because of his semi-divine nature he is favoured by the gods.

As the Greeks began the sack of Troy, he was commanded by the gods to gather a group and escape, then found a new city which would keep alive the traditions of the city that was about to be forever erased from the face of the earth. The Aeneads included his father Anchises, his friends Achates, Sergestus and Acmon and a number of other warriors and he carried with him the household gods of the city. After six years of wandering the coasts of the Mediterranean in their boats they eventually arrived at the city of Carthage. Here the queen, Dido, fell in love with him and proposed that they jointly rule the city. But the gods reminded Aeneas of his duty and the Aeneads slipped away in the night, leaving Dido so heartbroken that she placed a curse on her lover that would be the cause of the eternal conflict between Rome and Carthage, and committed suicide with a sword she had given Aeneas as a token of her love.

Later on, Aeneas descended into the underworld where he met Dido who had reunited with her husband, and his father who revealed his destiny was to found Rome.

Sailing on they arrived at a shallow port on the coast of the small kingdom of Latium, where they were welcomed by King Latinus—who had already received a prophecy that his daughter would marry a stranger from a distant land—offered his daughter to Aeneas. This union produced the line of the ancient Kings of Alba Longa who ruled for some four hundred years until Rome was established by their descendants, Romulus—from whom Rome takes its name—and his brother, Remus—whom he murdered. Julius and Augustus Caesar claim descent from this lineage, as does the legendary King Arthur of Britain, according to the Benedictine monk, Geoffrey of Monmouth.

We got to Anzio just as dusk was falling and the first lights were beginning to twinkle along the foreshore. It looked as if we would have reasonable protection in the lee of a marina wall, and as the weather forecast was still good, we anchored off. The flat coastline ran away into the darkness on either side of us.

It was here that on 22nd January 1944 the U.S. VI Corps assaulted across the beaches in an attempt to break the deadlock that had halted the Allies invasion of Italy in World War II. It eventually resulted in the capture of Rome, but the Germans were able to withdraw to a new defensive position further north.

The Italian campaign had already resulted in the capture of Sicily during July and August 1943. The fighting cost the Allies around twenty thousand casualties, the Axis fifty-five thousand casualties and one hundred and sixty thousand captured. Using Sicily as a springboard, the main attack on the Italian mainland was made at Salerno on the south west coast, with supporting attacks in Calabria and Taranto.

There was bitter fighting all the way up the Italian Peninsula until the Germans finally surrendered in May 1945. The casualties on both sides were horrendous. The allies suffered three hundred and twenty thousand, the Germans three hundred and thirty thousand. For the Italians it was more complicated, and worse: two hundred thousand invasion casualties, one hundred and fifty thousand civilians, thirty-five thousand anti-fascist partisans and thirty-five thousand troops of the Italian

Socialist Republic.

There were more infantry casualties to both sides during the Italian campaign than in the western front.

The rationale for the campaign was to draw Axis troops away from the Eastern and Western fronts. It did do this, but at terrible cost. The allies committed far more than the Germans. Nearly one and a half million against four hundred and forty thousand, four thousand aircraft against some seven hundred. And it committed the Allies to a series of 'meat grinder' operations in terrible terrain. At least some of responsibility rests with its staunch advocate, Winston Churchill.

We drank a toast to those who had fought, and to the pain endured by their loved ones. And thought how fortunate we have been, to have lived the life they helped make possible.

Away with the dawn the next day we anchored early off the beach at Gaeta fifty miles or so further on, and the next day we headed for Naples.

The Bay of Naples is one of the world's most famous destinations – partly because it was from here that so many Napolese sailed for the New World, carrying with them their memories of home. It has been the setting of real-world dramas since Roman times, more in the Middle Ages including the Borgias and scheming Popes and no fewer in modern times. Countless, books, plays and movies have been set in Naples and the off-lying islands.

It is a place you cannot help but love even though the waters inside the bay are a disgrace. Naples is often a rubbish dump and most days the smog is too thick to see the outlying islands. It can be difficult to find a marina berth close to the city, theft and damage are problems and it is certainly not a salubrious spot for a cruising sailor to relax.

However, no one comes here to relax, and the negatives are far outweighed by the positives. Vesuvius, Heraculeum and Pompeii are close by. The national museum and gallery are simply stupendous, the city and the people are vibrant and impossible not to love, life is passionate and exciting, the food mouth-watering.

We first anchored in the ancient harbour of Misenum, which is tucked just inside Capo Miseno, the northern headland of the Gulf of Naples. It is still partially protected by the remains of an ancient Roman breakwater, and around its shallow waters lie many reminders of when it was the base for a Roman fleet. We nosed in late in the afternoon, and except for a few small fishing boats moored along the shore, had it to ourselves.

We anchored somewhat gingerly, worried about fouling our anchor on a couple of thousand years of accumulated detritus. Generally, we try to avoid 'pulling in' the anchor in this sort of situation if it is not windy, as it increases the chances of hooking onto something bad. Most of these old mainland harbours have glutinous muddy bottoms and the anchor will bury itself anyway, and with any luck you will have a straight clean lift when leaving.

By the time we had settled in the sandstone cliffs were aglow from another golden sunset, and in the distance across the bay stood the great bulk of Mount Vesuvius. In these ancient harbours it is hard not to be touched by the past, particularly with a glass of red in your hand as dusk falls. The fading light smudges the marks of the passing centuries and all that remains are the ageless shorelines, the mountains and the timeless lap of the water.

In this marvellous spot there is also a very personal link to the past—letters written by one of Rome's great literary figures, Pliny the Younger, two thousand years ago.

During the famous eruption of Mount Vesuvius in 79 CE the commander of the Roman Fleet in the bay was the great lawyer, military commander, philosopher, naturalist and prolific author—most famously his natural history 'Naturalis Historia'—and authority on wine, Pliny the Elder. He was the younger man's uncle, and met his death attempting to rescue people from the shore below the exploding mountain.

The Elder had been a well thought of and disciplined young officer who on campaign in Germany in 55-58 CE disparagingly records that his commander was carrying around with him a silver dinner service weighing twelve thousand pounds! Excessive, I would have thought, even for the best of British regiments. He kept his head down during the reigns of Caligula and Nero and wrote nothing political. But after Nero's death in 68 CE he became an important confidant and official of Emperor Vespasian, who had also come up through the military.

His nephew, Pliny the Younger writes of his uncle:

'For my part I deem those blessed to whom, by favour of the gods, it has been granted either to do what is worth writing of, or to write what is worth reading; above measure blessed those on whom both gifts have been conferred. In the latter number will be my uncle ....'

Mount Vesuvius literally exploded, spewing thousands and thousands of tons of molten ash, pumice and poison gasses into the sky. A firestorm engulfed the surrounding area, suffocating the inhabitants and burying the towns of Pompei, Herculaneum and Stadiae. They remained covered until excavations began in 1748.

Staying with his uncle on this tragic day, his young nephew described the horrific events in two lengthy letters to a friend, which includes the following paragraph.

'You could hear the shrieks of the women, the wailing of infants, and the shouting of men: some were calling their parents, others their children or their wives, trying to recognise them by their voices. People bewailed their own fate or that of their relatives, and there were some who prayed for death in their terror of dying. Many besought the aid of the gods, but still more imagined there were no gods left, and the universe was plunged into eternal darkness for evermore.

Pliny the Younger also became an important personage and was a lawyer, author and magistrate. Hundreds of his letters survive and are an invaluable insight into the Roman governance of this period.

One provided the earliest existing record of Roman policy towards Christians.

In the Epistulae X.96. Pliny wrote—as the governor of Bithynia et Pontus, in modern Turkey, bordering the Black Sea and part of the Aegean coast—to the Emperor Trajan in January 113 CE, asking his advice. Pliny explains that he had conducted trials of suspected Christians who had been anonymously accused of rejecting Roman rule and gods. His investigations revealed no overt rebellious acts, only *'harmless practices and depraved, excessive superstitions'*. However, as he was worried about the spread of superstition, and having given them three chances to affirm their innocence, they had refused to do so. Should he order their execution?

Trajan replied. Do not allow anonymous accusations. Do not seek out Christians for trial. If the accused are guilty of being Christian, then they must be executed. But if they deny they are Christian and show proof they are not worshipping the Christian gods, they are to be pardoned.

Sailing further into the bay we found there are not a lot of safe anchorages when the tail end of the mistral blows in. We edged past the ruins of the famous resort town of Baia where the emperors Claudius and Nero both had luxurious villas. Volcanic subsidence has submerged a large part of the town and created the world's most stunning underwater museum.

But after a bit of searching we did find a pleasant spot to see out a few days of wet and windy weather behind the island of Nisida. The island is actually the steep rim of a submerged crater that wraps around a small lagoon. It still retains an extensive garden and is dominated by a sixteenth century castle. From the water it looked very appealing, although there seem to have been a few building additions that should have been knocked back by council.

In the 1st century BCE it was an exclusive getaway for a few of the rich and famous families of Rome. Probably the most well-known was Markus Brutus, made famous by the words *'et tu, Brute?'* gasped by his friend, benefactor and perhaps his father, Julius Caesar, as Brutus prepared to plunge his dagger into his chest in 44 BCE.

Brutus came from an aristocratic and well-connected family and had made himself rich, largely through opportunities provided by government appointments and money lending. His mother Servilia, was Caesar's long-time mistress. He served under Caesar in Gaul and was a popular and successful commander. But when Caesar marched on Rome and civil war broke out, he sided with Caesar's mortal enemy Pompey the Great. The ensuing war was decided at the Battle of Pharsalus, where before the battle Caesar had given specific orders that Brutus was not to be harmed and to be captured alive. The victorious Caesar forgave him, took him into his inner circle and appointed him to important positions. During this period, he and his wife Porcia—the daughter of the great orator Cato—used the estate on Nisida to plot with the other best-known assassin, his brother in law Cassius Longinus. Another famous visitor was the great orator and politician, Cicero.

After the assassination, Brutus and Cassius fled Rome and raised armies and eventually confronted Caesar's heir Augustus, and Marc Antony at the Battle of Phillipi in 42 BCE. In defeat Brutus committed suicide, as did Porcia when she heard of Brutus's death.

But the Battle of Actium, between Augustus and Antony, was still to come before the bloody civil war was finally ended.

Another owner of an estate on Nisida, quite possibly a previous owner of Brutus's estate, was the famous conqueror of the eastern kingdoms during the Third Mithridatic War a few decades before. Lucius Lucullous (118-57 BCE) was an impressive general whose victories over the mythically wealthy eastern potentates gave him an immense fortune—in those days, and for many many years to come for that matter—the generals kept the lion's share of the booty. He used his booty to establish a luxurious lifestyle, splendid gardens and stupendous villas. Pliny says he was 'Xerxes in a toga' and has given us the word '*lucullan*', meaning; lavish, luxurious, gourmet.

Plutarch says he '*quitted and abandoned public affairs, either because he saw they were already beyond proper control and diseased, or as some would say, he had his fill of glory and felt his struggles and toils entitled him to a life of ease and luxury.*' Fair enough!

In those days the small volcanic island was probably a priceless jewel, but prices would have suffered after Mount Vesuvius exploded a century later.

When the weather cleared we headed towards the old town where we were convivially squeezed into a marina close by the Castell Dell Oro. We hadn't been off the boat for quite a few days and were ready to explore the town, famous nearby sites and to sample the wares of some of the legendary restaurants with only an easy downhill walk home.

Three days later we decided that if we were ever going to leave, we had better get on with it, or we never would. We edged out of the marina, hoisted the sails and headed out.

You could spend a lifetime in the outer islands of the bay and never tire of their beauty. The light is magical and brings alive the pastels of the colourful villages, and the blues of the sky and sea. Procida and Ischia are irresistible with plenty of good anchorages off unspoiled towns, a million miles from the tumultuous streets of Naples. We spent a couple of weeks anchored on the south side of Procida and off Sant'Angelo on Ischia, rowing ashore each day to explore the narrow streets and enjoying unforgettably friendly service and seafood in the many restaurants.

A little further on, the island of Capri was not an easy place to visit in a yacht. There is a small marina, but you need to know the Pope to get a berth! There are one or two anchorages in very deep water and exposed to all winds. We had to settle on one of these, but I was not at all keen on leaving *Sea Dreams* unattended.

The second Roman emperor, Tiberius built a series of villas including the famous Villa Jovis and governed the empire from there. Thereafter it has always been a popular place to live. Although in 1535 the Ottoman Admiral Barbarossa Hayreddin Pasha—yes, the red-headed monster with a Turkish father and a Lesbos Greek mother—arrived in galleys probably built by conquered Greeks and raped and pillaged the island, and in 1553 the equally notorious Turgut Reis followed suit. The rich, famous, indulgent and powerful that have a connection to the island are far too numerous to enumerate – although one particularly amuses me. Maxim Gorky hosted Vladimir Lenin and Joseph Stalin at his 'institute' in 1908.

We continued south, hugging the rugged coastline framed by the high green mountains rising behind. Anchored off Positano we had a splendid view of the village clinging to the steep cliffs and smothered beneath the profusion of cascading pink bougainvillea. At Amalfi we were lucky enough to get a berth amongst the local fishing fleet and were able to do some exploring among the small hilltop villages and vineyards of the hinterland. We came back laden with wines, olives, prosciuttos and cheeses and even more in love with Campania. An Italian friend of ours maintains that there is still no such country as Italy, only a collection of regions. Everyone thinks of themselves as Tuscans, or Calabrians, or Sicilians, or Romans, or Campanians; Garibaldi wouldn't like it, but we think he is probably right. The divisions of ancient tribes, and centuries of rule by various noble houses, religious orders and communes are not going to go away anytime soon—just ask any Venetian or Sardinian.

We continued on to the small harbour at Salerno, which was the location of the main amphibious assault of the Italian campaign of World War II. It was overlooked by a ring of mountains which at first glance looked like a very dubious place to land a large army. Which was probably what the allied commander thought a few days after the landing of US 5th Army on 9 September 1943, and he was looking at defeat or withdrawal. They managed to hold on, but rather than a dash north they were faced with a slow war of attrition, and what many think was one of the most dubious operations in military history and there have been many of those.

The commander of the invasion force was Lieutenant-General Markus Clark, who had made a name for himself as a staff officer but had had no previous operational command in the war. He was a protégé of the Army Chief of Staff George Marshall and a friend of General Dwight Eisenhower, but he turned out to be a controversial choice for the job. He was widely disliked by those under him, a number of generals took the rap for situations created by the commander, a lot of men were killed.

Major General George Patton, who went on to become one of the most celebrated Allied commanders of the war was under Clark's command, and probably summed up the thoughts of many.

'I think that if you treat a skunk nicely, he will not piss on you – as often'.

After the war some of the men he commanded also made their thoughts known. In 1946 the U.S. 36th Infantry Division Veterans Association passed the following resolution.

'Be it resolved that the men of the 36th Division Association petition the Congress of the United States to investigate the river Rapido fiasco and take the necessary steps to correct the military system that will permit an inefficient and inexperienced officer such as General Mark W. Clark, in high command to destroy the young manhood of this country and prevent future soldiers being sacrificed wastefully and uselessly'.

We had a wander around and an aperitif beside the harbour, before dining on another wonderful seafood pasta while watching the night fall, the mountains fading from a lush green to dark shadows. In the morning it was southward again while the gentle northerlies continued to blow. Aeolus was being more than kind to us.

The high emerald mountains continued to march beside us, still sprinkled with charming villages, vineyards and stands of cypress. Two nights later we were ensconced in the marina at Tropea just north of the Messina Straits. We had a long climb up ancient, heavily worn steps to the old town perched high above the marina. When we eventually made it, we collapsed exhausted at a table on a fragrant balcony overlooking the town walls and the limitless ocean.

One of the culinary specialties of this area is swordfish, which unfortunately is hunted with much gusto in the local waters. Now, these are noble animals that can grow to around four metres and more and, weigh up to a tonne and a half. Unlike many sharks they have no interest in eating swimmers and it seems to me a great tragedy that such a creature should be served up as a popular delicacy.

Up until now I had avoided tasting them, but against my better judgement I decided to try a swordfish steak. Perhaps my prejudices ruined it for me. It was the only meal ever to come out of Mediterranean waters that I have had absolutely no desire for an encore. Since then I have taken notice of the generally glum and disappointed expression on the faces of swordfish eaters—so perhaps we should be campaigning to save these wonders, rather than bloodthirsty man-eating White Pointers. At least in areas where they eat swimmers.

The next day we left for the Aeolian Islands in the late afternoon so we would have a night-time crossing in which to appreciate the fiery spectacle of Mount Stromboli. It is still an active volcano and generally regarded as the world's most ancient lighthouse. Around midnight its glowing tip rose over the horizon and we joined the company of countless sailors who through the ages have been mesmerised by the sight.

Stromboli was first mentioned in the Odyssey: *'Then to the Aeolian isle we came, where dwelt Aeolus, son of Hippotas, dear to the immortal gods, in a floating island, and all around is a wall of unbreakable bronze, and the cliff runs up sheer.'*

Mythology gives Aeolus the Greek god of the winds, a number of homes but there is no reason to think that he did not live on the island from time to time, keeping the winds enclosed in a cave. The clouds of steam and fire pouring from the volcano were believed to be warnings of his intentions of releasing the winds to wreak their havoc. It is interesting to note that in modern times it has been discovered that the shape of the plume is related to atmospheric pressure, so perhaps the ancients were on to something.

Anyway, we found the islands to still be a bloody windy spot, not well served with anchorages. We anchored in a crowded and not well-protected bay at the island of Volcano, which was still smoking from time to time, and in the sunsets its pumice and ash-covered slopes did in fact look remarkably bronze.

With a gale in the offing we decided to head for a more secure anchorage at the Portorosa marina on the north coast of nearby Sicily. We anchored for a night protected by a sand spit below an imposing monastery on Cape Tindari before motoring up the protected inlet leading to the perfectly secure marina.

As background to our visit to Sicily I had been reading a history of the Mafia.

174

I had expected that towards the end of the book it would be revealed that they had finally been eradicated, and the island ushered into a new era of peace and prosperity. I had mentioned my hopes to a genial Sicilian we had met along the way.

'Ah, no.' He had laughed. 'They have actually grown and diversified. For instance, they negotiated the contracts for the installation of wind generators all over the island. If all the money had gone into generators, ha ha ha, the island would have been able to fly, ha ha ha. And they build and maintain a lot of the roads too, ha ha ha.'

Later when we hired a car to tour the island, we were able to insure everything but the wheels. The operator shrugged his shoulders when we asked why, but after narrowly missing death in some of the dangerous potholes of anti-tank ditch dimensions that were everywhere, we realised it would take a miracle to still have round wheels by the time we got back.

We were definitely in Mafia country. The chemist in the town adjacent to the marina was located *inside* the police station and the police looked at me suspiciously, their hands hovering near their sub-machine guns, when I entered in search of some Panadol. I didn't really look that dangerous—just a weather-beaten old Anglo.

The poor souls living nearby were amongst the most sullen, most lacking in civic pride I have seen anywhere. Ground down by the Catholic Church, the Mafia and destroyed periodically by eruptions of nearby Mount Etna. That said, if you do survive the roads—the Mafia have also saved lots of money on the lighting in the numerous dark tunnels—there are many rewards to be found.

The mountainous countryside is stunning, with many old villages sitting atop lofty pinnacles looking as if the centuries have just passed them by. Near a lonely farmhouse we were bemused to see a number of men, who could have been Mafia or just honest farmers, disembarking from beaten-up cars carrying baby goats under one arm and shotguns under the other. Was it a barbecue or a visit to a backyard butcher? We were reminded of that once when we bred angora goats, we would advertise to give away the baby males—who had no breeding value—as pets. Our ads were always answered by hungry looking men of Italian/Greek origin. Who could blame them, baby goat is delicious!

The island has had a tough history. Being so rich and close to Italy and a stepping-stone between Africa and Europe, it has interested lots of grasping people. The Romans and Carthaginians, Christians and the Muslims have waged bloody wars to possess it. Then for centuries and centuries it was a pawn of the noble houses of Europe. World War II drenched it in blood, the Mafia were always murdering people and fighting with those bastards from Calabria. Time Lapse Maps if you would like more detail.

But between all this there were golden periods.

The great city of Syracuse was founded in 734 BCE and at its pinnacle was described as the most beautiful Greek city in the world. In the twelfth century the island was ruled by the Hautevilles, a Norman family of Viking heritage. Under the enlightened rule of Roger II it became the '*most luminous centre of culture in Europe, a centre of scholars, scientists, poets and artists of all races and nationalities*'. Sounds like they may have been related to that other famous Norman family of Viking heritage – Ro's family, the Esmondes. Richard the Lionheart married a Sicilian princess on the way to the Crusades. I think that she came with some badly needed ships.

In a few days in a car it is impossible to do justice to the island. It is full of wonders, including seven UNESCO Heritage Sites. The Valle dei Templi in Agrigento, Villa Romana del Casale near Piazza Armerina, the Baroque towns of the Val di Noto, the Necropolis of Pantalica, Mount Etna, Palermo and the cathedral churches of Cefalu and Monreale, and of course the Aeolian Islands. There are hundreds of archaeological sites, castles, monasteries and countless breathtaking panoramas.

We spent a week away, confident that *Sea Dreams* would be well looked after by the local Mafia, who we presumed operated the marina or at least provided protection. It was certainly the most expensive we used in the Mediterranean.

All was well, a minor leak of hydraulic oil in our self-steering had been fixed, and we set sail for the Straits of Messina, the famous straits between Italy and Sicily. We passed by where the monster Scylla and the whirlpool Charybdis almost destroyed Odysseus. The whirlpool which in ancient times could swallow whole galleys, has been tamed—probably by changes to the sea bottom caused by earthquakes. But there is still a strong tidal race and at its peak it creates a large circular eddy, which is moderately disconcerting on a yacht.

We dropped the anchor near the old port of Reggio di Calabria framed by the jagged mountain backdrop. Here we felt the tug of the ancient tide, sipped some Sicilian red and enjoyed the sunset and the timeless passing parade. Thought of the countless souls who had sailed past this spot; rich and poor, famous or unknown, freeman or slave—all carried to their mostly unknown destinies.

But the destiny of one, at least, still interests me. In 71 BCE the rebel slave commander Spartacus, camped with his last 2,000 men on the adjacent shore. He had been hunted south by the Roman legions and had arranged with Sicilian pirates to be carried across the straits to Sicily. They betrayed him and he was forced to march

176

north and died in the final battle of what is now called the Third Servile War. Although there are legends he escaped and disappeared to live anonymously in the mountains of his native Thrace. I hope so.

We had the anchor up an hour before dawn, as we had a long way to go to our next stop halfway across the foot of Italy.

Our starboard navigation light, which had been okay when checked the previous evening had decided not to work. This was a very busy stretch of water and it was a bit of a risk sailing in the dark without one, but we were eager to get going. I could have tried to change the bulb, but it was a three-handed job while leaning over the pulpit in the dark, and the most likely outcome would be me dropping something vital overboard.

When as a youth commuting to and from university on a slow and smoky bus, I had once ploughed through an old second-hand copy of Charles Darwin's '*On the Origin of Species*' and for many years had been an unquestioning believer. However, recently I have been wondering. If it was all true why evolution has not yet produced three-handed sailors— and sometimes walking home at night I have realized that an extra leg would be handy also. Husbands can often call on a wife for an extra hand, but to do so often results in too much unsolicited advice and, a realisation you were doing it the wrong way in the first place!

Anyway, we headed off, hugging the shore and staying well out of the main shipping lane, while keeping a sharp lookout for unlit fisherman, lobster pots and nets. We had 180 kms to a fair-weather anchorage under Capo Rizzuto and for us that was a long day. There were a couple of small marinas along the way, but they were really too shallow for us, and the cruising guide mentioned robberies with aggravated violence and Calabrian Mafia smuggling routes, so we had decided not to visit.

We welcomed a gentle land breeze as the sun came up, and with the engine ticking over at 1300 rpm and the mainsail up we scooted along, admiring the coast and the gleaming white beaches, and olive groves around Melito di Porto Salvo as we breakfasted on bacon and egg rolls and mugs of coffee. The day brightened and with a steady hand I managed to change the navigation light without dropping anything. By late morning the breeze had freshened, and we had the genoa filling nicely and the motor switched off. Behind the beautiful coast the mountains were sprinkled with small stone and white-washed villages, and isolated farms.

By mid-afternoon we were well into the Gulf of Aquillace and the coast was now only a blue shadow along the horizon. The wind continued to strengthen from the northwest building a short choppy sea on our quarter. We reefed our sails and surged along, spray flying over the starboard deck as the waves rolled through. As

177

dusked started to settle we were very pleased to see the light on Cape Colonna off our bow and before darkness settled, we had the anchor buried in a sandy bottom behind the cape. Secure enough as long as there was no south in the wind and we were not impeding any Mafia business. Later the wind dropped out and a silvery moon lit our small bay. Not a sound other than the gentle lap of the water.

Up and away before sunrise, heading across the Gulf of Taranto for the small port of Santa Maria di Leuca on the tip of Italy's heel, about seventy nautical miles away—say ten hours. The port was still enjoying siesta when we arrived a bit before 3 pm and it was very crowded and there were no spare berths. However, we needed to top up with diesel and decided it was probably better to hang around and wait for the fuel wharf to open, rather than go away and anchor and have to come back.

Fuel berths, as I think I may have already mentioned can be nightmares, made worse by yachts such as ourselves hanging around waiting for service. Eventually it opened around 4 pm and after lots of milling about and shouting we were able to reverse in, top up and head out into the adjacent bay and anchor. Our nerves were a bit frazzled by this stage, but fortunately the sun was close enough to the horizon for normal routines to be observed immediately.

It was a quite exposed bay, but a beautiful one. Lined by the exotic and colourful buildings of the village, replete with crenulated turrets, domes, candy-striped brickwork, bell towers and promenades alive with lovely ochres and subtle pastels. A delightful mixture of Italian and Greek heritages. The hassles of the fuel wharf were soon forgotten, washed away by the golden beauty of the sunset, the aroma of seafood pasta from the galley and enough of the fine restorative Sicilian wine.

Perhaps the most famous visitor to this delightful village was Saint Peter, who called in here on his way to establish the Christian Church in Rome in the first century. But I imagine that just about anyone who was anybody, good and evil, from the first Phoenician mariners until the end of the age of galleys would have stopped in here, either before or after crossing the foot of Italy.

In the morning we rounded the southern tip of Italy and headed north along the coast, past Capo d'Otranto the most eastern point and into the harbour at the town of Otranto. There were swimmers enjoying the sandy beach overlooked by a jumble of old stone buildings.

We took our tender in and secured it in a small stone dinghy harbour at the southern end of the beach before setting off to explore the town and to stock up. We had not been ashore since Sicily and needed fresh vegetables and bread, and a sample of the local vino of course. The town was a delight, a beautifully landscaped esplanade, a cobbled old town, plenty of fresh produce from the surrounding fertile plains, inviting restaurants overlooking the anchorage and a happy cheerful throng of locals; all seemed to have relatives in Australia, surely, we must know Mario, Lorenzo or Gina in Melbourne etc etc.

In the twilight we came back in for a very enjoyable meal of fresh shrimps grilled over coals and a few glasses of fine Rosso di Cerignola, one of the many great wines of Apulia. Everyone was still happy, lots of laughter. Ro received several proposals of marriage, but, but there was still no knowledge of 'the man who invented red wine'.

There were strong northerlies the next day, so we did much the same again but added a visit to the museum and castle—culture had lost out to gastronomy the previous day. As with so many coastal villages of the Mediterranean it has had a hard and bloody history. After the Ottomans conquered Constantinople in 1453 their fleets began ranging further west, attacking European shipping and ravaging and pillaging the countryside. In 1480 Otranto was sacked by a fleet of Mohammed II, the citizens slaughtered or sold into slavery. Perhaps the young and beautiful were sent to the harem, or the young and strong to the ranks of the Janissaries – the sultan's elite troops. In 1537 our infamous corsair admiral Barbarossa, ravaged the town and in between there were countless lesser raids.

Our next stop was the famous old port of Brindisi. It was an important Greek city even before Roman times. Then it was linked to Rome by the Via Apia and this together with being the best port on the east coast, made it a major strategic hub of the Empire. Its importance had always made it a military target; it suffered during the Punic Wars, unfortunately took Pompey's side against Caesar, was captured by the Ostrogoths, recaptured by the Byzantines, taken by the Lombards, then the Saracens, then the Normans followed by the Venetians. Time Lapse Maps if you would like more detail.

It was probably always tough to get property insurance here.

Today it still has a somewhat unloved look. We took *Sea Dreams* into the inner harbour so that we could visit the end of the Via Apia and view the one remaining column marking the spot—there was once two, but one was stolen by the nearby city of Lecce, and the case has been before the Italian courts for 566 years. We decided we would come back in later on to celebrate the memory of the thousands and thousands of forgotten legionnaires who had embarked from here to fight in Greece or Asia, and those lucky ones who made it back.

However, shortly after returning to our boat we were visited by an officious naval officer who told us we were in a restricted area and to move on. The only sign of things naval was a rusting hulk of an old patrol boat which looked as it could have seen service in World War I, and a couple of slovenly sailors drinking with the locals in a nearby taverna. Oh well. We pulled up the anchor and took ourselves to the outer harbour where we anchored in a good spot off a modern marina.

We had just got ourselves settled when a lone German sailor, who we had never set eyes on, sailed very close under our stern and greeted us effusively as if he had surprisingly stumbled across a long-lost brother (and sister). We waved back politely, and he anchored nearby—really much too close for comfort. The next thing we knew there was knocking on the hull, and there was our lone sailor come for drinks—but bringing no wine. Oh well. We asked him onboard for a glass, but by the time we were starving, and Ro was clanging a few pots in the galley he had shown no signs of leaving. We made a half-hearted offer of dinner which he accepted before we had gotten the words out of our mouths. Eventually, after what seem a very long night and many bottles of wine, we managed to lever him into his dinghy and send him off.

It was only later that we realised how invaluable his very hard to understand reminiscences about his seven years in the Croatian islands, had been. He had marked our charts with his favourite places, and that proved very helpful.

Nonetheless, in the morning we were away very early, well before an unexpected breakfast guest could arrive. The day's destination was the industrial port of Bari about sixty miles north, where late in the afternoon we anchored in a concrete-encased outer harbor. We stayed on board, and after a somewhat noisy and restless night were away with the first light of a grey dull dawn.

Northwest along the coast again. The northerly wind was enough on our quarter for us to use the mainsail with the engine on low revs and we made good time along a flat and unremarkable coastline. There were a few small ports along the way, but none looked enticing enough for us to explore, and we wanted to make the most of the wind. We made good time again and reached our planned stop-over at Manfredonia, on the base of the Gargano Peninsula well before dusk.

We had intended to clear Customs and Police here before crossing over the Adriatic to Croatia. However, neither organisation could be bothered with us, and as there was not enough room to anchor in the harbour we kept going. We were now under the lee of the Gargano Peninsula which thrusts eastward into the Adriatic and gives some protection from the predominantly northerly summer winds. An hour or so later we came to an indentation in the coast, certainly not a bay, but as the breeze had now died out it seemed okay for the night.

It was a pretty stretch of the coast, hilly, with forests and vineyards and some pleasant-looking resorts along the beach front. All very peaceful until about 10 pm when a nightclub sprang to life, sending high voltage music, shatteringly loud across the water. A disturbed night until towards dawn when the music eventually stopped, but the raucous revellers spread down to the water's edge. It was time to go in any case.

We had about eighty miles to our entry point into Croatia, the small island of Lastovo.

Once we were underway, we got into our normal routine. Ro made some coffee then retired for a further nap, leaving me to enjoy the supreme beauty of the sunrise. The flush of pink in the eastern sky, the golden orb edging over the horizon, pale blue washing away the grey of the sky, the ocean now sparkling blue as a land breeze ruffled the water, the greens and ochres of the coastline growing richer, the first birds circling on the wind. The mainsail out and the genoa set.

About 8 am Ro reappeared with more coffee and, as it was going be a long day, a bacon—really prosciutto—and egg roll. I handed over the helm and left her to it while I had a nap on the leeward cockpit bench.

It became another perfect day. A clear sky and a fifteen knot north-westerly blowing straight down the Adriatic, giving us a lovely broad reach. The breeze picked up a bit and in the early afternoon Lastovo Island began to emerge over the horizon. As we grew nearer its nature emerged. Dense pine forests clothing rocky hills, sparkling waves breaking on the rugged shore. Wrapped in all the mystery of a new landfall.

~ THE ADRIATIC SEA 2009 ~

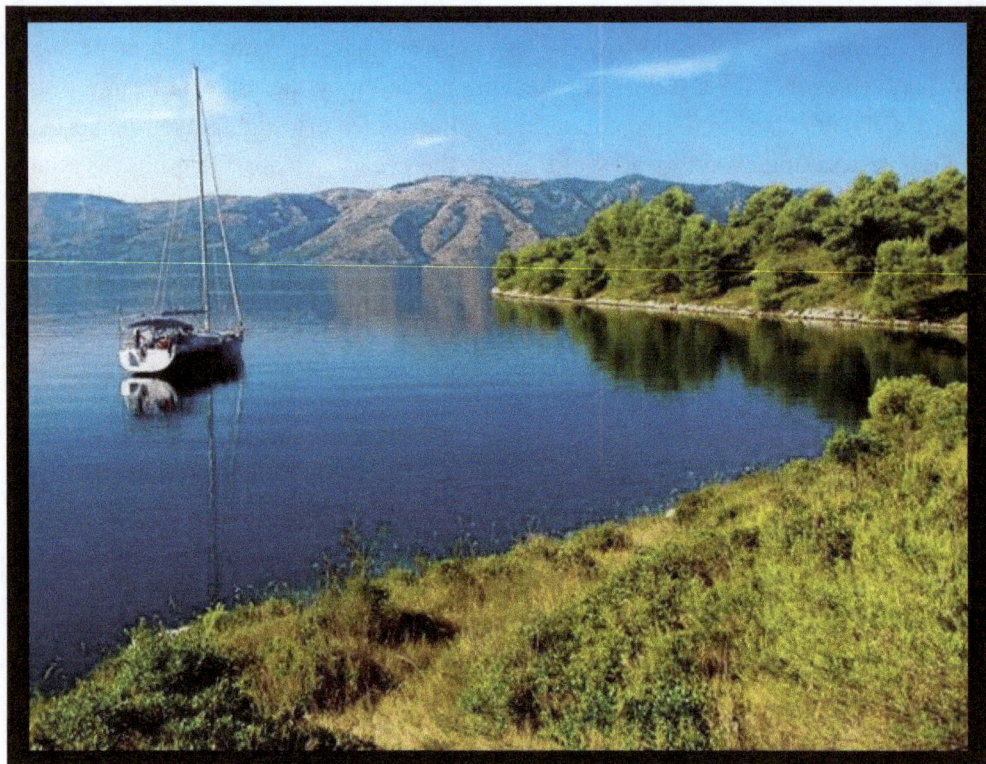

Sea Dreams near Stari Grad - Croatia

As we neared the Croatian island of Lastovo we sailed close to a strongly swimming loggerhead turtle. Its eyes were fixed determinedly ahead, but it still gave us a suspicious glance as we wished it good afternoon. The village of Ubli was in the large almost land-locked bay of Velji Lago, which was lined with pines and gave us protection from all winds.

It was mid-afternoon and there was not a great deal going on in Ubli. In fact, not a soul was visible. There were a few stone wharves with a couple of old wooden dinghies moored alongside, secured by weed-covered lines. A tired old dog tottered stiffly to the end of one jetty and fixed us with an indifferent stare. A Croatian flag fluttered above a dilapidated stone building, which we presumed was where we would find officialdom, and not far away was what appeared to be a small market.

We launched the tender, gathered our passports and ship's papers and set off to check in. Customs was in the dilapidated building beneath the flag, but the official sent us off to check with the harbourmaster and police first. We walked back around the harbour to the nondescript police station where a genial giant checked our passports and directed us to the harbourmaster where we paid the various taxes required to cruise in Croatia, then back to customs.

Customs now informed us we would have to bring *Sea Dreams* into the Customs Wharf. This we did and returned with our papers, which he duly stamped after we had paid some more fees. He then waived us off without coming anywhere near the yacht. But he ordered us to clear from the wharf before we did any shopping, so that he could bring in the next yacht that he would not look at. Presumably!

Anyway, it was all pretty painless, and we were free to go where we pleased for three months. Then we would have to leave the country for one night—the yacht could stay—and then be okay for a further three months.

We re-anchored and came back to investigate the town, replenish our perishables and most importantly check out the local wine. We contemplated the town's most important historical site, the well cared for foundations of the Basilica of St Peter, which was erected in the fifth or sixth century, and then ambled to the market. There was a delicious arrangement of local fruit and vegetables from the fertile gardens in the centre of the island, some local frozen fish and an adequate display of Croatian wine, including a local red, Plavic Mali and a golden-coloured local white, Rukatac-Saric.

The first Greek settlers started arriving in Croatia around the 7th century BCE and brought with them their wines and their vines. So, there is a long and valued viticultural tradition with many of the ancient varieties still popular today and thriving in the many micro-climates and diverse topography of the country.

The Romans arrived some centuries later and after a long period of bitter warfare the province of Illyricum was formally proclaimed in 35 BCE. Ubli was an important centre during the Roman period, for much the same reason we had come this way; it was a convenient stop-over between Italy and the Balkans. Having a large number of Roman legionnaires and sailors passing through would naturally have been very good for the wine industry on the island.

We loaded up our 'granny' trolley with our purchases and headed back to the boat, put the white wine in the freezer, up anchored and motored around the corner to a small landlocked bay that opened off Velji Lago, and anchored securely on a nice muddy bottom. It had been a long day. But what a beautiful safe place to have reached. A dense pine forest lined the shore, the only sign of man was some ancient ruins hiding in the shrubbery. The wind had dropped out completely and the water was now a mirror gleaming with the golds and dark emerald greens of the sunset. The sky was a dark mauve flecked with some lazy fluffs of gleaming white cloud.

We contemplated the serenity and de-corked a now nicely chilled bottle of Rukatac-Saric which proved to be excellent and contemplated the serenity some more. Our 'Sailing Directions' for Croatia details 777 anchorages, and there are plenty more which have not been included. More than enough for a lifetime, but unfortunately our plans only gave us two years.

After a second peaceful night we motored leisurely through the calm waters and deserted bays on the western shore of Lastovo and inspected the beautiful bay and village of Mali Lago-Lastovo. When the wind started to come up we crept through the narrow entrance into the small bay of Zaklopatica enclosed within steep rocky hills. The foreshore was lined with some old stone buildings in various states of repair, a hotel, a fishmonger with some fishing boats moored in front and a few tavernas (*konobas*). It was warm, protected from the wind and the water was clear over a sandy bottom.

We went ashore for a late lunch at a *konoba* called the *Augusta Insula*, where we dined on grilled squid and experienced the delights of our first Croatian '*Konoba*'. Over the next two years we came to really love Croatia—and much of the love grew while we dined, wined, gossiped and laughed while lounging at konoba tables overlooking stunningly beautiful and isolated bays. Without fail we were welcomed into the heart of these small family businesses, treated as friends and served fine food and wine. There were also many good restaurants in the villages and cities, but for us the memories we savour most are those from the small rustic stone and timber konobas in the scattered islands and remote bays.

After lunch we meandered around the quay, examining the old stone buildings until we came to the fishmongers. We were amazed and delighted to find a heap of freshly caught crayfish at prices that even such an infamous skinflint as myself was

184

more than happy with. We bought dinner and a supply for the freezer. After a couple of days, we were thinking we could happily spend the whole of summer here eating crays; falling in love with where we were was to become a habit. But our curiosity of what lay ahead drove us on, a little distance anyway. Around the coast a bit was the hidden harbour of Skrivena Luka.

We had only been anchored in the middle of this stunning inner bay for a few minutes when we received a visitor. Robert, the proprietor of the *Konoba Porot* and a resident of Melbourne during the Australian summer, had seen our flag and insisted that we dine with him that night. An invitation we were very happy to accept, and as the sun edged towards the mountains—very late sunsets at this time of year—we were sampling more Lastovo white while meeting some of Robert's family. His grandmother who supervised the garden and vineyard, from which would come the essentials of our feast. His mother the head chef, cheesemaker and baker. His younger brother, the fisherman, who provided the freshly caught anchovies and scarfish and the youngest brother the goatherd, waiter and water-taxi operator —if required by patrons who had become too cheerful to row. Robert was of course the host, winemaker and floor show.

There was no menu and no prices which, because of my miserly nature and particularly after our experience with Lenny in Sardinia, makes me a bit nervous. But in due course we were served up a feast, had a hilarious night and were pleasantly surprised by the bill.

You would like to know how the chef prepared the scarfish?

Stuff the fish with thyme, rosemary, parsley. Sautee granny's half-cooked chopped potatoes, diced tomatoes, some peppers, olives, capers and transfer to a baking dish. Lay the fish on top. Add a cup of broth, bake in a wood fired oven, basting periodically. Granny's fresh salad and Mum's cheese and crusty bread on the side. It was impossible to get away without a shot of Sljiovica— a plum liqueur much favoured by Croatians—or a homemade Limoncello, and in the end thought it polite to try both.

In the hot Mediterranean summers, our traditional attitudes to wine were changing, changing to such an extent that many of my old friends, mostly the old retired colonels and brigadiers who are quite insufferable wine snobs regard me as something of a wine drinking pariah.

It had started in Gruissan in France, where we discovered that the locals were quite happy to fill up plastic bottles of the current vintage from the local 'cave' for a couple of euros, and that this new wine was actually fresh and very enjoyable. In Spain we found how delightful the chilled and fruity Sangria could be and soon we preferred

185

our reds chilled also. The Italians have always watered their wine. Julius Caesar did not drink anything else.

But it was not until we arrived in Croatia, where watered wine actually has names, *gemist* and *bevanda* that we started to rub shoulders with drinkers who add water as a matter of course. So, soon we were chilling our reds as well as our whites and we were adding water, and the corruption was almost complete when we found we really enjoyed some ice blocks as well. Ro generally likes a dry white, and the final degradation came when I discovered a slice of lemon might do the trick. And sometimes I don't mind a fruity glass or two— well why not add your own fruit anyway, the Spaniards are not the only ones allowed to make Sangria.

Now I have tried to explain this to those crusty old colonels and brigadiers, but all I get are slowly shaking heads.

We caught a small bus into the town of Lastovo located in a verdant valley in the north of the island. It is home to around three hundred mostly mature-ish citizens, living in picturesque stone cottages surrounded by lush gardens and vineyards. If you are looking for a great spot to escape the world, perhaps with a stone cottage to do up, you should think seriously about here. Although you should realise that Croatians can be a bit prickly about foreigners buying up the best real estate. In one little town on the mainland we became friendly with a Croatian merchant marine captain who had a holiday home there. It was in a region not too far from the Bosnian border and there were quite a few burnt out cottages in the area.

'Were these burned during the war?' we had asked.

'No,' he replied with a shrug. 'Just the locals keeping prices down.'

This was well before they joined the EU so things may well have changed. Although in Sardinia, Corsica and Crete there can be problems, and in Greece, the tangled web of the law and property rights can make problems which are even more annoying than having your house burnt down.

And of course, in Spain it may just be demolished if building regulations have been broken.

Onwards. We had to make our rendezvous with our daughter, Charlotte and family, Charlotte last seen on *Sea Dreams* in northern Italy.

Mljet is said to be one of the most beautiful islands in the Mediterranean. It is also reputed to be the love nest of the beautiful Calypso, the seductive daughter of the god Poseidon, who bewitched Odysseus on his voyage home from the Trojan War and held him captive for seven years.

Whether it was Mljet or not, who really knows? But Homer's description of

186

the island pretty well captures today's beauty:

'Thick luxuriant woods grew round the cave, alders, and black poplars, pungent cypress too, and there, birds roosted, folding their long wings, owls and hawks and the spread beaked ravens of the sea, black skimmers who make their living off the waves. And round the mouth of the cavern trailed a vine laden with clusters, bursting with ripe grapes. Four springs in a row, bubbling clear and cold, running side by side, took channels left and right. Soft meadows were starred with violets, lush with beds of parsley. Why even a deathless god who came upon that place would gaze in wonder, heart entranced with pleasure.'

By the time we were close to the rocky foreshore and the thickly forested slopes of the island, the sea breeze was well and truly blowing. The outlying reefs were alive with dancing white waves and misted with spray as they dashed themselves on the rocks. It was quite difficult to pick our way through the swirling water of the channel and we would have been on the rocks in an instant if the motor decided to play up. We breathed a sigh of relief as the narrow passage opened into a protective cove, although the wind still gusted through the rigging at around twenty-five knots. We anchored close as possible to the protected shore, the anchor set firmly with fifty metres of chain pulled taut as a steel rod.

I sat for a while in the bow with my hand on the anchor chain testing for any anchor drag, my thoughts captured by our surroundings. The shore was lined with a luxuriant forest, dense and green, no sign of man. The water was clear and sparkling with a few sweeping gulls. One other yacht within sight. Homer's words were still not far from the mark.

Lost in my contemplation I was surprised when a motor launch passed close by our bow. It was crewed by a beautiful young woman standing at the helm who waved cheerily to me as she went by. Except for a floppy white hat, she was as naked as the day she was born—another Calypso? Was Poseidon concealed in the trees laughing at my amazement?

In the morning we motored around the coast for a few miles to Luka Polace Mljet. Here was an even finer harbour, with any number of anchorages in the forested coves and channels of the close-by islands. Along one shore were a number of old stone buildings, some *konobas* with tables spilling onto the quay and a couple of markets nestled below the ruins of an old castle. By nightfall we had the company of about twenty yachts, including a few large gullets of Turkish origin full of Danes and Germans having a great time, even before going ashore to the *konobas* and coming back even happier.

Shortly after midnight the merriment was extinguished by the unheralded arrival of a Bora, the much-feared katabatic wind of the northern Adriatic. These winds are created by cold air falling from the high ranges and are fiercest as they hit the coastal waters below the mountains, but they still blow strongly well out to sea. They are at their worst in winter. In December 1998 a wind speed of 120 knots was recorded near Zadar and, in 2003 near the Sveti Rok Tunnel 150 knots was recorded. Seven metre waves can be formed, fish are literally blown out of the water and at sea level the salty spray makes it almost impossible to breathe.

In summer winds over 60 knots are rare. But it is still a very unpleasant experience to be surprised by such a wind during the night, and we religiously anchored with good protection between us and the east, and to avoid the most notorious areas.

There was pandemonium for an hour or so. Inevitably some yachts dragged their anchors and entangled themselves in their neighbour's chain, leading to much shouting, cursing and accusation in fifteen different languages.

When yachts arrive to anchor, they invariably drop their anchor while facing into the wind. For yachts arriving at different times during the day the wind may be blowing from different directions, so when a strong wind arrives from yet another direction yachts can swing in different dangerous arcs. It is more complicated if you are anchoring and there is no wind, because yachts still drift around, and it is impossible to know where their anchors are unless they are pointed out to you. Also, if an anchor is 'dug in' for say, a northerly wind and a strong easterly arrives, there is every chance the anchor will be wrenched out and will have to reset before it holds again.

After an hour or so the *Bora* passed and gradually peace reclaimed the bay. We thanked the wind god Aeolus, for sparing us and retired for a short nap before dawn.

In due course we idled along the coast of Mljet to another very pretty bay, Luka Prozurska, and picked up one of the *Konoba Barba's* moorings. The general understanding in Croatia is that the mooring, or even a jetty, will be free of charge provided that you eat at the *konoba,* a great arrangement which we often took advantage of. However, in many popular spots you do have to pay just for a mooring. After our recent brush with a *Bora* I was a bit apprehensive about just how protected we would be, but I was assured by the proprietor when he came to present his menu, that the *Bora* would be no worry here.

As far as winds are concerned in the Med, there is no substitute for the vast pool of local knowledge that has been acquired over many centuries. Cities, villages and even isolated *konobas* and villas, have grown up in locations which over the centuries have been found to be fit for purpose. The factors driving the wind here are different from those in Australia, where the winds are formed and shaped by high and low-pressure systems rotating over the great southern oceans, somewhat moderated by the land and sea breezes of a relatively flat land mass. The main drivers of the summer winds of the Mediterranean are more stable. Large high systems form over the high mountains of Europe and Asia, and large low-pressure systems form in the warm waters of the Mediterranean and the Red Sea. Winds naturally flow from the highs to the lows and are more regular in direction and importantly, are then channelled and bent by the mountains and the high islands in a way that repeats itself year, after year after year.

Which of course doesn't mean that there are no catastrophic unpredictable winds generated by storm systems moving in from the Atlantic. There are, indeed, otherwise the old gods of the wind would never have gotten into the business of looking after sailors.

Our dinner of local scampi grilled over a wood fire was served by Barba's delightful eleven-year old son, who was fluent in English— he could do Australian— Italian, Spanish, German, Dutch, and of course Croatian. In the morning we walked across a small isthmus separating us from the larger half of the bay and explored the small quay, vowed to return when we had more time. We set off to visit a few special places before finding our rendezvous on the mainland coast with Charlotte and family, passing a bay just around the corner which was to become one of our favourite haunts.

Heading south towards Montenegro we loitered at Sipan and Lopud_islands. Both are beautiful with charming villages and secure anchorages framed by rocky headlands and thickly forested shorelines. There are rarely currents or undertows in the Mediterranean. Apart from making swimming much safer this helps keep the water very clear as there is nothing stirring things up. From the middle of May until September the water temperature is bliss, and very importantly for those like me who have grown up with a pathological dread of White Pointers, there are virtually no sharks. And none that are likely to dine on humans. This, and a naturally imposed limit on the catch of fish in winter, encourages a profusion of small fish, so swimming and snorkelling is a joy almost every day.

We were close to the coast now with the dramatic coastal mountains lining the eastern sky as we neared the Gulf of Kotor and Montenegro. The gulf is really a series of quite thin inter-connecting basins, similar in this respect to the marvellous waterways at Port Davey in Tasmania. It is certainly one of the most dramatic harbours in the world, tightly lined by high mountains, narrow-indented shores sprinkled with picturesque and ancient villages. In winter the mountains are covered

189

in snow, but in the height of summer it all had a very sub-tropical feel with profusions of cascading flowers and palm trees. After clearing Customs we anchored off the old town of Herceg Novi and went ashore to have a stroll around and dinner at a restaurant where we could keep an eye on *Sea Dreams*. There have been settlements around the Gulf at least since Illyrian times, and all the great Mediterranean powers realised that they could not ignore such a great and very defensible harbour halfway up the Adriatic. There are still a lot of fine-looking old villas and imposing churches and castles from the time it was a wealthy and important strategic centre. Unfortunately, there are a number of cement boxes of the Stalinist School of Architecture that sit rudely amongst the noble Venetian, Italianate and Art Deco gems.

After we got back my sleep was broken by thunder rolling around the surrounding mountains and the flickering of jagged lightning, and I was told to get out of bed and make sure all was okay. The rain bucketed down for most of the night, but in the morning the skies were clear again, and the air as fresh as the crispest day of spring.

In the morning we motored past the Church of Our Lady of the Rocks built on an artificial island in the second basin, which was created by sinking old and captured boats filled with rocks— and by some accounts, also bodies. Another legend is that the island was formed by returning sailors throwing a rock into the water at this spot in thanks for a safe homecoming. In any case the church was built around 1452, and even to this day at sunset on July 22 the locals throw rocks from their boats to widen the island.

At the top of the third basin is the beautiful old town of Kotor with its massive stone stronghold, and in the dangerous past, a chain across the narrows leading into the basin. In Venetian times it was one of their most important outposts, home to one of their fleets and a very wealthy city. These days it is impossible to sit on a yacht at the quay overlooked by the majestic Mount Lovcen, which soars seventeen hundred and fifty metres above the town, and not be awed by the beauty of the town and the immensity of its surrounds. But as an old infantry officer I could not help thinking what a bastard it would be to haul my pack and myself to the top of the immense crag.

It's one of those spots where people have lived since the earliest times, before the Greeks, and Romans discovered how marvellous it was. The Emperor Justinian built a fortress above the town in 535 CE. The Bulgarians, Serbs and Hungarians each controlled it at times before Venice took over in 1420. They ruled until 1797 having fought off the Ottomans a couple of times.

These days it is a UNESCO World Heritage site and a joy to visit. Lots of grand churches, a lovely Venetian ambience and the nostalgia of the old fortifications and what they meant. We naturally tried the local wine and some very tasty boar and fish stews, before our time ran out and we headed back to Croatia. We were planning to do an inland road trip at the end of the sailing season, and we knew we would have to come back to the wild mountains of Montenegro.

Charlotte and Stephen had leased a 16th century stone villa in a small inlet a dozen miles north of the ancient city of Dubrovnik which in the Middle Ages was one of the great powers of the Mediterranean, with a fleet only surpassed by Venice. Now, it is one of Europe's iconic destinations. The old city is a charming memory of another age, nestled within its great stone walls. It was quite badly damaged by the Yugoslav People's Army during the Croatian War of Independence 1991-1992. Artillery sited on the coastal mountains bombarded the city until they were driven off by the local forces—although the truth of the matter is that it was accomplished almost singlehandedly by the gregarious taxi driver who took us there! Most of the scars have been repaired and to wander through streets then watch the sunset from the ramparts, preferably while enjoying a local Vranac red wine or two, will leave memories for life.

Within sight to the south is the island where Richard the Lionheart, the King of England, was shipwrecked on the way home from the Crusades. Richard was a great and chivalrous warrior who had fought bravely, made friends with his opposing number the almost equally famous An-Nasir Salah ad-Din Yusuf ibn Ayyub better known as Saladin, and had negotiated a respectable treaty. But despite this he did have a really great talent for making enemies.

He and the King of France Philip II detested each other, and their mutual distrust was such that before embarking for the Crusade they both swore a papal oath that one would not return before the other, in case one returned and attacked the lands of the other. Philip broke this oath and returned early, which meant that when Richard eventually headed home, he could not pass through France without fearing for his life. At the siege of Acre Richard had mortally offended Leopold the Duke of Austria, a vassal of the Holy Roman Emperor. Richard had thrown Leopold's banner off the walls as he thought it was not fit to fly beside his own. So, most of the German lands were also a no-go area for him. As were most of the Italian states, and the islands Corfu and Sicily.

Eventually he attempted to make his way home disguised as a Knight Templar, travelling by way of the Adriatic Sea and then by horse over the Alps. He survived the shipwreck near Dubrovnik, but when he was close to Vienna he was recognised and imprisoned by Leopold on the charge of having arranged the murder of his cousin.

After almost a year he was ransomed for the astronomical sum of fifty tons of silver, which was about three times the annual income of the English crown and around thirty-two million dollars in today's money. I think that in our age of billionaires, perhaps fifty tons of silver has a better ring to it. Part of the reason the price was so high was that there were two other bidders. Philip of France and Richard's brother John both wanted him dead or incarcerated. Richard was a lucky man to escape with his life, but not long after he was killed fighting in France.

On the way we checked out the harbour at Slano just north of Brsecine, and found a great base for exploring this part of the coast. It was almost enclosed, there was plenty of anchoring room with a good muddy bottom, a small town with a market, a choice of *konobas* and a bus service to Dubrovnik. There was also a low-key resort near where we liked to anchor, and whenever we came back to this spot we tended to eat on the terrace with a good view over the bay and our yacht. We had lots of memorable dishes. A favourite was fish stuffed with herbs and softened dates and cooked over coals— could be wrapped in foil—and there were plenty of fresh mussels cooked in a variety of broths: cheese, mustard, wine.

When Charlotte and family arrived we decided to moor in the tiny harbour at Brsecine in front of their villa. There was not enough water at the small jetty for us to tie alongside nor enough room to anchor, but there was a large cement mooring block on the bottom with an embedded iron ring. The boys dived down and passed one of our mooring lines through the ring, and on the calm and sunny morning all looked perfectly secure.

However, one of the gods, probably Aeolus, but it could have been one of his untrusty off-siders must have been watching. The next night was calm until around 9 pm when a few gentle breezes wafted down the hill behind the villa and stirred the leaves of the lemon tree in the courtyard, below which we had finished dinner and had begun the first round of the Croatian World Texas Hold 'em Poker Championships with the family.

In the land of the *Bora*, and plenty of other places for that matter, I am always nervous when we are away from the yacht at night and it is anchored or moored as it was now and, the breeze was enough to raise the hackles on the back of my neck. Amid accusations of poor sportsmanship and nervousness and both, Ro and I grabbed our things, dumped them into the dinghy and got back on board in a hurry.

By that time the wafts had become gusts and I was having second thoughts about our mooring line through the rusty ring on the cement block, which in fact had quite sharp edges. We were blowing back towards the old stone jetty and if the line broke, we would be on the rocks in a nanosecond.

The gusts were blowing stronger and I could hear bloody Aeolus cackling in the hills above us. Go into the dark or stay? If the wind came up much more, we would not be able to go at all. On with the engine, Ro at the helm edging forward until I could free the line, the wind was starting to roar now. The line came free, more throttle as she swung the helm over, fingers crossed. Out through the gap we went, between the shore and the jetty.

Now the gusts were laying us over, even without the sails up, as we headed through the black night—and that bloody navigation light wasn't working again—to Slano and the safety of its lovely muddy bottom, where nothing would drag our great Spade anchor or break our 12mm chain. Would we have been safe on our mooring in Brsecine? If there was chain between the cement block and the boat all would have been well, but rope through a rusty ring?

Our friend, the merchant marine captain, opined that all would have been well. But I wondered if it was such a good spot why no locals had taken advantage of the unused cement block, and it was not the only one available either.

One of the striking features of the coast and islands of Croatia are the old free stone walls that once marked out the gardens, groves and vineyards of times long, long ago. What are now otherwise bare hills, are crisscrossed with a lattice work of walls which were once the markers of men's labour, their dreams and their wealth. The walls were all built by toil, the laborious collection of rock— perhaps with the help of a donkey—from the fields, day after day, year after year, century after century. So much rock that in places there was too much just to make the walls, and it was heaped in cubist structures that look from a distance to be small castles.

We often walked amongst these empty fields, many with ruined cottages or perhaps a villa, and it was hard not to come back on board without some melancholy thoughts about the transient nature of life. There are so, so many places that were once alive, full of hope, love and expectations and are now only empty decaying relics; the creators and their progeny now all long forgotten.

Now that we had our full crew on board we visited the nearby islands and Mali Ston where formidable fortifications were built across the Peljesac Peninsula to create a haven from Ottoman marauders. For centuries the villages along this coast were preyed upon by Muslim Corsairs and raiders coming westwards across the Balkans, but thankfully these days the area is much more famous for its red wines and oysters. The sailing was magnificent, afternoon sea breezes of twenty knots, clear skies and sparkling blue water. The sun was warm, the twilights cool and peaceful as the breeze dropped out, though I could not help keeping a suspicious eye on the high coastal ranges from whence we could be assaulted by a screaming *Bora*.

On the island of Sipan the 'Island of Eagles' we had a wonderful meal sitting within the stone walls surrounding the remains of an old tower built in 1577. Near the small harbour we were able to stock up on fresh bream, local figs, olives, almonds, tomatoes and citrus fruit and a few bottles of the local drop.

In due course we returned to Slano and Charlotte, Stephen and little Ferdi departed leaving us with Hubie and Rufus. The next day we picked up Ro's nephew, Andrew Rosewarne, with his beautiful Welsh wife Jane and their daughters, Sian and Catrin.

It was time to head north. We had a night in the beautiful anchorage of Luka Polace on Mljet on the way and then anchored near a large monastery on the south side of Badija Island in the Kanal Jezevica. In the late afternoon the water was delicious, and we all swam ashore to explore the pebble beach shaded by lofty pines and the monastery. It had been built by Franciscan monks in the late 14th century and is a fine representation of the style known as Dalmation Gothic. The monks are still in charge although they were evicted for a period during the communist era. They did not seem to mind the northern European naturalists enjoying their foreshore.

We returned to our boat to enjoy the twilight and the views to the great rocky mountains on the mainland, while the children competed at swimming and diving and later singing, dancing and reciting poetry in the first heat of 'Croatia's Got Talent'. After which we had another round of Texas Hold 'em and finally retired to bed utterly exhausted. The kids were all bunked down in the cockpit and it seemed to be nearly dawn before they stopped chattering and went to sleep. In the morning they were very hard to get out of bed.

Next on the itinerary was a visit to another of the Adriatic's jewels, the nearby medieval walled city of Korkula. It sits on a peninsula looking across the channel to the mountains. From a distance it could be a fairy tale village: red-roofed sun-bleached stone houses, walls and round turrets overlooked by the high spire of the fourteenth century Cathedral of St. Mark. It was built at around the same time that the great adventurer Marco Polo was born in a house that still stands, some three thousand years later. Legend has it that the town was founded by the Trojan hero, Antenor, after the fall of Troy. There is a quay and a small harbour, and it is all surrounded by beautiful clear turquoise water.

It was at the lovely old fortified port of Kotor that we first started to really appreciate the importance of the Venetian Empire to both the Mediterranean and to Western society. We had visited Venice a few times in the past, but I must admit that I had not looked beyond the marvels of the actual city itself. Perhaps understandably enough, as it is a unique and wonderful place, one of the great cities of the world for over a thousand years. One of the oldest and longest running democracy on earth, full of wonders of every kind, mother to an endless parade of historical greats in every field of endeavour.

But here at Korkula, was another of the many of the fortified hubs of the Venetian Empire that had dominated the Adriatic and Eastern Mediterranean for hundreds of years. In general, the Venetians were not interested in holding vast swathes of countryside— Crete was an exception—as they realised, they did not have the manpower to do so. Trade was their game—bringing the riches of the east to Europe and controlling the sea lanes over which they came. To do this they needed a powerful navy and fortified harbours where their trading ships could find sanctuary and from which their navy could patrol the seas. In these waters you are never more than around 100 kms—roughly a day's travel for a Venetian galley—from one of these still great and imposing fortresses, poignant reminders of the past, each with their own fascinating stories.

Venetian trade brought immense wealth to Europe: silks, spices, herbs, rice and other exotic foods, gold, precious jewels and pearls. Riches flooded into Venice and created the marvellous treasures, the palaces and cathedrals that still adorn the city, and financed her great fleets and the mighty Arsenal that built the ships. At full production the assembly line at the Arsenal could launch a fully equipped galley every day. In the city archives there is an amazing account of a sixty-ton galley being assembled from the keel up and launched during the time from seating visiting guests of honour at a state banquet to when they arose on their now unsteady legs. There were no unions to slow things down in Venice.

At the Battle of Curzola fought near the island in 1298, a fleet of one hundred Venetian galleys was nearly wiped out by a Genoan fleet and Marco Polo was taken prisoner. While in prison in Genoa he began writing the story of his travels to the court of the great Mongol lord and grandson of Genghis, Kublai Khan. A story that still enchants today.

It is easy to overlook how long and deep the relationship between the West and China has been. Asia first appeared on Greek maps in the 6th century BCE, and Alexander walked to India in 326 BCE. The Silk Road dates from Roman times and there are a number of suggestions of Roman expeditions towards the Chinese border. Christian missionaries were sent to China in 638 CE. The advances in science and technology during the Song Dynasty, 960-1279 CE were truly amazing and far ahead of the West. Water clocks, gunpowder, metalwork, firearms, the awareness of the existence of multiple galaxies, geological time, the nature of time and even soccer; the list goes on and on.

Venice and Europe were not only enriched by trade. The connection to the technologically advanced and sophisticated China brought ideas as well as the actual technology. Was it a coincidence that the European Renaissance began to bloom as trade with the east flourished? Was it a coincidence that some of the marvellous 'inventions' depicted in the sketches of Leonardo da Vinci were of technologies that had existed for centuries in China?

The link was not only the overland Silk Roads.

Chinese fleets had been following the monsoonal trading routes to India, through the Red Sea to Egypt for hundreds of years. For many years up until around the ninth century CE there was a canal from the Red Sea to the Nile River. It was first mentioned by Herodotus as dating from the 5th century BCE, and by Aristotle in the 4th century BCE. According to Strabo, in the 1st century BCE the canal was forty-six metres in width, wide enough to accommodate large ships, an opinion supported by Pliny in his Natural History. It is hard not to be entranced with the mysteries of the past as you lean on an old stone battlement and look out over the glimmering water and ancient mountains.

All too soon it was time for the Welsh choir to depart, and with only Hubert and Rufus as co-skippers we continued on our way towards Split where they were to be delivered back to their parents. Our route was along the Peljeski Kanal, the rugged mainland mountains on our right and the verdant shore of Korkula to our left.

We had not gone far when the roiling black clouds of a very ominous thunderstorm swept over the mountains and down the channel towards us. We hurriedly furled the sails and started the motor as we began to be buffeted by strong squalls, lightning and horizontal rain. There was a snug-looking cove on the nearby coast of the island, and we scuttled towards it, edging as close to the protected shore as we could. We dropped our mighty spade anchor and felt it dig in as the wind swept us backwards. Relative peace returned. The wind still howled overhead, and the rain drenched us, but we were out of the worst of it and in a good spot. The anchor held firm.

An hour later it was over, and by mid-afternoon we were ensconced behind Mala Kneza, a small island near the end of the channel. It turned out to be the sort of island we are always dreaming of owning. There was only one small stone cottage backed into a low knoll and surrounded by trees. It overlooked the placid water of our almost enclosed anchorage and the beautiful distant views. In front was a wooden dinghy with fishing nets drying on an old stone jetty. At dusk a small plume of smoke rose from the cottage's chimney and we could smell the aroma of fish grilling over a wooden fire. Shortly afterwards the soft glow of an oil lamp lit the vine covered

196

terrace. Silence, stars peeping through the inky sky, the loom of the rising moon. A lovely recluse, beyond care and worry.

But time was rushing by and our rendezvous with our crew's parents was approaching. A day's leisurely sail took us to the lovely town of Hvar on the western side of Hvar island. It was developed by the Venetians and is still protected by the great fortress they built overlooking the harbour. Today it is a fashionable place, thronged in summer by beautiful people enjoying the ambience, the fashionable shops and fine dining. Just the place to be when the most important birthday of the year was fast approaching—I could detect the gleam in Ro's eyes as we strolled along the jewellery shops in the boulevard.

Mooring in the harbour had been a bit traumatic. It is quite small; the old Venetians really only needed a place where they could tie up alongside, rather than a large body of water to anchor in. It was also open to the south and the afternoon sea-breeze, really not a great anchorage at all.

There was not enough room to actually anchor, all yachts had to pick up a mooring buoy and take a long stern-line ashore. We had done this successfully, which generally involves a bit of shouting at each other and were relaxing over a cup of strong coffee, when a French yacht pulled alongside and with no 'how do you do' tied up to us. Now, this is common along quays and jetties, and often schools of charter boats which arrive and leave together may do it in protected bays. But generally, a buoy is a one-boat thing—you pick it up and it is yours, it is designed to take only one boat.

Now we could not leave without casting the Frenchman adrift.

However, we were happy to go along with whatever the local custom was. We shrugged and half-smiled at our new neighbours, who during the whole proceedings had carried on as if *Sea Dreams* was some public convenience provided for their use.

Later, another yacht with a load of happy Italians tied on our other side and we were well and truly prisoners of our neighbours. It would be pandemonium if a *bora* blew in during the night. In ten years sailing in the Med there was only one other case where we moored up alongside another yacht on a single buoy. A few days later at another anchorage we invited a young Italian couple, who had been up and down a string of moorings and were looking lost and forlorn, to join us—but that was it.

I think because there is no other close anchorage to Hvar and visitors are so desperate to go ashore, normal practices go out the door. During our two years in Croatia we came back a number of times with friends and found it best to anchor well away in a quiet corner of the Clementi Islands and take a high-speed water taxi in or anchor on the other side of the island and come across by car.

But it was always a joy to stroll through the town, vibrant with visitors from all over the world and full of the things that normally attract people in search of a Shangri La. Expensive boutiques and jewellery, lovely old buildings, marbled streets, the old fortress, and of course good eating. I saw recently that the town had obtained its first Michelin rating, but the food was pretty extraordinary in 2009 and certainly not so cripplingly expensive as that place Lenny found in the Maddalenas. The hills behind the town are patchworked with the old stone walls, which made me maudlin, thinking of all the work and love that went into making the terraces that in the end are only ruins. The hardness of history. The fields are still alive with herbs growing wild and the views breathtaking, either out over the seemingly endless expanse of the blue Adriatic or east to the rocky mountains of the island of Brac and the mainland behind.

The night stayed calm and we had no trouble mooring wise with our neighbours, although they were certainly noisy. But we didn't notice that until we stopped being noisy ourselves about midnight, and the grandchildren had cleaned us up at 'Texas Hold'em'. We had to wait around until mid-morning before there was any sign of life on the French boat and we were able to cast off and leave. Looking back on it, I cannot understand why I was so unusually patient. Perhaps the contented ambience I was enjoying after a fine dinner ashore and having selected a beautiful handcrafted silver bracelet for the important birthday coming up.

We pushed on and had a few days on the coast at Trogir with Charlotte and Stephen before they reclaimed our crew and headed back to France. Trogir is a very attractive town with stately buildings, parks and esplanades on a small island connected by bridges to the mainland on one side, and on the other side to a larger island. Islands have always been popular places to build villages in this part of the world. Although you could still be ravaged by pirates it made it much more difficult for marauders on horseback. So, it is no surprise that there is evidence of habitation here that dates back to the stone age, long before the Greeks recognised its potential in the 4th century BCE. Unfortunately, rapacious Moors arrived in their galleys in 1123 and sacked the town, but by 1420 it had re-established itself as a prosperous trading centre. Then the Venetians swooped on it and held it until 1797. The streetscape reflects all this, numerous imposing medieval buildings including a fortress and tower and the marvellous cathedral built around the end of the 12th century.

We found a very convenient anchorage near the tower where we only had about two centimetres between our keel and the glutinous mud below, but we could almost step ashore. Roger Wainwright had arranged for an old army friend to show us around while we were here. David Rowe had come to Croatia as part of the UN Peacekeeping force after the Balkan war. He had done his job, fallen in love, married and decided to stay on. David and his wife, Daria, had a charming loft apartment with a roof garden overlooking the waterfront and we had a few amusing days with them and exploring the old town.

The days were drawing in. There was a hint of winter and southerly storms in the air —the sailing season was nearly over, and it was time to begin putting *Sea Dreams* into winter quarters.

The fine city of Split was also founded by Greek colonists around the 4th century BCE and has been a place of note for nearly two thousand years. It still has the aura of an old imperial capital. The harbour is surrounded by impressive boulevards and imposing buildings, all set against the backdrop of rugged mountain ranges. In 305 BCE the Roman emperor Diocletian, a local boy who had joined the legions and risen through the ranks to the pinnacle of power, and then proved smart enough to be the first emperor to voluntarily retire—most emperors were assassinated before they had the chance—built a magnificent palace on the foreshore of the harbour. Here he spent his retirement tending his garden and giving the odd word of advice to his successors. He proved to be one of the great Emperors, reforming an empire that was on the brink of collapse and enabling it to remain intact until the Western Empire was conquered by German tribes in 476 CE.

Diocletian was one of twenty-two Roman emperors who came from the Balkans, all of whom were put in power by the legions. It is interesting to note that after Augustus's reign not one legion was raised from Italy south of the river Po. The legions were of the empire, not Italy. Even in Caesar's time the best legions, with which he conquered most of Europe, were raised mainly in Spain. After Caesar no emperor could reign without the legions behind him.

Western history tends to equate the fall of Rome with the fall of the Roman Empire. In fact, the capital of the empire was moved to Constantinople by Constantine in 330 CE and remained there until it finally disintegrated following its sacking by the Venetians and Crusaders in 1204 and capture by the Ottomans in 1453.

Diocletian's palace was a huge and opulent fortress surrounded by nearly eight hundred metres of walls between fifteen and twenty metres high. Water was supplied by an aqueduct nine kilometres long. Much of the original palace still remains and is an intrinsic part of the city, which is a marvellous polyglot of the ancient and fine Venetian architecture, which helps create a vibrant and irresistible ambience. There is an original stone-vaulted subterranean passage running from the waterfront promenade beneath the western wall that is a bustling shopping arcade—

surely the oldest existing arcade in the world. During the Middle Ages the city was a lonely Venetian bastion surrounded by the high-water mark of the Ottoman Empire, but it was never taken. Eventually the Turks were driven off and the city continued to prosper as a trading centre, its port linked to the interior by a pass through the high mountains.

Lenny and Helen Griffin arrived in *Fourth Dimension* shortly after us. The next day we were also reunited with Rob and Jan Flew on *Le Pelican*, a lovely sixty-foot French yacht. Eugene and Jenny arrived, along with Dave and Jill Henry on *Sweet Chariot* and we shared some boisterous meals along the waterfront.

Autumn was definitely being nudged by some chilly southern weather and it was time to go. We handed *Sea Dreams* over to Igor Gazin at the marina who was to take care of her during the winter and took a taxi to the ferry terminal, driven by 'Taxi Igor' who had an unpronounceable surname. We had gotten to know Taxi Igor quite well and had become firm friends. He was always driving us to the supermarket and picking up and delivering friends and family to the airport. He had kept us abreast of the local scandals and corruptions and the tempestuous goings on in the three-storied home he and his wife shared with his parents and his brother's family. Like many Croatians he was a huge man, about two metres tall and weighing in at some 130 kgs, but he had a cheerful sunny disposition and gossiped like a fishwife. He was able to keep us on top of the mayor's stormy romance with his young mistress, the fights between his mother and his brother's wife, who was greasing who in order to get approval for a large waterfront hotel and the likelihood of a new war in the Balkans.

Despite our friendship, it had not crossed our minds that there would ever be any discounting of a fare. I don't think that a taxi driver has ever done such a thing in the whole history of taxi driving— it's just not done. Imagine our amazement when, after dragging our bags from the boot, he held up his huge hams, palms outward, and with a gentle smile refused to touch our money.

We had an uneventful night-ferry passage across the Adriatic, and after a night in Ancona we headed north by train. We had our usual problem finding our carriage and seats—Italian trains do not seem to arrange their carriages in any discernible order and seat numbers are also arranged without reference to normal numerical sequence—but eventually we settled in to enjoy the trip. The beauty of parts of Italy takes your breath away, however the architecture along the coastal track north suggests that there was nothing much more complicated than a cement box built for quite a while—certainly not since Garibaldi's time. It is a blessing that the train stations at Bologna and Florence are close to the centre of these great cities, and to alight from the train is to step into another world. The station at Venice is certainly not so convenient and required quite a long portage of suitcases and an expensive water-taxi fare to our apartment on the waterfront of the Grand Canal opposite St Marks. I had already discussed the sale of our home in Hobart to pay for the two weeks stay, but nevertheless thought I may as well just enjoy it! The canal lapped our front terrace and there was an expansive walled garden at the rear.

Venice's history is diverse and spellbinding. It forged an unimaginably wealthy empire on the back of trade and naval might and for most of its long history it was a democracy—of sorts. It was from here that Marco Polo set sail for China in 1271 and where the world's most famous lover Giacomo Casanova was born, as were Titian, Tintoretti, Verdi, Canaletto, Guradi, Bellini and other greats too numerous to name. The city sits in the Venetian Lagoon which is around a thousand square kilometres in size and contains over thirty islands which all have a life of their own and a story to tell. Thankfully most of these islands and still backwaters are relatively untouched by tourism. It is possible to amble untroubled around almost deserted backstreets and waterfronts where the restaurants serve spicy Venetian dishes, and to wind your way home in the darkness with only your own footsteps echoing off the empty pavements.

Seafood, naturally enough for a city of the sea, has always been a staple of Venetian cuisine, traditionally marinated or salted to preserve it for long periods. From the earliest times rice was imported from Asia and Arabia and has been a dominant staple ever since, as have been the spices first imported to Venice along the Silk Road over a thousand years ago. There are countless variations of risottos combining seafood and vegetables, including Risi Bisi and Risotto Nero.

To me, the remarkable fact that all the architectural marvels of the city have been built supported on wooden poles driven into the mud of the islands and lagoon is the one which amazed me most. The creation of such wonderful architectural gems moulded by the traditions of Italy, Byzantine, the Moors and Arabia captures the essence of the Venetian people themselves, their brilliance, ingenuity and tenacity. The church of Santa Della Salute built in the seventeenth century is a good example, built on over a million wooden poles each over four metres in length and standing today a proud and beautiful memorial of a time in history.

A day in a galley from Rosinj would have seen the ancient mariners back home to Venice. I can only imagine the sense of incredible relief that must have been felt by the blistered, chafed, wearied rowers, who had pulled heavy wooden oars against the northerlies from long-distant ports. They were all free men on the Venetian galleys, and their spirits must have soared as they pulled through one of the channels into the safety of the Venetian Lagoon and spied the spires of Saint Mark's Basilica gleaming in the late sunshine.

It was these galleys, captained and manned by the free citizens of the city, which created her great wealth. Enough to fund a mighty empire and construct on an isolated swampy mosquito-infected archipelago at the top of the Adriatic, a city which for the best part of a thousand years was one of the world's truly great cities. It has arguably done more to foster, inform and defend the western traditions than any other place on earth. Except for Constantinople, which for over a thousand years was the custodian and defender of Greco-Roman-Judean traditions. Without Constantinople all would have been consumed by the armies of Islam.

But despite all that is good and great in the history of the Most Serene Republic of Venice, in 1202 CE it took part in one of history's greatest betrayals. An act so monstrous that it almost destroyed Europe. In this year a European Christian army embarked in a Venetian fleet and set sail for Jerusalem to liberate the holy city from its Muslim Conquerors. This was the fourth crusade.

Even before the fleet set sail there were money problems. Despite large donations from the Pope there was not enough to finance the army and to pay for the fleet that the Venetians had built for an agreed price. With hungry crusaders in Venice and the large fleet not paid for it looked as if the crusade would collapse and Venice would be bankrupted.

A partial solution was reached. The Venetians under their Doge would join the crusade if first the crusaders would help recapture the Venetian city of Zara, which had been taken by Hungary. This was accomplished and the city sacked. The Pope was outraged and excommunicated the entire expedition.

Then a complete solution presented itself. Prince Alexios Angelos, the son of the recently usurped Byzantine Emperor—who had been blinded and thrown in prison—approached the crusader leadership with a proposal. They enthrone him (don't worry about Dad) in place of the usurper, and he would help finance the crusade, supply additional troops and submit the Church of Constantinople to the authority of Rome.

Constantinople was the largest, most powerful and richest city in the world. It had been founded as the capital of the Roman Empire by the emperor Constantine nearly a thousand years before and still controlled a mighty empire. It was immensely rich and had been the centre of the Orthodox Christian church for all those years.

The proposal was enthusiastically accepted by the leaders of the crusade who were mostly Franks (Norman-French – the Esmonde family were originally Norman-French and they were crusaders, but I don't think it was this one) and tended to despise the eastern church as much as they did Muslims. It was not just the money, it would be a great solution to the longstanding schisms and festering hatred between the 'Latins' who owed allegiance to the Roman Pope and the 'Greek' Christians who followed the Greek Orthodox tradition. In due course the fleet set sail, neglecting to tell the soldiers that they were heading for Constantinople rather than Egypt, and their target was a Christian capital rather than a Muslim army.

It is best if I keep the rest of this story until we ourselves reach Constantinople in a later chapter.

In late April the following year we arrived back in Split looking forward eagerly to continuing to explore one of the world's great cruising grounds. After much discussion the cruise director decided that in the first three months, we would do a loop to the top of the Adriatic along the Dalmatian coast, through the Konati Islands, Istria and back to Split. We would then spend late summer and autumn enjoying the nearby offshore islands with a number of friends arriving from Australia. Then we would hire a car and do an inland road trip through the mountains to Sarajevo. Then, as winter settled, back on the train through Milan, Torin and Chambery to Charlotte's magnificently restored chalet on the shores of Lake Annecy in the French Alps. In the unlikely event I had the stamina to survive all that, the French Texas Hold 'em Poker Championships and long games of chess with the grandchildren would certainly finish me off.

On the first day of May we sailed out of Split, heading for the small fishing village of Maslinika a few hours away on the western tip of the island of Solta. The mountains behind the old city were framed by a clear blue sky, it was great to be alive and on the water with some wonderful sailing ahead of us. Although sunny, the wind had a sharp edge and it was not until after lunch that we peeled off our wet weather jackets.

The harbour off the village was fringed with pine trees and shielded by several offshore islands, which gave it security from the boisterous afternoon sea breeze. In the late afternoon we went ashore for a stroll through the forested and rock-walled hills behind the town. They were rich with the scent of pine and herbs and the groves of ancient olives. Towards dusk we sauntered back to the village clustered around the waterfront, to investigate the friendly *konobas* offering an excellent range of seafood, including some impressive lobsters. As a special treat we shared one, chopped and sautéed in garlic, chillies, basil and white wine and served with pasta. Magnificent! This naturally required a local wine and the recommended variety was a Dobricic, a rich herb scented dark red that has been grown on the island since ancient, probably Greek, times. A memorable dinner, which included some dips from the owner's olive trees which were also many centuries old and a honeycomb dessert from the *konoba's* own hives, rich with the aroma of—the herb—rosemary. Everything grown on the island.

The ancient Greeks brought their winemaking traditions to the Croatian islands two thousand five hundred years ago, and many of their varieties still thrive and have found perfect matches in the three hundred odd micro-climates throughout the islands and in the mountains and valleys of the mainland. Of course, the islands sat astride perhaps the ancient and medieval worlds' most dynamic trading routes, linking Venice and Rome to the Asia. This provided a huge export market—and not only for wine—and a continual infusion of ideas and technologies.

On the opposite shore of the village a Venetian castle dating from the early 18th century has been renovated into a very pleasant hotel, which we were invited to on one occasion. The next evening towards dusk we were relaxing in the cockpit before going ashore for an evening at the quay, when the melodious sounds of a choir drifted across the calm water. The singing continued as we rowed ashore and when we had chosen our *konoba* for the evening we discovered the choir was ensconced in a walled courtyard at the rear. After a wine or two we poked our noses out and found not a choir, but a group of about twenty gregarious women. They had finished lunch a few hours ago were just singing and having a good time—have you noticed how attractive Croatian women can be—before the launch of a biography of a famous Croatian feminist by one of their number. They were impressed that we were such ardent supporters of the feminist cause ourselves—well, you have to be polite—and with two very liberated daughters ourselves—true. The real celebrations would be later they said, would we like to come? What man could resist celebrating with twenty gorgeous women, and Ro seemed to think it was a good idea too. The book launch was at the fine old romantic castle. The celebrations started there and my memories of the rest of the night are a bit jumbled.

We left the next morning and overnighted behind the peninsula at Primosten Luka, and then on to Luka Grebastica a deep inlet a few miles further north and settled down to wait for a mechanic who we hoped would fix our water-maker for us. We anchored not far from a very impressive fortified wall that was built right across the peninsula on the north side of the anchorage in 1497 to provide a safe haven from Janissaries. The wall is around a kilometre long and six to nine metres high and is just another indication of the immense effort the people along this coast were prepared to go to, rather than surrender their lives, freedoms and religion to the Ottomans. Don't forget those in the Balkans who had already been conquered were required to pay a tax of thousands Christian children each year to the Sultan in Istanbul. How many rocks would you be prepared to cart, how much sweat would you spill to save your son and daughter from being a plaything in the harem or a castrated official or perhaps worst of all, a Janissary who once he had been converted and forgotten where he came from, may well be back to murder all your family.

By nightfall there was still no sign of our mechanic. It's the same everywhere in summer, if you are a mechanic you are among the feted elite of the coasts. In fact, if I did have a third hand and could understand how things work, I would definitely be one myself. While we were complaining, two French yachts came into our bay, it was still half-light, and dropped anchor. There was some toing and froing and revving and one of them eventually upped anchored and left. There was some confusion and shouting on the front deck of the remaining yacht. Their anchor went down a bit and was pulled up again. More loud muttering and swearing in French. Then they also pulled their anchor up and they disappeared into the gloom. We forgot about them and the bloody mechanic who hadn't turned up.

But, about 11.00 pm we were awoken by shouts from the shore and a torch being waved. The shouts changed from Croatian to Croatian/English—it was our mechanic. What a man, who cares if the work is done at midnight. By 1 am all was done, and I rowed him ashore, laden down with our profuse thanks and wad-fulls of our cash. We went back to sleep happy.

The next morning as we were getting ready to go, two burly hard-bitten gangsters approached us in a large dilapidated old wooden dinghy. They were irate about something, shaking their fists and shouting in Croatian. As they got a bit closer, I was relieved to see the dinghy was full of nets and fishing gear. Ah, they weren't pirates after all, just irate fishermen. They reached us and standing up, they grasped our gunnels and anchor chain and continued to fume. Well, they may not have been pirates but they were becoming increasingly threatening. I could now make out one of the words. 'Policija, Policija,' they were shouting. Even someone like me who had failed year three French could work that out. And now they were rubbing their thumb and index finger together in the universal signal for 'give us some bloody money'.

Meanwhile quick-thinking Ro had gotten our Croatian agent Igor Gazin, who I think she had a crush on, but who fortunately for me was besotted by his very beautiful young wife, on the phone. We handed them the phone and they shouted at it and waved their fists for some minutes before handing it back.

Igor explained that we were accused of ripping up their fishing nets to the value of four hundred Australian dollars.

Those bloody French yachts mucking around in the gloom last night. They were the culprits and had fled the scene of the crime.

We explained to Igor and handed the phone back to the fishermen. More loud conversation in Croatian. But it was pay up or front the local officialdom and cops, which would be a bureaucratic nightmare and take days and days, and in any case, we now felt sorry for them.

We handed over another wad of cash to the now smiling and kindly fishermen, pulled up our chain and anchor, to which not one strand of fishing net was attached or ever had been. Ah well, worse things could happen. It was nowhere near as expensive as that bloody dinner in the Maddalena Archipelago that Lenny had organised!

About 100 kms north of Split the small island of Zlarin lies among a cluster of islands nestling off the mouth of the Krk River, which leads inland to the Krk National Park. The island is heavily forested with a small population and protects its quiet ambience by allowing no cars. If you are doing some shopping here, it's a question of finding a spot to park your wheelbarrow. There were a couple of *konobas* on the quay and a fine view over the placid sun-streaked waters to a scattering of quite palatial old Venetian palazzi. The next day was very pleasantly spent following the winding Krk River upstream until we came to the village of Skradin sitting beside a large calm pond below the gushing waterfalls where the river cascades out of the mountainous interior.

On the way back to the sea we stopped at the ancient city of Sibenik sitting alongside a broad reach of the river that has provided a fine harbour for sea-goers since antiquity. There is a large esplanade and many fine buildings, including the splendid Cathedral of Saint James built in the 16th century. Most people with a passing interest in religion will be aware that for the sake of man's souls, the medieval church employed many, many quite innovative ways of raising money. Papal Indulgences and Forgiveness of Sins for instance. The clergy at Sibenik employed a blunt form of a blackmail. If you did not donate, your image would be carved into decorative friezes on the outside of the cathedral. Six hundred years later plenty of these parsimonious skinflints still face the ridicule—or possibly admiration—of posterity. Myself, perhaps I would have been keener to donate to the four strong fortresses that were built to keep marauders at bay.

We had another few days pottering around the islands near Zlarin and were amused one day when a large Turkish gullet full of German nudists anchored close to us. It seemed that the only rule was that you dressed for dinner. Unfortunately, I cannot find a link to any suitable images.

Going further offshore we anchored in the gorgeous bay of Uvala Stupica Vela on the island of Zirge where we were overlooked by the ruins of a Roman fortress built around the 5th century. It was, and still is a fertile and picturesque island and being located on the outer edge of the ribbon of islands probably made it both more attractive and more vulnerable. The Ottomans almost wiped it out completely in 1472 leaving hardly a soul alive. From the old fort there is a lovely view over the pine covered hills and the sparkling blue waters, and it is hard to imagine that the bloody times of the past really did happen.

There are over a hundred islands in the Kornati Archipelago which runs in a broad ribbon along the Dalmation coast from Sibenik to Zadar. They are mostly within a national park and make one of the most beautiful and interesting cruising destinations in the world. In summer a sailor's delight with many remote and uncrowded anchorages, pristine water, fresh breezes—and unfortunately the odd *Bora*. There is a sprinkling of *konobas* serving local fish and Kornati lamb that has been left to run wild over winter and fatten—a bit anyway—on the spring growth. All of course, grilled over smoky fires and washed down with great wines from the Dalmation coast. Most of the islands are almost treeless, their forests long ago sacrificed to build the fleets of Venice and satisfy the needs of the farmers and villages during the harsh winters, when gale force winds howl off the icy mountains of the Balkans. They have been inhabited since the Neolithic Age. For centuries they were vulnerable to ravages of the fleets of Muslim pirates and in other times they have been home to local pirates preying on passing trading ships. If piracy had a homeland it could well have been among these islands or along the adjacent coast.

The island of Zut has some very good anchorages, and on the protected shoreline of one we found one of our very favourite *konobas*. I do have to admit that the list of our favourite *konobas* and *tavernas* is about the same size as telephone directories used to be for a medium-size city. We spent a few days anchored off the Konoba Sabuni with Rob and Jan Flew on *Le Pelican*, enjoying the absolutely amazing colours and sweetness of the waters in the bay before being ferried into the *konoba* for dinners of fish, scampi and squid roasted and grilled in the huge brick fire place in the kitchen.

As with all the Kornati islands it is a marvellous place to potter. There are reminders of the past everywhere. Old stone walls marking out long deserted fields, stands of battered olives clinging tenaciously to the hard, rocky soil, fields scented with wild herbs hiding among the tough island grasses, old vines clinging to life behind crumbling walls. Here and there families have managed to hold onto old farms, at least for the summers. There are stout wooden launches moored beside stone jetties and with the approach of evening tails of smoke drifting into the darkening sky and the gleam of candlelight from behind curtained windows. The sense of long ago pervades. The struggle against the harsh climate to eke out a living from the threadbare soil, to survive the depredations of the sea's marauders.

The village of Vrulje is the largest village on the actual island of Kornati. It consists of about half a dozen homes, a small market, a couple of *konobas* and is deserted in the winter. It has a nice stone quay, but not nice enough to lure us from an anchorage in the clear waters of the bay, where we had a great view of the rugged treeless hills with miles and miles of old stone walls marking off the ancient farms, and where now a few sheep and donkeys roamed.

When we rowed ashore, we found we had to choose between the *Konoba* Robinson and the *Konoba* Vrulje. We were a bit suspicious why anyone wanting to lure customers to an authentic Croatian experience would give their *konoba* an English name, perhaps they were appealing to English soccer hooligans. So, we went with the Vrulje and we were certainly not disappointed. There was no menu. When we were ready to order our host walked us along to his brother's fishing boat, which had docked when we were about halfway through a small carafe of *domace` vino,* and we inspected the catch. On advice we selected a red snapper that was still giving a dispirited flap of its tail and a red mullet. We returned to our small wooden table looking out over the bay and in due course the fire in the *konoba's* wooden oven was lit. But it was some time before the rocks were hot enough to grill and it was quite dark, and we had eaten far too much freshly baked bread and olive dip and drunk too much *domace` vino*, before the crispy-skinned succulent fish was served. But nevertheless, it was superb, and we had had plenty of time to chat to the host's mother about old times on the islands and watch a flock of cats patrolling the quay and annoying a large Alsatian dog on the back of one of the boats.

The next morning, we followed an old path lined on each side by free stone walls into the hills behind the village. It wandered through a gnarled old olive grove and some hardy vines that are grown as low bushes to mitigate wind damage, before it led to an ancient tower on the top of one of the hills.

Sailing on, our course took us through a labyrinth of small islands sheltering on the western side of Kornati. Here and there were the remains of old fortresses perched on top of rocky crags, and in some of the bays an old farmhouse or neglected church. We wound our way to an anchorage in the large bay of Telascica on Dugi Orok Island.

We were rendezvousing here with Helen and Lenny on *Fourth Dimension* and I was pleased that the only *konoba* had a simple menu with prices displayed. My scar from the meal in the Maddalena's still itched a bit at night! In due course they arrived with one of their sons and his girlfriend and we had a fun night. The proprietor was amazed that Lenny's grandmother was born on a nearby island! But having established that lie we were looked after as though we were one of the family.

It was a remote and enchanting spot, encased in high hills and pine forests. Local folklore is that Edward VIII romanced his bride to be, Wallis Simpson here on board the yacht Nahlin. The *Dubrovnik Times* records that while on the nearby island of Rab the couple enjoyed a skinny dip and are credited with introducing nude bathing to Croatia. If they were able to come back to the islands, they would no doubt be delighted at what they did for tourism in the Adriatic.

The weather was delightful and the winds gentle. Just enough breeze to amble along and they took us to anchorages at Molat, Ist and Silba islands. The island of Losinj is only a few miles north of the Kornati's, but it is another world, though equally beautiful with its heavily wooded landscape and the colourful Venetian façade of the bustling port of Mali-Losinj. The port is almost totally enclosed within the encircling arms of the lush island, with only a narrow channel at the northern end for yachts to sneak through. It is quite deep and protected from all winds—I fell in love immediately as we nosed through the channel and the beautifully protected haven opened before our eyes.

We spent a while here, coming and going, sometimes anchoring but mostly enjoying the fun and bustle of the town quay. The village dates from the 14th century and was an important ship building centre and a stopover, two days out of Venice for the trading galleys. By the time we arrived the sailing season was in full swing and although at heart we are peace and quiet sort of people, it was impossible not to enjoy.

We, or at least Ro, got off to a good start. Coming in late one morning we had taken a berth in the small marina at the quay and were just settling in when a disreputable-looking yacht blundered into the adjoining berth. Its sails were badly furled, ropes were trailing everywhere, and a number of unshaven drunks were lying around the noonday decks. Perhaps one was a corpse. Bloody hell I thought, it must be a group of Manchester United fans, but when I heard mutterings in German, I realised they were probably VfB Stuttgart fans. I went below to check on the whereabouts of the baseball bat I keep to ward-off drunken soccer hooligans.

Nothing much happened in the afternoon. The bedraggled sloths gradually awoke and sauntered off towards the nearby taverns. At a respectable hour we headed in for an aperitif ourselves and were drawn towards the shaded deck of a restaurant from which emanated the joyous sounds of Mozart's *Le Nozze Di Figaro*. We ordered a carafe of white and some ice and enjoyed the music. After a while the Mozart stopped and was replaced by some lyrical Irish music which I am particularly fond of. I put my head in the door to see if the volume could be turned up a bit and discovered that the music was actually coming from a group of unshaven drunks voraciously wielding various fiddles and wind instruments in the back corner. We moved inside to enjoy things more and in due course got to talking to the musicians, who to our amazement were the fine fellows off our neighbouring yacht. They were in fact not soccer hooligans at all, but members of the Berlin Symphony Orchestra. Later as we were drifting off to sleep, Ro was serenaded by a beautiful rendition of *Rosemarie I Love You*. Those guys really knew how to win my girl's heart. She was almost weeping when they set off the next day, with a lone violinist standing on the foredeck playing her favourite tune, again.

Losinj prides itself on its cuisine. *'Its essence is the capture the tastes and smells of the clear ocean waters which surround it, the expansive natural herb gardens on the island with over two hundred varieties and a tradition that goes back nearly a thousand years – to when trading ships first introduced the east to the west'.* No false modesty there. Fish are plentiful, the local shrimps from Kvarner Bay are claimed to be the best in the world, lobsters, mussel, squid and octopus abound. Fresh local salad vegetables and plentiful local wine. Some special dishes we enjoyed included: red scorpion fish *brodeto* with polenta, sea bass cooked with wine and olives, bream marinated with sage and wild onion, spicy crab soup, island lamb roasted 'under the bell', octopus with broad beans and fennel and tuna with agrimony and olive oil.

So, as you can see, we spoiled ourselves outrageously. Each evening the restaurant owners started rubbing their hands together as we strolled along the quay searching through the displayed specials and agonising over the choices. But in the early mornings and again in the afternoon we covered many, many steps exploring the over two hundred kilometres of laid pathways that wander through Losinj and her close neighbours, winding their way through sweet smelling forests and glades, small hamlets, protected bays and stunning outlooks. There was diving in caves and on reefs and just swimming in the irresistible water. We discovered lovely Baroque churches and bell towers, the Fritzi and Bishop's palaces, the Museum of Sacred Art, the relics of Saint Gaudenziz, the wooded park at Cikat with trees brought back by homesick sailors from all over the world, and around nearly every street corner or bend in the pathway something else to remind us how wonderful life was.

Pula was an important town in Illyrian times and has been occupied during the two and a half millennia since. The Romans built a great city here from 44 BCE and there are still a number of reminders of its magnificence. We anchored offshore from what is said to be the best-preserved amphitheatre outside Italy and it is indeed something to wonder at. A short stroll through the city takes you past other fine reminders of the Roman's—Hercules's Gate, a triumphal arch, a theatre and a temple to Augustus to name just a few. Today it is very much a working port so it's not the place for a quiet weekend of skinny dipping, but the anchoring is good, and the Roman ruins are some of the best in the Mediterranean.

Further on Rovinj is on the eastern coast of the northern Adriatic in Istria, a day of so travel by galley from Venice. It was an important part of the Venetian Empire for five hundred years. A secure port for their galleys travelling through the pirate infested waters of the Adriatic and a strategic defensive outpost against invasion. It still looks and feels very Venetian and is commonly called the jewel of Istria, which it is. In summer dawns and again as the sun sets over the glimmering ocean it has a golden glow. The ochre and yellow pastels of the terraces are an impressionist's canvas and the imposing spire of the mighty Saint Euphemia's Basilica sparkles above the city like a jewel encrusted lighthouse. Originally it was situated on a small island separated from the mainland by a narrow channel. But in 1763 the city must have decided it needed a plush plaza rather than a moat, and it was filled in.

The city is now a famous centre of the arts, and in summer the old cobblestoned streets are home to fine collections of art, jewellery and fashion. I enjoy a little shopping, but I certainly don't have the endurance required to keep up with some, so fortunately the plaza had plenty of shaded tables with nice views over the harbour and the passing parade. The cuisine is very Italian, and delicious. Plenty of spicy pizzas and pasta, a wide range of local seafoods, local Istrian hams and sausages, fresh veggies including truffles and wild asparagus. And for those who enjoy an occasional wine, it could be here that the Italian and Croatian traditions coalesce - if there is such a place in the shadowy world of oenology. A friend of ours has a business card announcing his profession as a 'non-discriminating oenologist.' In his case this is a downright fib as he is definitely an insufferable wine snob, but it pretty well sums up my attitude. I like it all. Anyway, we spent a few days exploring and doing a bit of 'non-discriminating oenology'.

The magical Brijuni Islands lie just offshore and we spent a few days exploring this enchanted wonderland. The islands have a long history of being a good place to come to and has been yet another escape for many of history's rich and powerful. Rich Greeks, Romans, Venetians and central Europeans all sought sanctuary here. After World War II the Yugoslav communist dictator Josip Broz Tito established a villa on the largest island and enjoyed it each summer until his death in 1980. Tito's Villa still stood grandly beside a sheltered bay, protected by various ageing watchtowers for machine gun carrying sentries, which have been necessities for communist dictators ever since there were the first communist dictators. Although a dictator, he was probably the greatest resistance leader of World War II and as an unaligned national leader was an important figure during the Cold War. He is reported as having hosted over one hundred national leaders at the villa as well a plethora of the stars of stage and screen.

Tito was born in the northern Croatian village of Kumrovec in 1892. At that time, it was in the Kingdom of Croatia-Slavonia, a part of the Austro- Hungarian Empire. He was an activist from an early age and a unionist by the time he was eighteen. As a factory worker/unionist/organiser he travelled through Europe agitating for the overthrow of the system. In 1913 he was conscripted into the army and before he was seriously wounded and captured by the Russians, he had become the youngest sergeant-major in the Austro-Hungarian army, a regimental fencing champion and man who was famous for his enjoyment of wine, women and song.

In 1917 he escaped from a work camp in the Ural Mountains and made his way to Petrograd and fought for the revolutionary forces in the Russian Civil War. At the age of twenty-seven he married a beautiful fifteen-year-old Russian, Pelagija Polka Belousova, and returned home in 1920 to the newly established Kingdom of Yugoslavia. He joined the Communist Party and was elected to his district committee in 1924 and in due course became a professional revolutionary who was at times imprisoned for his activities.

He was a delegate to the Seventh World Congress of the Comintern and rose through the ranks. Notably recruiting over a thousand fighters for the Spanish Civil War, of whom 671 were killed and 300 wounded, although he didn't serve himself. In 1937 he was appointed General secretary of the Communist Party of Yugoslavia.

Germany invaded Yugoslavia in April 1942 and Croatia proclaimed itself an independent state, the Kingdom of Croatia. When the King fled the German invasion, Tito was named as President of the National Committee of Liberation and the partisans and Tito were formally recognised by the allies at the 1943 Tehran Conference. In May 1945, after the German forces were driven out after a bloody and bitter resistance, he announced the provisional government of the Democratic Federal Yugoslavia. A later election gave him an overwhelming mandate. Initially he had close ties to Stalin and was a strongly orthodox Marxist. Dissidents and religion were suppressed, and he maintained an aggressive policy towards the West, reclaiming Istria and Zadar and attempting to take Italian Trieste.

There was a famous and acrimonious split from Stalin in 1949.

'Stop sending people to kill me. We've already captured five of them, one of them with a bomb and another with a rifle... If you don't stop sending killers, I'll send one to Moscow, and I won't have to send a second.'

212

Then followed the brutal suppression of Russian communist sympathisers, tens of thousands were sent to labour camps, and relations were not relaxed until after Stalin's death in 1953. His independent status enabled him to extort aid from both sides during the Cold War and he was instrumental in the creation of the Non-Aligned Movement. Internally he experimented with profit sharing and workplace democracy in formerly state-owned enterprises and, in 1953 self-management became the basis of the entire social order in Yugoslavia. Internationally his policy was of neutrality during cold war and a liberal travel policy that in 1967 abolished nearly all visa requirements.

The New York Times view: *'Tito sought to improve life. Unlike others who rose to power on the communist wave after WW II, Tito did not long demand that his people suffer for a distant view of better life. After an initial Soviet-influenced bleak period, Tito moved towards radical improvement of life in the country. Yugoslavia gradually became a bright spot amid the general greyness of Eastern Europe.'* 5 May 1980.

That said, he was still a dictator with a secret service modelled on the KGB and watchtowers with machine guns protecting his island paradise.

A Slovenian Constitutional Court pronouncement captures the conundrum.

'The name 'Tito' does not symbolise the liberation of present-day Slovenia from fascist occupation during WW II .... But also, grave violations of human rights and basic freedoms, especially in the decade following WW II.'

His love life remained tumultuous until the end. He separated from the beautiful Pelagija in 1928, and only one son of five children survived. He later married several times and had numerous affairs, the best-known being with Jovanka who became his wife when she was twenty-seven and he fifty-eight.

The days were flitting by and reluctantly we headed south. On the way we called at Krk Island, Rab Island, Zadar and Luka Drvenik and before the summer solstice we were back in our berth at noble Split, watching the sun rise above the coastal ranges and illuminating Diocletian's great palace. On board our beautiful *Sea Dreams* there was lots of hustle and bustle as we prepared for friends and reviewed our plans for the rest of the sailing season.

Milna on the nearby island of Brac became another favourite place. It was an ideal spot to spend our last night at sea with friends before we dropped them back at Split on their way back to the real world. With Eric and Eileen Tang, Carmel and Phil Thomson, Eugene and Jenny Esmonde, Margie Hansen, Sue and Don Clark we enjoyed meals along the quay, watching yachts come and go while the warm candle-lit dusk settled over us. Sometimes it could be quite busy, but if we avoided the days the charter fleets came by, we could normally anchor in the small basin in the centre of the town. But otherwise there was always a spot at the quay. We have other friends who wintered their yacht here for a number of years and found the slower pace more relaxing than the frenetic rush of Split.

Charlotte and family and friends rented a villa close by and we spent a lot of time here and anchored in nearby Uvala Lucice, across a few hills on the other side of the island.

Milna is close to Hvar Island where on the northern shore there was another place we grew to really love. Stari Grad was settled by Greeks in the 8th century BCE and is one of the oldest towns in Europe. It was the main town on the island for nearly two thousand years, but despite having a great anchorage it was a bit out of the way for the Venetian galleys. Here we could pick up a mooring right in the middle of town in a beautiful and safe situation, or within an hour find a deserted anchorage in a tree-lined bay, where although the anchorages have been used for two and a half thousand years, they still have a fresh virginal ambience. Stari Grad suited us. There was always a mooring available if we got there before lunch and we discovered a *konoba*, with a walled courtyard shrouded in a canopy of bougainvillea, that served fine seafood from the wood-fired oven and tasty *domace vino* made from the owner's vineyard on the island.

I don't think that octopus has really captured Australian palates, and although I admit that great tentacles the size of a forearm and covered with carbuncle-like suction pads don't look very appealing, it is a shame that so many are missing out. It is tasty and very flexible: grilled, baked or as a stew or in a salad it can be delicious. Here is the method used for an octopus salad by our favourite *konoba*. Very simple. Cook the tentacles in boiling water for ten to fifteen minutes. Strip the skin and dice. Chill and marinate in white wine for a day or so. Serve with fresh salad. The secret is in the garnishing—you do need olive oil, vinegar, balsamic vinegar and perhaps something hotter, blended to your taste. The flesh tends to be bland but dressed up it is very seductive. Which is why if you are grilling it, it is best done over an aromatic smoky fire.

Stari Grad was a good base from which to explore the island. There were mokes and cars for hire and there was a newly built road, of more or less modern specifications, which ran across the spine of the island to Hvar town. Although it was steep and winding it only felt moderately life threatening. There were even some tunnels that cut out the most hair-raising bits. We normally took our guests across on this road, but once we decided to come back on the old road. But this turned out to be unsuited for the faint-hearted, so we only took it the once. Most of the winding stretches along the steep mountainsides, alive with a profusion of wildflowers, were only wide enough for one small car and there were no lay-bys for passing and no safety rails. For every hundred metres forward we seemed to be reversing fifty, with those on the abyss side of the moke white-faced with terror.

There was another road running along the length of the island which connected to two more pleasant stone villages, Vrboska and Jelsa. The road beyond Jelsa is still of historical interest. The official version is that it was built by Napoleonic era engineers and is pretty much in its original condition. This could be true, but personally I lean towards construction during Roman times. The old works and cuttings were impressive examples of what can be done with picks and shovels, but although it would have been wide enough for four legionnaires to march abreast, it looked a bit narrow for French wagons and cannon. In any case no one has ever seen the need for any safety fences, and again we also found our passengers white-lipped and not all that talkative.

Only a few hundred metres outside the town it is still possible, after all this time, to see the outlines of the gardens the Greeks established over two thousand years ago. Absolutely amazing, and the soil is still rich and fertile, producing the luscious salads we almost lived on— together with an octopus or two.

With Don and Sue Clark we took the sea breeze to Vis, about twenty miles further on and yet another beautiful and fertile Croatian island. A mountainous hinterland and a coast line indented with some exquisite bays and beaches where the water was clear enough for the sand to glisten ten metres under our keel. When we arrived there the sun was starting to slide towards the mountains, and we dropped anchor off the village of Kut, in the large harbour of Viska Luka. This was also an important Venetian port in the Middle Ages and much of its Venetian heritage is still here to admire among the stone cottages along the quay.

We dined at the Val restaurant, on the palm shaded esplanade where we were welcomed by the delightful owner, Luce Knego. The favourite dish was the local sardines sautéed in garlic and parsley in hot oil, seasoned with salt and pepper, cooked over a gentle heat; the favourite wine was a *Bogdanusab* white from a vineyard on the hill behind the harbour.

After a night at Kut we sailed around the northern side of the island to the small village of Komiza on the western end. In the bay there was not all that much protection from the west and we ended up anchoring in as close under a stone jetty as we could and, taking a long stern line ashore to an old stone bollard that looked as if it had been built to take some monstrous medieval warship. In the night we were visited by a *Bora* bucketing in from the east and screeching down the mountains. Lots of strain on the stern line and I ended sitting up most of the night. The next day a westerly built up a swell in the bay, and although we got a little protection from the stone jetty it was uncomfortable with a lot of pressure on both the anchor and the stern line.

Perhaps there was the reason we were the only yacht anchored in the bay.

Nevertheless we loved Komiza. It sits in an amphitheatre of mountains and is overlooked by a quite majestic 13th century monastery, sitting in stately solitude on a knoll covered with gardens and vineyards. Along the quay there were plenty of friendly *konobas* overlooked by an old stone fortress and a lofty Venetian tower. In fact, this small harbour was indeed a metaphor for the history of the islands—the boisterous sea, the dominating Catholic faith, the everlasting threat of war and piracy, the Venetian Empire and stout-hearted people who were as strong as their self-sufficient stone villages.

Nearby was the scene of an Italian naval imbroglio in 1866 at the Battle of Vis. A large Italian fleet sent to capture Venice was crushed by a smaller Austrian fleet. On returning home the Italian admiral claimed a great victory, but later when the truth emerged, he was tried for cowardice. Meanwhile, victories by Italy's allies France and Prussia meant that the French emperor Napoleon III had become the ruler of Venice. Italy, despite having not contributed much to the war effort demanded Venice be given to them, prompting a famous quip by the French Emperor: '*If the Italians lose another battle, they will be demanding I give them Paris.*'

We meandered through the islands until the end of August. We then left *Sea Dreams* safely moored in the marina at Split and headed into the Balkan hinterlands towards Sarajevo, where the assassination of the Archduke Franz Ferdinand and his wife the Duchess Sophie in 1914 provided the spark that lit the inferno of World War I and a century of slaughter in and beyond Europe.

Our route took us through the village of Mostar in southern Bosnia-Herzegovina, a few hours pleasant drive into the hinterland behind Split, and we arrived in time for an early lunch of a platter of dips and strong Turkish coffee at a cafe overlooking the Neretva River. It was a lovely autumn day—enough sun to enjoy the terrace and admire the surrounding mountains framed by a clear blue sky and cusping the picturesque village.

The area was inhabited in pre-history, and in the early 1400s a fortress was built to control the trade route to the east, where it crossed the river. It was captured by the Ottoman Turks in 1468, and on the orders of Suleiman the Magnificent the iconic Old Bridge was built in 1474. From that time onwards, the village took its name, Mostar, the Turkish for 'bridge keepers.'

216

Evliya Celebi, the celebrated seventeenth century Muslim scholar and traveller, recorded his impressions: *'the bridge is like a rainbow arch soaring up to the skies, extending from one cliff to the other ... I, a poor and miserable slave of Allah, have passed through sixteen countries, but I have never seen such a high bridge. It is thrown from rock to rock as high as the sky.'*

Mostar was incorporated into the Austro-Hungary Empire from 1878 until the end of World War I when control passed to the State of Slovenes, Croats and Serbs, then to Yugoslavia. After World War II it belonged to the Independent State of Croatia, then again to Yugoslavia. Independence from Yugoslavia was unilaterally declared in 1992 heralding vicious divisions and fighting along ethnic lines. Tragically the Stari Most (Old Bridge) was destroyed in November 1993 but was rebuilt and reopened in July 2004. Two thousand were killed in the Bosnian-Croatian war before international efforts brokered a settlement.

As with most the villages we had visited in the Balkans that had been caught up in war some of the scars of the fighting remained. But not enough to spoil the ambience of the village, the colourful mosques and the vibrant market with its strong echoes of western Asia.

The plan had been a stop for lunch and a quick walk around, but we dallied a bit and it was well into the afternoon before we got away, heading into Montenegro and through the rugged Black Mountains to the city of Niksic. The winding road ran through deep valleys shrouded in dark pine and around hard craggy mountains that in winter are covered in deep snow. This is country that for most of history has been home to brigands and revolutionaries and bear and wolf packs still roam the back country.

There was very little traffic and we really wouldn't have been all that surprised if we had been waved to a halt by heavily moustached horsemen with carbines slung over their blanketed shoulders. Night was starting to fall by the time we arrived at Niksic.

It had been a long day and we were very happy to check into our hotel and find that it had a welcoming bar and bistro that served all that we needed to revive us. The earliest record of the city was of a Roman camp in the fourth century before being taken by the Slavs a century later. The Ottomans arrived in1455, but little evidence remains of their long occupation. In the morning we detoured through the hard country, past an old stone fortress to Ostrog Monastery and on to Zabljak the highest town in the Balkans. It is surrounded by a stunning national park, shimmering lakes and noble mountains. It suffered badly in the Balkan Wars and was largely destroyed except the old Church of the Holy Transfiguration.

217

It was another long day by the time we arrived at the capital of Bosnia and Herzegovina, Sarajevo. After getting lost for a while we finally stumbled onto our hotel, found what seemed to be a safe spot for the car and checked in. Dusk was falling by that time and we set off to find a comfortable table where we could wash away the cares of the day and soak up the atmosphere of the old town.

Sarajevo lies in a valley surrounded by mountains and was founded by the Ottomans in 1461. It too was incorporated into the Austria/Hungarian Empire in 1878. In 1914 it had been a stronghold of the Empire, located about a day's ride from the border with Serbia. Relations between the two fluctuated between poisonous on a good day and murderous, but a tenuous peace existed following the 1912-13 Balkan Wars. The Balkans is a very ethnically divided area, with age-old racial hatreds compounded by centuries of suppression by the Romans, Byzantines, Bulgarians, Ottomans and Austria-Hungarians. And made even worse by the religious hatreds between the Latin and Byzantine Christian Churches and Islam that their oppressors brought with them. The gradual decline of the Ottoman Empire had opened the door to national independent movements and encouraged the expansionist ambitions of the Austro-Hungarians, the Bulgarians and the Russians. The border of the Russian Empire was now tantalisingly close to the Dardanelles and the spiritual home of their Christian Orthodoxy, Istanbul. The realisation of a long-held dream seemed almost within their grasp.

Beyond the tinderbox that was the Balkans, Europe had been poised on the brink of war for years. Great Britain was concerned by the balance of power in Europe and for her naval superiority which guaranteed her empire. Germany, a latecomer to both European and colonial power wanted to seize the pre-eminence that seemed to be hers by right. For centuries the Russians had pushed their empire south and west and also saw a grander imperial future for themselves. France still believed in the exceptionalism of their culture and that the imperial power of Napoleon was theirs by right. Their defeat in the Franco-German War and the loss of Alsace-Lorraine was a festering ulcer. The Austro-Hungarian Empire was a crumbling edifice, the last citadel of the once mighty Habsburgs.

The House of Habsburg was for much of the second millennium the most powerful and distinguished family in the world. It had accumulated power through marriages as well as by sword, and it had provided the Holy Roman Emperors from 1438 to 1740, Kings of Bohemia, Germany, Hungary, Croatia, Illyria, the Mexican Empire, Portugal, Spain—Jure uxoris kings of England and Ireland, and rulers of numerous Duchies and Principalities.

There were two main branches of the family. The senior branch ruled

218

Habsburg Spain from 1516 to 1700. At its zenith it controlled the Americas, the East Indies, the Low Countries, much of France and Germany, the Portuguese Empire and parts of Africa. The cadet branch of the family ruled the Austria-Hungarian Empire, which in 1914 ruled an area that included today's Austria, Czech Republic, Hungary, Slovakia, Slovenia, Bosnia-Herzegovina, Croatia and much of Poland and Romania.

Such was the background to the momentous event which occurred in this undistinguished city in the mountainous interior of a minor Balkan country, on 28 June 1914. An event that changed the world forever.

After dinner we strolled the short distance along the dimly lit street to the old stone bridge crossing the shallow Miljacka River. Below us the waters of the river flowed past with barely a murmur. The pavements along the riverbanks were deserted, sparsely lit by weak yellow streetlights that left the sky an impenetrable blackness. There were no memories in the night air of the assassination of the heir to the Habsburg crown, the Archduke Franz Ferdinand and his wife the Duchess Sophie, who were shot by a young Serbian revolutionary, Gavrillo Princeps.

One of the principal actors in the great catastrophe that was to unfold was Count Leopold Berchtold. Born in 1863 he was the great grandson of Marie-Therese Berchtold, nee Peterswald, a distant ancestor of our family. Marie-Therese was the mistress of the beautiful , Schloss Buchlovice that had been built by her ancestor Jan Peterswald. Already rich and well connected, Count Leopold married the heiress of one of the richest aristocrats in Hungary, Countess Ferdinanda Karolyi in 1893. Entering the diplomatic service, he was ambassador to Russia from 1906 to 1911. In 1908 he hosted a secret meeting between the foreign ministers of Russia and Austria-Hungary at Schloss Buchlovice, where the Russian foreign minister gave secret Russian acquiescence to the annexation of Bosnia and Herzegovina. In 1912 at the age of forty-nine, he was appointed the Imperial Foreign Minister of the Austria-Hungarian Empire—at the time the youngest to hold such a post in Europe. His tenure coincided with the Balkan Wars of 1912-13, the increase of Russian influence in the Balkans and escalating Serbian ambitions.

The assassination of Archduke Franz Ferdinand at Sarajevo was the culmination of rising tensions between the Empire and Serbia and perhaps in response to earlier criticism, he became, along with the army commander, a leading advocate for war against Serbia. After debate, it was decided to present Serbia with an ultimatum and on 21 July he presented the Emperor with a ten-point ultimatum which was sent to Serbia on 23 July. According to his wife, he had been unable to sleep the previous night as he agonised over whether his terms may have been too weak and would actually be accepted by the Serbs! The Serbs did accept nine of the ten conditions but refused to allow the Empire to take part in the investigation of the assassination, asserting it would be a severe violation of their sovereignty.

On Berchtold's recommendation the Empire made the decision to enter a state of war with Serbia on 28 July. Six months later he was forced to resign over his more moderate stand for trying to avoid war with Italy. Opinions on his policies and role in the precipitation of war cover the whole spectrum, the only point of general agreement being that he along with all the other diplomats in Europe did not see the catastrophe lying in wait.

He spent the remainder of his life as a much decorated (Knight of the Order of the Golden Fleece, Grand Cross of the Order of Saint Stephen) grand seigneur and died in 1942 at one of his grand estates at Pereszne in Hungary. In the 1969 film, *Oh! What a Lovely War*, he was portrayed by actor John Gielgud.

Much has been written about the assassination of the Archduke and Duchess Sophie, and their love affair and morganatic marriage which meant that their children would never have inherited their father's crown. Countess Sophie Chotek and Archduke Franz Ferdinand fell deeply in love and began a secret relationship in 1894, when he was thirty-one and she twenty-six.

Although very much a member of the European nobility her pedigree was not such that she was regarded as a suitable match for the future ruler of the Austro-Hungarian Empire. To be eligible to marry a member of the imperial House of Habsburg she would have needed to be a member of one of the reigning, or formerly reigning dynasties of Europe. The Emperor Franz Joseph at first refused to approve the marriage, but in 1899 finally relented provided their descendants would have no rights to the throne. They were married in 1900.

There was in fact a lot of royalty in Sophie's background. These included princes of Baden, Hohenzollern-Hechingen and Liechtenstein, Albert IV Count of Habsburg and Elisabeth of Habsburg sister of King Rudolf I of Germany. Also tucked away in the background was one of her less famous great grandparents, Marie-Therese Berchtold (nee Peterswald) mistress of the beautiful Schloss Buchlovice in the Czech Republic and also a great-grandmother of Imperial foreign Minister Count Leopold Berchtold.

We remained on the old bridge for some time, searching for some answers to the most tragic question in the history of the world. How did this single act of terrorism in the Balkans in 1914 set in train history's bloodiest century of warfare?

~ THE BLOODIEST CENTURY ~

Australian War Cemetery in France

By 1914 advances in technology and a European arms race had created large and heavily armed national armies and navies, whose power and destructive capacity were unimaginably beyond those of even the recent past. Europe was ruled by governments which were oligarchical rather than democratic and largely controlled by unelected

221

elites. These elites included the powerful aristocracies of the old empires, industrialists, diplomats, militarists and even their national churches. The armies were mostly commanded by old generals who had no comprehension of how vulnerable their soldiers would be in the modern battlefields.

The 'voice of the peoples' had very limited effect on Government. None of the belligerents, including the United Kingdom, were really democracies. Enfranchisement was only extended to the following percentages of those eligible to vote today. France 29%. Germany/Prussia 22%. Belgian 23%. Serbia 23%. Austria 21%. Britain 18%. Rumania 16%. Russia 15%. Italy/Piedmont 8%. Hungary 6%. Although this gave the people *some* voice, the old royal families and aristocracies in Russia, Germany and Austria still controlled executive government and were still extremely influential in Britain.

There were four major military powers in the world. Russia, France and Britain were signatories to the Triple Entente which was an agreement of friendship and understanding, without military guarantees. But beneath this edifice, the militaries of Britain, France and Belgium had well developed plans for military cooperation and promises of support implied in secret at ministerial level. There was a formal treaty between France and Russia, the Franco-Russia Alliance of 1894 which guaranteed mutual military support from any mobilization of a member of the Triple Alliance. Germany, the fading Austria-Hungarian Empire and Italy were signatories to the Triple Alliance which offered mutual military support in the event of an attack by another great power. Fatally, these arrangements made Russia, France and Germany hostage to events in the Balkans, a region teetering on the edge of anarchy.

The comparative mobilised wartime strengths were as follows. *The Triple Entente* 5,726,000. *The Triple Alliance* 3,485,000. Primary and Secondary industrial capacity, financial capacity, fuel supplies, merchant marine capacity and, all the other necessities for waging war were even more in favour of the *Triple Entente*.

The *Triple Entente* nations enjoyed an enormous advantage over the *Triple Alliance* countries. This was recognised with trepidation by Germany, but conversely, in British eyes Germany remained a long-term economic rival and still had the military potential to control all Europe, particularly if Russia was taken out of the equation.

By 1914 there was a pro-war faction in every country in Europe. Despite England having elected a Liberal Government in 1906 on an anti-war platform its foreign policy was in the hands of a pro-war faction.

France and Russia were sworn to fight to support Serbia—an unstable Balkan nation in a sea of instability, over whose national ambitions they had little control.

The Russian government and the Russian Orthodox Church saw themselves as the rightful heirs to Constantinople. Its recapture, gaining access to the Mediterranean and increasing its power in the Balkans by pursuing a pan-Slavic policy supporting Bulgaria and Serbia, were at the heart of their foreign policy. The weakness of the Ottoman Empire and the instability in the Balkans fed the old Russian dream of capturing Constantinople. These ambitions put Russia at odds with Austria-Hungary and her ally Germany, while at the same time the alliance with Britain and France enhanced her opportunities of achieving these aims

The close relationship between Russia and France had been abetted by the Kaiser who let lapse the Russian -German Treaty 1887 leaving Germany isolated.

Despite her strong position Britain still harboured fears and suspicions of Germany's imperial ambitions and her historical attitude towards alliances can be summed up by the following. *'The Queen cannot help feeling that our isolation is dangerous'*. Queen Victoria 1896. And Lord Salisbury's prescient reply. *'Isolation is much less dangerous than the danger of being dragged into wars which do not concern us.'*

The terms of the *Triple Entente*, signed with her traditional overseas rivals Russia and France, safeguarded the UK's empire. The cessation of the German naval build-up left the UK in command of the seas and there was no realistic direct threat to the UK from Germany in Europe or overseas. But, diplomatic—including the role played by Edward VII—and military planning with France created a, 'Dangerous Liaison' that was beyond the terms of the *Triple Entente* and kept secret from Parliament and the people. And, Sir Edward Grey and a pro-war lobby feared a Europe dominated by Germany.

Belgium's neutrality was guaranteed by all the Great Powers in 1839. A noble intention, but 80 years later it put the fate of Europe into the hands of the Belgium king, King Albert I. His decision to uselessly sacrifice his soldier's lives, after German guarantees of Belgium's integrity on the cessation of fighting, precipitated the UKs entry.

Kaiser Wilhelm's hatred for Edward VII and his inept diplomacy fed Russian hostility and did nothing to resolve long-term issues with France, particularly Alsace and Lorraine. His guarantee to go to war in support of Austria-Hungary in the event of a war between Russia and Austria-Hungary, given that both nations were almost certain to be drawn into war in the Balkans, meant Germany's fate was in the hands of the Emperor Franz Joseph, Tsar Nicholas II and the unstable Balkan states. And, the German pro-war lobby saw the relative strengths of Russia and France increasing against their own and believed that a pre-emptive war would be their best chance

The actual assassination of Archduke Franz Ferdinand and his wife Sophie has been generally viewed as the work of a small group of crazy terrorists belonging to 'The Young Bosnian Movement'. More recently, because of their relationship with the Serbian Black Hand Society and links to Colonel Apis, the head of Serbian Military Intelligence, the assassination is now widely viewed as one of many acts of state-sponsored terrorism carried out all over the Balkans by Serbian factions—directed at the non-Serb populations as well as Austria-Hungary—with the objective of the expansion of the Serbian state. If it was a state sponsored murder it certainly adds justification to Austria-Hungarian anger at being excluded from the investigation of the murder.

The most commonly accepted scenario following the assassination is that the great European powers fumbled their way into World War I, but it was still all Germany's fault!

We all blundered into war.' David Lloyd George. British WWI PM.

Britain had signed the *Entente Cordiale* with Russia and France, but this did not bind them to war. But a pro-French faction in the British cabinet, led by the Foreign Secretary Sir Edward Grey had implemented secret plans for, and promised, military assistance to France. Despite this secret agreement both Sir Edward Grey and King George V continued to imply to Germany that Britain would remain neutral in any European war. The British pro-war ministers in cabinet realised that neither the Government or the British people would support a war in which either Britain, Russia or France was the aggressor

Sir Edward Grey was an ardent Francophile, innately hostile to Germany and he became a major facilitator of the war. In 1908 the editor of *Daily News* A. G. Gardiner offered the following opinion of Grey: *'The inflexibility of his mind, unqualified by large knowledge, swift apprehension or urgent passion for humanity, constitute a peril to the future ... the slow movement of his mind and his unquestioning faith in the honesty of those on whom he has to rely render it easy for him to drift into courses which a more imaginative sense and a swifter instinct would lead him to question and repudiate.'*

And Lloyd George's opinion: *'....he lacked the knowledge ...vision, imagination, breadth of mind and that high courage ... which his immense task demanded ...'* he was *'a pilot whose hand trembled in the palsy of apprehension, unable to grasp the levers and manipulate them with a firm and clear purpose ...*

By 1914 Europe was on the edge of war. In May, Colonel Edward Mandell House, a respected adviser to the President of the USA Woodrow Wilson delivered the following assessment: *'The situation is extraordinary. It is jingoism run stark mad. Unless someone acting for you can bring about a different understanding, there is some day to be an awful cataclysm. No one in Europe can do it. There is too much hatred, too many jealousies. Whenever England consents, France and Russia will close in on Germany and Austria'*

However, this was more intergovernmental belligerence and not widely mirrored (the Balkans exempted) in the general public of Europe. The eminent British historian, Niall Ferguson concludes: *'The evidence is unequivocal: Europeans were not marching to war but, turning their backs on militarism'. The Pity of War.*

In Germany there was widespread concern about their situation. Field Marshall Alfred von Schlieffen, the former Chief of the German General Staff and famously the architect of the German war plans, saw the situation as thus.

'At the given moment, the drawbridges are to be let down, the doors are to be opened and the million-strong armies let loose, raving and destroying, across the Vosges, the Meusse, the Niemen, the Bug and even the Isonzo and the Tyrolean Alps. The danger seems gigantic'.

And the Reich Chancellor Bethman Hollweg: *'If there is war with France, the last Englishman will march against us.' '...the future belongs to Russia, which grows and grows and weighs upon us as an ever heavier nightmare ...'*

Meanwhile the Kaiser who made no secret in his pride of his British blood and in whose arms, Queen Victoria had passed away, who had been made a Field Marshall in the British Army on Victoria's death, had already let a treaty with Russia lapse.

He had proposed: *'... We ought to form an Anglo-German alliance, you keep the seas, while we would be responsible for the land; with such an alliance not a mouse would stir in Europe ...'*

Such was the political landscape when Archduke Franz Ferdinand was assassinated on 28 June. A timeline to war was as follows:

17 July. Three weeks after the assassination the Chancellor of the British Exchequer, Lloyd George, stated that the assassination was *'no more than a very small cloud on the horizon ... and you never get a perfectly blue sky in foreign affairs.'* On 23 July he spoke of how Anglo-German relations *'were very much better than they were a few years ago.*

23 July. Austria/Hungary presents demands to Serbia.

24 July. Belgium mobilization order issued.

25 July. 1pm Serbia Mobilises. 9.30 pm Austrian partial mobilization against Serbia.

26 July. Russia orders partial mobilization. (Remember Russia had secretly

approved of the annexation of Croatia-Herzegovina in 1908-09)

27 July. Britain offers mediation. This is accepted by Germany but, rejected by Russia and France. Britain proposes Italy, Germany and France meet in London, but Germany rejects.

28 July. After considering Serbian response Austria/Hungary declares war on Serbia.

28 July. Russia begins full mobilization.

28 July. The Netherlands declares neutrality.

29 July. Churchill orders the navy to war stations without government approval.

29 July. Telegram from Czar Nicholas to his cousin the Kaiser. '*I appeal to you to help me ... I Forsee that very soon I shall be unable to resist the pressure exercised upon me and that I shall be forced to take extreme measures which will lead to war...*'

29 July. Kaiser to Czar. Advised he would do all he could to establish a dialogue between Austria and Russia and ... '*I hope confidently that you will support me in my efforts to overcome...*'

29 July. German Foreign Minister Bethman Hollweg offers that '*provided Britain did not take sides against Germany, Belgium's integrity will be respected after the war.*'

30 July. Telegram from France to Russia with Poincare's approval '*in the precautionary measures and defensive measure which Russia believes herself obliged to resort, she should not immediately proceed to any measure which might offer Germany a pretext for a total or partial mobilization of her forces.*'

30 July. Kaiser to Czar. '*My ambassador is instructed to draw the attention of your government to the dangers and serious consequences of mobilization ... If, as it appears from your communication and that of your Government, Russia is mobilizing against Austria-Hungary ... the whole burden of decision now rests on your shoulders, the responsibility of peace or war.*' The Czar responded that he would send his personal emissary, General Tatishchev to Berlin to broker peace. But unknown to the Czar the general was arrested on the orders of Sazonov the Russian foreign minister, a man with a close relationship to the pro-war factions in the French and British governments. Under pressure from Sazonov and the military the Czar changed his position and confirmed his orders for general mobilization.

30 July. Kaiser and Bethman Hollweg send telegrams to Austria-Hungary pleading with them to accept mediation. Austria-Hungary gives assurance not to annex any Serbian territory or violate Serbian sovereignty.

31 July. British army begins mobilizing without government approval. '*Thousands of feet tramped the Channel-wards; regiment after regiment with full kit wound*'

through the London streets as the bells from tower and steeple called the folk to prayer. In Whitehall crowds parted to let a regiment march through. They marched on past the War Office and the Admiralty, but no one knew their ultimate destination.

31 July. The Kaiser sends another telegram to the Czar. *'It will not be I who am responsible for the calamity which threatens the whole civilised world. Even at this moment it lies in your power to avert it. Nobody threatens the honour and power of Russia, which well could have waited for the results of my mediation.'* Nicholas could have chosen to wait for a resolution between Serbia and Austria by the Kaiser's mediation, which both he and Austria were confident could solve the Balkan problem without war. In a note the Kaiser wrote that day. *'I have no doubt about it: England, Russia and France agreed amongst themselves to take the Austro-Serbian conflict as an excuse for waging a war of extermination against us ... the stupidity and ineptitude of our all is turned into a snare for us ... the net has been thrown over our head ... we are brought into a situation which offers England the desired pretext for annihilating us under the hypercritical cloak of justice.'*

31 July. Kaiser proclaims the 'Threatening danger of War'.

I Aug. Alexander Isvolsky the Russian ambassador to France sends a telegram to St Petersburg. *'The French War Minister informed me, in hearty high spirits, that the Government have firmly decided on war, and begged me to endorse the hope of the French General Staff that all efforts will be directed against Germany'.* France mobilises, Italy, Denmark, Sweden, Norway declare neutrality. Germany and the Ottoman Empire sign a secret treaty. At this point Serbia, Austria, Russia France, and Britain had begun military measures of some sort, only Germany had not.

1 Aug. At 5 pm after waiting twenty-four hours for a reply from Russia demanding that Russia stop all military movements on their border Germany declares war on Russia and mobilises. Germany proposed that it would respect Belgium sovereignty in exchange for the promise of British neutrality. Grey replied that *'for the present there was not the slightest intention of proceeding with hostilities against Germany.'* This exchange was never revealed to the House of Commons.

1 Aug. Betham Hollweg to Reichstag: *'We have informed the British Government, that as long as Great Britain remains neutral, our fleet will not attack the northern coast of France, and that we will not violate the integrity and independence of Belgium. These assurances I now repeat to the world'*

2 Aug. Germany invades Luxembourg.

2 Aug. 7 pm Germany requests Belgium permission, within 12 hours, for passage of German troops. King Alfred of Belgium appeals for British support.

3 Aug. 11 am British mobilization commences without approval of Parliament.

Germany declares war on France.

3 Aug. Britain sets Deadline to stop German invasion of Belgium at midnight 4 Aug.

4 Aug. War formally proclaimed by King George V.

How should the blame be allocation?

Firstly, what should have been just another localised Balkan spat became a continental war when Russia mobilised (which by treaty brought in France) and became a world war when Britain entered. There was a disastrous breakdown of European diplomacy every step of the way, and a criminal abdication of their duties by the governments and elites of Europe. That all were Christian countries, with powerful churches intimately interwoven into governments and the social fabrics, points to a colossal betrayal of humanity by the Churches.

Secondly. The alliances existing in 1914 encouraged the pro-war factions in the *Triple Entente* to act while they held a strong military position. The pro-war faction in an isolated Germany believed their relative weakness would continue to grow.

Thirdly. The Triple Entente belligerents had firmly held historical ambitions. France to reclaim Alsace-Lorraine. Russia to obtain Istanbul. Serbia to establish a dominant Serb state in the Balkans. Britain the removal of an imperial rival.

Fourthly. The leading actors were mostly flawed men with flawed agendas. Particularly the Tsar and the Kaiser who, although holding autocratic powers, were manipulated by others. Also, Sir Edward Grey, the British Foreign Secretary and the pro-war clique who led their country to its suicide. Churchill's reputation is hardly enhanced by the following. *'I think a curse should rest on me – because I love this war. I know it's smashing and shattering the lives of thousands every moment – and yet – I can't help it – I enjoy every second of it'.* Winston Churchill to Violet Asquith on 22 February 1915. Or the Bishop of London, A.F. Winnington-Ingram, in his Advent Sermon preached in 1915 *'... a great crusade – we cannot deny it – to kill Germans: to kill them, not for the sake of killing, but to save the world; to kill the good as well as the bad, to kill the young men as well as the old, to kill those who have shown kindness to our wounded as well as the fiends who crucified the Canadian sergeant, who superintended the Armenian massacres, who sank the Lusitania, and who turned machine-guns on the civilians of Aershott and Louvain – and to kill them lest the civilisation of the world should itself be killed.'* And...*The Church can best help the nation first of all by making it realise that it is engaged in a Holy War ... Christ died on Good Friday for Freedom, Honour and Chivalry and our boys are dying for the same things ... You ask for my advice in a sentence to what the Church is to do. I answer MOBALIZE THE NATION FOR A HOLY WAR.* Or, General Haig (a member of the Church of Scotland, to his wife on the eve of the Battle of the Somme). *'I feel that every step in my plan has been taken with the Devine help'.*

Fifthly. Did Britain fight for freedom? A bit rich seeing that its authoritarian rule controlled the largest empire the world had seen (including Ireland which the UK held brutally by force of arms) and only a low percentage of her own population had the vote. Belgium was a brutal colonialist power who had raped and pillaged the Congo.

In any case the toll of this apocalypse was: eight million soldiers dead and twenty million wounded, diseased, mutilated or poisoned by gas. Twenty million civilians killed or wounded and many of the survivors starving in the rubble of cities, towns and the countryside. It left Russia ruled by a murderous, unstable communist regime, soon to be taken over by Joseph Stalin. Europe was a smouldering ruin, a whole generation had been decimated, millions were unemployed, economies shattered, and social unrest was widespread. And in perhaps the greatest tragedy of the whole bloody war, the peace terms imposed by the victors created the political atmosphere that made the rise of Hitler, or someone like him, inevitable.

World War I heralded the collapse of the great European and Ottoman Empires and the emergence of the creeds that would rock the world—fascism and communism. World War II shattered the remaining empires and helped spread communism throughout Europe, China and the old colonies of Asia to the point where the existence of Western democracy seemed in peril.

Hitler's rise to power in Germany was abetted by weak governments and the continued inept diplomacy of the other European powers, particularly the UK who found itself in the most isolated position since Elizabethan times. After years of appeasing Hitler while at the same time disarming themselves, the decision of the British Prime Minister Neville Chamberlain in 1939 to draw a line in the sand by guaranteeing Poland's integrity—with the enthusiastic support of Winston Churchill—was one of the worst strategic decisions in British history.

'I said at once, 'The Unnecessary War.' There was never a war more easy to stop than that which has just wrecked what was left of the world from the previous struggle'. Winston Churchill, who was crucially involved in the start of WWI, oversaw the disastrous Gallipoli campaign and led Britain into WWII.

Britain had let her armed forces run down to such an extent that it was in no way ready to fight a major war at that juncture. However, it could have put itself in a position that it could not have lost a war against Hitler. It still had a powerful navy and was churning out fighter planes that would have given it complete control of the skies over the English Channel at, what these days seems an impossible rate; of 496 Hurricanes and Spitfires in July and 467 in August 1940.

It was also extremely hypocritical of England and France to guarantee the freedom for the Poles while still retaining huge colonial empires in Asia and Africa that were held by military force. Where the native population had no rights of self-government and limited personal freedoms. But I suppose they were only natives; in Churchill's view Gandhi was a '*a seditious fakir .... striding half naked up the steps of the vice regal palace....*'

In 1939 Poland was a military dictatorship that had just taken part in dismembering Czechoslovakia and was refusing to allow Germans living in lands that had been German for hundreds of years, to re-join Germany. Chamberlain and Churchill knew that British and French guarantees were worthless, they simply did not have the military capacity to intervene in Eastern Europe. But the guarantee encouraged Poland's intransigence, particularly on the question of Danzig, a city that the British themselves recognised should be returned to Germany, and Silesia which had been settled by Germans and been part of Bohemia and the Austrian Empire since the fourteenth century.

It meant that the decision to go to war was placed in the hands of an erratic Polish dictator, Colonel Joseph Beck, over whom the British and French had little influence, in an area that was not of vital interest to either nation. It meant that what may have been a Polish – German war — in which there were rights and wrongs on both sides—of brief duration, became a world war that resulted in sixty million deaths.

Churchill's decision to go to war over Poland, and then to pursue the war alone after the fall of France, cost Britain her dominions and two million service casualties. It left her bankrupt and lost her the greatest empire the world had seen—perhaps Hitler's role in liberating Asia and Africa has been overlooked. The winner was Joseph Stalin. It enabled him to create the vast USSR, seize much of Europe and sponsor Mao Zedong's communist regime in China, which in the four years of 'The Great Leap Forward' alone, killed forty-five million, of his fellow countrymen. What the shape of the world would have been if Stalin had been left to fight Hitler alone, is one of the great 'what ifs' of the 20th century.

The recklessness of Churchill's decision is highlighted when you consider the vastly different international landscape that had formed since World War I. Then, Britain at the height of her power and her dominions including India, Canada, Australia, New Zealand plus France, Russia, Italy and Japan would have been defeated by Germany but for the USA's entry into the war.

In 1940 France was defeated, Russia, Japan and Italy were German allies and the USA was determinedly neutral. It is also worth remembering that although Communism was a highly marketable creed internationally, it is very unlikely that Hitler's fascism would have been.

At the end of World War II, Joseph Stalin, a communist murderer who in the process of establishing his regime had exterminated at least forty millions of his Russian countrymen, ruled much of Europe. Poland, the country whose liberty was the immediate reason for Britain and France going to war, was to remain under a brutal Soviet dictatorship for fifty years. In this tragedy Poland was not alone. Estonia, Latvia, Lithuania, Hungary, Romania, Yugoslavia, Bulgaria and Czechoslovakia, all Christian nations, were under Stalin's rule.

Ernie Peterswald, my father's elder brother was wounded on the western front in World War I, and his son John was a pilot who was shot down and captured in the Italian campaign in World War II. Dad's youngest brother, Keith fought in Africa and the Pacific in World War II.

Elsewhere in Europe, in the aftermath of the war, socialist political parties dominated the national stages of most of the free nations, vying with communist parties for popular support. Into the 1950s Russia's magnificent war effort seemed to have been the precursor to great social and economic advances. Stalin's Five Year Plans were the envy of the democracies, still trying to dig their way out of war debts, and the lingering effects on social and economic life of the Great Depression. The USSR was perceived by many, particularly by the left, as a worker's paradise, and Stalin's gulags were hidden behind the shadows of the 'Iron Curtain'.

The conventional military balance in Europe was massively in favour of the USSR and no sane analyst could imagine that western forces could delay, let alone defeat, a Soviet advance to the Atlantic from their frontier running through the heartland of Europe. The West's only defence was a nuclear one – and there were many in the West, perhaps most, who thought that a nuclear war was too high a price to pay to defend the western democracies. The great liberal virtues of the democracies seemed to many of their citizens to be poor fare, compared to the equality, justice and economic security supposedly provided by the communist states.

The ascendency of communism in Europe, was matched in the emerging nations in Asia. In 1949 Stalin's prodigy, Mao Zedong gained control of China and established a communist regime that was even more brutal than that in the USSR. Communist regimes now extended from within a few miles of the Atlantic, across all Europe and Asia to the Pacific. communist doctrine demanded the worldwide spread of communist rule by force and shortly after the war the world found itself enmeshed in the 'Cold War'.

In 1948-49 Russia tried to force the allies out of Berlin, necessitating the Berlin airlift. Between 1950-53 the Chinese and North Korean communists fought the UN to a standstill on the Korean Peninsula. Tibet was taken over by the Chinese in 1950 and by 1959 communist movements were fighting in Malaysia, Indonesia, Laos and Cambodia. In the Americas a communist regime was established in Cuba in 1959, and guerrilla movements were fighting in Peru, Chile, El Salvador, Bolivia, Haiti and Nicaragua. Guerrilla wars were being fought in Africa. All these wars were fought with Russian or Chinese aid with the overreaching aim of communist world hegemony.

The end of World War II brought the end of the colonial era and sparked the rise of nationalist movements all over the world. The western democracies, because of their economic, scientific, political and military development from the industrial revolution onwards, had been the colonisers, creating huge empires ruled from their homelands in Europe. Even before the war's end, Sukano and Hatta had proclaimed Indonesian independence, and in 1949 the Netherlands formally transferred sovereignty to the Indonesian Government. Ho Chi Minh had done the same for the Democratic Republic of Vietnam.

The rise of the independence movements eventually forced Britain to give independence to her colonies with reasonably good grace. Independent democracies were established in India, Pakistan and Bangladesh and in Africa with varying degrees of success. However other Europeans nations refused to give up their colonies without a fight. None more so than the French in Asia whose actions were shameful and resulted in the beginning of the First Indochina War in 1946. In most cases communists were able to ride to power as nationalist independence movements—a disaster for the emerging nations with democratic ambitions.

The brutality and economic incompetence of the communist regimes in China and Russia at the time were not widely exposed until the late 1980s. The truth would not be apparent until the collapse of the bankrupt USSR in 1996 and the final unveiling of its criminal, murderous and corrupt government. In the post war period, Stalin and Mao were idealised in both the West and the East. In these years the great freedoms of the west—to be able to elect governments, to worship or not according to your conscience, to own private property including private homes and the means of production, to speak and move freely in pursuit of individual happiness, the rule of law, seemed trumped by promises of nationalization of assets and centrally planned economies and a life in a worker's paradise.

This was the world that I grew up in, and by 1965 there was a wide feeling that the times of the great western democracies were drawing to a close. However, by this time I had become a passionate believer in democracy and the rule of law that had developed in the West over the last seven hundred years. I was influenced by Sir Arthur Bryant's great book, 'Set in a Silvery Sea' and 'The History of the English Speaking Peoples' by Winston Churchill. They are both moving accounts of the great democratic institutions that had been nurtured in the United Kingdom and exported to the world. It was impossible for me to admire the social, legal, political and economic achievements of democracies and also believe in the sort of regimes that Stalin and Mao had created.

By now enough of the ugly truths had leaked out to expose the regimes for what they were, if you were prepared to accept the evidence. Australian servicemen had fought the Chinese Communists in Korea and shortly afterwards in Malaya. Czechoslovakia had been overrun by the Russians, and the West was under the constant threat of a nuclear war.

~ VIETNAM 1969 ~

Vietnam had become an independent nation astride the Red River Delta in 939 CE and its capital Hanoi, was founded in 1010. While fiercely fighting to protect their independence from China, they extended their control southward. The Kingdom of Champa in central Vietnam was absorbed and they reached the Mekong delta in the mid-eighteenth century. For most of this century two families, the Trinhs in the north and the Nguyens in the south struggled for dominance and it was not until 1802 that the Emperor Gia Long established a dynasty that survived—under French rule from 1883—until 1955. The imperial capital was established in Hue in central Vietnam. Indochina War had commenced. By 1953 the People's Army of Vietnam (PAVN) had become a formidable force, capable of waging both conventional and guerrilla war. Morale was high and it was receiving considerable support from the Soviet Union and China, in the form of arms and material, training, sanctuaries and supply lines.

In 1954 the French were defeated at the Battle of Dien Bien Phu. In the same year the 'Geneva Accords', sponsored by the UN and attended by representatives of all the interested parties, including the Democratic Republic of Vietnam (the Communist North) and the State of Vietnam (French Vietnam which would become South Vietnam) split Vietnam into two halves. The Viet Minh were required to return to the north, while those Vietnamese who wished to move to the south to avoid communist rule could do so. Some one million Vietnamese did migrate south, including many who wished religious freedom. the formation of an intelligentsia which led the struggle to gain the freedoms and political values of France for their own country.

Discontent and opposition to the French continued to grow during the twentieth century, despite all efforts of the French to suppress it and resulted in the growth of a Moscow-aligned communist movement—in due course the leader of which was one Nguen Sinh Cung. Born in 1890 he spent from 1911 to 1941 in London and Paris where he became a founding member of the French Communist Party. In 1920 he studied at the School for Toilers of the East, in Moscow and became a professional revolutionary with many aliases. In 1929 and 1930 he helped form the Indochinese Communist Party and eventually adopted the alias Ho Chi Minh: 'the Bringer of Enlightenment'.

After the fall of France in 1940 the Japanese took effective control of Vietnam and Ho Chi Minh emerged as the leader of the Vietnamese communists. In alliance with other nationalist groups he formed the Vietnam Independence League, which was generally known as the Viet Minh. During the war the Viet Minh continued a low-key guerrilla war against the Japanese but concentrated on crushing rival groups so that when the Japanese were defeated and surrendered on 2 September 1945 Ho was in a position to declare the establishment of the Democratic Republic of Vietnam

(DRV).

After France took over the country the ruling elite in Vietnam was predominantly French, although there was still a number of wealthy Vietnamese landholders. There was only a small indigenous middle class, but the vast majority of the people were either unemployed or rural labourers. A few Vietnamese received a French education which eventually resulted in

However, France had no intention of surrendering her Indochinese colonies and began military operations in late 1946. The DVR leaders retreated into the mountains and the First

A free and fair referendum was to be held to decide the fate of the entire country.

In 1955 Ho Chi Minh, following communist doctrine implemented 'land reforms' in North Vietnam. Thousands who were classified landowners and farmers were imprisoned and 're-educated' and their property confiscated. Many more fled to the South. The prevailing view in the West was that there could never be a 'free and fair' referendum if the communists were involved, and that any election they won would be the last one held. Which is exactly what did happen.

In the South a former mandarin of the Nguyen dynasty was named Prime Minister of the State of Vietnam by the Head of State Bao Dai in 1954. The following year, after winning a rigged referendum, he established himself as the president of the Republic of Vietnam (RVN). Partly because of the guerrilla movement fostered by the North, partly because the Catholic Diem regime discriminated against Buddhists and largely due to the personalities of the regime, it rapidly became a virtual police state and lost the support of wide sections of the population. In 1957 North Vietnam organised and supported a guerrilla war in the South, and in 1959 the USA sent its first military advisers to support the independence of South Vietnam.

By 1962 the USA commitment had grown to 11,000. By 1965 it was 200,000 and by 1966 there were around 400,000 of whom 6,000 were killed and 30,000 wounded in that year. Australia's first commitment was thirty advisers in 1962 and in 1965 a battalion (Ist Battalion Royal Australian Regiment) and a support group totalling 1100 men was committed. In 1966 this was increased to a task force of two battalions and logistic support totalling around 1100 men, including conscripts.

On 18 August 1966 Australian troops fought the Battle of Long Tan which for Australia was the largest action of the war. It was fought in a rubber plantation close to the Australian base at Nui Dat, between Viet Cong and North Vietnamese units planning to attack the base and D Company 6 RAR supported by cavalry, artillery, mortars and helicopters. Eighteen Australians were killed and twenty-four wounded, while the much larger Viet Cong force lost at least 245.

By early 1967 the size of the Australian Task Force had been increased to three battalions. On 17 February 6 RAR and A Squadron 3rd Cavalry were involved in vicious fighting during Operation Bribie. During March to May 1967, an eleven-kilometre barrier minefield designed to separate and to shield Phuoc Tuy villages from enemy units was built. This proved to be a disaster as it could not be protected from enemy soldiers and, hostile villagers 'lifting' the deadly M16 'Jumping Jack' landmines provided them with what proved to be their most potent weapon. When trodden on the mine would jump up a metre or so and explode with a deadly radius of around 25 metres. A conservative estimate is that between May 1967 and November 1971, 1 ATF suffered fifty-five killed and 250 dismembered by mines stolen and used against them. This was close to half of the casualties during this period and, inflicted a great deal of trauma on the wounded and their loved ones, and all those involved in the hideous incidents.

The Vietnamese New Year or Tet, celebrating the arrival of spring is the most important celebration in Vietnamese culture. It is an occasion for pilgrimages and family reunions, forgetting about the troubles of the past and looking to a better future. On 30 January 1968 while the country was honouring this ancient tradition, the Viet Cong launched a major nationwide offensive. It was a dramatic escalation of the war, and although the Viet Cong initially had some high-profile victories, it ended in a devastating military defeat. But it was a major propaganda victory for them and, fuelled anti-war sentiment in the West. In Phuoc Tuy, the Australians were involved in bitter fighting, including around the villages of Trang Bom, Baria and Long Dien and later in major operations near Bien Hoa/Long Binh.

In May and June Australian and New Zealand forces fought major battles in the defence of Fire Support Base Coral and Balmoral, some twenty kilometres north of the city of Bien Hoa. Fire Support Bases were heavily defended positions for artillery, mortars and armoured units which supported infantry operations within the range of the artillery. Coral and Balmoral were situated astride a route used by NVA and VC forces approaching or departing Saigon and Bien Hoa and from which the allies conducted aggressive fighting and ambush patrols. The North Vietnamese launched several strong attacks in an attempt to destroy the bases, and during a twenty-five-day period the Australians fought their costliest and most protracted battles of the war.

In February 1969 the HMAS Sydney carrying the 5th Battalion Royal Australian Regiment, dropped anchor at Vung Tau in South Vietnam after a voyage from Sydney Harbour. I had joined the battalion as the second-in-command of a rifle company the previous October and it was three years since I had graduated from Duntroon, most of which I has spent with the Pacific Islands Regiment in Papua New Guinea.

After joining the battalion in October 1968, it seemed no time at all before I was at Garden Island in Sydney Harbour waiting to board the HMAS Sydney, an aircraft carrier converted to a troopship. There were crowds of well-wishers mingling with the soldiers. A military band was playing. On the surface there was a carnival atmosphere, but behind the music lay the tensions of impending separation. Love fought fear, smiles and laughter, tears and tight embraces.

Princess Charlotte, whom I had seen so little of, nestled in my arms and I wondered what the future held for us both. My mother held my arm, the pain of her cancer a memory beneath her fear of my going. Ro smiling through her tears. A handshake and an arm across my shoulder from my father.

It was time to go. Climb the gangplank, waving as the ship pulled away, the music from the band, the ship's horn. The sparkling water of the harbour, the wide Australian sky, blue and cloudless. People in boats waving, through the Heads, the coastline just a shadow on the far horizon.

It took us a week to reach Vietnam. The trip across was a surreal experience. The rush and the turmoil of the final months, the thousands of administrative details, the drama of actually getting afloat, replaced by a stately progress across the seas. The days were spent firing at targets off the back of the flight deck, lectures and physical training. At night Mike Battle and I were invited to join the ship's poker school, which allegedly had played for every night the ship had been afloat. In due course we arrived at Vung Tau and by the time it was light we were ashore and in a convoy of trucks heading for Nui Dat, the defensive base of the Australian Task Force, about thirty kilometres inland.

The enemy the Australians faced when we arrived in Phuoc Tuy in 1969 were the 5th Vietcong Division of which the majority of the soldiers were North Vietnamese regulars, and the 33rd NVA Regiment. Below these were two regular battalions, the D445 Provincial Mobile Battalion recruited locally and the D440 Battalion, again mainly NVA regulars. They generally operated as guerrilla forces, mostly avoiding direct confrontation unless that could be achieved in a situation in which they thought they held all the aces. They used the jungle and the mountains as safe havens from which they could launch hit and run attacks and intimidate the villagers. At a local level there were local guerrilla units recruited and supported by villages, with full and part time guerrillas who may or may not have been farmers by day and fighters by night. They were all commanded from the Central Office for South

Vietnam.

The first thing I need to say is that I had a very lucky war. 5 RAR was a well-trained and commanded battalion where the lives of all its members were jealously guarded. For me there were no 'this is it' moments even if there was some apprehension at times. My company commander, Major Ray Harring, was a man who inspired trust. He was in his early thirties, a wiry man who was never ruffled. He was to command B Company with aggression and courage, but foremost in all he did, was his respect for the soldiers he led.

Just before the major battle of the battalion's tour was fought at Binh Ba in June, I was posted to a job where virtually the only danger was falling out of a helicopter. I came home with no physical or mental scars.

However, not everyone was so lucky. Despite excellent medical evacuation by helicopter, the casualties sustained by 5RAR were twenty-five killed and 202 wounded, nearly a third of the strength of the battalion that arrived. These figures relate to physical wounds—who will ever really know what the mental scars, the non-battle physical damage from injury and disease have been. That said, I don't think the average digger in 5RAR would have swapped for the Battle of the Somme, or Guadalcanal, or the Buna/Gona Campaign or Stalingrad.

The questions of the morality of the war have tormented all who took part. They are still with me after half a century. At the heart of the conundrum are a number of perhaps irreconcilable positions. The right of the Vietnamese people to form an independent self-governing nation, including the right to live in a Communist dictatorship if that is their wish. And on the other hand, the existential threat posed to the Western Democracies in the second half of the twentieth century by the spread of Communist Totalitarian Dictatorships. At the outset the United States clearly supported the end of colonialism. They wanted the French out of Indo-China nearly as much as the Vietnamese did. But they hated and feared the spread of communism.

It would be inhumane not to be appalled by the brutality of the war and shocked by the many nightmarish images of it: women and children fleeing flaming villages, the massacre at My Lai, Buddhist monks incinerating themselves, a Vietnamese general executing a prisoner with a shot through his head, the corpses in muddy paddy fields, forests denuded and poisoned with Agent Orange. It was right to loathe the thought of a son, a brother, a daughter or a sister being killed or maimed in the quagmire. But was it not also right for many Vietnamese, both in the north and south, to want a life in a free and democratic country and not endure the nightmare of rule by a Stalin or a Mao, who slaughtered millions upon millions of their countrymen?

For Australians, the Cold War and the international spread of communism was a real and proximate threat to our country and our democratic ideals. The alliance with the USA was vitally important to our national security. Was the war a price worth paying for our security and freedom? Was it right that so many of the Australians who fought were so young and many were national servicemen who were only nineteen or twenty and had no choice? They were wrenched from the lives they had planned, to be sent to a dirty jungle to fight and die in a dirty war before they even had the chance to vote for or against the politicians who decided their fate.

These were the Australian soldiers who my Commanding Officer the remarkable Colonel Colin Khan DSO wrote so movingly of:

'I saw a rain and sweat drenched man in green,
Laden like a pack mule, twenty-one going on fifty
Cutting his way through the jungle by day to attack the enemy,
Then laying all night in the paddy fields or on trails on ambush.'

The one emotion that has remained constant over the half century since the war, is my absolute and unchangeable admiration for these young men. They served with bravery, devotion, mateship and stoic good humour, they exemplified all the best of our nation. They deserve our continuing gratitude and respect, and most have carried emotional or physical scars from what they went through — including the odious and cruel opprobrium heaped on them by the voracious anti-war movement.

Many were angry, but because of their bravery and loyalty to their mates and units, they fought on. However, the poem *'We the Unlucky'* — Dedicated to Jimmy Webster who gave the lot for a land that forgot ... published on the 5 RAR website— speaks for many of those who served.

'They said it was Australia's war, they lied.
It belonged to those that served and died;
Australians didn't really care,
Or maybe they didn't want to know;
Rather watch the footy show.

They taught us how to kill a man in a far off distant land
They said the enemy was over there;
We had to stop the commie plot.

I'm still pondering thirty years on,
Trying to work out what went wrong;
I don't sleep well at night,

Still trying to work out what was right.

I'm still crying for the friends that died,
And for what!!!
Our real enemy was here all the time,
The Government, DVA, the lot!!!

Our war still goes on,
Thanks a bloody lot.'

The spirit of social protest the war empowered in Australia and abroad flowed over into all aspects of life and encouraged a social revolution. Attitudes to sexual freedom, birth control, abortion, marriage and divorce, rights and entitlements were profoundly changed. Malthusians and Marxists found a new generation of militant supporters. Australia's place in the world was changed. The war was our first military involvement independent of the UK and was formal recognition that we must look to the US for our security. A socialist government, with Gough Whitlam as Prime Minister was elected, and the Labor Party was in power for the first time in many years. Both good and bad have come from these events.

I think that most who served would now also deeply mourn the many deaths amongst those we fought and share the anguish and sorrow of their loved ones. The battlefield count, of those of our enemy who were killed in action by 5 RAR during that second tour was 370 and in excess of 146 wounded. How many more, whose bodies were not recovered from the battlefield or were killed by airstrikes, artillery fire or died through disease or chemical poisoning, we will never know.

The Commanding Officer of 5 RAR Lieutenant Colonel Colin Khan was universally liked and admired. As a young lieutenant he had fought in the Korean War and had proved he was a brave and resourceful fighting soldier. He had been badly wounded by machine gun fire and his life had only been saved at the cost a lung. He was decorated for bravery. He was a proven commander, very approachable and his first concern was always for the lives and welfare of his soldiers; who in return would have done anything for him. Naturally, he was universally called 'Genghis' but it was much more as a term of respect and liking than as any comparison of the blood thirsty nature of the legendary Mongol.

The Australian base sprawled over an area of the old rubber plantations surrounding Nui Dat Hill and was protected by twelve kilometres of barbed wire with strong-posts and mine fields. The area outside the wire was cleared allowing good fields of fire. Our battalion area was on the northern edge of the base and provided comfortable accommodation in six-man tents shaded by the rubber trees. There were showers, canteens and messes. Generally, a rifle company could expect to spend a few days a month enjoying these comforts—the rest of the time was outside the wire – sleeping on the ground, eating hard rations, no ablutions.

We commenced operations after a couple of weeks of sorting ourselves out and acclimatization.

The following are edited extracts from 'The Year of the Tigers, South Vietnam 1969-70, edited by Michael Battle and David Wilkins:

'On 1 March 5 RAR deployed on Operation Quintus Thrust in an area of operations (AO) to the west of Nui Dat in an area that included the northern and eastern parts of the rugged Nui Dinh mountains. The paddy fields at this time were cemented by the sun and the vegetation on the coastal flats was tinder dry. The thick clumps of thorn covered bamboo proved to be a formidable obstacle to A and D Companies, as they deployed west on foot and in APCs to the west of the AO.

The mission of the battalion was to conduct Reconnaissance in Force operations to harass enemy forces and deny them base plate positions within range of population centres.

At 0800 2 March, 105 Field Battery fired artillery preparation prior to a helicopter assault into Landing Zone (LZ) Marie by C Company, followed by Battalion Headquarters and B Company. In the afternoon the patrolling companies discovered fresh signs of enemy movement and located a 107mm rocket launching site.

On the night of 3 March A, C and D Companies reported contacts in their ambushes and sweeps in the morning confirmed eleven enemy killed and indications of others wounded. Lieutenant H Doyle of D Company was wounded and later repatriated to Australia.

The next four days saw the companies continuing their operations with scattered light contacts. Both the RAAF Iroquois and the Army H13 helicopters flying in support received ground fire. 12 Platoon D Company killed two local guerrillas in a contact at 0655 hours 5 March. By last light on 8 March the battalion, less B Company, had consolidated in an assembly area in preparation for the next phase of the operation. B Company had harboured with a troop of tanks and a troop of APCs.

On March 5 the battalion began to assemble for the next phase of the operation, the cordon and search of the village of Phuoc Hoa Long which nestled close to the perimetre of Nui Dat base. It was known that the village was often

242

infiltrated by Vietnam Cong on resupply and intimidation missions.

At midnight, under a half moon, D Company led the battalion across the open paddi and through the bamboo to the perimetre fence of the village of Phuoc Hoa Long. The village nestled under the southern perimetre of Nui Dat base and was often infiltrated by Viet Cong guerrillas on resupply and propaganda missions. An extensive political and military communist infrastructure was also known to exist among the 5,100 villagers. 5 RARs task was to cordon and search the northern hamlets of the village.

C and D Companies were to form the cordon and A and B Companies were to conduct the search. D Company was led along the dark corridor of trees and banana plantations by 10 Platoon. At 0150 hours heavy firing shattered the stealth of the approach. 10 Platoon reported firing from the Regional Force post at the northern end of the village. At the same time 11 Platoon came under AK47 (a communist weapon) fire from their right flank.

The American Liaison Officer managed to stop the firing as soon as it was realised that elements of 10 Platoon had stumbled into a Regional Force minefield. However, by this time casualties had been sustained from both mine explosions and small arms fire.

Artillery fired continuous illumination while casualties were recovered from the minefield by RAAF Dustoff helicopters. One helicopter spent forty minutes hovered above the rescue party providing illumination with its landing lights. This was an extremely dangerous operation, as there was the chance that the down blast of the blades would detonate more mines and the helicopter was very vulnerable to ground fire.

Three members of 10 Platoon were killed. The Platoon Commander 2nd Lieutenant B Walker, the Platoon Sergeant B Smith and Section Commander G Gilbert.

While this calamity was unfolding the remainder of the battalion continued with the operation and by 0730 hours the sweep and search was underway. A and B Companies prodded their way around the many small gardens and searched 263 houses. This type of operation proved exhausting because of the ever-present threat of mines, booby traps and snipers. 1700 villages were screened by intelligence units of which eleven were detained as suspected VC infiltrators.'

This operation represented some of the enduring problems with the war, ones which have beset every anti-guerrilla war in history.

The first was the need to win and hold the support of the villages, while at the same time providing security for them and preventing Viet Cong infiltration. Many of the villages in the province had been established by North Vietnamese Catholics who had fled the north in 1954 and were our natural allies. As much as anything this type of operation was designed to help them secure themselves from Viet Cong intimidation.

However, surrounding, searching and screening a village was not a way to win hearts and minds. We hated it as much as the villagers, there was an air of a Gestapo operation about it, and the possibility of booby traps preyed on everyone's nerves.

The operation was an introduction to some of the defining elements of the infantry war in Vietnam. Most operations ran for around a month and involved continuous dawn to dusk fighting patrols carrying heavy (around 40Kg of gear and weapons) loads over long distances in hot and humid weather. They were very physically demanding, bloody hard and exhausting work. Most infantry soldiers lost between 10% and 15% of their body weight during the tour and everyone was fit and lean to start with; dysentery, heat exhaustion, fevers of unknown origin, malaria, infections were a daily presence. Once on operations the next contact with the enemy was always only a heartbeat away, the next step could explode a 'jumping jack' mine. Every night's harbour was in a situation where any movement in the darkness outside the camp was a threat. Sentry duty and radio piquet's meant that sleep was short and broken – averaging three to four hours a night, lying on the ground in wet or sweat soaked clothes that were worn for weeks at a time. This meant that everyone was under extreme mental and physical stress from the moment they stepped outside 'the wire'.

We had all subconsciously been programmed by the ubiquitous, Pavlovian sounds of helicopters. The sound of which, for the rest of our lives, would in an instant take us back to the jungles and the paddy fields. The sound meant flying to operations, insertions or extractions from risky helipads, casualty evacuation, gunship fire-support in action, resupply in jungle clearings, or if it wasn't us then some other poor bastard not too far away, was copping it.

Not that there was a great deal of rest back in base on the three days a month (on average) that they were back in Nui Dat. Pickets still had to be mounted twenty-four hours a day, clearing patrols at dawn and dusk, preparation made for the next operation. There was always a lot of noise; artillery, mortars, helicopters, firing on the rifle ranges. And, and, and there were beers that had to be drunk in the company boozer, noisy boisterous camaraderie to try and forget the danger and the strain of operations for a few short hours.

Operation Federal Overlander (Edited extracts from The Year of the Tiger).

244

'As a result of a significant enemy threat the Battalion was deployed to help protect the large US bases in the Long Bin, Bien Hoa area. HQ 1 ATF with 4 RAR and 9 RAR had been deployed forward into an area of operations some 4000 metres east of the massive Long Bin post. This base had been developed into one of the largest military complexes in the world and at the time was subject to regular rocket attacks.

On 10 March 5 RAR relieved 9 RAR at Fire Support Base Kerry and took over the responsibility for the area of operations (AO) Arunda while 4 RAR was operating in the adjoining AO Belconnen.

The major threat was assessed as being the 5th VC Division to the north east of our AO. 3/274 VC Regiment was thought to be south of AO Belconnen but was severely decimated. The 275 VC Regiment was to the north west. Elements of 33 VC Regiment were thought to be actually in our AO and elements of 95A VC Regiment were on the northern boundary.

Friendly flanking units around our AO were the 36 Ranger Battalion (US) to the west, I Division (US) to the north west, 3/1 Air Cavalry (US) to the north and a mobile strike force to the east.

On the morning of 10 March, A, C, and D Companies with Battalion Headquarters were ferried by CH47 Chinook helicopters into the dustbowl that was FSB Kerry. B Company with A Squadron 3 Cavalry arrived from Nui Dat at 1010 hours. By 1600 hours the relief was complete.

For the next ten long hot days the companies carried out saturation patrolling without significant contact. It was thought that the numerous small contacts made by 9 RAR in the previous weeks had been reconnaissance parties preceding a major attack on the US bases.

On 20 March D Company and a Tactical headquarters swept the 'Fried Eggs' feature without contact.

Throughout this period the fire support component of the command post was working overtime on clearances sought by innumerable zealous fire support units. At one time the annihilation of D Company was prevented when allied radar spotted an 'enemy' mortar base plate in the D Company position and requested a clearance for a Divisional bombardment.

Perhaps because of the heavy patrol program no enemy were contacted the main enemy units were denied reconnaissance routes and were forced to the north and north east of the battalion.'

Edited extracts from Year of the Tiger.

'On 27 March the Battalion redeployed into AO Manuka so as to deny the enemy the use of extensive bunker systems known to be in the area and to attempt to

245

destroy HQ T7 (MR7) the headquarters controlling VC operations in the provinces of Long Binh, Long Khanh, Phuoc Tuy and Bin Tuy. As the operation progressed other elements of 274 Regiment and D525 Sapper Battalion were found to be in the area.

Most contacts during this phase were against small groups of enemy in bunker systems. In two instances though, ambushes were initiated against large enemy groups. Generally, the enemy reacted to our contacts vigorously, quickly returning fire with RPGs and automatic weapons. In the main bunker systems encountered in the south of Manuka the fire was particularly heavy.

The MR7 base camp was located by 11 Platoon on Good Friday, 4 April. The platoon was patrolling from the company base and found numerous fresh tracks. The forward scout heard enemy voices and at the same time spotted a bunker ten yards to his front. Grenades were thrown into the bunker and at the same time the enemy was engaged with heavy small arms fire. The enemy reacted quickly with heavy machine guns, RPGs and automatic weapons, pinning the platoon down. Two soldiers, Privates White and Pike were wounded.

A heavy machine gun was continuing to lay down heavy fire on the left flank of 11 Platoon.

12 Platoon, which was three hundred metres away moving through another bunker system, was sent to help. But as it moved onto the right flank of 11 Platoon, it too came under heavy fire.

Helicopter gunships had been urgently requested and at this stage they arrived overhead and began laying down heavy suppressive fire to within fifteen metres to the front of the platoons. This enabled the two platoons to pull back, bring with them their dead and wounded, while all the while being subjected to continuous fire from the enemy.

While this was happening two diggers were displaying exceptional heroism. Private Fitch, a stretcher bearer, discarded his rifle and moved continually, under heavy fire, to give first aid to the wounded although he himself was seriously wounded in the stomach. He was later awarded the Military Medal. Private Burridge, a machine gunner, continue to fire belt after belt of ammunition into the enemy positions although this attracted heavy RPG and machine gun fire on himself. His actions contributed greatly to the successful pull back.

D Company regrouped and with tank support successfully assaulted the bunker system. It was found to comprise a large command post, a hospital bunker and twenty-eight well used and maintained fighting bunkers. Later a Hoi Chanh (a Viet Cong who had come across to the allies) revealed that at the time of the contact the VC commander of MR7 had been in conference with three of his regimental commanders.

On 8 April 5 RAR returned to Nui Dat, all the companies having defeated elements of units which were regarded as amongst the enemy's best. The operation had disrupted HQ T7 and forced them to move out of the area, seriously disrupting any intended enemy offensive.

Between 12 -18 April individual companies were deployed on Operation Deerstalk. The only contact was made by B Company some 4000 metres to the southeast of Nui Dat. At 2045 hours, enemy movement was heard to the rear of an ambush position occupied by Company Headquarters and 5 Platoon. A sentry, Private A Remeljej, fired a burst of M16 killing one enemy some twenty-five metres from the perimetre. The enemy immediately replied with heavy automatic fire and RPGs, which was suppressed by M60s from 5 Platoon returned fire. Casualties had been suffered and the Dustoff helicopter was called in.

Further enemy movement was heard in front of the eastern flank and was engaged with artillery fire from Nui Dat and the Dustoff came under fire from that direction. Shortly afterwards the enemy moved off in an easterly direction.

During April there were growing numbers of reports of enemy buildups in the area of the Ho Tram Cape. The headquarters of D445 Battalion with two companies was reported in the area east of the 'Long Green'. Aerial reconnaissance had also found that the beach in the area was being used to land supplies for VC forces in the Nui May Tao mountains.

With 9 RAR in the western half of the Long Green, 5RAR was deployed on Operation Surfside, into AO Coogee which covered an area from Xuyen south to the coast.

The plan was to establish Fire Support Base Bruiser using Battalion Headquarters and D Company on 22 April. Followed by the insertion by landing craft of B and C Companies onto the beach at the south eastern edge of the AO, at first light on 23 April. They who would then sweep inland to locate and destroy the HQ of D445 Battalion while A Company was inserted into the fire support base by helicopter and deployed as a blocking force.

Weather conditions forced the cancellation of the sea born insertion and B and C Companies were deployed by truck, and the search for HQ D445 began as planned. Over the following days there were twelve contacts with small enemy groups. It became apparent that although there may have been two VC companies in the area they must have broken into small groups who were intent on avoiding contact.

Three hundred enemy bunkers were found and mostly destroyed. However, booby trapping by M16 mines and grenades caused some serious wounds, among the *diggers, and it was slow and dangerous work.*

On 25 April 2 Platoon reported that there were four suspicious vessels about 1000 metres off the coast. By nightfall there were thirty darkened sampans within fifty metres of the beach and it seemed that a large landing of men or stores was imminent. Although these were waters prohibited to civilian vessels, orders were given to hold fire until an actual landing was made, to avoid any possibility of civilian casualties.

There was a large Junk further off shore which appeared to be trying to make contact with someone ashore with a signaling lamp. Shortly afterwards the fleet moved quickly out to sea.

In a further effort to come to grips with the VC, the area of operations was extended into the Long Green. A Company had immediate success with an ambush which resulted in the enemy kia, one of whom proved to be a company commander from D445. There were some other small and indecisive contacts, but the major enemy units remained unlocated.

After overnighting in Nui Dat the battalion commenced Operation Twickenham on 2 May. It was inserted by APC and foot into the new area of operations, which included the rough mountainous area of the Nui Thi Vai and Nui Toc Tien mountains, southwest of Nui Dat. The Nui Thi Vai mountain had been a no go area for years and was reputed to be a strongly fortified VC stronghold.

Aerial photography showed some of the enemy positions. Some were caves that had been quite famous tourist attractions during French colonial days, and were now quite possibly strongholds, hospitals and administrative areas. Although there was a lot of evident activity on tracks and intelligence reports of enemy activity, there were no identified enemy bases.

On the morning of 3 May the battalion headquarters group moved to Fire Support Base Susan, just off Route 15 which ran along the fringe of the AO. Then A, B and C Companies went into ambush positions around the fringe Nui Thi Vais on foot, while D Company came in by APC.

It soon became evident that the track A Company was on was part of a major system leading in and out of the northern valley. They ambushed numerous groups of enemy, inflicting nine kia in four days. That these were fanatical and brave VC fighters was confirmed by the following incident. An enemy officer was wounded in a contact with 1 Platoon late on 6 May. 2 Platoon moved into ambush in the vicinity and that night heard yelling and moaning to the front of their position and were fired on three times. In the morning they sent out a patrol to investigate. Seventy yards out they were fired upon. Their answering fire silenced the shooter. The Viet Cong was found to have had both legs shattered in the contact the previous day, but still had managed to drag himself away, put tourniquets on his upper legs, fire into the ambush, prop himself against a tree beside the track, and then although near death through loss of blood, to fire at the searching party. A courageous man!

Courage was also the order of the day when A Company was met by elements of D67 in the northern valley. 1 Platoon was met by an aggressive group of VC firing from prepared positions in caves. Lieutenant John Lee took a small group and set off up the steep rocky slope to reconnoiter the enemy position. About halfway up his party was hit by heavy small arms fire, grenades and RPGs. The platoon commander was in a fire lane and was hit, and the remainder of the party were pinned behind a rock ledge. Sergeant A. B. McNulty was sent from 3 Platoon with a section to provide fire support. When he arrived at the scene he decided to move to the right flank and move up the slope with his section to locate Lieutenant Lee. Neither air or artillery fire support could be used because of the location of Lieutenant Lee and the proximity of our own men.

It was obvious that the VC were going to stay and fight. B and C companies were moved into cut off positions on the south and east. D Company was sent up the mountain with orders to assault the enemy from above.

Sergeant McNulty reached the group that was pinned down and extracted them using fire and movement.

Throughout this time the group had been subject to heavy fire, including AK47s, RPGs and claymore mines. On his own initiative Lance-Corporal K.C. Bell dashed across a known fire lane towards the platoon commander and was shot in the neck and cheek. Undaunted and criticizing the enemy's firing in the most colour full Anzac tradition, he indicated that he was ok. Two other soldiers dashed forward, under cover of heavy M60 fire, dragged him to safety.

By this time, flame-throwers had been brought up and Corporal W. Ward attacked the enemy position and, although he immediately came under fire, it enabled Privates Williams, Donnelly and Leahy to dash forward and drag Lieutenant Lee back over twenty metres of open ground. The group then withdrew to the company position.

It is impossible to adequately describe the heroism and loyalty of all those involved in this fight, which had gone on for seven hours, and it is miraculous that there were not more casualties.

During the night the enemy position was heavily bombarded with artillery fire, and in the morning D Company assaulted it. During the night the enemy had slipped away, avoiding the companies in blocking positions. However, they had captured a well prepared base including a substantial workshop with a furnace and tools.

While this operation had been going on a significant threat had again developed against the large US base at Long Binh and the battalion was redeployed at short notice.

On 13 May it was moved by air and road to an area of operations near Long Binh (not far from the old AO Arunda) and commenced patrolling designed to thwart any enemy thrust through the AO towards Long Bin. The only real contact made during this operation, which lasted eight days, was on the evening of 13 May when 3 Platoon met ten VC on the corner of the Trang Bom rubber plantation. One VC, who later died of wounds, was captured.

Once again the forecast attack faltered. It was widely acknowledged that 5 VC division had abandoned the offensive when they heard of the arrival of the 'Tigers'.

The battalion was returned to the south to complete Operation Twickenham in AO Illawarra.

The headquarters group reoccupied Fire Support Base Susan while two companies returned to the Nui Thi Vais and two to the nearby Nui Dinh complex.

C Company took to the ridges of the Nui Bao Quan and Nui Dinh ranges and successfully dislodged a large enemy group from what was their long standing sanctuary. When a large number of women and children were identified among the VC soldiers they were allowed to slip away without pursuit or attack by air or artillery.

On 1 June the Battalion returned to Nui Dat'.

Shortly after getting back to Nui Dat, I was having a beer in the officers' mess when I was surprised by a tap on the shoulder by Genghis, who led me away to a quiet corner, where a steward brought us both another drink. He then broke the news that the battalion had been ordered to provide a captain to be operations officer at the Task Force Reinforcement Training Unit, and he had decided to send me. I opened my mouth to protest, but he held up his hand and smiled. 'I'm not asking, Bob. They need an experienced officer, and it will be good experience for you. And most of the captains will be rotated to new jobs before long anyway. Now come and have another beer.'

So, my eight-month stint with the battalion was nearly over. I had mixed feelings. 5RAR was a great battalion and a privilege to be a part of. But the job as 2ic of a rifle company and being the perpetual understudy to a company commander, even to someone as good a man as Ray Harring, was frustrating at times. I had learned a lot from Ray. He understood his men very well, and what it took to get the best out of them. And they knew he was on their side.

My new job would have some big pluses. It would certainly be safer and much more comfortable. I would not have to dig a shell scrape every night and sleep rough and filthy. I'd be able to shower, eat hot fresh meals, have a cold beer or two each night. My replacement, an old friend from New Guinea, Tamo Rae, eventually arrived and I departed to my new life amongst much ribbing about becoming more of a 'pogo'.

Generally, a 'pogo' is someone further away from the action than yourself.

The man always in most danger on operations is the forward scout of the leading section. He is the most likely to be shot or to tread on a mine. The second scout—often the section commander when numbers were down—is the next most likely. Those close behind him, including the platoon commander and radio operator who are both expected to keep their heads up and run things if someone is firing at them, are also favourite targets. Generally, company headquarters will be treading warily through the jungle a hundred or so metres behind the forward scouts or could even be in a relatively safe 'harbour', so from the platoon's point of view company headquarters are pogos, particularly the 2ic who is towards the rear of that gaggle.

Now, battalion headquarters were generally in a relatively safer (most of the time) Fire Support Base or even in Nui Dat itself, so they are pogos to those closer to the 'pointy end'- even to company 2ic's. Task Force Headquarters, always safe in the middle of Nui Dat can only look down their noses at the logistic elements enjoying the comfort and amenities at the seaside paradise of Vung Tau.

My new job was on the other side of the task force, and amongst other tasks was responsible for the defence of part of the perimeter of the base. But there was no denying I would be more of a pogo, but I could argue not as bad as Task Force Headquarters or Vung Tau. At least I would be dry and well fed.

Mid-morning of 6 June I was lounging behind the large desk in my new office, enjoying a nice mug of coffee. The wall behind me was covered with large maps of Phuoc Tuy Province, Nui Dat and the area adjacent to us that was our responsibility, and various reports, tables, summaries and programs necessary and proper in any military office. In an adjoining office I could just hear the faint squelch of the high frequency radios and the murmur of quiet conversation. I was in immaculately clean jungle greens; my boots were polished and the memory of a fine full English breakfast with lots of nicely toasted freshly baked bread had not yet been banished by the anticipation of a tasty lunch. I had enjoyed a deep and uninterrupted sleep on a wire bed with a comfortable mattress beneath a mosquito net in my commodious tent, safely protected by a sandbag wall, alert sentries and the extensive barbwire and mines of the Task Force perimeter fence. I had not noticed if it had rained or not, before I showered and loitered across to the mess to be served by the attentive mess orderlies.

Ah, it was a fine war.

At about 1000 hours a radio operator poked his head around the door and informed me that D Company 5RAR, and the rest of the Ready Reaction Force, had been mobilised and sent to Binh Ba, a village a few kilometres north.

The thought that good friends, including Mike Battle the 2ic of the company, were about to put their lives on the line immediately took the gloss off life. Shortly after B Company was deployed and my worries increased.

The Battle of Binh Ba one of the major Australian engagement of the Vietnam War was beginning.

The following paragraphs are extracts from an account of the battle by Raymond Gallacher, a writer and lecturer from Glasgow, which is published on the 5RAR Association Website.

'The village of Binh Ba was at peace in the early morning. It was a community of plantation workers and was prosperous by the standards of South Vietnam in 1969. The homes were of brick and the roofs were tiled. Gardens were well tended and trees provided some shade. Only the military presence was out of tune with the scene. Route 2 cut past the eastern side of the village and military traffic was commonplace. In particular Australian and New Zealand military traffic was part of the everyday life of the people of Binh Ba, as they had the fortune of being only four kilometres from the Australian base at Nui Dat.

A centurion tank and a recovery vehicle moved slowly north up Route 2 from Nui Dat. The commander of the centurion had been told that Binh Ba was free of Viet Cong and its political elements and that (friendly forces) were in control of the village and surrounding hamlets. The tank crew had every reason to believe their journey would be without incident.

A RPG round flashed out from cover and hit the centurion square on its turret. The shot was from close range and the rocket penetrated the hull and rocked the tank on its suspension. The centurion was a good tank. It had been designed by the British for service against the Soviets in Western Europe. But this RPG crew were either experienced or lucky and the centurion, call sign 2 Zero Delta, was incapacitated; the radio operator was wounded and the turret would not traverse. With no infantry support available 2 Zero Delta was in a vulnerable position. The armoured recovery vehicle behind it ground forward firing its .30 calibre machine guns into any likely looking spot. It was a big-hearted moved by the crew of the poorly armed service vehicle, but fortunately no further RPG rockets came from the village. When the firing of the .30 calibre weapons stopped the village seemed as quiet as ever. 2 Zero Delta ground further north towards the nearby post of at Duc Thanh. It seemed to be the end of a small incident, the kind that happened every day in Phuoc Tuy province. A report was sent to Nui Dat where the incident was considered to be worth investigating. It was yet another stray shot in a long war but this one would not fade away and Binh ba would become the scene of an intense battle for forty-eight hours.

Ist Australian Task Force (1ATF) had arrived in South Vietnam with the simple instruction, 'Take over Phuoc Tuy'. 1ATF had put its stamp firmly on the area of operations with a strategy of a strong physical presence in the hills, jungles and villages of the province. Patrolling, ambushing and continual pressure had been put on the 274 and 275 VC Main Force Regiments. There had been large set-piece battles too, not just the encounter at Long Tan but also the defense of the Fire Support Bases Coral and Balmoral in 1968. 274 and 275 Regiments and their local elements had been severely mauled on every occasion. There was now a gradual understanding that North Vietnamese Army units were in the area and may be in some strength. As always in the Vietnam War, intelligence was the most difficult of games.

5RAR was on its second tour of Vietnam and was a tested formation. The soldiers were a mixture of Regulars and National Servicemen – an arrangement that caused friction in other armies but not amongst the Australians. They had been involved in the battle of Long Tan in 1966 and now in June 1969 they were at the Nui Dat base again. They were resting between operations and glad to be away from the large-scale manoeuvres to enjoy what amusements life at 'The Dat' could offer. For individual soldiers it meant days of individual housekeeping, maintaining equipment and cleaning kit, or perhaps listening to the radio; maybe music or 'Chicken Man'. A Company was enjoying some short Rest and Convalescence leave in the seaside town of Vung Tau where the other companies would also rotate through over the next several days.

10 Platoon D Company commander 2nd Lieutenant John Russell, remembers. 'We had been on operations for some time. Some of us were feeling pretty run down and we were looking forward to getting some sun on our banks'.

It was not all housekeeping however. D Company was also the Ready Reaction Company for the Task Force, on 30 minutes notice to move. Small arms were ready, their equipment was ready and their ammunition and rations were packed.

Major Murray Blake, commanding D Company had concerns of his own. Many of the company were on promotion courses or training that put them out of use and he was left with light resources if the blue light started to flash. So far however,

253

early on the 6th the diggers were having a tranquil day.

For the armour, both the tanks of 1st Armoured regiment and carriers of the 3rd Cavalry Regiment, even a day at Nui Dat was hard work. The vehicles had to be maintained due to the pressure on them from their arduous journeys to support other operations where 6 RAR and 9 RAR were in action. In particular, there was always damage to contend with from the bugbear for all the units in Vietnam – mines.

Others in Phuoc Tuy province were having anything but a peaceful morning. 6 RAR was newly arrived in country and was engaged in operations ten kilometres to the north of Nui Dat. What should have been warm-up patrols evolved into heavy fighting. The pressure from 6RAR's operation was having a direct effect on the enemy and pushed across NVA supply lines. What the Australians did not know was that they were also disrupting the movement of an NVA battalion. As resistance increased 6 RAR was in need of support and the Centurions were lending their ever valuable fire support.

The Centurion tanks had not always been considered so indispensable. It had been thought there was no place for them in Vietnam in this war of patrolling and ambush. The tankers had been given the unkind nickname 'The Koalas' as they were not to be shot or sent overseas. But the armour had proved their worth firing canisters in defense of FSB Coral, and the APC's had been crucial at Long Tan, and the tanks, in particular, were always welcomed by infantrymen during bunker clearance.

A Centurion tank with a recovery vehicle had been sent to the aid of 6 RAR but at eight o'clock had been stopped, literally, in its tracks at Binh Ba.

Binh Ba was well known to the task Force. This village of plantation and farm workers had a population of about one thousand and would, in normal times, have been quietly prosperous. The prosperity and proximity to Nui Dat base made the village a target for Viet Cong tax collectors as well as assassination squads. As part of the hearts and minds ethos the Australians had occupied the village in a benevolent way on 5 RAR first tour when Binh Ba had welcomed a platoon with mortar support. There is even a painting showing gifts being given to the villagers. Perhaps inevitably, the needs of more complex operations meant the Task Force soldiers could not be spared for security duties and the village was handed over to the Regional Forces. Intelligence reports now suggested that two Vietcong platoons had infiltrated the village and that the RF were no longer in control.

Brian Bamblett was told that D Company were to go and investigate the situation at Binh Ba. 'Our kit and ammunition were already packed. We knew we were on standby and that anything could happen. I admit I did feel an adrenalin rush. After two years in Vietnam I just thought, 'Here we go again".

Bill O'Mara and Greg Dwiar of B Company were aware of D company's preparations and did not expect it to amount to much. They were the backup rifle company and they fully expected to have lunch in the relative comfort of the Dat. Bill O'Mara was a keen photographer and made a mental note to keep his camera handy, just in case anything 'interesting' happened. For Greg Dwiar who was a relative new arrival in Vietnam, he was getting used to the everyday tasks of platoon life and trying to fit in with his new mates. So far, for Greg, it had been nothing but routine. He had only been in the platoon for two days and was still feeling his way around.

D and B companies may have been enjoying a little peace but there was little of any sort of tranquility in the rest of Phuoc Tuy province. As described above 6 RAR's fighting had intensified as it pushed over one hornet's nest after another.

Major Blake considered the intelligence available and it seemed that two Viet Cong platoons had infiltrated the village and that the RF were no longer in control. Presumably it was an RPG crew from one of these platoons who had fired on the Centurion. Colonel Colin Khan, Major Blake and the other experienced hands of 5 RAR were aware of the unreliability of sources of intelligence. Intelligence gathering and analysis in Vietnam was a perennial problem. Local Force VC already fed back superb intelligence from observation and infiltration. Their assassination squads, now probably at work in Binh Ba and the surrounding hamlets, would clear up any they thought guilty of collaboration. Large-scale intelligence from aerial observation was generally of little value as both Main force and local VC could hide their movement by keeping in thick cover. The cleared areas including the famous Light Green in the shadows of the Long Hai Hills, were frequently mined by the Viet Cong to inhibit allied movement. Forming up and actual assaults by Main Force regiments were often under the cover of darkness. Both the intelligence war and the ground war were like a chase in a dark labyrinth. Surprise was never far away.

Nevertheless, the philosophy of the war was not the immediate problem of Murray Blake or the men of D Company. They gathered their weapons, shrugged on their webbing and headed towards the APC troop. The ready reaction force would consist of not just the infantry but also the M113 carriers and a troop of Centurions. The column moved up Route 2 to Binh Ba with as much speed as the tracks would allow. They arrived and formed up south of the village by 10.30 hours.

The shooting had already started. The Regional Force troops were already engaged in fighting but their reports were confused. The reports of contacts did seem to belie and estimated infiltration of two platoons. Around the village the rubber trees had been cleared and at times as much as 800 metres was exposed. When D company and their carriers pulled up in the cleared area south of the village, they soon

255

discovered that some enterprising enemy had found them within range.

But the opening moves were those of social upheaval so typical of the war. John Russell saw 'A great stream of people coming down the road: men, women and children. The RF were evacuating the village. The diggers could only wait and watch helplessly. The more experienced hands also saw that the evacuation was an obvious escape route for Main Force and Local Force VC. The most frustrating aspect for Allied soldiers all through the conflict was the habit of enemy fighters changing into civilian clothes and mingling with the civilians in order to escape final capture. This was a deliberate tactic that ensured that the ATF had to tread as carefully among the news cameras as they did with the mines.

For Murray Blake, local politics was an immediate problem. He was still in conference with the Vietnamese Village Chief. He remembers this as the main cause of any delay in bringing his force to act on the enemy in Binh Ba. But the village would be ruined by the 20-pounder guns of the Centurions and the inevitable infantry assault. Damage to property could be substantial if the Australians met any resistance. It would obviously be a propaganda victory for the Viet Cong no matter what. The ATF Ready Reaction Force began forming up east of the village but still in the area of the cleared rubber trees.

Meanwhile the RF had consolidated a position well north of Binh Ba. We can only speculate as to the preparations of the enemy within the village at this time.

In the cleared ground the diggers were aware of their vulnerability. Brian Bamblett and his riflemen arrived on their APCs, before dismounting he saw 'figures running at the edge of the village. I could see no pith helmets or floppy hats, no red stars. I couldn't see whether they were VC or NVA. They were just running figures. Then I saw a smoke trail from an RPG. The APCs used bursts of .50 calibre to chase them off.' An experienced man, Brian looked over while D company got itself organised.

At 11.20 Major Blake was told by the District Chief, 'Do what you have to do.'

A solution had been quickly thought out. D Company with the support of tanks and carriers would form up with Route 2 as the start line and assault east to west. The combined force would roll through the village streets and clear the enemy. The Reaction Force advanced towards the village, four tanks under the command of 2nd Lieutenant Brian Sullivan led the way while Captain Raymond De Vere's ferried D Company behind.

At 300 metres the RPGs were within their effective range. The commanders of the Centurions were already firing at houses where they suspected the rounds were

256

coming from. The enemy were trying to effect flanking moves. Although his view was limited, Brian Bamblett was aware of firing coming from the south. Firing was indeed coming from this direction and the tanks were firing canister in return. The operation was heating up.

As always the soldiers of the ATF were not without friends. 9 Squadron Royal Australian Air Force were on call to support the assault. The light fire team of two Bushrangers (an Iroquois helicopter fitted with mini-guns and rockets) were to soften up the enemy and prevent any escape from the village. They would follow the simple method of sweeping in the direction of the Australian assault. As always the plan would change as events unfolded. The Bushrangers would expend their ordnance many timed over in the hours to come.

Binh Ba was not large, just 200 metres north to south and about 500 metres west to east. It had a grid system of four roads running through it. The initial plan was simple. Tanks, APCs and infantry would advance to each block of houses. The infantry would clear the houses with support from the armour. A mopping up force would bring up the rear. The Bushrangers would attack the retreating enemy.

As the Australians pushed through the village, resistance was stiff. Tank commander Brian Sullivan discovered that the well built houses could absorb a lot of fire power and were providing good cover. He found that firing a 20-pounder high explosive round through the wooden doors, or if possible the wooden window shutters, would kill everyone inside without causing too much destruction and leaving rubble behind. Despite superb support from the tanks and suppressing fire from the carriers of 3rd Cavalry both men and vehicles were coming under increasing amounts of small arms fire and more dangerously for the vehicles, the RPGs.

Nick Weir, commanding one of the APCs remembers, 'We received quite a shock when we came under sustained heavy fire from the first houses as we entered the village.' Nick's other abiding memory was the sight of the French plantation owner, 'He was swearing and spitting at us. All he was worried about was his rubber business'.

The assault troops found themselves vulnerable to a determined enemy, well concealed in the built up area. RPG crews roamed the village and the destruction of houses and the physical furniture of the community merely provided them with more cover. The level of firing did not even seem typical of the VC but was the beginning of an indication that there was an NVA presence. Each small group of D Company pushed forward and contact after contact was made. The APCs and tanks expended thousands of .50 calibre and .30 calibre rounds at every suspected doorway or point of fire. The Centurions' heavy guns were turned on any hardened position. For

Murray Blake, 'The enemy were everywhere, it was like you see in the movies. I even saw blokes dragging a 12.7mm machine gun up. The other problem was that there were still a lot of civilians around. I saw my men stop firing and run to move frightened civilians out of the way.' He still remembers this very visibly.

John Russell felt it was, 'Chaotic. There was an awful lot of firing from the armour. I was aware that we were getting low on ammunition, especially grenades.'

At the end of an hour three tanks were disabled due to damage and crew casualties and Binh Ba had still not been taken. Memories are confused and each man holds only fragments of the battle in his mind. One Centurion was temporarily abandoned while the kit slung on top of it burned. D Company and the armour pulled out to the south and then around to the western side of the village.

Murray Blake saw it mainly as a problem of supply. In particular, the Centurions needed ammunition resupply and there were lots of casualties from small arms and splinters. In the APCs Nick Weir was, 'Surprised by the violence of the action.

From Brian Bamblett, he felt he had been, 'Kicked out of Binh Ba.'

Nevertheless, the priorities were now ammunition resupply and reinforcement. There was no question of not going back into the village. Murray Blake recalls. 'We had to. We just had to go back in.'

The situation at Binh Ba required reinforcements. Back at Nui Dat news was coming in that there had been a big contact at the village. B Company 5 RAR had been put on standby. They were now given orders to move.

In Vietnam there was no slow approach to the face of battle. Modern transport moved a man within an hour. For B Company then, they began their day listening to Hendrix and the Beatles on the American Forces Network and by lunch they were climbing aboard a carrier and heading towards the shooting.

Moving from Nui Dat to Binh Ba took no more than 20 minutes.

The soldiers of B Company were to ensure that no enemy were to leave the or enter the village. They deployed in the outskirts of the village in the rubber.

B Company pulled up and spread out about 300 metres from the village. Using route 2 as the border of their right flank and its carriers spread out over some 400 metres in their first blocking position. Their left flank looked on the edge of the rubber plantation. The area was mostly flat and had no obstacles apart from the occasional tree stump. It gave a perfect view. Some of the men stood up on top to get a better look at the contest in front of them.

Apart from the smoke and the small arms fire the most obvious sights and sounds were the Bushrangers, and the noise of their mini-guns. They made a high-

pitched ripping noise as they spat out cannon shells at the enemy.

D Company was now formed up on the west of Binh Ba. They would assault again. This time the infantry, carriers and tanks would move from west to east. A fresh troop of tanks moved up into position and the APCs would give close support. The infantry would lead off at 1400 hours. They would clear the houses supported by X Troop 1st Armoured Regiment. But with the enemy now in a dense defensive position created by the damage of the first assault it would be a bitter time. One of the problems was that the villagers had bunkers built under or near their homes. Sadly, this was a response to living and working in a war zone. Every point of concealment would have to be searched and pacified. It would be nerve-racking work that only the infantry could do. There was no evidence that the hit-and-run guerrillas had evacuated the village – it was to turn from a mechanized battle into one of hand-to-hand fighting.

Each infantry platoon had one tank and two carriers in close support. The platoons were kept broken up into house clearing teams each of three men. The infantry would lead the assault and the tanks and APCs would follow, with the APCs at the rear spread across the full width of each flank. Tanks would be called up whenever they were needed. This sensible arrangement would suffer from the first contact with the enemy and the confusion of losing control by line of sight. Control of the house clearing teams and control of the supporting vehicles would now be a problem. Although small, it was still a built up environment where observation was restricted and confusion arises quickly. The teams were to clear one row of houses at a time. If the all went to plan they would step through Binh Ba one fire team and one house at a time.

D Company moved forward again, they were mounted in carriers at first because the first open space would be when they were at their most vulnerable.

Closing with the houses the infantry dismounted and contact was immediate. John Russell looked along the extended line of infantry. At first he thought 'There aren't that many of us and we're taking fire already'.

Brian Bamblett was aware of the amount of firing in all directions. Private Wayne Teeling was shot dead as his platoon reached the first line of houses. Sergeant Brian London of 10 Platoon ran to the rear of the closest centurion and picked up the telephone on the chassis. He had been warned they never worked. Typically, it wasn't. He climbed up and shouted down the hatch. Brian asked for one round of high explosive into the first building. Brian Bamblett remembers it as canister. The house rocked under the blast and the diggers ran forward and assaulted. Six NVA dead were found in the ruins. This pattern was repeated again and again.

John Russell found that 'There were already dead and wounded in the houses.

259

One man, an NVA soldier came out with his hands up. He was showing me his wound. I sent him back to be taken prisoner.

The fighting was fierce and confused. Communications and control were lost frequently. The Australians pushed forward with or without direct orders. Sometimes junior ranks would lead and often a private soldier with no more than a few month's experience would lead. More experienced men were not always around but someone would always come forward. Another corner and another room would be taken. The battle was a minute-by-minute venture by private soldiers and NCOs. For Brian Bamblett, 'It was split second choices and close in fighting inside houses and inside rooms.'

By now, it was obvious the fighting was far above what could be expected from two platoons of VC. A US Air Force forward controller, call sign Jade Five, offered to help but Ray de Vere was confident enough that the Australians could manage with their own resources. De Vere directed rocket and mini-gun fire onto targets that could not be pacified and that were causing the advancing diggers to falter.

John Russell and his men had now reached the center of the village. As they approached a Town hall like building John saw that there were enemy wires running out of it. He had the presence of mind to cut them. Going inside, he said, 'We were fired on. I got stuck in the house and dived behind a low dividing wall. The NVA threw a grenade after me. It went off and I was wounded, but still conscious. The NVA put their heads around to see if I was dead'. John Russell opened fire. Unlike his enemies, he walked away and continued to fight until he was sent back because of his wounds. He shared an APC with the deceased Wayne Teeling on the way back to Nui dat.

By last light the firing had lessened and the last of the houses were being cleared. As most of the buildings were now hardly recognizable, the fight had gone underground. The diggers pulled open the coverings of bunkers built close to or within houses. Many of the enemy walked out, they were deafened and shaken by the day of non-stop concussion. They added to the physical and moral confusion by changing into civilian clothing in order to escaped.

The assaulting company was equally rung out. As darkness fell, they were exhausted. But if anyone could sleep they would have to sleep through the artillery. Harassing fire was arranged and 105th Field Battery was given a huge list of targets. They were to prevent the orderly retreat of the NVA and more importantly to prevent them from forming up again.

As for the night, apart from the crump of artillery on its harassing tasks, the diggers spent the night peacefully. As one described it, 'Deliciously cool'. Some men rested if they could.

The men of B Company and their carriers formed an all-round defensive position, a large circular laager with the APCs and riflemen facing outwards'.

The following paragraphs are extracts from an account by Bill O'Mara B of B Company 5RAR.

D Company was Ready Reaction Company and already at Binh Ba when B Company was sent to join them early afternoon 6 June 1969. We travelled the five kilometres from Nui Dat in APCs (Armoured Personnel Carriers). As we got closer to the village we could see the damage inflicted by the armoured units, artillery and helicopter gunships.

As we moved over the ground cleared of rubber trees we could see part of the village alight.

Late in the afternoon our platoon (6 Platoon) set up a night harbour on the edge of the rubber plantation. As usual our M60's (machine guns) were placed at 4, 8 and 12 o'clock and we each took our turn during the night for sentry duty of a couple of hours per two men.

It was raining slightly, just enough to give another uncomfortable night, so I had put up my hoochie. Then, foolishly removed my boots after I'd done my turn on sentry. This was something I'd not done before and was never to do again.

We had a rude awakening at daylight, when a force of NVA soldiers approached our position. Most of us were asleep (me included) when our sentry on the M60 exchanged 'waves' with the NVA. Realization dawned and I was woken by the sound of our sentry belting out waves on the machine gun and had a hard kick from my 'bed mate' Peter Wardrope.

Not the best of time to have your boots off ... but they were ... and I returned fire with a couple of magazines from my M16. I recall the green flash from the enemy RPGs (Rocket Propelled Grenades) and the sound of shrapnel into the rubber trees. I have no idea how long this lasted, but long enough to be scared.

Eventually dragged my boots on (laces still undone) and with other platoon members walked up to the area we were being attacked from by the NVA. No bodies, no blood trail and as none of our platoon had been killed or wounded, assumed that the NVA like us, had all fired too high. I found this amazing, but guess that's what can happen in the heat of the moment. Later the same day, myself and another were given the grisly task of burying six enemy bodies. I recall they were Viet Cong (dressed in black) and not NVA soldiers from the early morning engagement.

Later that day we were positioned closer to the village for a 'sweep' and I managed to take the photo of our guys just before we set off over the cleared ground

261

with APCs.

> *As we prepared for this final sweep, we were told it would be with APCs. In my ignorance I thought it meant we would be in single file with the APCs for protection. But ... that's not the way it's done. We spread out between the APCs and swept across maybe 100 yards of open ground before entering the village. We were not fired upon.*
>
> *We conducted house to house clearing but I personally never found anyone alive. The damage had been well and truly done.*
>
> *As we surveyed 'The Mess' in the village, a photographer on top of one of the Centurions asked us if we could re-enact some footage with grenades into houses etc ... we made our feelings felt!*
>
> *Many years later a report was broadcast on the ABCs television program 'Nationwide' with a soldier's claim that we had massacred women and children. This was simply not true and can only imagine that the former soldier who had made this claim was not at Binh Ba. The older men, women and kids were let out of the school house unharmed at the end of the battle. I reported the facts to Frank Cranston of the 'Canberra Times' within days of the false accusation.*
>
> *The Battle of Binh Ba finished at 0800 hours on 8 June.'*

126 NVA and VC were killed. The 1st Battalion 33 Regiment was badly mauled. They had initiated a plan which they hoped would pull the Australians into a largescale ambush. They had been determined and had the strength and firepower to inflict heavy casualties and their heavy defeat speaks volumes for the training, bravery and expertise of 5 RAR who used their superiority in fire power to devastating effect.

It is a miracle that more Australian lives were not lost. It is to the eternal credit of the medevac system and of the skill of the medics, nurses and surgeons. Wounded soldiers who were lifted by helicopter, literally from the battleground, who were still alive when they reached Nui Dat or Vung Tau only minutes later, had an excellent chance of surviving. Many diggers survived wounds that in early wars would have seen them dying on a stretcher in the jungle or the trenches.

I soon settled into my new job and remained in it until I returned to Australia in January 1970. The steady stream of infantry reinforcements coming from Australia to the Task Force all came through our hands. It was our job to ensure they were up to speed and had done some operational work before they were thrown into the high-risk environment of the battalions. Generally, there were three platoons, who were run by battle experienced lieutenants and NCOs and they did lots of weapons training, a lot of anti-mine training, physical training and range work. They manned our section of the perimeter, did the morning and evening clearing patrols and ambush patrols a kilometre or so out from the wire. I had a team of experienced Warrant Officers and Sergeants who formed a training cadre to actually conduct the training.

After a couple of weeks each platoon would do a 'hot insertion' by helicopter. In consultation with Taskforce HQs I would choose a landing zone (LZ) where there would be very little chance of landing on top of any VC.

Iroquois helicopters transports and gunships would be ordered, together with whatever fire support I could organise —which on a quiet day could be very substantial. On one occasion, as well as our own artillery, we had US fighter bombers and a US battleship supporting us. I would go aloft in a Sioux helicopter (this was the only exciting part of my job) to coordinate the action. I would call in the big guns of the battleship which pounded the surrounds of the LZ, then the fighter bombers, then the artillery, then the gunships and finally as I still hovered to one side watching this awesome display, I would call in the troops to the LZ, which had almost certainly been safe beforehand but now had no living creature within cooee. All at a cost exceeding several Sydney New Year's Eve fireworks, which ever since have not done a lot for me.

Three or four days later the platoon would be collected and flown back to base.

Apart from my days in the air, life was pretty relaxing. Most days at dawn and dusk I would stroll around the perimeter to check all was as it should be and during the day spend some time watching training. Once every few weeks I would go out with one of the ambush patrols, just to remind myself how comfortable life was.

There was very little danger involved in these ambushes, and from memory I cannot recall there being a 'contact' during my tenure.

But there had been an accident a couple of years earlier which was a reminder to us of the tragic consequences of something going wrong.

In 1967 an ambush was set in what was a similar situation to our nightly ambushes and it resulted in the death of five civilian, 'bamboo pickers' including two teenage girls and a young boy.

It has been the subject of considerable investigation and there is no doubt that it was an accident, and no blame can be attached to the soldiers involved, who were commanded by a friend of mine. None the less it was a calamity for both those killed and their loved ones, and very much so for the soldiers involved.

The circumstances were as follows. The ambush was set in an area widely known to be a 'no go' area for civilians and a vital area for the defence of Nui Dat base. Australian soldiers had a duty to themselves and their comrades to assume any unidentified movement in the area was hostile.

In the misty half-light of dawn, a group dressed in black clothing and apparently carrying weapons, approached the ambush position. The leading figure appeared to raise a rifle and aim at an Australian machine gunner, who opened fire and others followed. Within thirty seconds, when there was no answering fire and judging from the tone of the screams, the platoon commander sensed that there was something wrong and ordered ceasefire. While shots were still being fired, he rushed into the 'killing zone'. He was too late to avoid the casualties but organised a quick medical response and 'Dustoff'.

The ambush still torments all those involved and is something they will never recover from. And their torment has brought misery to their friends and loved ones.

The ambush that they mounted was exactly what our unit, always with inexperienced soldiers, was doing every night. The need to avoid a repeat was always on our minds.

It was reinforced for me after I had been there a couple of months. There was a similar incident involving my old company, and one civilian was killed. Task Force HQs pulled the name of an investigating officer out of a hat, and it was me. It was difficult interviewing soldiers that I knew well. It was terrible visiting the village and family of the dead man to ask the questions that could only ever have one answer and face their understandable hostility and the heartbroken mother.

Most of my days were in my comfortable office drawing up programs and rosters, writing reports and drafting orders for this and that. Some nights I would get together with Mike Battle or Peter Knight or others passing through for a few beers or a game of cards.

As the year progressed, and in Phuoc Tuy Province at least it seemed the war was very much swinging in our favour, an increasing number of Viet Cong came across to our side. Vietnamese going the other way would have been, of course, deserters. But coming our way they were Hoi Chans, or 'Ralliers'. After their initial debrief they were lodged with us, where we could keep an eye on them until they were judged to be genuine and give them enough familiarity with our methods for them to be able to go on operations with Australian troops.

If they had been officers or senior NCOs, they became part of our mess, and most evenings we would share a beer and have a chat – as far as our language skills would allow. We all got on well, certainly our 'ralliers' did not want any bad reports going up the line. I became quite friendly with an ex-company commander of D445 Battalion, a fresh-faced young man who spoke reasonable English and was with us for a couple of months before he was sent elsewhere, never to be seen or heard of again. I cannot imagine things turned out well for him. If he did survive the war, it's unlikely he survived the purges that followed it; another regret, among the many that cannot be laid to rest.

On a more light-hearted note. Some of the senior staff at Task Force Headquarters were invited for a social day and 'conference' at the famous Le Cercle Sportif in Saigon. This was a 'racquet' club that had been a legend for decades. Somerset Maughan probably wrote about it, and if not, he should have. It was famous during the French era, and for those of you familiar with the film *Emmanuelle*, it was to this sort of club that the senior officers probably imagined they were invited to.

As a face-saver, in case they actually had to play tennis, they needed a tennis player to go along. So, I was rung up and ordered to present myself at the helicopter pad with tennis gear and racquets. When I politely mentioned that I had not actually brought these items to the war zone, I was told to come along anyway. They hoped I would be able to borrow some gear, so that the valuable helicopter seat I was taking up was not wasted.

When we landed, we found that the glamour of the French period had long since gone and there was not a Frenchman to be seen, let alone a Frenchwoman. There were lots of American and Vietnamese brass around, and I was sent off to represent Australia, in borrowed gear, on a court guarded by tanks parked at each corner, their cannons and machine guns pointing outwards—there were probably more tanks here than at most of the bloodiest battles of the war—while the brass safely retired to the bars. I was let inside for lunch. Great food, but none of the generals and brigadiers seemed interested in talking to a junior captain. More tennis after lunch, and after successfully safeguarding our nation's sporting reputation I was the only sober passenger on the flight home.

Many of the nights in the 1st RTU officers and sergeants' mess were spent playing cards. A number of exotic and dangerous forms of poker were played, for quite high stakes. A favourite was called 'Whores and Fours and One-Eyed Jacks' wild. Of course, the 'whores' are the queens, the 'fours' are fours and the 'one eyed Jacks' are the jacks of spades and hearts —the jacks of clubs and diamonds have two eyes, if you haven't noticed before. 'Wild' means you can nominate a 'wild' card to be anything you want. Thus, you can end up with five aces all of one suit. Which I learned early on, at considerable cost, beats a Royal Routine Flush, which up until that moment I thought unbeatable as long as you were not 'looking'. The money we gambled was a US military currency which was only valid in Vietnam and was designed to make it harder for large quantities of US dollars getting into the wrong hands. Periodically all the currency on issue would be cancelled and a fresh batch issued. So, if you were holding a large amount of the military currency—never me—it could become worthless overnight. Anyway, it was all good fun, and if you lost you could console yourself that it could be worthless in the morning, anyway.

'Five Hundred' was another favourite, and one night we embarrassed ourselves while enjoying a quiet game. In the distance there was an explosion, which could have been a mortar shell landing. There were always explosions at night from artillery or mortars firing actual 'missions' or more commonly 'harassing fire' which was really just another name for dropping a few rounds into some empty jungle somewhere. Then a second later another explosion, then another—definitely getting closer and louder, then another, much louder now and then another. Bloody hell, we dropped our cards and sprinted towards a trench. No more explosions, we shook ourselves off, checked with the duty officer that all was well with our ambush patrol, returned to our table, collected the scattered cards, dried the spilt drinks and continued playing.

The next morning, after my full English breakfast I reported to my comfortable office, and while enjoying a cup of coffee it occurred to me to investigate the disruptive explosions of the night before.

There was nothing in the Task Forces records of the night that explained the interruption to our game. Later on, I managed to discover that US B52 bombers (a remarkable airplane that today still looks as fearsome as it did fifty years ago) had dropped bombs supposedly some kilometres south of us. So that was what had caused us to spill our drinks and dive for the trenches. I have never been able to explain to myself why we were so suddenly alarmed. It was not as if we were not used to noises in the night—I thought it may have just been too many beers.

But in recalling this night I did some research.

Our normal artillery shell contained 2 kg of explosive. A B52 bomb contained 180 kg of explosive. Now, I was only ever a simple infantryman, but that says to me that the bomb probable made ninety times as much noise. Hence the panic, that amount of noise can sound very close at night if it interrupts a card game. That was the only time I can recall a 750 lb bomb explosion. But personally, I still think the bomber must have been a bit lost and a lot closer to us than he should have been.

We had, a few times, stumbled through the awesome craters that a bomb load created. It is very hard to recreate the surreal scene of devastation; the huge flooded craters, the shredded jungle, tangled and uprooted. We camped in such a place one night, and the area seemed to teem with spiders and scorpions, as if these poisonous arachnids were the only survivors of the holocaust.

My brother-in-law, Eugene Esmonde, an artillery officer who served twice in

Vietnam, recounts another humorous incident involving a mutual friend. The friend was ordered to take his platoon on a 'sweep' to check on some suspected enemy activity. They went out, navigating by compass—sometimes, it is not all that hard to actually march in a circle when you do this in difficult country) and an hour or so later approached what appeared to be an enemy camp. They attacked. At the same time company headquarters reported they were being assaulted. Do I need to say more? Luckily no harm was done.

In February 1970 I flew home, very glad to be in one piece and to be lucky enough to find two beautiful girls waiting for me at Mascot.

About this time many families of the 5 RAR soldiers would have already received the following: *This is to inform you that .... is no longer the sweet unspoiled boy who left Australia fired with patriotism and a zest for adventure, the man with a mission. He is now older, leaner, wiser, water soaked, and slightly crazy, so get the women off the streets, hide all the beer and grog, put a chain around the fridge and you must impress on him the following:*

- *The house is respectable – he doesn't have to organise some blokes into a work party to paint the place in the Unit's colours.*
- *This man has survived the worst that the far east has to offer; mud, rain, heat, dust, sand, monsoons, typhoons and loneliness.*
- *He may look strange, and act even more strangely, but after the time he has spent in Vietnam this can only be expected.*
- *Pay no attention if he smears all his food, including sweets, with Soy sauce, or mixes raw snails in his potatoes for flavor.*
- *NEVER say anything about powdered eggs, 'C' rations, fresh bread, de-hydrated potatoes, milk, ice cream or cold tea.*
- *He will gaze in awe and fascination at blonde haired Aussie girls, blue eyes, trams, sheets (especially clean ones) hotels and tight sweaters. Remember his only contact with round eyed white women has been via the centre pages of Playboy Magazine, and he will probably think all girls have staple holes on their stomachs.*
- *NEVER ask him 'Does it ever rain in Vietnam'.*
- *If he stands there and mutters 'Choy Oy, Uc Dai Loi, Xin Loi, Be Nie, Boom Boom, Number One, Dung Loi, Number Welve or other strange words ignore him and never ask what they mean.*
- *Act as if nothing has happened if he 'pees' in the gutter, this has been the normal custom for the last year.*

☐ *If he stands there flushing the toilet or turning lights on and off, humour him. These are all novelties to him, and if he heads to the back of the garden with a shovel with a strained look on his face just point him to the nearest convenience.*

☐ *If he won't get up at a reasonable hour, just stand near his bed and whisper 'Lights on the wire' and watch him leap out of bed with a strangled cry and grovel under the carpet.*

☐ *Be careful not to say. 'I wish it would rain', 'You buy me a Saigon Tea' or "It'll be on the next Jeparit'. He cannot be held responsible for his actions.*

☐ *Force of habit could cause him to denounce all in authority, abuse anyone on sight, sleep with his boots on, grind his cigarette butts into what may be your carpet. Humour him.*

☐ *Keep him locked up when the postman arrives each day. He could become violent, race out, flatten the postie, upend his bag, search him and it, then demand why he hasn't received a letter.*

☐ *Tell him not all cabbies and shop keepers are scoundrels, Vietnam is a long way away, the mosquitoes will not hurt him, everybody loves him and draught beer is not poisonous.*

☐ *He may not look or act it, but he is your very own. Given time he will become accustomed to civilised living again. Do not send anymore letters or parcels to .... as this crazy looking, bloody eyed, mud splattered, damp, dishevelled, lovable soldier is on his way back to you!*

Signed ....WO2   CSM C Coy 5RAR

On a more serious side, it would not hurt anyone to reflect on the powerful poem by Jack Gennings (66-67, 69-70).

Vietnam War

To all, family or friend,
This was a war that may never end,
Home we are from the stench and stink,
How many will need to see the shrink?
Every man woman or kid,
Wondering what we really did.

Victorious we were not,

But to the very end we gave our lot.
Infantrymen without a front line,
Treading carefully, watching for a mine.
Every man a soldier,
At nineteen years old, but much bolder.
Trained for the steaming jungle,
Hoping each step we will not bungle.

Not much chance to really sleep,
Too much at stake, our lives to keep.
Asians, friend or foe, looking the same
This is not a bloody game.
Maybe when we are home away from here
We may relax and have a beer.

Why were we sent to this place?
To go back home and be called a disgrace?
Australian girls, families and wives
This is why young men lost their lives.
Remember all our unfortunate mates
We'll have a roll call at the pearly gates.

Or,

'Where The Rubber Grows' by Robert Cavill (A soldier of 5 RAR).

There is a forest in the north,
And its trees weep white;
Where the rubber grows.

In drifting mists of morning light,
They stand right dressed;
As soldiers know.

These men of the south,
Sought shelter from the storm, lay still;
In the mud beneath them.

With shattered trunks and broken limbs,
The weeping white trees;
Did proclaim them.

In white dripping silence came a gentle weeping'
Away to the south;
Where the wattle grows.

Brothers carry pride in the past, for sought and seeker held fast,
When the trees bled white;
Where the rubber grows.

The first Australian moratorium march, in which 120,000 participated throughout Australia took place in1970.

By early 1972 most Australian combat forces were withdrawn.

On 27 January 1973 the 'Agreement on Ending the War and Restoring Peace in Viet Nam' was signed.

In 1975 the 'Ho Chi Minh Offensive' was launched by North Vietam. The US Senate refused to honour the US guarantees provided as part of the agreement. Saigon was captured on 30 April 1975.

Total Casualties

The USA lost 58,220 soldiers killed and 304,000 wounded (amputations and crippling wounds were 300 percent higher than WWII).

Vietnam: 2 million civilians killed.

The North Vietnam and Viet Cong: 1.1 million soldiers killed and over 600,000 wounded.

The South Vietnamese: 250,000 soldiers killed and 1.17 million wounded.

Australia: 500 soldiers killed and 3,129 wounded.

Was this war an unnecessary one?

From the country that did so much to bring us WWI and WWII the French attempt to regain their colonies in Asia was outrageous.

The USA had the choice to fight in Asia or not. But once they were entangled, our national security made it imperative we supported the nation that had saved us in WWII, and we hoped would stand by us in the future. Was our participation in the war morally justified? Firstly, we fought alongside many Vietnamese who were willing to die fighting and many of whom had already fled from the communist north. Secondly, the spread of aggressive militant communism in Asia endangered the right of many nations, including our own, to exist as free and democratic countries.

I have sometimes wondered what all those brave and tenacious Vietnamese who fought and died for the communists, would have thought if they had known Vietnam would remain under an oppressive communist regime, with no free elections, no responsible government, no rule of law and no private ownership of land for so many years, and of the purges and retraining camps which accompanied them. Their thoughts would no doubt be confused by the newly flowering capitalist economy which is spreading wealth and well-being amongst their descendants.

For my part, I hope with all my heart they enjoy health, happiness, prosperity and in due course their freedom. I look back in sorrow at the great tragedies of the last century and hope, forlornly I fear, they will not be repeated.

But forty years after I had arrived home from Vietnam, Ro and I were back on *Sea Dreams* and about to enter Greek waters. What could I possibly complain about?

~ GREEK WATERS 2010 ~

Sea Dreams and mighty 'Spade' anchor.

A gentle north wind, scented with the aroma of resin and wood smoke from cooking fires along the coast, carried us south. Croatia, Montenegro and Albania lay in our wake. In the darkness, lit only by the thin crescent of a new moon, the island of Erikoussa was a shadow on the horizon. Othoni, her more imposing neighbour was away to the west and the last of the Albanian coast, marked by some lonely lights lay a few miles to our east.

We were near the island of Kerkyra or Corfu as it is commonly known. The seductive island that in Greek mythology was the love nest of the god of the sea Poseidon and the beautiful damsel Kerkyra, after whom the island took its name.

If you are sailing in Greek waters for any length of time, even in this modern age where many think the gods have long since lost their powers, it is still impossible not to rub shoulders with the old Greek gods. Every mountain that looms on the horizon, every glade along the winding roads, every forest, every stream that bubbles through a rocky chasm or lies calmly beneath a grove of olives, the very sea that tosses your boat, has a story of them to tell.

The king of the gods, who lived on Mount Olympus in northern Greece, was Zeus. Poseidon, and Hades the king of the underworld, were his brothers along with a number of siblings of lesser importance—Hera (also his wife), Hestia, Demetre and Chiron. More about them later.

Zeus was not a loving and forgiving god such as is said to be the Christian god. He had overthrown his father, Cronus, in The Battle of the Titans and although he could be wise, fair and prudent, he was unpredictable. He was easily angered and destructive, hurling lightning bolts and violent storms at those who crossed him. He was lusty and amorous and fathered hundreds of divine and semi-divine children from too many goddesses and beautiful human women to count. His wife was also his sister. Some of his divine children were Aphrodite, Apollo, Artemis, Hermes, Athena and mortal/semi-divine include Heracles, Perseus, Helen (of Troy), Dionysus, Argos, Polyeuces and many more.

His brother, Poseidon, was also a passionate guy and by our standards at least, a bit unhinged. Probably his most famous dalliance was with his sister, who turned herself into a mare to avoid his advances. He responded by becoming a stallion and the result of their union was the horse, Arion. His union with his wife produced Triton who was half-human and half-fish. Other progeny included Theseus and Atlas.

These old gods often descended from their lofty mountain, in various guises, to share the stage with their human subjects, to batter them with misfortunes, storms and calamities, seduce them or reward them with riches and glory.

Now, back to Corfu. It is the most northern of the major Greek islands in the Ionian Sea. Ahead of us lay the Gulf of Corinth, the Aegean Sea, the coast of Turkey and our destination by the end of summer, the vibrant Turkish port of Marmaris.

273

Shortly before midnight, eager to drop our anchor and have a celebratory wine, we carefully nosed our yacht into a shallow bay on the southern side of Erikoussa, only to find we could make no sense of our surroundings. It seemed to us that we were still a long way out, but our GPS position put us close to shore and in only three metres of water. It was dark, visibility was not too good, and we were becoming a bit worried about running aground.

I soon learned that when you are a bit lost in Greek waters its best to blame the charts rather than your wife or your GPS. The GPS position is generally right, but the old charts which may have not been updated since Roman times, have lots of things a bit wrong. It was not uncommon for the chart and our GPS position to disagree violently, often by large distances that could show us sailing through an island or over a rocky headland or an island would appear where none was marked at all. This can be a bit disconcerting even in daylight and the objects you are trying to avoid are visible and above water, but definitely daunting at night if it is a submerged reef you need to miss.

Eventually we were satisfied we were safe enough, even if we didn't know exactly where we were. So, we dropped the anchor, thankfully poured a wine and let the beauty of the calm night settle over us. It had been a very long day. And it had been a long journey that had brought us here.

As children, Ro and I had both been touched by the wonder of the ancient Greek world. By the early sagas of the voyages of Jason and Odysseus, the fall of the Trojans, Minoans and Mycenaean', the Persian Wars, the rise and fall of Athens and Sparta and the conquests of Alexander. The old gods, the great names—mystical and real, the beauty of the ideas and inspiration of their art.

Socrates, Plato and Aristotle were the fathers of Western philosophy; Homer, Hesiod, Herodotus, Sophocles, Aristophanes gave us the foundations of our history and literature; Pythagoras and Euclid our mathematics. Incredibly, around 490 BCE Leucippus and Democritus gave us atomic theory, that the universe was composed of two elements, the atoms and the void. The pinnacle of our sporting ideal is still the Olympian, our scientific method was introduced by Thales of Miletus and his followers, physics and engineering was pioneered by Archimedes. No artists have surpassed the works of Praxiteles or the exquisitely decorated vases and frescoes of the Minoans. How lucky we felt to be the masters of our own yacht, free to explore what now lay before us. To sail in these waters, walk in the places where our modern age was born, to be able to marvel at what still remains.

In the morning we found we were a long way off, but the sea was still calm with only a gentle wash on the shore below a high rocky rookery. Gulls wheeled overhead and deep green cypress pines were silhouetted on the spine of the island. The water was a clear emerald and refreshingly cool as the early sun peeped over the rugged mountains of the mainland.

The only sign of life was an old fisherman in a small boat a few hundred metres away.

Over the next few days we made our way through the calm blue waters along the north and east coasts of Corfu. There were many enticing coves surrounded by groves of olives and stands of beautiful cypress pines, and a sprinkling of inviting villas.

We had arrived in the spring and the island was a luscious garden; lupins, geraniums, crocus, hellebores and gladioli were sprinkled in the fields and groves. Morning glory covered hedges, fences and trellises. There was a profusion of roses, sea holly, sea lavender, oleander, orchids, and herbs. Cypress pines—known locally as the fingers of god—grapes and olives dominate the landscape, while carobs, figs, and holm oaks abound.

With our old shipmate, Margie Hansen, who was on board with us and who has been a commercial flower grower for longer than any of us like to remember, we spent many enjoyable hours investigating the lush hinterland. Generally, this meant meandering from one convivial seaside taverna to the next clutching posies of herbs and discussing ideas for dinner. We all liked cooking, but we mostly felt a moral imperative to support the local economy, particularly fishermen, restauranteurs and vintners.

The island was settled by colonists from Corinth around 730 BCE, and because of its richness and situation at the mouth of the Adriatic has always been a tempting prize. Behind the beauty lies a cruel history. For thousands of years the early Greek city states, the Romans, Vandals, Ostrogoths, Slavs, Byzantines, Venetians, Turks, Moors, Normans and Franks, pirates and despots, have all fought over her and drenched the island in blood time and time again.

Venice became master of the island in 1215 CE, as a reward for taking part in the sack of Constantinople. We were anxious to see the mighty fortresses they had built to protect this rich and beautiful gem of its far-flung maritime empire. The beauty of Venice herself is open for all to see, but to appreciate the power of this great—but certainly mercantile and brutal democracy it is necessary to venture far afield.

So, it was with great anticipation that we arrived at Gouvia Marina, not far from the port and town of Corfu one Friday on a lovely spring afternoon. The staff were struggling to throw off the somnolence of a long lunch and a peaceful siesta and were returning to their duties.

We were about to learn that entering Greece by yacht, even if you are just a gentle soul intent on enjoying the food, wine and ambience is nearly always a very testing experience. Bear in mind that on the way out of Montenegro the three of us had been cleared by courteous customs officers, at one office in the harbour, in ten minutes at 3 am.

Our 'Cruising Guide' confidently assured us that the marina would handle all arrivals and departures and was by far the best place to go through customs formalities. Unfortunately, the marina staff knew nothing about this. All they knew was that the office of the 'Port Authority' at the marina would be open tomorrow, and they would take care of things. The next day, after waiting quite a while, an attractive young woman in jeans and tank top arrived around 10 am. and opened the office. Alas, she could not help us until we had cleared customs, the port police and the civil police at various offices in town. She did not think much would open over the weekend, or on Monday as it was a public holiday.

Nevertheless, we thought we should try and took a taxi into town where— guided by a knowledgeable driver—we checked out two customs offices. But both were locked and there was no sign of life. We tried again on Sunday. At 9 am on Monday we taxied in again—in the hands of another driver who had helped many others clear in—but again both offices were locked and deserted.

However, a cleaner working adjacent to the second building directed us to a rear gate that was well hidden from pesky people like ourselves and was manned by four security guards. After pleading to be admitted they escorted us inside through a back entrance—still no sign of life other than a tea lady and more cleaners. After a long wait an official in casual clothes arrived and dismissing our explanations of locked offices, dressed us down for not checking in on Saturday. We were then directed to the port police and after spending an hour or so cooling our heels in an empty waiting room we had our papers stamped and they sent us off to the town police. By now it was lunch and then it was the siesta for the authorities, so it was not until late afternoon that we were back at the marina where we needed to get our papers stamped—again.

Over the next few years we were to find that dealing with most Greek officialdom—although others literally gave us the wine from their tables—can sometimes threaten your sanity.

Finally, we were very pleased to be able to pull down our quarantine flag and hoist the Greek flag from our starboard spreader and set off to explore Corfu and her famous fortresses.

We spent some days anchored below the Old Fortress, a huge Venetian castle on the headland adjacent to Corfu city. Neither Suleiman the Magnificent in 1537 nor Sultan Achmet III in 1736, both with huge armies and fleets, had been able to subdue this mighty stronghold. Reefs in the shallow water surrounding the walls made a sea-borne assault impossible. This left only frontal assaults over a series of walls, a wide canal and more walls all dominated by the high castle walls with cannons sited to bring enfiladed fire on the attackers.

Logistics also played a vital role. These huge Muslim armies and fleets could not be resupplied once winter fell and wild storms severed the supply lines and threatened to wreck any fleet outside a secure port. In fact, it meant the fleet and army could only begin to assemble in Istanbul in March or early April. They then had to sail to Corfu—or Rhodes, or Malta or whatever their target was and get the job done by September, or head home before they were starved or wrecked.

Our anchorage was in a beautiful setting. The city above us, the mountains in the distance, the looming bulk of the fortress, but in the dusk it was not hard to imagine the din of battle and the cries of the dying and wounded as men fought for their lives and the glory of their gods.

Corfu town is a very pleasant place and we enjoyed exploring it together. It is friendly and bustling and still reflects its diffuse cultural and architectural heritages. Crowded with pleasant places to eat; on shaded terraces or in the cool winding streets of the old town, serving great Greek food, often with a lingering hint of their Italian traditions. Away from the town the country roads wind through a picturesque landscape, with sometimes breath-taking views over the rugged coastline and the ever-present ocean.

I was having trouble with my Greek, as I do with all languages. Particularly confusing for me was the word for 'squid' - *calamari*—which is one of my favourite seafoods no matter how its cooked—and the word for 'good morning'—*kalamera*. Locals were continually bemused when I greeted them with a cheerful greeting of 'squid' or attempted to order a 'good morning' for dinner.

We spent a couple of weeks on the island and the adjacent Greek mainland with Margie before she was scheduled to head back to Tasmania and the demands of her beautiful flowers.

We sailed across the Corfu Channel to the Greek mainland and anchored for a couple of nights in Middle Bay near the small village of Mourtos one of a number of anchorages formed by a cluster of small islands off the village.

A little further north we found an isolated and picturesque anchorage in an estuary bounded by a sandy wetland on the north shore and a narrow promontory on the south. There was a fine view of the jagged mountain ranges of Greece on the hazy blue horizon. Flocks of migrating flamingos, flying elegantly in an extended file after the long journey from Africa, arrived not long before dusk and settled in the marshes. We were in a regular stopover—ducks, geese, storks, golden orioles, shrikes and swallows and others were among the regulars.

We headed back to the north-eastern coast of Corfu, sailing parallel to the Albanian coast, to Saint Stefanou Bay. The head of the bay was lined with tavernas protected by a rocky mole extending from the southern shore, while its headlands were covered with olives and cypress. The swimming was delicious, the water had lost the chill of early spring and was warm and clear, the food and local wine just as good.

Nearby was another pleasant anchorage in Kalami Bay—I think the name relates to 'nice in the morning' rather than 'good squid fishing'. Ashore, the White House Restaurant offers fine meals, warm friendly service and a table, which we commandeered each night, perched on a flat rock-shelf lapped by the sea. Nearby was a natural rock pool holding the restaurant's abundant supply of seafood. All was overseen by the beautiful Daria—a Russian model who had married into a Greek family who have owned the villa for more than a century. For a while it was the home to the Durrell family and has been made famous by the naturalist and conservationist Gerald Durrell's '*My Family and Other Animals*'. His brother, the prolific novelist and travel writer Lawrence is best known for '*The Alexandria* Quartet' and perhaps '*Prospero's Cell*' a captivating guide to the landscape and manners of Corfu.

In due course Margie flew off and shortly afterwards two other old friends, Roger and Tina Wainwright arrived on the overnight ferry from Venice. Roger and I were at Duntroon together, also many more years ago than we like to remember. But we still enjoy recalling, with great hilarity, many of the stupid exploits of those days, although our wives are not too excited about our often-repeated exaggerations. After a few drinks Roger and I generally start boasting about having been the best tennis doubles partnership of our era at Duntroon, the army, the services and after a few more, the best of any era. He in fact was a champion Australian Rules rover, who won the ACT best and fairest award as an eighteen-year-old. After retiring he has devoted much of his life to the welfare of veterans and has been a longterm president of the 5RAR association and deserves much more thanks and recognition then he will probably get. Like me he was lucky enough to meet his intended while he was a cadet.

None of our reminiscences are ever complete without a mention of the Regimental Sergeant-Major of our times, the wonderful, legendary Warrant Officer Class I Tom Muggleton. Tom was responsible for drill and discipline and kept an eagle-eye on the comings and goings of cadets from his office. Any infraction of his concept of perfection would bring forth a bellowed sally.

'Smarten up, Sergeants Wainwright and Peterswald, y're marching like bloody painters.' Or 'Am I hurting you, Sergeant Wainwright? I should be, I'm standing on y're bloody hair. Get it cut!'

We tried a few more of the local restaurants—more inappropriate *Kalamera*s and *Calamari*s from me. The weather was mostly pleasant, but still unsettled with some southerlies refusing to surrender to the approach of summer. One afternoon a violent, but thankfully short-lived thunderstorm with winds of forty knots, whipped up breaking waves while we were anchored in an exposed bay in the channel.

It was time to move on, and dropping off Roger and Tina we headed south stopping, overnight at Lakka, a pretty bay on the northern tip of the island of Paxi a few miles from Corfu. The water of the bay is famous for its beauty, which is something when in Greece the water is rarely less than exquisite. The anchorage was indeed magical with the sun playing on the surface creating brilliant translucent blues and greens, and every detail of the sandy bottom clear as clear.

Unfortunately, it is nearly always crowded in summer, and the approach of a late thunderstorm caused some consternation and arguments over anchoring rights— as usual, French and Italian boats against all comers. When the drama was over most headed off to the tavernas in the top of the bay and World War III was averted.

The eastern coast of Paxi is also beautiful — headlands covered with stands of the dark green cypresses enfolding small bays and beaches dotted with charming villas. We called into the sleepy village of Gaios, anchoring in a superb sandy passage on the inside of a small island.

We would have been happy to spend all summer here, sheltered from the afternoon sea breeze, friendly tavernas overlooking the passage, plenty of *calamari* and *kalamera*. However, we were on a mission and in the late morning a couple of days later we took the sea breeze to the port of Preveza, about thirty miles away on the mainland. The north wind came in on time and we had an invigorating reach across the sparkling blue water, the afternoon's white horses dancing around us as we arrived at the entrance to Preveza.

There is a dredged channel leading through the bay to the entrance to the town and the extensive Gulf of Kolpos. The channel passes through the shallow waters of a bay where one of history's great dramas, the Battle of Actium was played out.

The battle was the final act in the struggle for the control of Rome, that had begun when Julius Caesar crossed the Rubicon river in 49 BCE. After overthrowing the republic, he was acclaimed dictator but was assassinated by republican loyalists in 44 BCE.

It was this battle that won Caesar's heir Octavian—retitled as Augustus—one of Rome's greatest rulers, the throne of the Roman Empire, and he established imperial rule that was to last for the next millennium and a half. It eventually inspired the creation of the position of Holy Roman Emperor in Europe, and the ascension of Charlemagne to an institution that was to last until Napoleon overthrew the last emperor. It ranks in importance with history's greatest naval battles: Salamis, Aegospotami, Lepanto, the defeat of the Spanish Armada, Trafalgar and Midway.

After Caesar's death Octavian and Caesar's loyal general Mark Antony formed an alliance and eventually defeated the republican forces. They then divided most of the Empire between themselves. Octavian ruled the west, Antony the east, where he soon fell under the spell of the Egyptian queen and Caesar's former lover Cleopatra. They had first met in Tarsus, in modern day Turkey, and it is reputed she soon turned the foremost general of the empire into a 'strumpets fool'.

The alliance between Octavian and Antony did not last, and by 31BCE they were at war, with their armies in fortified camps in the vicinity of modern-day Preveza.

Antony's army was encamped on the southern entrance to the Gulf of Kolpos, with his ships bottled up inside by Octavian's fleet. Antony would have preferred the battle to be fought on land, but he was eventually forced to try and break Octavian's blockade.

The battle was still in the balance when Cleopatra and her Egyptian ships broke away and made a dash for the open sea. Seeing his lover deserting, Antony once the bravest of men, threw away his honour and fled after her. They reached Egypt, but in the end their only escape was to take their own lives. Cleopatra famously clasping an asp to her breasts and Antony falling on his sword. Octavius 'tidied up' his hold on power by murdering Caesar's young son by Cleopatra, Caesarion.

We anchored for the night in a cove to the northeast of Preveza only a short stroll from the site of Octavian's stronghold before the battle and the site of the ruins of the great city he created to mark his victory. In the darkness of the still night there was no hint of the bloody drama of that long-ago day. Were the shades of the thousands who were slaughtered or drowned still hovering in the shadows around us, or long since gone to the Elysian Fields or Hades.

The next day we sailed further on *Sea Dreams* into the gulf and enjoyed four days in a snug bay on the south side of the Gulf of Kolpos. Nearby there was a large Venetian fortress built on the ruins of earlier strongholds and overlooking the village of Vonitas. Behind the village a patchwork of fields and groves ran up to the foothills of high mountains. It seemed a rich and gentle country.

Our next stop was the mountainous green island of Lefkada. We motored out of the Preveza channel in the early morning so we could enter the Lefkada Canal, which has a difficult entrance choked with sandbars, before the sea breeze made things harder than needs be. Many sailors believe the channel is deliberately badly marked to create business for the local tow boats—personally I think it is more likely caused by idleness than malfeasance—but then again there is a long history of piracy in these waters. It is also said that yachts are dragged off the sandbars on a daily basis – and as we have personally met two such stranded skippers this seems very believable.

All went well, there were no breaking waves at the entrance and the narrow canal was calm and adequately marked. All was overlooked by the old Castle of Aghia Mavra which was built around 1300, captured by the Ottomans in 1487 and retaken by the Venetians in 1500 and is still standing sentinel. The canal has been in use since ancient times and was once of great strategic importance, providing a short and secure route to and from the Ionian.

Shortly afterwards, we passed through the swinging bridge—technically a ship so that the island retains it 'island status' which attracts some financial benefits, linking the town to the mainland and took a birth at the friendly Lefkada marina. It was a short stroll to the village square and the bustling streets around the town centre.

Over the years the town has been ravaged by earthquakes and this has had a pragmatic effect on the town's architecture—most buildings are constructed of galvanised iron above the ground floor. This gives it a somewhat dilapidated air, but the good humour and courtesy of the townsfolk make it a most congenial spot to enjoy a wine—the island is famous for its Vertzami grapes—and to dine on local seafood as dusk gives way to the now sensuously warm night, filled with laughter and chatter.

Earthquakes have in fact plagued Greece throughout recorded history. The country sits astride the African and Eurasian tectonic plates and the relative movements cause periodic calamity. Sparta suffered twenty thousand deaths in 464 BCE, thousands in Crete in 365 BCE, thirty thousand in Corinth in 865, many thousands in Crete in 1303, thirty thousand in Rhodes in 1481, hundreds in 1865 in Rhodes, in Lesbos and Cephalonia in 1867, over eight thousand around Chios in 1881, six hundred in Filiatra in 1894, two hundred and fifty-five in Atalanti in 1894, five hundred in Lerissos in 1932, eight hundred at Zakynthos and Cephalonia in 1953, over one hundred in Athens in 1999 are the major ones. In between there have been literally hundreds of quakes and tremors which have taken lives and caused extensive damage.

On checking who was responsible for this havoc, I found it was none other than the lusty Poseidon whose responsibilities included earthquakes as well as the sea.

281

No wonder he has a reputation for being a surly bastard!

Again, we left reluctantly, and motored along the canal in the early morning to the   Ionian Sea. Although, if at the time I had been aware of the earthquake statistics we may well have headed back to Croatia. It was calm and the sky a pale blue, promising another warm day.

There is a four-knot speed limit in the canal, unless you are in a large motor cruiser and flying Greek or Italian colours. In which case you can drive at whatever speed you like, and need have no concern whatsoever for the safety and comfort of others! However, courtesy demands you should give a cheery wave to acknowledge the adoration of those unfortunates you have swamped in passing.

We had been looking forward to arriving in the Ionian. Apart from being interesting to explore the weather was supposedly ideal. Our cruising directions informed us that at this time of year it was 'calm at night and in the morning, with a relaxing 'gentleman's breeze' in the afternoon that dropped out in time for drinks'. Just our sort of weather!!

Shortly after leaving the canal in the still early morning, the ruffling water heralded the arrival of a strong westerly. And so, the pattern was set: for six days out of seven there were strong north westerlies, blowing twenty to twenty-five knots, night and day and funnelling around the islands making secure anchorages hard to find.

We spent two days at Vliho Bay on the east coast of Lefkada Island, a picturesque and sheltered spot, while waiting for the wind to drop to gentlemanly strengths and swimming in the warm inviting water.

Being disappointed by the weather tends to be part of sailing—no one is going to make a summer holiday location work by advertising that the weather there is crappy—although some hardy friends have still bought in Norway and the Arctic. This was certainly not the first time we had been misled. Witness Queensland's boasts of 'beautiful one day perfect the next' —more like 'strong winds with dangerous tidal races today, stronger winds and thunderstorms tomorrow'.

As the wind showed no signs of abating we motored around the dramatic coastline past lots more lovely cypress and olives, patches of flowering bougainvillea and gardens, to Skorpios Island. Famous in modern times as the recluse of Aristotle Onassis and Jackie Kennedy. We anchored in the clear blue water of a sheltered cove with distant views of the high rocky mountains of the Greek mainland. There were a few yachts with us during the afternoon, but by nightfall we had the lovely ambience all to ourselves.

From the water the island was enchanting, with lush vegetation and manicured lawns. But the exotic charm was not enhanced by the overt presence of security guards patrolling the shore. Onassis bought the island for a few million in the fifties, and it is rumoured that the family have recently knocked back more than a hundred million. Cannot blame them from ensuring riffraff is kept at arm's length.

We moved on, exploring the many fjord-like anchorages in nearby Meganisi Island and the adjacent coast. The wind was still strong and outside of the anchorages we struggled along with our sails reefed and keeping a careful watch for the ferocious 'bullets' roaring down from the high steep mountains.

We stopped for a couple of days in the large bay at Vasiliki at the southern end of Lefkas, where the wind was howling straight over the bay. There was reasonable protection off the sandy beach at its head, although there was still an uncomfortable chop two hundred metres out. It was the wind surfing capital of the world, great entertainment, but I think those speeding past at only slightly subsonic speeds resented having a potential death trap anchored in a path they presumed was exclusively theirs, which it definitely was not.

The run south to the island of Ithaca with the wind off our stern quarter was exhilarating. After passing three Venetian watchtowers at the harbour entrance we anchored off the pretty village of Kioni. It was still over twenty knots in the harbour, and it was not easy to get the anchor set in the quite deep water. As the afternoon wore on a number of other yachts had difficulties, we were lucky none dragged onto us.

Now, can I talk about careless anchoring? Not wishing to be pedantic of course.

On most yachts coming into anchor from the still paternalistic Mediterranean countries, with macho cigar-smoking skippers at the helm, there is usually a beautiful woman standing at the bow. She is posed in a skimpy or topless bikini while the skipper does a lap of honour selecting an anchoring spot. The beautiful foredeck hand nonchalantly drops the anchor when ordered, disdainfully lets out a bit of chain, poses a little more, then sways sexily to the stern, enjoying the admiration from surrounding yachts—oops, I hope that doesn't sound a bit sexist. Meanwhile the skipper will do a couple of chin-ups, comb his hair, check the set of his collar, jump in the tender and roar off at great speed to book a table for lunch. If the tender had wheels, it would be burning rubber as he returns to collect his crew.

That's careless anchoring.

Later, when the skipper and crew are well into a long lunch ashore a stiff sea breeze comes in. Their yacht swings and collides with another yacht or drifts off, bludgeoning the surrounding yachts out of the way. There will be loud and acrimonious discussion about whose fault it was, the skipper or his beautiful foredeck hand, before a dinghy roars off in pursuit of the drifting yacht.

Now if I can be pedantic for a moment . . . again.

Anchoring is not a trivial afterthought on arriving somewhere. It is an absolutely essential sea craft. Not anchoring carefully is much the same as leaving your front door open in say, San Pedro Sula in Honduras - perhaps not that bad, but say Kabul or Karachi. Sooner rather than later something bad is going to happen. The wind will come up at the wrong time or a storm will blow through on a black and miserable night, and the anchor will drag, and you will be on the rocks.

It can be a laborious business. And in more maternal societies ruled by women, such as my own, it is the man who must set and retrieve the anchor, usually in the late afternoon or early morning when the angle of the harsh Mediterranean sun beats off the water, into the face of who-ever is standing in the bows. In the afternoon a strong wind will greatly increase the sun damage.

On our boat the boss flatly refuses to be involved, maintaining that she has no intention of aging prematurely. So, it's always me up in the bows early to have a good look around as we come in, leaving the boss posing behind the wheel where she can admire the view from beneath the shady canopy.

The first thing—of course—is choosing the right anchorage, one that will give you safety in the forecast weather. Then—also of course—choosing the right spot in the anchorage; some parts are always more protected, there may be weed on the bottom, you want to be close to the best taverna etc etc.

So, I courteously direct Ro to an empty spot with a radius of at least the length of chain to be dropped, bearing in mind that in calm weather some anchors may not necessarily be out in front of already anchored yachts. Ghost to a gentle stop and if possible, drop the anchor onto a clean bottom with no seaweed, at the moment your boat stops moving forward. Let the wind carry you back, or gently reverse as you lay out a couple of boat lengths of chain. Clamp the chain and let the drift of the boat 'set' the anchor and get its first grip on the bottom.

Keep a hand on the chain to get a feel of the bottom; with a bit of practice you can tell if it's fine or coarse sand, mud, weed, rocks etc, and ensure the anchor has set. Pay out more chain and let the wind carry the boat back some more, it may need some gentle reverse. Keeping tension on the anchor chain so that the anchor continues to be pulled into the sea bed.

When you have let out the right length of chain—at least three times the depth you are anchored in—check that all looks good and you will be clear of everyone if the wind swings. Attach a springer between the chain and a cleat so that the anchor winch does not carry all the weight.

Signal the boss to gently reverse again, giving just enough power to ensure the anchor is well dug in, but not so much that it is prematurely pulled out of the mud. Keep your hand on the chain so that you can feel if it's dragging.

Then hang round the bow to keep an eye on things, identify some points on shore that you can use later to check your position, and see if anyone is gesticulating or shouting at you; Germans can be very pedantic about anchoring over their anchor chain.

Switch the motor off. If the water is not too deep and the weather not too bad—in other words, if it is calm, hot and you feel like a swim—put on flippers and mask and swim out to check the anchor is dug in and check what the bottom is like. There may be something which will foul the anchor if it drags back—old mooring chains are everywhere—or resets at a different angle during a wind change.

Now that's careful anchoring.

I think the reason the average French boat only heads out of the marina to anchor two and a half times a year is because after two days most women realise it is not worth pursuing a relationship with some cigar-smoking bully if the price is being an anchor maid who will be shouted at a lot and your skin is likely to be ruined by the harsh sun and wind.

But if you are a cruising yacht and you plan to hang on an anchor for weeks and months on end, good anchoring is the only way to stay sane. If you have a big, oversized and well-designed anchor, enough chain and you know your anchor is dug into a good bottom you can sleep peacefully; at least until the wind or tide change and the boss kicks you out of bed to check things.

Back to Ithaca. It is most famous as the home of Odysseus the hero of Homer's epic sagas, the '*Iliad*' and the '*Odyssey*'. It was from here he set off to the Trojan War after getting advice from the beautiful goddess Athena who had a soft spot for him and returned after nearly two decades of war and travails, just in time to slaughter a number of suitors who were attempting to steal his crown and his wife, Penelope, who understandably had just about given up on him.

And although the site of his palace has never been definitely identified—and from time to time other islands have tried to claim ownership of Odysseus—it was most likely on the mountain just behind our small bay.

This enhanced the ambience of a wonderful twilight. It was rich with the aromas of the sea, the surrounding forest and wood fired cooking that made dinner on the small rocky quay, with the beautifully complexioned love of my life, one of those occasions which do really seem timeless and unforgettable.

And yes, the wine of Ithaca was a good as Odysseus was always saying. But again, I got the feeling that it was not here that red wine was first invented.

From Kioni it was an hour around to Vathi the capital of the island. The huge harbour is a flooded crater with a dramatic narrow entrance through the surrounding lofty mountains, which Homer describes as being more suitable for goats than horses. As with all the Ionian it is earthquake-prone, and the architectural inspiration of the village is also somewhat on the existential side. Nevertheless, it is a lovely spot to explore and we had some fine meals overlooking the harbour.

The gusty winds persisted, but we took a little comfort from assurances by a local taxi driver that it was 'most unusual' and would calm down before long. But before too long we realised Greek taxi drivers always lie about the weather—see Charmaine Clift's insights later on in this chapter.

It was too windy the next night to go ashore, and it was still strong when we decided to head for Kefalonia where we anchored in Andisamis Bay, finding a small corner that gave us some protection. The island is the setting for one of my favourite books about the Mediterranean, *'Captain Corelli's Mandolin'* (*Birds Without Wings* is also great) by Louis de Bernieres and the island has a justifiable reputation for great beauty, stunning women and fine wines.

De Bernieres captures the essence of the island: *'The half-forgotten island of Cephalonia .... it is an island so immense in antiquity that the very rocks themselves exhale nostalgia and the red earth lies stupefied not only by the sun, but by the impossible weight of memory. The ships of Odysseus were built of Cephalonian pine, his bodyguards were Cephalonian giants, and some maintain that his palace was not in Ithica but in Cephalonia.'*

'(the light) .... is completely virgin, it has overwhelming clarity of focus, it has heroic strength and brilliance. As though straight from the imagination of God in his youngest days when he still believed that all was good. The dark green of the pines is unfathomable .... The ocean .... azure and turquoise, emerald, viridian and lapis lazuli ....and easier to see through than the air in any other place.'

Of course, it goes without saying that it is home to the most beautiful women in the islands. He explains that over the years so many men have been forced to emigrate to find work, that only the most beautiful of the girls can find husbands and these pass their beauty on.

Our anchorage was also beautiful although some of the strong wind still curled around into our small cove and, we had to anchor close in and hang alongside the rocky cliffs of the shoreline to get any protection. We were in fifteen metres of exquisitely clear warm water, and the reflections from the ochre coloured cliffs were stunning. The wind dropped out in the early evening and we enjoyed a still night and lovely morning until an easterly came up and forced us to move on.

We had planned to visit the village of Poros near the southern end of Kefalonia, but there was not much room in the harbour. The wind was still strong enough to jeopardise our relationship if we tried to find a berth, and in any case, Ro did not want me mooning over the beautiful ladies of the island.

The wind was a blustery twenty-five knots on our nose on the way across to Zakynthos and we were thankful when we arrived at the anchorage just off the sea wall at Nikolaos harbour, where a craggy granite island gave protection from the northwest. There was a gull rookery among the cruel grey cliffs, and we were serenaded by the shrill cries of the whirling birds as dusk settled, with the wind still whistling through the rigging. After three days we had had enough of the music and the wind showed no signs of easing.

I checked the cruising guide again – *'calm in the morning, a gentleman's breeze in the afternoon and a still peaceful night'*. Hmmm.

Due to its richness and strategic position the island has also had a bloody history. It was sacked by the Athenian fleet during the Peloponnesian War, later conquered by Phillip of Macedon, then the Romans and was always subject to attacks from pirates and passing fleets. It was ravaged by the Goths, the Vandals, Saracens, Normans and the Turks who depopulated the whole island. Sadly, a history shared by so much of the eastern Mediterranean.

Finally, from 1489, it enjoyed a period of prosperity and stability under the Venetians, who needed the island to protect their trade routes and who established lucrative horticulture — mainly currants—and viticulture industries in the island's fertile soil and left behind one of the most beautiful cities in the Ionian. There are still a wide range of vines on the island, including Robola, Skiadopoulo, Katsakoulis and Pavlos. Some memorable wines are made by the commercial wineries on the island as well as in most back yards. However, there were no signs that the person who invented red wine had passed this way!

The French ruled the island from 1797 until it passed to the British after the defeat of Napoleon, and finally to Greece in 1864.

The wind was still brisk when we decided that we had to press on and, following the route taken by Odysseus when he set off for Troy, we headed for Katakolon on the west coast of the Peloponnese and just a short drive to Olympia.

The first Greek games were held at Delphi before moving to Olympia in the 8th century BCE, which was then the site of the games for more than a thousand years and, were of course the inspiration for the modern Olympics. The ancient Olympics were not always pure, even though there are no recorded problems with performance enhancing substances. But something does seem a bit 'off' when the Roman emperor Nero won the singing and chariot events in 67 BCE. The games were abolished in 393 CE and the site destroyed on the orders of the emperor Theodosius following urging from the Christian church, which abhorred the pagan nature of the games.

It was the site of the Greek sculptor Phidias' twelve metre bronze statue of Zeus circa 432 BCE and one of the wonders of the ancient world. The circumstances of its disappearance are still the subject of debate, possibly destroyed by fire, but most likely by Christians at the site or in Constantinople.

We had not been able to decide whether to continue in Odysseus's wake and sail around the south of the Peloponnese or to go through the Gulf of Corinth and the Corinth Canal. After a chat with the harbourmaster, who thought we would be crazy to take the southern route while the winds were what they were, we decided to go through the canal. This would let us visit some important sites on the way, including the ancient site of Delphi and the city of Missolonghi, the location of a watershed event in the Greek War of Independence.

So, from Katakolon we headed north to Kyllini and anchored under the protection of the long breakwater. It was a quiet night with just some wash from ferries coming and going. Today the town is a backwater, but during the 13th and 14th centuries, it was a major port and an important commercial centre. It is overlooked by a forbidding castle built by the Franks and expanded over the centuries.

We left Kyllini early, and with the help of a morning land breeze we gambolled across the Gulf of Patras and were off the canal leading into Missolonghi at midday. The coast here is mostly low-lying marshland with shallow water extending quite a way offshore. It was all eyes on deck as we edged apprehensively into the shallow muddy canal that leads to the town; we were very much a blue water boat and not too happy having only a metre of so under the keel.

The Missolonghi lagoon had a forgotten world feel about it, with ramshackle fishing shacks festooned with drying nets, perched precariously on stilts along the muddy foreshore. In due course it led into a generous basin, with the nondescript city fringe along the eastern shore and a large boatyard opposite. The water was calm, the bottom glutinous and we had distant views of the mountains in the north. Safe and secure rather than glamourous, but nearly two hundred years ago it was the scene of dramatic events that led to the reunification and independence of Greece for the first time in over two thousand years.

By the 19th century, Greece which had previously been a province of the Roman and Byzantine Empires for a millennium and a half, had endured a further four hundred years of Muslim rule. In many aspects this rule was pragmatic, freedom of religion was generally allowed. The main concern of the Sultans was to maximise their harvest of wealth, resources and manpower from their subjects—the fate of their souls was not something they worried over too much. But taxes were brutally collected. The tax which caused most resentment and hatred was the Devshirme, the provision of young boys and girls who would be forced to convert to Islam and serve the Ottoman Empire, many as elite soldiers (Janissaries) or in the harems of the Empire.

But even after nearly two thousand years of enslavement the spirit of freedom and independence was still very much alive in Greek hearts. Abroad, there was a Greek diaspora promoting independence and at home there were thousands prepared to fight for it. In 1821 unrest against Ottoman rule had begun to gather pace. But it lacked co-ordination, finance and trained soldiers and there was still no tangible support from European governments or widespread support in Europe for their cause.

But in 1823 one of the great romantic adventurers of the ages sailed into Kefalonia.

With a father known as 'Mad Jack' who had married two heiresses and squandered their fortunes, a grandfather who was Vice Admiral 'Foul Weather Jack' and had circumnavigated the world, and a granduncle known as the 'Wicked Lord' it is not surprising that Lord Byron inherited, along with his literary genius, some very wild genes.

His mother wrote that as a young man he had no disposition she knew of, other than love. His romantic conquests, with no discrimination for sex and age—including his half-sister and many young men - at a time when homosexuality was illegal, and the penalty was a death sentence—became legendary. His three years at Trinity College were a tapestry of passionate sexual liaisons, boxing, horse riding and gambling. In the family tradition he amassed debts, enjoyed a wild and adventurous Grand Tour where he moved from love affair to love affair and was famous for swimming the Hellespont.

He became a celebrity when the first two cantos for Childe Harold's Pilgrimage were published in 1812 and went on to become the most brilliant star of the dazzling world of Regency London.

For many years he had been a passionate supporter of Greek independence and his arrival in Kefalonia marked the beginning of his plans to play an active role in the Greek War of Independence. He sailed his own warship, which had cost him a fortune, to Missolonghi in 1824. He was planning an attack on the fortified port of Lepanto when he contracted Malaria and died on the 19th April. His fame and the tragedy of his death did much to promote the Greek cause and much credit must go to him for the eventual winning of independence. A statue to honour Lord Byron has been erected at Missolonghi and we had come here to pay our respects.

The town was also the site of one of the pivotal battles of the war. Over the centuries there had been several uprisings against the Ottomans. In the earlier years the European powers were totally occupied in their own survival and in no position to assist, and later as the Ottoman empire began to crumble, they were reluctant to sponsor independence less it stirred up trouble in their own colonies. Russia was interested in what was going on because of the connection through the Orthodox Church and her interest in gaining access or controlling the Dardanelles – but Europe, naturally enough, preferred the status quo rather than Russian control.

By the early 1820s there was widespread fighting all over Greece, and a number of massacres which helped ignite European support.

The third siege of Missolonghi began in April 1825 and by the spring of 1826 Egyptian and Turkish forces had captured the marshes around the city and cut off their supplies. The Greeks refused to surrender and tried to break out. On 22 April three thousand Greek men tried to cut their way out and allow six thousand non-combatants (mainly women and children) to escape. Some fighters succeeded in getting through, but four thousand of the women and children were captured and sold into slavery. Most of remainder blew themselves up rather than be captured.

This tragedy changed attitudes everywhere.

The American philosopher Samuel Howes wrote: '...*damning proof of the selfish indifference of the Christian world. You may talk to me of national policy and the necessity of neutrality, but I say a corpse upon such a policy.*'

The symbol of the murder of young innocent Christian women at the hands of the Turks became the symbol of the war. In 1826 Russia, Britain and France finally intervened, the war was won, and the national enslavement ended.

We enjoyed two peaceful nights anchored off the city. We visited the statue of a romantic, swashbuckling Byron. It seemed to capture his larger than life character and at dusk when we returned to *Sea Dreams*, we drank a toast or two to the great man.

The next day we passed through the waters where the Battle of Lepanto between the navies of Christian Europe and the Ottomans, was fought in the summer of 1571. It was the most important sea battle since the Battle of Salamis in 480 BCE where the Persians were thrown back from the possible conquest of Europe and, is up there with the most important naval battles of all time.

A Christian defeat at Lepanto would have given the Muslims unchallenged control of the Mediterranean at a time when their armies were pressing deep into

Europe. It could have meant the end of Christian Europe. It was also important technologically, as it was the first naval battle where cannon and firearms decided the outcome, changing the way war was fought at sea.

The fleet of the Christian League was commanded by Prince John of Austria, although most of the fleet was from Venice (one hundred and fifteen of two hundred and six galleys), as well as from Genoa, Spain, the Papacy and other nations. The Ottoman fleet comprised one hundred and eighty-nine galleys and eighty-six Galliots. In all over two hundred thousand men, including thirty-seven thousand Christian slaves, fought for their lives.

Prince John, who was a hardened warrior warned his men there was no paradise for cowards, while the Turkish Commander Ali Pasha offered his Christian slave rowers their freedom if he triumphed. His men were assured that in death there awaited a place in paradise where they would each be attended by seventy beautiful virgins.

At the end of a bloody day the Christians, much superior in cannons and firearms, were victorious. The larger high-sided Venetian galleys played a brave and decisive role in the battle. They placed themselves ahead of the Christian fleet so that the Muslims had to try and capture them or expose themselves to the Venetian cannon before they could come to grips with the rest of the Christian fleet.

Thirteen thousand slaves were saved but some eight thousand Christians and thirty thousand Muslims, requiring the services of over two million virgins, perished. It is impossible to sail past this spot without giving thanks to the brave sailors of the Christian fleet who, with their victory preserved the heritage of Europe and the Greco-Roman world. Sad to reflect that like most great battles that at the time seemed to have saved the world, it may have in the end have been futile.

By the time we reached our destination for the night, the island of Trizonia, the wind was boisterous again, and we were glad of the shelter in the almost enclosed harbour. It had died down by 7.30 and we went ashore to investigate the charming village that spread across a narrow isthmus between the harbour and the channel separating the island from the mainland

There was a marina, of relatively modern, but shoddy construction on the inland shore adjacent to the village, and we tied up our dinghy alongside a crumbling and rust-streaked cement wall. On the way in we were bemused to find the two masts of a sunken ketch protruding at a drunken angle from the water inside the marina. It all had a dilapidated and unloved look. A number of shabby yachts, some with signs of life and others deserted, looking as if their sea days were long since over.

It turned out that the EU had built a number of similar marinas in Greek waters with the aim of attracting yachts to various islands and villages without existing facilities. In most cases the construction was shoddy—surely the Mafia could not have been involved—and for some reason there was no management or municipal control. They were simply used as extra berthing for local runabouts or by vagrants who wanted free berthing for their unseaworthy craft.

Our spirits were lifted however, as we strolled the short distance through the village to the far shore. The mountains on the mainland were glowing in the rich golden light of the late sun and were framed between the blues of the channel and the pinks and blues of the sky behind. Many years later this beautiful scene is as fresh in my mind's eye as it was on that evening, the colours as vivid as they were that night.

There were four or five restaurants overlooking the translucent water of the small quay and the picturesque fishing launches tied alongside. They were convivial places, blackboard menus, local wine and seafood cooked in wood fired ovens, salads from the island's gardens. There was always a handful of yachtsmen passing in or out of the Gulf of Corinth, all ready with a laugh and a story to tell. It was quite late as we rowed back to *Sea Dreams*. A calm dark night, the yacht's masthead-light a welcome beacon to guide us home.

We lingered for the best part of a week. The island, apart from the graveyard that the marina had become, was utterly charming. On our return five years later, the masts of the sunken ketch were still a forlorn decoration.

The village of Galaxidi was an easy day's run up the gulf and we anchored off the town, overlooked by an elegant cathedral. Towards sunset a strong northerly forced us to move across the bay and we ended up in a rather forlorn and empty spot where shallow water forced us to anchor in choppy water a long way out. There was not a sign of life to be seen—no lights, just the dark hills.

Early the next morning we entered the also somewhat dilapidated marina at Itea and tied up alongside the breakwater. An officious port official spent most of the day hanging around to tell arriving yachts—all two of us—to report to his office at 7 pm to complete paperwork and have our transit logs stamped. The same official was at the office at appointed time, but we had to wait an hour for his attention. Why we could not have completed the papers as we arrived, which would have been a much easier procedure, is a mystery. However, when we topped up our fuel the very friendly driver of the mini-tanker brought us a bottle of his homemade wine—light red with a gentle aroma of roses. The irritation of officialdom, the charm of the common man.

Our main reason for being at Itea was that it was just a short distance from Delphi, and we headed up Mount Parnassus before the sun was too high the next morning. Delphi had a major influence on life in ancient Greece for the best part of two thousand years. It was originally the site of a temple dedicated to the god Apollo—a son of Zeus and his wife/sister Hera. But over time the prophesies of the head priestess, the Pythia gave it such importance that few great endeavours were undertaken without first consulting her. Most leaders who wanted a glimpse of their future made the arduous trip to Mount Parnassus. Or if they were really important, they may have sent a minion on their behalf. Here are some of the prophesies that have survived the passage of three millennium or so.

The Oracle is credited with having predicted the Trojan War, which was fought sometime around 1200 BCE.

The historian Herodotus records that the Spartan king Lycurgus consulted the Pythia in the 8th century BCE before introducing a constitution that combined dual kingship and a free population with equal shares of land. The following advice was also given: *'Love of money, and nothing else, will ruin Sparta.'* The Spartans rejected coinage until the expenses of the Peloponnesian War forced them to accept it.

In the 6th century BCE the great Athenian law-maker Solon was advised: *'Seat yourself now amidships, for you are the pilot of Athens. Grasp the helm fast in your hands; you have many allies in the city.'* Solon passed up the chance of dictatorship and created a constitution which gave trial by jury, a graduated tax system and forgiveness of debt. All of which helped create an Athenian middle class. The town magistrates swore to uphold his laws on pain of paying for a gold statue dedicated to the Oracle of Delphi, equal in weight to themselves.

The famous king of Lydia, Croesus, was advised that his kingdom would be safe until a mule became king of Media. Thinking himself invincible he made war on Media having forgotten that their king was half-Mede and half-Persian and could therefore be considered a 'mule'.

Early histories credit the Delphic priestess Themistoclea for the moral doctrines of the great philosopher and mathematician Pythagoras.

During the 5th century BCE with the approaching invasions by Persia, the oracle's advice was keenly sought a number of times by the two most powerful Greek states, Athens and Sparta. The advices were as usual enigmatic and obscure, but later seemed prescient.

'Either your famed, great town must be sacked or the whole land .... shall mourn the death of the king of the house of Herackles. The Spartan king, Leonidas died at the Battle of Thermopylae. *'Pray to the winds. They will prove to be mighty allies of Greece'.* At the naval battle at Salamis the wind disrupted the Persian fleet and the Greeks triumphed.

Around 440 BCE the Oracle opined that there was no one wiser than Socrates.

The great philosopher modestly replied that either all men were equally ignorant, or that he was the only one aware of his ignorance *(what I do not know I do not think I know)*. Giving rise to the most famous of Delphic mottos: *'know thyself'*.

In 403 BCE Lysander the Spartan admiral and victor of the thirty years of the horror of the Peloponnesian War was warned of *'.... the serpent, earthborn, in craftiness coming behind thee'*. In 395 BCE he was killed from behind by Neochorus, who had a serpent painted on his shield.

In 359 BCE the Oracle told Philip II of Macedon: *'... with silver spears you will conquer the world'* and in 336 BCE told his son Alexander the Great *'You are invincible my son.'*

Cicero perhaps Rome's greatest orator was advised: *'Make your own nature, not the advice of others, your guide in life.'*

The Emperor Nero certainly one of Rome's most infamous rulers visited the Oracle in 67 CE, having amongst many other atrocities murdered his mother (also his lover) a few years earlier, was told: *'Your presence here outrages the god you seek. Go back, matricide! The number 73 marks the hour of your downfall!'*

Being a man who took criticism badly, he had the Pythia burned alive. He was only thirty years-old and, seventy-three seemed a long way off. But shortly after, a revolt by the seventy-three-year-old Galba removed this piece of human excrement from the throne.

While Hadrian was still a young man the Pythia advised him that he would become emperor, and later told the emperor Diocletian that Christianity would lead to the destruction of the empire. The first certainly came to pass, and many would agree with Gibbons regarding the second.

Almost the last recorded prophesy was given to the Roman emperor Julian the Apostate in 362 CE and predicted the end of the Oracle: *'Tell the emperor that my hall has fallen to the ground. Apollo has no chapel left, no prophesying bay, no talking stream. The stream is dry that had so much to say.'* The next year the temple was closed on the orders of Emperor Theodosius I and never reopened. Within five years the Emperor was dead and fifteen years later the Visigoth Alaric had captured Rome.

Reading through the old prophecies it is hard not to be impressed by them. They come down as so subtly phrased—a feminine subtlety, allowing a wide range of interpretation which anticipates realities and the aspirations of anxious and ambitious people. They generally favour a cautious path. There is an accurate appreciation of who is asking for advice and why. They display a knowledge of the world as it was, in some cases displaying an amazing historical and geographical knowledge. The delivery of the prophecies was dressed up with smoke and mirrors and superstition,

294

but behind it all were shrewd and astute minds.

For many centuries the Delphi precinct was protected by treaties between the city states guaranteeing its sanctity, and the Pythia showed great commercial acumen as well as diplomatic and philosophical perception. It had the best business plan—other than conquest and pillage—devised to that date. The lucrative business of being able to see the future and pass on the advice of Apollo were not the only strings to their bow.

They had the Olympic franchise until the games were moved to Olympia, but then still maintained a probably equally important athletics event. Most of the Greek states kept their treasuries there, where they were protected by treaty and it was always a great tourist attraction.

In modern equivalents it was a bit like one entity controlling all the banks, as well as having a monopoly of religious interpretation—now split between dozens of organizations—and running the Olympic Games and the various world cups of soccer rugby etc etc.

No wonder it was shut down shortly after Christianity became the official religion of the empire, and Constantinople and the Vatican fought over the religious spoils while refining their own business plans. They added things the Pythia would have loved to be able to sell—the Divine Right of Kings to rule, granting sanctity to marriage and legitimacy of birth.

Delphi is in a stupendous site, and although mass tourism does detract from the spiritual aura it must have had in ancient times, it does still feel close to the old gods. To climb up the winding track through the remarkably inspiring ruins of the temples, amphitheatres, vaults, grottos and the arena is perhaps to be as close to the spirit of ancient Greece as it is possible to be. Standing at the top and looking over the shadowed valleys and mountains below, it is impossible not to be moved by what once was.

Pressing further up the dramatic coastline we explored a number of bays that looked good on the charts, but they were all plagued by katabatic winds howling down from the mountains and poor anchorages. We had a couple of windy nights at the eastern end of the Gulf of Corinth and decided to head for the Corinth Canal.

The canal was completed in 1893 and is about seven kilometres long and twenty-two metres wide. It makes a tremendous difference for a sailing boat that would otherwise have to circumnavigate the Peloponnese Peninsular—which, particularly in winter can be a hostile place for a yacht. For frail ancient galleys it was a graveyard, and for this reason a canal has been a dream since ancient times. The tyrant, Periander, in the seventh century BCE was the first to actually turn a sod, but in the end, he opted for a stone carriageway to hall boats across. The remains are next to the canal to this day.

Many other notables, including Julius Caesar, floated the idea. Nero, probably still smarting over the Pythia's insult, personally swung the first blow of a pickaxe in 67 CE. When he died a year later the workforce of six thousand Jewish prisoners had dug about a tenth of the way across, but the project was given up. In fact, it wasn't completed for almost another two thousand years when the first vessel sailed through late in the 19th century.

Fortunately, it was a calm morning when we arrived at the westward end of the canal, where there was a considerable delay waiting for the canal to be opened for traffic heading east. It is only one-way traffic and boats are required to form in convoy, freighters first and yachts last. It takes the best part of an hour to pass through and at places the 'cut' is through spectacular cliffs.

A strong sea breeze greeted us at the other end and the windy terminal where dues are paid was a bit of a bun fight. Yachts must dock and pay over the counter—payment by internet would have saved a lot of time and been much more convenient—but not a strong consideration for Greek officialdom. We decided to recommend to the EU that the vast horde of officials sitting on their bums shuffling paper should be put onto maintaining the crumbling walls of the canal.

With the sea breeze on our quarter we set of to explore the Saronic Gulf the large body of water lying between Athens and the Peloponnese. The water was a dancing blue, the sky cloudless and the shoreline ahead a mystery calling us forward, and before long we had forgotten our irritations with officialdom.

The hazy blue lump away to our north-east was the island of Salamis. In 480 BCE, what could be history's most important naval battle, the Battle of Salamis was fought in the straits between the island and the Athenian mainland. The ships of the Greek city states opposed a Persian navy as it was poised to snuff out Greece's golden age, and with it the great heritage it was to leave the world—in government, philosophy, science and the arts.

The invasion had been some years in the making. In 490 BCE there was an earlier invasion led by the Persian King, Darius, but it had been defeated by the Athenian army at the Battle of Marathon fought 42.195 kilometres east of Athens. In 481 BCE Xerxes, who had succeeded his father, demanded the Greeks acknowledge him as their overlord. The Greeks refused, and remarkably as some states were still technically at war with each other, managed to form an alliance. Xerxes advanced with a huge army and fleet, the army crossed the Dardanelles on a bridge of ships and advanced south along the Aegean coast. The famous Battle of Thermopylae was fought between the two armies, and the Greek fleet was forced to retreat to the straits between the island of Salamis and the Athenian mainland.

Athens was evacuated and captured by the Persians. Themistocles, the commander of the Greek fleet—of some three hundred and seventy ships—was determined to fight the much larger Persian fleet—various estimates from six hundred to twelve hundred ships—and enticed them into the narrow waters of the straits, where the Persian numerical advantage was mitigated. This tactic worked, assisted by a strong wind which came up as the Persian fleet turned into the narrow strait. They became disorganised, lost their cohesion and fell prey to the bronze rams of the larger Greek triremes with fully armoured hoplites aboard. Probably half the Persian fleet was destroyed, against a few dozen of the Greek fleet.

The Greek triremes of this era were generally around thirty-five metres in length and six metres wide and painted and embellished with eyes and figures to conjure up frightening and dangerous apparitions. They carried a crew of some thirty officers and marines and around one hundred and seventy sailors who manned the three banks of oars. In short bursts they could reach speeds of ten knots and their manoeuvrability made the large bronze tipped rams fixed to the bows a deadly weapon. For journeys running before suitable winds they carried a sail.

A fleet of these vessels moving in formation would have evoked the same fear and omnipresence that a modern aircraft carrier battle group does today.

In the aftermath Xerxes retreated back to Asia with the bulk of his army. The portion he left was decisively defeated the following year at the battles of Plataea and Mycale, and it would be two thousand years before Greece fell to another empire from Asia – the Ottoman Turks.

These victories ushered in the golden summer of classical Greece and the flowering of democracy in Athens. But alas, it proved to be the penultimate act of the greatest Greek tragedy of all. Only seventy years later, in the spring of 404 BCE the Spartan admiral Lysander sailed a vast armada of warships crammed with thirty thousand warriors, into the port of Piraeus to finish the horror that was the Peloponnesian War. It had lasted nearly thirty years and in proportion to the numbers involved, both in actual combatants and the general population devastated by fighting, disease and famine, it was perhaps the most tragic war in history.

Its harsh lessons have fascinated military historians ever since. It was a civil war fought between a democracy and a feudal oligarchy, a great naval power that ruled the seas against an army all thought invincible on land. One side was immensely rich from trade and tribute from its allies and colonies, the other a rural backwater which even eschewed the use of money. There were great battles and sieges and bloody guerrilla warfare, and commanders whose names still ring down through the ages.

It was all recorded by the historians, Xenophon and Thucydides, who was also a commander and combatant in the war, and a philosopher who predicted that human nature is unchanging and presents us with lessons of what can happen in war at any time, and in any place. The tragedies engulfed the rich and famous as well as the lowest. Pericles, the spiritual and political leader of Athens, died of the plague, as did his sister and two of his sons. Another son and a gifted commander, Pericles the Younger, was executed as a scapegoat after the bloody battle of Arginusae. His nephew, Hippocrates, fell at the battle of Delium. The greatest family of Athens virtually wiped out.

Athens, the city that has been the inspiration of so much of what is good in western culture, would not be its own master again until 1826 CE, two thousand four hundred and thirty years later.

Back onboard *Sea Dreams*, humbled and saddened by our thoughts we followed the southern coast to Korfos Bay passing lots of fish farms tucked into small bays, with ramshackle cottages perched precariously nearby. On the way we were nearly run aground by two large fishing boats who at one stage had come around a point ahead of us, travelling in our direction.

Now, who has 'the right of way' at sea is a complicated set of rules.

Our general rule is to get out of everyone's way on the basis that most people driving big boats believe that 'might is right', fishing boats think no one else should be on the water, and a lot of people in small boats are hyper-sensitive about what they think their rights are and may or may not know the rules anyway. If they are Greek or Italian they naturally have right of way in any case, even if they are flying a USA flag—an extraordinary number of yachts, skippered by swarthy well-tanned men with lots of gold jewellery, are registered in the state of Maine because of a popular tax dodge known by virtually every boat owner in the Mediterranean, but apparently not to tax officials.

In this instance we saw the two boats quite a way off and on their present course, they would pass well to our left. They were flying no flags or symbols to warn of any peculiarities—towing nets, divers over-board, anchoring etc etc. The 'right of way rules' were all in our favour. We were under sail, we were on starboard tack, we were downwind, we were passing on the correct side, we were giving them a wide berth and making our intentions absolutely clear.

Keeping half an eye on them we kept going. The shore was still a fair way off.

Shortly afterwards the two boats swung towards us again. We turned further to get out of their way. The rocks on the shore were getting closer now and we became a little bit worried. They turned in a bit more. We edged closer into the shore to give them more room. The rocks were dangerously close now.

Then they swung towards us again!

We could now see that they were towing a net strung between the two boats, and they were intent on trawling as close to the shore as they could. Bugger anyone in their way.

There was no way we could avoid them and the shore. Our only chance was to spin around and out-pace them. We spun the wheel and gunned the motor. Fortunately, they were only travelling at a couple of knots and in a few minutes, we were clear and could detour around the outside of them. Shaken but safe.

A casual wave from a deckhand as he threw a butt in the water as we passed. Angrily we called the European Central Bank and demanded they immediately foreclose on all their Greek loans and kick the bastards out of the EU!

Later, after we had cooled down, we rescinded this order.

The next night was spent in a small deep anchorage on the south west of the island of Agistri with lovely views of the mountainous mainland. We anchored in twenty-four metres and could not put out as much chain as we would have liked because of limited swing room. Before the strong sea breeze abated a Russian motor-cruiser anchored close by and shortly afterwards dragged its anchor and jammed itself across our bows, threatening to damage our pulpit and entangle our anchor chain.

There was much shouting in English and Russian, but only limited communication, before the Russian helmsman— I think only a visitor as the skipper had rushed off to shore as soon as the anchor had been dropped – actually perhaps he was a Greek or Italian? —eventually jammed his boat into gear, gunned the motor and surged forward, leaving quite a bit of his stainless steel work hanging off our anchor chain.

Remarkably we were unscathed. Absolutely no remorse or hint or apology from our transgressor. We thought of calling our old mate, Vlad Putin, but decided to let the matter pass. We didn't want to get a name as whingers.

Next morning we anchored for a while in Perdika Harbour on Aigina Island and visited the harbour before spending the night in a bay on the west coast with three large motor yachts for company. We had been hoping to find a long term anchorage on the island, but they all seemed a bit precarious, and after a quick conference we cut short our intended stay and headed off to Poros which had lots of good reviews.

We were not disappointed. The entrance to Poros harbour is a dramatic channel through rocky mountains covered in pine and olives, rising precipitously from the deep offshore waters. Once through, the large enclosed harbour is exposed, with the picturesque village of Poros climbing up the slopes of the small island at the eastern end. There are a number of anchorages around the large harbour, ranging from the quiet and secluded bays in the western end to frenetic spots close to the town, at anchor or on the town quay.

Poros is a lovely and friendly town, with a long quay lined with shops and restaurants. It is a great place for coffees or to loiter and dine on the local seafood in the languid warmth of mid-summer evenings. On the southern side, another narrow channel leads to the open sea and is thronged with yachts coming and going, pleased to have the joys of town or eager to find the freedom beyond.

We spent some weeks here as friends and family came and left, and before long we were intimates along the waterfront and the narrow twisting laneways and had taken the town into our hearts.

Sally Cerny from Hobart arrived on the ferry from Athens after having to fight her way from the airport during one of the violent strikes that had become a feature of Athenian life in the summer of 2011. But it takes more than that to faze the irrepressible Sally, and she arrived as beautiful and vivacious as ever.

Based here, where there was some protection while the meltemi was at its strongest, we sailed to Hydra and Dhokos and spent some time in Port Helio before sailing further into the Argolic Gulf.

The township of Hydra is very beautiful and has always been popular with tourists, so much so that these days it is almost impossible for private yachts to berth in the harbour. A few years before, while Georgie and Simon had been working in Ireland, they had spent a couple of weeks here on a friend's yacht and had been captivated by it.

We anchored in a nearby harbour and the girls went to town while I protected *Sea Dreams*. They eventually came back, very pleased with themselves and the compliments they had received from the lotharios on the quay.

For us the island had always been associated with poet/singer Leonard Cohen and the Australian writers, Charmain Clift and George Johnson who had lived and written here in the 1960s. Re-reading Charmain's stories reminded me of what an astute observer of human nature she was, and perhaps why you cannot trust Greek taxi drivers as far as the weather is concerned.

This is a passage about Manios, a Greek friend:

'His behaviour has continued consistent. Manolis is pliable. We have found ourselves picnicking in a hailstorm on his assurance that it was bound to turn out a beautiful day. We have wasted many expectant hours waiting for events and people and information that have never materialised. The bus has left the station. The ship, alas, weighed anchor two hours ago. The party is not tonight, it was held last week.*

If either of us express a wish (often, indeed, we have no need to express it; Manolis merely assumes that we will) he instantly assures us of its imminent gratification, not from any conviction but from a sincere desire that things may turn out as we hope. He sees nothing illogical in this. It is an expression of his friendship.'

On other Greek friends at Hydra: *'The price of the house was one hundred and twenty gold pounds, as had been agreed earlier during lengthy and mysterious negotiations between Socrates and the barber. Rather to my surprise there was no last-minute attempt by either of them to raise it by ten pounds or so. Perhaps experience is deceitful after all, and one has become unnecessarily devious in business dealings with Greeks'.*

Leonard Cohen bought a home in Hydra in 1969 and described it to his mother: *'it has a huge terrace with a view of dramatic mountains and shining white houses. The rooms are large and cool with deep windows set in thick walls. I suppose it's about 200 years old and many generations of seamen must have lived here .... I live on a hill and life has been going on here exactly the same for hundreds of years. All through the day you hear the calls of the street vendors and they are really rather musical .... Early morning is coolest and therefore best, but I love the heat anyhow, especially when the Aegean Sea is only 10 minutes from my door.'*

In the 1960s, when we were young and in Vietnam and remote Papua New Guinea, the music of Leonard Cohen, (and Bob Dylan, Simon and Garfunkel and Cat Stevens etc etc) were the sounds that kept the rhythms of our souls alive. At the time I had no idea Cohen's seemingly magical lyrics only related to drunken carousing on the quay of Hydra and, a bird surveying the harbour from newly installed overhead electric wires. Anyway, to hear any of his songs still takes me back to my youth.

To read his widely published epitaph to his old muse and love, Marianne (Ihlen), who was on the verge of passing away after a separation of some thirty years, is enough to make a hardened old sailor choke: *Well Marianne it's come to this time when we are really so old and are falling apart and I think I will follow you very soon. Know that I am close behind you that if you stretch out your hand, I think that you can reach mine. And you know that I've always loved you for your beauty and your wisdom, but I don't need to say anything more about that because you know all about that. But now, I just want to wish you a very good journey. Goodbye old friend. Endless love, see you down the road.* Leonard Cohen.

Back to our Hydra where the only form of transport is still only donkeys. We had a lot of trouble retrieving the anchor from the fouled bottom, it was hooked on an old anchor or chain, but eventually it came up and we headed to the quieter and perfectly clear waters of Dokos island where the only life on shore was goats and turkeys

301

fossicking on the rocky slopes. We played a lot of our old music, enchanted by the memories and our timeless surrounds.

The next day we had a great run with the northerly behind us until we were nearly at Porto Helio a rusticated sort of Monte Carlo, replete with big boats and ferocious water taxis. It has a lovely entrance with magnificent villas set in forested-landscaped gardens running down to the channel. Once inside we anchored in the centre of the large bay off the restaurant strip. It was dead at midday but came alive and boisterous after dark.

The port attracted more than its share of 'rich and famous' in large 'gin palaces', and together with the water taxis, were naturally not required to obey any of the rules which applied to us lesser folk, as they sped past leaving large wakes behind. A lot were boats registered in Maine USA. I read recently that the Greek government had confiscated five thousand luxury boats for tax evasion. Some government official must have got wind of my impending disclosure!

There was a particularly captivating anchorage behind Nisis Khinitsa at the entrance to the harbour and we spent some days there. The water was exquisite, though there were still ubiquitous water taxis driven by Formula One racing car drivers on holidays. There were other very attractive bays in the channel between Spetsai Island and the mainland.

Further up the Argolic Gulf we anchored behind the lovely Korakonisia Island, with some impressive villas on the shore and then went on to Ormos Drepanou the deep inlet behind Ak Khaidhari. It was guarded by the ruins of an old fort on the headland that had a romantic air as it was lit by a golden glow as the sun set behind the high mountains of the Peloponnese. It was home to a small fishing fleet, and we dined on fresh fish washed down by a few glasses of house white. With two such beautiful women as Ro and Sally, we were always ushered to the best table on the water's edge and surrounded by attentive waiters.

In due course we idled back to Porto Helio where Sally left us to fight her way back through Athens to Tasmania and a few days later the regular summer crew from France arrived, our daughter Charlotte, husband Stephen and sons, Hubie, Rufus and Ferdi.

The northerly *meltemi* builds to a peak in August and as we worked our way back to Poros we battled fairly constant winds gusting up to forty knots. We were glad to be back in the relative protection of Poros, although outside the winds showed no signs of abating.

At one stage when the sea had come up a bit, we thought it would be prudent to tie Ferdi —aged six years—on with a safety harness. Why, he complained, was he the only one to be forced to go down with the ship if it sank. A good point, he has a future in the law. This was the fourth season for the elder grandsons, and they took the occasion with the aplomb of the veterans they are, having worked their way up from assistant rope men to helmsmen.

At the end of August, we were by ourselves again and took *Sea Dreams* alongside the quay to fill our tanks and stock up ready to head across the Aegean to Turkey. Now, filling up with diesel and gas can sometimes be a problem.

In the Western Mediterranean fuel wharfs are often few and far between and nearly always crowded. This means queues must be formed. But alas, as I may have mentioned, queuing is not a concept that is recognised by many sailors. The British, Germans, Dutch can queue. The French can queue sometimes. For the Spanish, Italian and Greeks queuing is for the lesser races.

At the best of times queuing in a boat is difficult. You cannot form a line as you would in a car queuing, say to board a ferry. Boats on the water can form a bit of a queue, but because of wind and tide there is more milling than queuing. Which means if you are trying to protect your place in the pecking order, you need someone in the bow to tell the Spanish, Italian and Greek boats to bugger off. Fortunately, Ro is good at doing this— without bad language of course—but it is still stressful work. This is compounded because in countries where the afternoon siesta is sacrosanct (need I spell out which countries) from midday until three-ish you can guarantee an impatient melee of yachts forming each and every day from two-thirty onwards.

So that in a nutshell is the situation with re-fuelling. After the first year I found it much easier to go ashore in the dinghy and bring a few ten litre cans back from a normal service station. No queuing, the walk was good, the fuel was generally cleaner, and I could filter it myself making sure it was perfectly clean. And it saved Ro's voice. A bit anal? Possibly, but dirty fuel is the biggest cause of engine stoppage in a yacht, and we did not have any problems.

However, thank Zeus, refuelling is one thing in which the Greeks are world leaders. If you tie up at a town quay a mini tanker will bring the fuel to you.

Gas was another matter. All the Mediterranean countries use different sized and shaped gas bottles and, the people who sell diesel never sell gas. The gas dealer is always in a hard to find back street a long way from the quay and, will rarely be able to fill or exchange your style of bottle, requiring the purchase of a new one.

So, we backed into the quay at Poros, where a mini tanker does the rounds a couple of times each day and, the very helpful driver also took our gas bottles away and filled them for us. That night we celebrated our imminent departure at our favourite restaurant, where first and last drinks are on the house, and where the owner was trying to talk me into migrating and running for mayor. We were talked into another night at the quay, but the day after that, all alone again and sad that the family had left, but happy to be moving on, we sailed through the narrows and into the wide blue heaven that is the Aegean on a bright summer's day.

Our plot was to head across the Saronic Gulf to the Athenian shore and anchor in a small bay on Cape Sounion. We were anxious to visit the famous Temple of Poseidon that has sat on this grand rocky prominence for two and a half thousand years. It would be hard to find a more magnificent spot for a temple in honour of the god of the sea. From here, on a clear day, you can see the islands of Kea, Kythnos and Seriphos running away to the southern horizon like great blue battleships, to the southwest across the gulf are Aigina and far off, the outline of the mighty Peloponnese mountains.

All around the blue see sparkles, light dancing off the waves.

Only Zeus was higher than Poseidon in the pantheon of the Greek gods. As god of the sea he was obviously of great importance for sailors, even more so as he had a say, along with Aeolus the god of the winds, in storms, lightning and that sort of thing. You would not want to go to sea without both them in your corner.

The natural beauty of Cape Sounion and the magnificence of the ancient weather-beaten temple, the mythical ambience, all make it a place that must stir your heart and leave an indelible memory. The philosopher Martin Heidegger had these words to say: 'these few standing columns were the strings of an invisible lyre, the song of which the far-seeing Delian god let resonate over the Cycladic world of islands' and 'this single gesture of the land suggests the invisible nearness of the divine and dedicates to it every growth and every human work.'

Lord Byron felt much the same on a visit in 1810: *'Place me at Sunium's marble step*
where nothing save the waves and I may hear our mutual murmurs sweep...'

Cape Sounion has enjoyed a prominent role in Greek mythology. It was from these high cliffs that King Ageus who gave his name to the Aegean Sea, threw himself to his death when he mistakenly thought the black sails of an approaching ship meant that his son Theseus, had been killed in his battle with the Minotaur on Crete.

The coastline and the approximately two thousand islands of the Aegean Sea are crowded with reminders of the rise and fall of ancient empires. The Phoenicians, Ancient Egyptians, Lydians, Carians, Trojans, Minoans, Myceneans, Greeks and Romans have all left memories. Nearly every bay, every mountain, every island has a story to tell. The waters have carried fleets of invaders and traders since the dawn of history. Ancient galleys, triremes, Viking long ships, cogs, round-ships and the great sailing ships that opened up the oceans of the world, have all ploughed her waters. Some brought rape and pillage and some wealth and trade.

The wind was a comfortable fifteen knots and we were hopeful the worst of the meltemi was over for our crossing as we headed for the island of Kea. We anchored overnight in a nice anchorage away from most other yachts, at Ormos Vourkari. The hills around us were hard and weather-beaten, with the odd goat searching the foreshore for something to nibble. At the mouth of the bay a white, blue-domed church gazed impassively out to sea. A last swim in the heavenly water, chilled local white, a golden twilight, calamari grilled on the barbecue, a rising moon, a gentle night. Thank you, Poseidon. Thank you, Aeolus.

By mid-morning the wind was with us and we followed the east coast of Kea for a little way before swinging away to Syros where we anchored at Finikas, an attractive and affluent port on the south west coast of the island. The gleaming villas and apartments lining the bay would do justice to any prestigious locale— not all the money lent to Greece disappeared into bottomless holes.

A hard to believe but true fact is that the Greek median household wealth is twice that of Germany (Google voxeo.org). Much is held in the family home, and right through Greece and the islands the housing stock is great, both in terms of the actual build as well as the stunning locations of many.

We dined ashore at a small waterfront restaurant and later that night the wind came up again and we spent the next three nights with the meltemi whistling through the rigging. Too strong for both of us to leave the boat and too strong to head off. I stayed aboard while Ro caught a bus into the capital of the island for shopping and photography and came back in love with the island and its people. Probably more offers of marriage.

We left with a moderate forecast but found the wind uncomfortably strong once we cleared the southern point of the island. It was a testing sail to Mykonos, reefed sails and a churning sea on our beam. We had intended to have a night or two at Rinia on the way, but the anchorages were too wind-blown and desolate for our liking.

Instead we anchored below the wind mills at Ornas bay just south of the town of Mykonos. We had the company of plenty of large super yachts also trying to escape the wind. We must have not been recognised, as by nightfall we had received no invitations to dine or for drinks from any of the various crown princes and tycoons surrounding us. Oh well, we wouldn't have accepted anyway; it was too bloody windy.

The island is billed as the island where 'anything goes' and we were anxious to get ashore to celebrate Ro's birthday. But the wind continued to howl and again we were reluctant to leave the boat, particularly with nearby yachts dragging their anchors. Even our mighty 'spade anchor' attached to one hundred metres of heavy chain, slid across the bottom for fifty metres before it found something deep enough to dig into.

After three restless nights of buffeting we took advantage of a lull to head south to a more protected spot on the island of Paros a morning's sail away. After an exciting run under our reefed genoa we anchored at Ormiskos Lanyer off a lovely sandy beach, and bliss, enjoyed a reasonably quiet night with our anchor well dug in on a white sandy bottom.

But in the morning our old mate was back and we had a boisterous run to Naxos where we anchored off a beach behind Cape Prokopion. I was still not happy about leaving *Sea Dreams,* but as the island claims a close association with our favourite god, I decided I had to take the chance. Dionysus or Bacchus as he was otherwise known, was the god of wine, vegetation— especially vineyards—and generally having a good time; the monotheistic religions, particularly Christianity and Islam miss out on something not having specialists in these areas. I also know plenty of atheists who could do with some divine help to cheer them up!

He was the son of Zeus, conceived during a love affair, much to the disgust of his jealous wife Hera, with the beautiful human, Semele. The love of his life was his wife, the goddess Ariadne, who he first met on Naxos after she had been deserted by Theseus. But being who he was, and irresistible to women, he had dozens of children with his many lovers. The most notable being Hymenaios, the god of weddings, Kharities the goddesses of the graces, Methe the goddess of drunkenness, Priapos, the goddess of garden fertility, and Thassa, the goddess of orgies. You would have to think that the 'man who invented red wine,' would have to have passed this way – surely.

We set off to visit the remains of the temple built in Dionysus's honour around the 6th century BCE. Afterwards we rewarded ourselves with an early dinner of spicy goat stew while overlooking the glimmering sands of the beach, and our beautiful yacht pulling gently at her anchor as she lay in the sparkling water. Mandilaria, a red variety has been grown here and in some of the other islands forever, and we shared a bottle of fragrant rich red from the Promonas winery. Hints of pepper and blackberry, excellent, and we decided to take a few back for the cellar. But, still no clues of our man!

In the morning we were off again. To the island of Schinoussa. Some poor souls were trying to beat up against the wind, and we were glad it was them and not us. In due course we were happily anchored, with a line ashore, in the narrow inlet of Mirsini. It was a beautiful spot with good all-round protection, and we enjoyed a wine in the cockpit as the sun set and with the wind blowing over our stern, had no worries about the anchor.

Happy and contented we strolled around to the nearest taverna. And were served inedible squid by a surly overweight young woman. Worse, there was no red wine. We understood why we were the only customers.

The next day we made an arduous hike to a 15th century Venetian watchtower overlooking the east coast of the island and were keen to rehydrate ourselves by the time we got back. We tried the other taverna in our bay and enjoyed the convivial atmosphere and a couple of carafes of the proprietors white, made from his own Assyrtiko vines. As the wind was still unpleasantly strong, we went back for another round the next night.

An Italian yachtsman we met there, said that our next stop, Astipalaia, was the windiest island in the Aegean.

'What about Mykonos?' we asked.

'For us, that island does not exist.' he replied.

We understood.

However, we could not dally. We had to be in Bodrum in Turkey in time to meet our younger daughter Georgina, and her family. It was a windy run to Astipalaia passing Amorgos island on the way. The waves were broken, lumpy, and uncomfortable.

After inspecting a few bays, we anchored in Skhinounda Bay, which was a pleasant spot with a gently shelving sandy bottom. There was only one other boat with us, and that turned out to be Australian. We had coffee together and after chatting for a while discovered, proving that old adage of the world being a small place, that we had a mutual friend in Tasmania.

The wind tested our anchor during the night and again we found ourselves dragging a bit. The sandy bottom was only a shallow cover over the rock below, and our trusty 'spade' anchor could not dig in sufficiently. It was only the second time for years that we had 'dragged' and a good reminder not to be complacent. We moved in closer to the shore and found a spot where it could dig in securely.

The village of Skala Astipalaia, dominated by a formidable Venetian fortress built around 1413, overlooks a snug harbour protected by a stone breakwater. It is a lovely spot, the views from the fortress over the surrounding ocean, the mountains dotted with white churches, the vineyards and the gardens are something to cherish. There are orchards rich in tangerines and oranges and good dining around the quay. We enjoyed some local reds made from Agiorgitiko vines which are abundant on the island.

Once again, we would have loved to have stayed longer; it is a marvellous island, uncrowded, sparkling white, the air fresh and sweet with the smells of the boisterous ocean. After three nights we took off for Kos, where we planned to clear customs before entering Turkey at Bodrum. The meltemi channels down this stretch of water and it was not a comfortable crossing, with the wind at twenty-five knots gusting up to forty, and a broken spume flecked sea. We were thankful when we rounded the south eastern tip of Kos into calmer waters.

We met Lenny and Helen Griffin on *Fourth Dimension* in a sheltered cove on the western end of the island and dined that night at the 'Sydney' taverna, where our hosts were a gregarious couple of young Sydney-Greeks. A most enjoyable and fun night. Lenny sometimes rejoices under the nick name 'Moses', when he opens his mouth the bullsh** rushes out, and sometimes things get a bit out of control.

The next morning, we had a perfect run along the south coast, dancing through small white caps a mile offshore, to the pretty village of Kos on the eastern tip. Kos is famous for being the home of the lettuce of the same name, and a fine thing to be famous for, although I must admit I had not put the two together until we visited the island.

Of more cultural significance, in ancient times it was the home of Hippocrates the father of medicine, who gave us the Hippocratic oath that continues to bind physicians two and a half thousand years later. In the centre of the town is the Tree of Hippocrates which marks the place where he is supposed to have taught, and the ruins of his school at Asklepieion are nearby.

Many of his anagrams are eternally simple and prescient.

'Let food be thy medicine and medicine thy food.'

'Whenever a doctor cannot do good, he must be kept from doing harm.'

'Natural forces within us are the true healers of disease.'

'Walking is man's best medicine.'

The town is built around an ancient harbour dominated by a crusader fortress and surrounded by comfortable places to eat and watch the ebb and flow.

The anchorage off the town was a bit windy, but nothing too much to worry about. We had a meal ashore at one of the tavernas overlooking the sea and the nearby coast of Turkey and in the morning, we girded our loins and set off to get our clearances out of Greece. It was not an easy job; we toiled through four different departments— some a couple of times—scattered around the town, being vetted and stamped . . . and charged! It was not until mid-afternoon that exhausted, we had finished. Poorer but happy, we retired to a taverna for a beer.

The highlight of the day occurred on one of our visits to the Port Police. A very pretty young cop in her flatteringly dark blue uniform, her pistol in a low-slung holster— not unlike Jennifer Lopez in one of her cop roles—asked Lenny, a vigorous sixty something who was being Moses again, to meet her at a taverna at midnight. Was she joking or just very short sighted? Was Helen invited? As the old saying goes 'if it is too good to be true . . . '

Lenny left for Bodrum with us, perhaps casting a wishful glance astern.

In the twilight we anchored under the towering walls of the old castle at Bodrum. The power these ancient fortresses once projected is now an almost forgotten memory, the castles themselves a reminder of the tragedies that befell them all.

Arriving at the coast of Asia is arriving at probably the greatest fault line of history. This is where the Mycenaean Empire and the Trojans fought, where ancient Greeks collided with the Persian Empires of Xerxes and Cyrus the Great, along which Alexander the Great marched to Egypt, from where the Romans launched their fatal campaigns against the Parthians, beside which the Crusaders marched, where the Christians of Europe and Byzantium fought the armies of the Prophet, where the Ottomans marched to conquer mighty Constantinople.

All along this shore lie memories of all these great eruptions, and of the gods to whose music men danced. There are no remains of the first gods who existed along the coast for many, many thousands of years before those of the Hittites from somewhere around 4000 BCE. Later they were followed by the somewhat shared pantheon of gods of the Greeks, Carians and Lydians.

The Greek gods are omnipresent during Jason and the Argonauts 'Search for the Golden Fleece' written around the 15th century BCE, and writing around the 8th century BCE Homer certainly has the gods overseeing the Trojan War fought around the 12th century BCE.

The early stories of the first of the monotheistic religions, Judaism, were probably composed in the 6th century BCE and placed Moses the bull**** and the exodus, around the 13th century BCE. The Greek gods were probably taken to Italy with Prince Aeneas and his fellow survivors from the sack of Troy.

Jesus was born around 5 BCE and Saint Peter established the Christian Church in Rome in 44 CE. It was legalised and the Orthodox Church established by Emperor Constantine in 313 CE. In 380 CE Christianity was made the official religion of the Roman Empire by Emperor Theodosius, but the Roman and Byzantine branches remained mutually despising congregations thereafter.

The Archangel Gabriel first embraced Muhammad in 610 CE, and from this time until at least a hundred years after the Muslim's conquered Constantinople in 1453, the coast was the setting of a constant and bloody battle between Muslim and

Christian.

The castle of St Peter at Bodrum was built by the Knights of the Order of Saint John (also known as the Knights Hospitallers) and was constructed from 1402. Unfortunately, over time much of the stone and marble from one of the wonders of the ancient world, the great Mausoleum of Harlicarnassus was stolen for the walls. The castle, incorporating a very interesting marine museum, has now been restored to much of its former magnificence. Anchored below it in the dusk is to be taken back in time, and the Muslim calls to prayer are another reminder of the transient nature of man's power.

For over a century it was the second most important castle of the Order and was a refuge for Christians from all over Asia Minor forced to flee the advance of the Muslim armies. Over the years it was continually strengthened, repelled many attacks, and was never taken. However, when the mighty Suleiman the Magnificent, with an army of 200,000 men forced the capitulation of the Order's headquarters in the nearby island of Rhodes in 1522 it was handed over to the Muslims as part of the surrender terms. With it went the castles on the islands of Kos, Kastellorizon and Symi which had fought on for a hundred years after the fall of Constantinople.

These days the Order is popularly regarded, along with Crusaders generally, as being an anachronistic band of religious bigots who meddled unsuccessfully in an area where they had no right to be. Nothing could be further from the truth. Moses was in the Levant 2,000 years and Jesus 600 years before Muhammad. The area was part of the Christian Kingdom of Byzantium from 380 CE. The Muslim faith was not founded until 610 CE at the earliest and was spread by the sword in lands that had been Judaic or Christian for at least many centuries.

The Order was founded in Jerusalem around 1023 CE. They built mighty fortresses, fought and died in all the battles in the Holy Land until the Christians were finally driven out in 1291. They then established themselves in Rhodes, built a mighty fortress again and fought until they were driven out. Then they re-established themselves in Malta in 1530 and built yet another great fortress. During this period, they were a mainstay of Europe's maritime defences, particularly after the fall of Constantinople. Their list of battle honours is without peer.

Their bravery and tenacity at the Great Siege of Malta in 1565 and the Battle of Lepanto in 1571 undoubtedly saved Europe. And they were still fighting during the Siege of Candia in 1668. They saved Europe from Muslim conquest and we all owe them our admiration and gratitude.

Bodrum is sheltered from most of the meltemi and provided the wind stays in the north there is a lovely anchorage in front of a strip of waterfront restaurants, with a busy bazaar behind. On our first run ashore, we chose a restaurant with a small jetty for patrons and we were cordially assisted out of our tender, ushered to a table and served with a sumptuous feast. All was good, the fresh-eyed seafood artistically arranged on ice, tasting dishes for your perusal, full-bodied local wine. There are over a thousand varieties of wine grapes in Turkey.

Over time it had become our habit, if we were anchored off, not to chop and change waterfront restaurants too much. If we are happy with one, we keep coming back, and in many cases have developed friendships that have flourished over seasons and on the Internet for years afterwards. But this is not the only consideration. When you climb into your dinghy for the trip ashore, you are aware that the eyes of all restaurants are on you. They all want your business. But if you dined with them the previous night, they cannot help being a bit miffed if you make a very public declaration and choose a competitor. The smile for a returned visit is always heartfelt, and even the shrug of the shoulders from the neighbouring businesses have a hint of good-humoured acceptance of dining loyalty.

Anyway, we had a number of very happy meals at the Denizce restaurant, and each time after losing our good senses, could not resist the many famously named handcrafted leather coats, shoes, shirts, jeans and Rolex watches in the nearby bazaar. All still going strong back in Australia a decade later.

The town dates from at least 484 BCE when it was established by Dorian Greeks and there is a lot to inspect and admire. Although much of its former glory is lost a lot of the classical stone and marble has been recycled into what stands today. A humble grime covered foundation stone in the bazaar may have once, many centuries ago, have been part of one of the world's most beautiful and greatest structures ever built.

The ancient historian Herodotus was born here. Two of history's most renowned warlords left their mark. The city was sacked by Alexander the Great in 334 BCE and besieged by Suleiman the Magnificent who took the Muslim Ottoman Empire to the gates of Vienna.

There was plenty to see and we enjoyed ourselves greatly as we waited for our new crew of Georgina, Simon, Joseph and Eleanor to arrive, coming in each evening to our small jetty. Then we had a couple more days in Bodrum while the crew inspected the fortress and the bazaar before we up anchored and headed south along the Turquoise Coast for Marmaris and as many stops in between as we could manage. The autumn weather was wonderful; a gentler wind, the nights a little longer and cooler.

A couple of hours down the coast we anchored off the beach at Alakisla Buku, where the water was still warm and crystal clear and thick forests cascaded down the slopes of the mountains to the water's edge. We were back into our old routine: barbecue at sunset, a few wines, some very serious World Championship Texas Hold 'em Poker or chess with the grandchildren and their parents.

At picturesque Cokertime we all went ashore for a feast of some great Turkish food at Captain Ibrahim's and inspected carpets being woven on hand looms. The next day we idled along to a lovely bay at Oren Belediyesi where another round of the poker championship was played, and Joseph and Eleanor went to sleep in the cockpit to the gentle murmurs of the sea.

There are a number of beguiling anchorages with names to titillate the imagination, near the head of the Gulf of Gokova where it would be easy to spend a month or more. It is out of the main channel of the meltemi and encased by dramatic mountains and lushly forested hills.

Great places include Cleopatra Island famous for its glistening beach—which according to legend, was imported by Cleopatra for her dalliance with Mark Antony—dazzling water and panoramic mountain views. There are still some Roman remains including a small theatre and it's certainly a wonderful place to dally.

During World War II the British special forces operated out of the secret wooded reaches of English Harbour while a Russian fleet gave Russian Harbour its name. But there are many others, all delightful in their own way and some with summer restaurants specializing in freshly caught sea bream and sea bass which are prolific in these waters.

Knidos, a small harbour partially protected by ancient crumbling breakwaters, sits on the once strategic south western tip of the gulf. On the hills above, the skeleton of an old city, dating from around 360 BCE still haunts the rocky slopes. It was a great city for a thousand years and, has now been a ruin for fifteen hundred years.

In was famous as a centre of the arts and culture. The ruins of two large amphitheatres still dominate the bay, along with the remains of a temple of Dionysus which once held the sculptor Praxiteles's statue of the naked Aphrodite, the most famous and beautiful statue of all time. Sadly, it was lost to history—the main suspects being, again, the censors of the early Christians of the Byzantine era and the city declined into ruin, despite being in such a good position for ships travelling north to wait for the *meltemi* to abate. It was damaged by earthquakes and could not rejuvenate itself; perhaps taxes were too high and too much was spent on the arts and not enough on commerce and defence. A not unknown scenario in the Med.

The weather had been calm and sunny since the new crew arrived and we were able to anchor outside the harbour at Datca and watch the coming and going of the gullet fleet.

We sailed deep into the gulf of Hisaronu and anchored in the enchanted cove of Keci Buku behind a small rocky island crowned with the ruined walls of a crusader fort built upon Byzantine ruins. In the morning the children led the assault on the walls, only to be turned back by a team of archaeologists ensconced in the citadel. Recovering, it was peaceful in the bay, surrounded by steep pine-clad hills and blue-hazed mountains in the background.

The passing days prodded us onward, and we headed to the town of Bozburun. In a deep sheltered bay with an island nearly covering the entrance, it proved to be a charming and friendly town built around its small harbour. Joseph and Eleanor pillaged the waterfront and befriended the charming Sunny, who did not quite sell us carpets. But the following year he did sell us the where-with-all to redecorate the forward cabin in a more eastern style.

We were nearing Marmaris, and sadly close to losing our young and vigorous crew. The last night out was spent at Serce Limani, an enclosed bay lined with steep rocky mountains and in the morning we sailed the short distance to Marmaris, where we planned to leave *Sea Dreams* 'on the dry' until the next spring.

Further travels are described in *The History of the World - From the Back of a Boat – Vol 2*. The search for the man who invented red wine continues. Ahead lie the coasts and islands of the Aegean Sea, a voyage that may challenge your views of our past and, through the vast network of inland waterways of Europe. More of our early life in PNG, how we became Tasmanians and discovered our own history. We hope you have enjoyed the voyage so far and that we see you back on board shortly.

The Whole Crew

~ ACKNOWLEDGEMENTS ~

I was lucky enough to fall in love with a beautiful young woman while I was a cadet at Duntroon. This has been a story of our experiences together, and although sometimes Rosemary may not have been with me physically, she was always there in spirit and love. I could not have sailed, lived my life, or written this story to tell about it, without her.

Thank you to all our family who we have shared so many good times on board. Particularly our daughters: Charlotte, her husband Stephen and sons, Hubert, Rufus and Ferdinand. Georgina, her husband, Simon, and children, Joseph and Eleanor. John (Poppy) and Hazel Peterswald, Wendy Peterswald, Richard and Francis Peterswald. Owen and Toni Esmonde. Eugene and Jennifer Esmonde, Deborah and Kevin Scott, Gill and Colin Rosewarne, Viv and Tim Cresswell, Godfrey and Kirsty Esmonde. Andrew and Jane Rosewarne and daughters, Sian and Catrin.

Many friends have shared a wine with us on the aft deck. Thank you. Particularly Don and Sue Clark, Lenny (who tragically is now with one of his many 'grandmothers' in a paradise somewhere far away) and Helen Griffin, David and Jill Henry, Mark and Remy Towers, Eric and Eileen Tang, Margie and Paul Hansen, Sally Cerny, Phil and Carmel Thomson, Roger and Tina Wainwright, Max and Viv Doerner, Margie Murray, Vince and Megan Thompson, Mike and Dianna Battle, Peter Langford, Peter and Susie Knight.

Thanks also to the 5th Battalion Royal Australian Regiment Association and president Colonel (Retired) Roger Wainwright for permission to quote extracts from the publication *The Year of the Tigers – The Second Tour of the 5th Battalion RAR in South Vietnam, 1969-70* (Edited by M. R. Battle and D.S. Wilkins).

Thank you very much to the distinguished Australian author, Annie Seaton, for her advice and help while editing *The History of the World – From the Back of a Boat. Vol 1*

www.ingramcontent.com/pod-product-compliance
Lightning Source LLC
Chambersburg PA
CBHW062009090426
42811CB00005B/793